JOHN McCORMACK

John McCormack, 1912. Photograph by James T. Bushnell. Courtesy of the Library of Congress.

JOHN McCORMACK

A Comprehensive Discography

Compiled by
Paul W. Worth
and Jim Cartwright

Foreword by
Gwendolyn McCormack–Pyke

Discographies, Number 21

Greenwood Press
New York • Westport, Connecticut • London

Library of Congress Cataloging-in-Publication Data

Worth, Paul W.
  John McCormack : a comprehensive discography.

  (Discographies, ISSN 0192-334X ; no. 21)
  Bibliography: p.
  Includes index.
  1. McCormack, John, 1884-1945—Discography.
I. McCormack, John, 1884-1945. II. Cartwright, Jim.
III. Title. IV. Series.
ML156.7.M35W7 1986   782.1'092'4 [B]   86-403
ISBN 0-313-24728-5 (lib. bdg. : alk. paper)

Library of Congress Catalog Card Number: 86-403
ISBN: 0-313-24728-5
ISSN: 0192-334X

First published in 1986

Greenwood Press, Inc.
88 Post Road West, Westport, Connecticut 06881

Printed in the United States of America

The paper used in this book complies with the
Permanent Paper Standard issued by the National
Information Standards Organization (Z39.48-1984).

10 9 8 7 6 5 4 3 2 1

To the Giants of McCormack research and discography,
on whose shoulders we have gratefully stood for
many years, this book is cordially dedicated:

        James Sheehan

        Leonard F. X. MacDermott Roe

        Robert Webster

            and

        Philip Roden

Contents

Foreword

I think that many people remember my father as a famous singer of ballads and Irish songs, which he loved, but this discography gives an idea of how varied his repertoire really was.   It is a wonderful compilation of his records, many of which bring back such happy memories to me. Often after dinner we would all sit around the fire and sing with him. I sometimes went with him when he was making records and can still remember what a perfectionist he was.   He would not pass a record if it had the slightest note that he did not consider right.   He always made those again. I think some of his records with Fritz Kreisler - who was a dear family friend - are among the loveliest he made.

I feel his records were so popular because he sang with his heart as well as his voice.   I congratulate Paul Worth and Jim Cartwright for compiling such a wonderful discography.   I feel very touched that so many people still remember my father and love his records.

Gwendolyn McCormack-Pyke

Preface

Four decades after John Count McCormack's death his art is still
cherished and lives on in nearly 800 recordings. The celebrations in 1984
in honor of his centenary and the many published tributes which appeared in
that year made it apparent that interest in this great tenor remains high.
Clearly he is not just another singer from the so-called "Golden Age," remembered only by elderly contemporaries and a few collectors of antique records.
McCormack was beloved as was perhaps no other singer of his time. Today his
audience consists mainly of listeners born after he had died. Through the
medium of the long playing record, introduced after his death, his singing
continues to reach and touch the hearts of millions.

The present discography updates and supplements earlier ones and
provides features not previously available. Absent from prior works
was an accurate listing of long playing reissues and an adequate treatment
of McCormack's unpublished but extant recordings and alternate takes. Absent
also was an accurate documentation of his recordings on film and of the transcriptions of radio broadcasts that have survived. In addition to remedying
these needs, this new discography supplies information on the composers, lyricists, and assisting artists for the recordings. It also contains details
regarding playing speeds of original records and recording locales. Finally,
it corrects a number of errors and omissions in previous publications.

In the chronological listing, which contains all of the discographic
data, one discerns McCormack's artistic development. His recorded repertoire
reflects to some extent the variety of his wide-ranging concert repertoire
over the four decades of his career. It is fortunate that his recordings are
still so readily available, and it is the compilers' hope that this guide will
enrich the listening of audiences today and in the future.

In a discography this large there will be, perhaps inevitably, fugitive
omissions and inaccuracies, though we have made our best effort to eliminate
them. Where we have succeeded in this effort we are indebted to many;
where we have failed we hope to be informed by those who are able to do so.

In the interest of periodically updating this discography, we invite
corrections and additions from all interested parties. Such information may
be sent to the compilers in care of the publisher.

Acknowledgments

A discography of the recordings of John McCormack is of such a magnitude that it is in reality the culmination of the work of many. We would like to acknowledge first of all the assistance provided by those to whom we have dedicated this effort. Without their pioneering work the task would have been quite unmanageable. We express at the outset our thanks and appreciation to James Sheehan. His assistance to previous discographers of McCormack was significant and largely unsung, and that provided to us quite valuable, especially for having been given on short notice. We owe a debt also to Leonard F. X. McDermott Roe's two discographies, which have long been the standard reference works on the subject. The discography and essay by Philip F. Roden and Robert L. Webster on the McCormack Odeon recordings is a model of such research and remains nearly as useful today as it was when it appeared nearly thirty years ago. We are glad to acknowledge our debt to their work. The first major discography of McCormack was published as an appendix to *I Hear You Calling Me* by Lily McCormack. It was compiled by Philip F. Roden also, and we found it a helpful companion to Roe.

Our thanks and appreciation are especially deep to William R. Moran for taking time away from his own immense projects not only to answer a multitude of questions patiently, but also to check all of the Victor information in our draft on an item by item basis against his own research. This eliminated many errors and uncertainties on our part. We acknowledge as well his contribution of the data on playing speeds and alternate takes taken from forthcoming volumes of *The Encyclopedic Discography of Victor Recordings* which he and Ted Fagan are compiling (for Greenwood Press). Discography as serious research owes a great debt to the work of Mr. Moran, as do the many discographers whom he has helped personally, and whose ranks we now join.

We extend our thanks to the Listings Division of RCA Victor for allowing access to the original files of the Victor Company and for the unfailing courtesy and assistance by the staff on more than one trip to consult this material.

We are thankful as well to Alan Kelly for sharing with us his knowledge and research concerning the complex history of the Gramophone Company in its early years. This was provided cheerfully and in great detail, delaying his own ongoing research on that subject, and we have profited a great deal by his many letters.

We acknowledge with gratitude the assistance of Ruth Edge, Manager of the EMI Archives at Hayes, for much information taken from files we were unable to consult personally, as well as the help provided by the resources of EMI and its staff. Likewise our thanks go to the written Archives Centre of the British Broadcasting Corporation and its staff, particularly Jeff Walden, for responses to our inquiries.

We are particularly grateful to Brian Fawcett-Johnston for sharing with us his research on McCormack's recordings, as well as for answering a host of questions about them. We offer additional thanks for his allowing us to preview his discography of the early recordings. We have been singularly aided, as have McCormack's fans everywhere, by the ongoing McCormack reissue project on Pearl records under his supervision.

Several individuals gave generously of their time and expertise to annotate an early draft of this discography and deserve acknowledgment along with our thanks for their painstaking assistance: Howard Sanner, Harry Butler, Christopher Sullivan, Kenneth Steenson, Fred Grundy, John Bolig, and John Powers.

Richard Warren, Curator of the Historical Sound Recordings division of the Yale University Library, gave us valuable and extensive reports on the holdings of that institution and answered many questions with promptness. We are grateful to him as well as for the efforts of his staff. We offer acknowledgment and thanks for the use of the Collection of Mr. Mrs. Laurance C. Witten II at the Yale Collection of Historical Sound Recordings and to the officers of that university for their support of this branch of their library's activities.

Our appreciation and thanks go to Mrs. Bertha M. White for sharing with us the results of her years of research on McCormack's career.

We are grateful to Miles Kreuger for providing much accurate information regarding the movie Song O' My Heart, correcting several misconceptions that had been previously published and revealing details about the separate and lost 70 mm version.   Thanks also go to Patrick More for his assistance with the microgroove reissues of McCormack's recordings and for sharing with us his research on the various alternate takes of many recordings.

We offer thanks to the Library of Congress for permission to reproduce the photograph of John McCormack from their collection. We are similarly grateful to the Gentlemen of the College of Arms for permission to reproduce the McCormack Family Crest. We acknowledge with our thanks Jane Ybarra for her careful rendition of the Crest for this volume.

To all individuals who responded to our inquiries and gave generously of time and knowledge in support of this project by providing data, corrections, advice, and recordings, we here recognize their help (alphabetically) with our sincere thanks and gratitude:

1. Richard E. Barnes (Dallas, TX)
2. Steven C. Barr (Toronto)
3. BBC Archives (Reading)
4. Blackwell's Music Shop (Oxford)
5. John Bolig (Dover, Delaware)
6. Liam Breen (Dublin)
7. Harry Butler (Studio City, CA)
8. Bill Collins (Davis, CA)
9. Robert Conn (Kirbyville, TX)
10. George Creegan (Steubenville, Ohio)
11. Peter F. Dolan (New York City)
12. Frank Drake (Chicago)
13. Ruth Edge (Hayes, England)
14. Ted Fagan (Palo Alto, CA)
15. Brian Fawcett-Johnston (Kent, England)
16. Dave Fitzgerald (Hayes, England)
17. Neil Forster (Foxboro, Massachusetts)
18. George Frow (Kent, England)
19. Syd Grey (Sussex, England)
20. Fred Grundy (London)
21. Keith Hardwick (London)
22. Louis Harrison (Austin, Texas)
23. William Henderson (Glasgow)
24. Lawrence F. Holdridge (Amityville, NY)
25. Larry Hooper (Austin, Texas)
26. Stephen Jabloner (Los Angeles, CA)
27. Donald Janda (Austin, Texas)
28. Anton Johannes (Pine Bush, NY)
29. Shiro Kawai (Japan)
30. Alan Kelly (Sheffield, England)
31. John Keveny (Maywood, New Jersey)
32. Larry Kiner (Redmond, Washington)
33. David Kirby (Hollywood, CA)
34. Miles Kreuger (Los Angeles, CA)
35. Michael Leone (Houston, Texas)
36. Emrys Mathews (Llandeilo, Wales)
37. Garrett MacSweeney (Ontario)
38. Timothy Massey (London)
39. Jeremy Meehan (Youghal, Eire)
40. Karl Miller (Austin, Texas)
41. William R. Moran (La Cañada, CA)
42. Patrick More (Vernon, Texas)
43. Charles I. Morgan (Gwent, Wales)
44. Jim Morrison (Youghal, Eire)
45. Padraic O'Hara (Ballina, Eire)
46. Pavilion Records (Pembury, Engl.)
47. Bill Park (Bedford, Texas)
48. Mrs. T. Peedell (Oxford)
49. Bernard B. Power (Ontario)
50. John Powers (Floral Park, NY)
51. RCA Victor, Listings Div. (NYC)
52. Bob Rose (Voce Records, Oakland)
53. Howard Sanner (Hyattsville, MD)
54. Ronald Seeliger (Austin, Texas)
55. James Sheehan (Yonkers, NY)
56. Kenneth Steenson (London)
57. Norman Stewart (London)
58. Christopher Sullivan (London)
59. Francis Traynor (Glasgow)
60. Jeff Walden (Reading, England)
61. John Ward (Rossendale, Lancashire)
62. Richard Warren (Yale University)
63. Robert L. Webster (Dublin)
64. Bertha M. White (Toronto)
65. Ed Wilkinson (Oakland, CA)
66. Peter Welland (Hayes, England)
67. Thomas Woodcock (London)
68. Witten Collection (Yale University)
69. Yale University Library (New Haven)
70. Jane Ybarra (Austin, Texas)

Finally, we thank those people not already cited, whose publications are listed in the bibliography, for the help provided by their research. We thank as well those whose names we may have inadvertently omitted.

The McCormack Family Crest. Courtesy, the Gentlemen of the college of Arms; rendered by Jane Ybarra.

The Art of
John McCormack
and the Phonograph

The recorded legacy of John McCormack is unique among famous singers in preserving the sound of his voice over a period of thirty-eight consecutive years. During this period that sound changed as the singer received vocal training, his voice matured, was strengthened through a strenuous useage that was unparalleled by any other classical singer, and finally deteriorated because of the effects of illness and age. The changing sound of McCormack's voice also conveys an incomparable artistry which he applied to his ever evolving repertoire from simple Irish folk songs to sentimental ballads to *bel canto* and *verismo* opera to classical arias by the great masters to popular songs from Tin Pan Alley to German lieder and French, English, and Russian art songs, eventually not merely encompassing but also mastering a wider range of musical genre than any other singer on disc.

John McCormack's recording career began in 1904 when he was twenty years old and before he had received formal vocal training other than as a member of the Palestrina Choir of the Dublin Pro-Cathedral under choirmaster Vincent O'Brien. A few other great singers had recorded that young, mainly sopranos, since female voices tend to mature earlier than male: Maggie Teyte made her first recordings at age eighteen; Rosa Ponselle at twenty-one. However, though both of these sopranos had extremely long recording careers, there were gaps of several years when they did not record at all. Leaving aside Jussi Bjoerling's youthful recordings as a boy soprano in a family trio, most tenors have not recorded until their mid to late twenties: Caruso first recorded at age twenty-seven though he would no doubt have done so earlier had the record industry itself been more developed, Martinelli at twenty-six, Gigli at twenty-eight, Melchior (though as a baritone) at twenty-two. Through McCormack's records the development of his voice and artistry can be followed year-by-year throughout his professional career and into the early years of his formal retirement from the concert world, until three years before his death in 1945.

By 1904 acoustical recording of the human voice, if not of the accompaniment, had been developed to a point hardly inferior to that of twenty years later. Indeed, in a number of instances the later acoustical recordings seem to have definitely retrogressed in certain ways, so far as realistic voice reproduction was concerned. Nellie Melba's 1904 G & T discs reveal a roundness and sweetness tone not usually captured by the later Victor and HMV recordings, where her voice sounds both harder and thinner even though no such changes in her vocal quality were noted by the critics who reviewed her live performances of the period. Luisa Tetrazzini's early Zonophone discs, primitive as they are, reproduce her voice more vividly than her later HMV and Victor records. This phenomenon was not confined to sopranos. Tenor Alessandro Bonci's voice is more accurately reproduced by his early Fonotipia discs than on his later Edison and Columbia recordings. The superiority of the earlier recordings probably results in large part from their being recorded at a closer proximity than the later discs, where the singer was positioned further from the recording horn so as to avoid the highly modulated grooves which were subject to excessive wear when played on the equipment available at the time, but there are other causative factors as well. The quality of voice reproduction obtained from both wax cylinders and G & T discs circa 1904 played with appropriate modern equipment is quite satisfactory as acoustical recordings go *if the records are not worn or*

damaged.   Unfortunately, most of the very early McCormack discs and cylinders
that have survived *are* worn or otherwise damaged, which accounts for their poor
sonics when re-recorded to LP.   Copies of these early records in good condition,
if properly reproduced, give an accurate idea of the singer at the very beginning
of his career.

John McCormack's solo singing career may be said to have begun on 14 May 1903
when he won the tenor gold medal for his performances of a Handel aria and "The
Snowy Breasted Pearl" in the Dublin *Feis Ceoil*.   He was engaged to sing at the
Irish Village of the Louisiana Purchase Exposition at St. Louis during the summer
of 1904.   After returning from the United States he made his first records in
London that autumn, nearly all of traditional Irish songs.   The earliest were a
series of ten Edison cylinders made for the National Phonograph Company on 12
September 1904, the first of which was "The Snowy Breasted Pearl."   Nine days
later he recorded his first discs for the Gramophone and Typewriter Company,
Limited.   Some of the discs recorded by G & T were issued under the pseudonym
"John O'Reilly" on the affiliated Zonophone label.   His first operatic recording
was "Eily Mavourneen, I See Thee Before Me" from Benedict's *Lily of Killarney*,
made for the Edison-Bell Consolidated Phonograph Company on 3 November 1904 along
with some of the same Irish songs he had already sung for other companies.
These Edison-Bell cylinders were the first McCormack recordings to be made in
multiple takes, four each of ten titles.

Unlike Violinist Jascha Heifetz's first Victor recordings made when he was
still in his teens or Rosa Ponsell's Columbia records of Italian operatic arias
made when she was in her early twenties which can withstand comparison with
records by any other violinist or soprano regardless of age, McCormack's first
records clearly show that he was no prodigy.   As his subsequent career would
lead one to expect, the essentially untrained voice was a good one, the basic
timbre already unique and the sound beautiful – clear evidence of natural gifts.
The lower notes were produced in a somewhat constricted manner, the higher notes
strenuously attacked.   The art with which the already attractive voice was used
was, despite unmistakable signs of an inborn musicality, at an embryonic stage.
The attempt to maintain a legato line, in itself wholly praiseworthy, led to a
slurring of the words (often indistinctly articulated or pronounced in a curious
deadpan manner) and to the use of an exaggerated *portamento*.   The lack of clear
diction created a certain rhythmic slackness, exacerbated by a sort of
generalized languishing "soulfulness" that took the place of more specific
feeling.   Finesse was totally lacking.   These early McCormack recordings are
primarily of curio value.

Using payment received from his autumn 1904 recordings, McCormack went to
Milan to study voice with Vincenzo Sabatini.   Judging the young tenor's voice
already well placed, Sabatini set him to work exclusively on scales and
excerises.   Shortly before his return to Ireland in the summer of 1905, he was
finally permitted to study two arias.   Thus was laid the groundwork of his
superb technique.   When McCormack was in London, either during the summer of
1905 or 1906, he made his last Edison-Bell cylinder, "Home to Athlone."

The young singer had applied himself to his studies with diligence and
mastered the Italian language as well as the rudiments of correct vocal
technique.   Upon his return to Italy at the end of September 1905, Sabatini
deemed him ready to audition for the opera.   His successful début, in Mascagni's
L'Amico Fritz, took place at the Teatro Chiabrera, Savona, on 13 January 1906.
He was twenty-one years old, the same age as Rosa Ponselle when she made her
operatic début at the Metropolitan.   There followed additional operatic
appearances, including the lead tenor role in Dupont's *La Cabrera* which
McCormack, adhering to the almost stereotypical pattern of the young opera
singer trying to make good, learned on short notice when the scheduled singer
became ill.   For these early operatic appearances in Italy, McCormack used the
stage name "Giovanni Foli," the "Foli" being an Italization of the family name
of his fiancée, Lily Foley.

McCormack returned to Ireland at the end of May 1906 and married Miss Foley.
The couple honeymooned in London where the tenor made six Sterling cylinders,
again all Irish songs, for the Russell Hunting Company, Limited.   Two of these
were re-recorded to vertical-cut Pathé discs.   In August the young couple went
to Italy to enable McCormack to make further opera auditions, including an
unsuccessful one for Giulio Gatti-Casazza, impresario of La Scala, during which
McCormack's voice cracked on a high C.   Like the young Caruso, McCormack had
some difficulty with his very highest notes at this early stage of his career.
Both tenors later gained security on top, though high C never became the favorite
note of either and both tended to avoid it in the later years of their careers.
Lily became pregnant and since John had failed to secure any regular engagements

in Italy, in early autumn of 1906 they decided to return to London.
    The young musician appeared as a supporting artist in several concerts and
sang in a few *soirées* in great houses, but with Lily expecting a child, the
couple was sorely in need of funds.   The tenor approached the Gramophone and
Typewriter Company, Limited about making further recordings for them but was
brusquely informed by Fred Gaisberg that any additional records he might make
would be useless to the company.   Fortunately, Arthur Brooks of the rival
International Talking Machine Company did not agree with Gaisberg's negative
assessment of McCormack's commercial potential, and offered the tenor a six-year
contract to make Odeon discs.   This was McCormack's first long-term recording
contract.   While the first Odeon records reproduce the voice well, the
accompaniments sounded almost ludicrous, being blatantly brassy with an
especially prominently recorded tuba playing *forte* throughout.   All of the 1906
Odeon discs were of the familiar Irish songs except for McCormack's first Odeon
operatic title, the duet "Ai nostri monti" from Verdi's *Il Trovatore*, recorded at
the second session on 5 December 1906.   The contralto in the duet was his wife
Lily, who was not pleased with the sound of her voice on records ("...it sounded
much more like a foghorn," she recalled in her biography of John), and the duet
remained unpublished.   No test pressings are known to have survived.
    The 1906 recordings dramatically reveal the tremendous improvements in both
voice and artistry that had taken place under Sabatini's tutelage and also
through hearing performances by many of the greatest musicians of the period at
La Scala (where Arturo Toscanini was house conductor) and the Royal Opera, Covent
Garden (where the likes of Melba and Caruso appeared regularly).   They are the
first McCormack recordings that can be heard with unalloyed pleasure.   The flat
sounding pronunciation and slurred articulation of the words was largely gone,
though not yet replaced with McCormack's later unequalled combination of
naturalness and expressivity in the singing of the English language.   The
English was usually intelligible but retained the pronounced Irish accent which
it never lost.   The pure legato remained, having been shorn of obtrusive
portamento.   The phrasing was more secure and although the songs were sung in a
relatively straightforward manner, there was more musical detail.   The voice was
freer and rounder in tone throughout its range.   *Forte* high notes had more
solidity and ring, and the incomparable soft singing of high notes began to be
employed.   McCormack's vocal technique had not yet become second nature however,
and the listener to his records from this period is occasionally made aware of
the conscious manipulation of the vocal mechanism.   McCormack had by this time
received all the formal vocal training he would ever have, providing the
technical and musical foundation which his own hard work and innate talent were
to develop within a few years to a peak of artistry equalled by few, if any,
other musicians.   To have accomplished so much during such a short period of
study (less than a year of lessons with Sabatini before his debut) is unusual
but not unheard of.   Helen Mitchell Armstrong experienced a similar
transformation during her fourteen months of study with Mathilde Marchesi in
Paris before her operatic debut under the name which was to become world famous,
Nellie Melba.   Melba was no doubt the more polished artist at the time of her
début, but she was then twenty-six and had received several years vocal training
in Australia before becoming a Marchesi pupil.   McCormack was only twenty-one at
the time of his début and had received virtually no training before his brief
period of study with Sabatini.   His development of his gifts on his own without
benefit of further instruction is in marked contrast to most singers who remain
tied to their teachers, an extreme case being Beverly Sills, who continued having
voice lessons with the same teacher for over thirty years.
    In March 1907 John McCormack first appeared at a Ballad Concert at Queen's
Hall, London under the auspices of Arthur Boosey, publisher of popular ballads by
such composers as Samuel Liddle, Stephen Adams, and Charles Marshall.   These
concerts featured a number of young artists soon to become well known, including
violinist Mischa Elman and contralto-profundo Clara Butt.   Here McCormack was
able to sing an occasional operatic aria in addition to the ballads being
"plugged" for their publisher.   In 1907 he recorded a few of the ballads for
Odeon, along with yet more Irish airs.   The band playing the accompaniments for
the June 1907 recordings was relatively restrained, at least while McCormack was
singing, and the players "let themselves go" only between the verses.   By
November of that year, even a few muddily recorded woodwinds and strings were
allowed into the recording studio.   Fortunately, McCormack's voice was still
able to emerge from these discs with crystal clarity even if the accompaniments
did not.
    On 15 October 1907 John McCormack made his Covent Garden début, in the role
of Turiddu in Mascagni's *Cavalleria Rusticana*.   His next part was to become his

most famous: Don Ottavio in Mozart's *Don Giovanni*.   So successful were his
appearances that autumn that he was engaged to appear in the prestigious Royal
Opera season which took place during the late spring and summer of 1908.   At
age twenty-three he thus became the youngest leading tenor in the long history of
the Royal Opera.   McCormack's first published operatic disc was of the
"Siciliana" from the opera of his Covent Garden début, recorded on 31 January
1908.   Unlike the theater performance, the recording was sung in English
translation.   The 1908 Odeon recordings reflect his expanded activities on the
opera stage and in concert: eleven arias, many ballads, some Italian songs, and
the seemingly inevitable Irish songs, all displaying his increased confidence and
sensitivity.   Still, his vocal technique itself was not yet completely perfected
and the 1906 - 1908 recordings reveal an occasional hoarseness on a low note
immediately following a loud high note, indicating a strain on top that
momentarily affected his vocal cords, especially in more demanding music.
    In 1909 he made no recordings until September, by which time his voice was
at a peak that was to last until his near-fatal illness in the spring of 1922.
By the autumn of 1909 his voice was matured and under perfect control,
displaying none of the vocal flaws heard on some of the earlier recordings.
The singing now sounded as if it were done with utmost ease.   The voice moved
from one end of its extensive range to the other with complete freedom and
clarity of tone throughout.   The loud notes were effortless, full, rich, and
ringing.   The high B's and B-flats had such solidity as to almost suggest those
of a spinto rather than a purely lyric singer.   The *mezza voce* tones retained
their focus and purity, in marked contrast, for example, to Pavarotti's husky
sounding attempts at soft singing.   Among tenors on records, only Gigli could
match their tonal beauty, but in Gigli's singing the soft tones were somehow
separated from the louder ones, as if the singer posessed two different voices.
McCormack could go from *mezza voce* to full voice with no abrupt change in quality
in passing from one to the other: his voice was completely integrated.   The
inborn urge for a pure legato which had led in his early days to use of a greatly
exaggerated *portamento* now resulted in the development of a breath control,
perhaps only equalled by Martinelli, in which the longest phrase could be
sustained on a single breath.   McCormack's vocal technique had become so firmly
ingrained that it allowed the artist almost unlimited freedom to express his
musical intentions, even though the intentions themselves were not yet fully
formed.
    Most of the 1909 recordings were of ballads.   Only five arias were
recorded, including remakes of titles recorded the previous year.   What proved
to be the last Odeon session, on 7 September 1909, was a marathon in which the
tenor recorded twenty-one sides, including two Tosti songs sung in beautiful
Italian.   McCormack's Italian was purer than any other language in which he
sang, not excluding English.   The very last Odeon disc, "Celeste Aida" from
Verdi's *Aida*, demonstrated the increase in the size and resonance of McCormack's
voice.   He never sang the role of Radames in the opera house, but this was
among his favorite arias at the time, and he sang it at William Ganz's Diamond
Jubilee Concert at Queen's Hall on 26 May 1908, at which the most celebrated
diva of the ninteenth century, Adelina Patti, emerged from retirement to make one
of her rare appearances.   McCormack's recording of "Celeste Aida" clearly
demonstrates his near idolatry of Enrico Caruso.   It is obviously patterned
after the Neapolitan tenor's 29 March 1908 Victor recording, even to the
inclusion of the unwritten upper mordant sung on the syllable "ci" in the phrase
"ergerti un trono vincino al sol," with which the E-flat in the fifth measure
from the end is ornamented.   Alas, McCormack's slavish imitation of Caruso also
included his taking the final high B-flat *forte* even though he would, as
demonstrated by his singing of the note in other music, have been one of the few
tenors capable of singing the note *pianissimo* as marked.   Aside from this minor
disappointment, it is an unusually impressive achievement for an essentially
lyric tenor, and, with nineteen known microgroove incarnations to date, the most
reissued of all McCormack's records.
    Coloratura soprano Luisa Tetrazzini, who had made her sensational Covent
Garden début the same season as McCormack, had been partnered by the Irish tenor
in many notable performances at the Royal Opera, and the two had become warm
friends.   Madame Tetrazzini had enjoyed a similar success at Oscar Hammerstein's
Manhattan Opera in New York City and she persuaded Hammerstein to engage
McCormack.   He made his highly acclaimed United States operatic début as Alfredo
in Verdi's *La Traviata* with Tetrazzini on 10 November 1909, the opening night of
what turned out to be the final season of the Manhattan Opera.   Calvin Child,
director of classical artists and repertoire for the Victor Talking Machine
Company, happened to hear McCormack in one of the Manhattan Opera's performances at

Hammerstein's Philadelphia Opera House.   Child was so impressed by McCormack's singing and the audience's enthusiastic response to the young tenor from Ireland that he asked him to make test recordings for Victor.   In addition to the incomparable Enrico Caruso, the Victor catalogue of 1910 listed recordings on the prestigious Red Seal label by tenors Carlo Albani, Florencio Constantino, Charles Dalmorès, Fernando DeLucia, George Hamlin, Riccardo Martin, Antonio Paoli, Georges Regis, Leo Slezak, the late Francesco Tamagno, Ellison Van Hoose, Even Williams, and Nicola Zerola.   The most celebrated of these tenors in the United States, Caruso, Slezak, and Tamagno, had either spinto or dramatic voices, leaving a gap in the catalogue which McCormack could fill by recording the lyric and *bel canto* arias for which his voice was best suited.   Also, none of the other Red Seal tenors were Irish, another gap for McCormack to fill by recording the songs of his native land.   Child's interest was doubly understandable.

On 3 January 1910, John McCormack went to the Camden, New Jersey studios of the Victor Talking Machine Company and recorded two sides: "Fra poco a me ricovero" from the Tomb Scene of Donizetti's *Lucia di Lammermoor* and "Killarney."   So successful were these test recordings that Victor, after negotiations in which the affiliated Gramophone Company (probably under instruction from Fred Gaisberg) refused to pay half the sum involved, bought out McCormack's contract with the International Talking Machine Company, which still had two years to run.   The two Victor test recordings were then assigned regular matrix and take numbers and commercially issued as Red Seal records. Additional recording sessions were immediately scheduled around McCormack's frequent operatic performances with the Manhattan Opera.

Despite Victor and HMV's success in putting the most celebrated artists under exclusive recording contract and in making the most money selling records and Victrolas and Gramophones on which to play them during this period, their recording process itself was in some ways less perfect than that used by their competitors.   McCormack's acoustical Victor and HMV recordings, like those of other musicians recording for these companies at the time, possessed certain noticeable defects that mar the reproduction of his voice.   In addition to the basic non-linearity of frequency response common to all acoustical recordings, the process used by Victor and HMV added extraneous noises, such as a grating roughness or faint rattle, to notes of a certain pitch on a given disc master. Sometimes this affected only loud notes of this pitch and would appear as the volume of the note increased and disappear as it decreased.   These extraneous sounds were artifacts of the recording apparatus and are found on all copies of the disc in which they occur, thus they are not to be confused with the noise and distortion arising from wear of a particular record.   This distorted marring of tonal purity may be heard on several of the loud F's below high C in Melba's 1913 Victor record of "Comin' Thro' the Rye."   The very same note is heard without distortion in her 1904 G & T recording.   Another example occurs on Pasquale Amato's high F-sharp in the duet "Su dunque! sorgete" from *Aida* with Johanna Gadski.   During the acoustical era it was customary to use different recording heads and horns for recording different different types of voices and instruments.   The acoustical recording heads and horns used by Victor and HMV for recording McCormack added extraneous noises to notes lying in the interval of a fifth below tenor high C.   A few of the many examples occur on the following loud high notes: F and G in "Three O'Clock in the Morning" (1922); F-sharp and G-sharp in "Luoghi sereni e cari" (1924); G in "Adeste Fideles" (1915), "Il mio tesoro" from *Don Giovanni* (1916), and "Little Town in the Ould County Down (1921); and B-flat in "Per viver vicino a Maria" from *La figlia del regimmento* (1910) and "Paul's Address" from *Natoma* (1912).   In the Donizetti aria the extraneous noise may be heard to vanish as McCormack executes a diminuendo. These peculiar sonic defects are not heard in McCormack's earlier recordings. By the time he was recording for Victor his voice had increased in power and it might be conjectured that it now over-taxed the recording diaphragm in a way his less developed voice had not done earlier.   However, this explanation seems unlikely since later recordings of other singers whose voices had already developed their full power when their earlier recordings were made exhibit these same defects, not heard on their earlier discs.   Melba's records have been mentioned as examples of this and Emmy Destinn's pre-1910 discs are likewise free from this defect heard on some of her later Victor records from the 'teens.   The most probable explanation is that the damping of the recording diaphragm was reduced in an effort to secure greater sensitivity to facilitate the recording of larger accompanying orchestras.   This permitted slightly more realistic sounding accompaniments but at some cost of fidelity and evenness of response.   Since McCormack's voice was especially distinguished by its smoothness and even emission, it is particularly disconcerting to hear these momentary distortions of

his pure tones which might hardly be noticed in records of a less polished vocalist.
     John McCormack was most active in opera during the years 1909 through 1913,
particularly during 1910.   During the 1909 - 1910 season he sang forty-seven
complete performances with the Manhattan Opera.   In 1910 he made more operatic
recordings than in any other single year, eighteen sides in all.   These include
Donizetti arias sung with extreme vocal finish, his beautiful Italian flowing
forth in a legato stream on a seemingly unending breath.   McCormack was a
"modern" singer in that he eschewed the late nineteenth century mannerisms, such
as the obtrusive fast vibrato that characterized the singing of Fernando DeLucia,
Alessandro Bonci, and Francesco Tamagno.   His tone by this time had become
wonderfully free and full, exquisitely modulated, with phrasing that was the
epitome of musicality and good taste.   The latter quality may be appreciated if
McCormack's recordings of two arias from the *Lucia di Lammermoor* Tomb Scene are
compared to Beniamino Gigli's or Richard Tucker's.   Gigli and Tucker tear the
musical line to tatters with exaggerated theatrical sobs, gulps, and gasps.
McCormack sings with a restraint and dignity that are a far more poignant
expression of Edgardo's grief at the death of his beloved.   After all, Donizetti
was a *bel canto*, not a *verismo*, composer!   Even Caruso's marvelous 1904
recording of "Una furtiva lagrima" from *L'Elisir d'Amore* seems a bit
narcissistically indulgent when compared to McCormack's elegant version.   Of
unusual interest among these 1910 Donizetti recordings is Tonio's aria from *La
Fille du Régiment*, which McCormack translated into Italian as "Per viver vicino a
Marie" and interpolated into *La Figlia del Reggimento* at the suggestion of
Charles Gilibert.   It is sung with consummate vocal control.   Madame Tetrazzini
naturally sang all her roles in Italian, including those from the French operas
Lakmé and *Les Pecheurs de Pérles*, so McCormack, who partnered her in these
operas, also learned them in Italian and recorded excerpts in that language.   At
this time he must have been more comfortable singing in that language than in
French, for he also recorded the tenor arias from *Carmen* and *Faust*, as well as
the final trio from the Gounod opera, in Italian.
     The *Faust* trio was one of the three ensembles recorded for the Gramophone
Company in May 1910 with the great Nellie Melba.   Perhaps because HMV had
refused to share the cost of securing McCormack's release from his Odeon
contract, it recorded him only in ensemble during his years at Covent Garden.
The ensembles with Melba are not especially successful.   McCormack was late in
arriving at the studio, so the story goes, which irked Melba.   Soprano and tenor
exchanged harsh words.   The resulting tension shows in the singing.   To make
matters worse, in the second take of the *Faust* trio, both McCormack and
Sammarco, the Mephistofeles, held the final note longer than the *diva*.   Of these
Melba-McCormack collaborations, only the *Rigoletto* quartet was published during
the soprano's lifetime.
     Since McCormack and Luisa Tetrazzini were such close friends, performing
together frequently in London and New York City and both under exclusive contract
to Victor/HMV, one wonders why they were never teamed in the recording studios of
either company.   They did record for Victor on the same days, 16 and 17 March
1911, but Tetrazzini was in New York City and McCormack in Camden.   For such a
prolific recording artist, Madame Tetrazzini made singularly few non-solo
records, in fact her only published ensembles were the *Lucia* sextet and the
Rigoletto quartet, both with Caruso.
     Despite their manifold musical and vocal beauties, John McCormack's 1910
operatic recordings are not ideal.   There is a lack of dramatic impetus such as
can be found in recordings of Caruso and Martinelli.   Most opera singers are
naturally more effective on stage than in the recording studio.   Marcella
Sembrich's studio recordings of arias, such as "Una voce poco fa" from Rossini's
Il Barbiere di Siviglia, are often devoid of musical authority and in spots
reveal a lack of mere vocal competence shocking in such a celebrated singer.
To a lesser extent, the same thing can be said of most of the studio-made
recordings of the legendary Lillian Nordica.   Modern listeners would have no
tangible appreciation of the true attainments of these sopranos had not Lionel
Mapleson, Metropolitan Opera music librarian, recorded a few fragments of their
live Metropolitan Opera performances on primitive wax cylinders.   A couple of
short excerpts from *La Fille du Régiment* prove Sembrich to have been an
accomplished and vivaciously charming *soubrette* capable of singing with genuine
brio.   The Mapleson cylinders of Nordica singing Meyerbeer and Wagner more than
sustain her great reputation: the commanding authority and soaring ease with
which she takes the high C's in the *Siegfried* finale contrasts markedly with the
tentative vocalism heard on some of her commercial recordings.   Evidently both
of these ladies needed the guidance of a competent conductor and the presence of
an appreciative audience to act as the catalyst that released their full musical

and vocal potential.   In more recent times, the studio recordings of Renata
Tebaldi and Jussi Bjoerling, beautifully sung though they are, lack the passion
of their actual stage performances.   Tebaldi's commercial recordings of *La Forza
del Destino* and *Tosca* contain no hint of the white heat generated in her live
performances of the operas conducted by Dimitri Mitropoulos available on
privately issued discs.   There are no recordings of McCormack in live opera
performances so it is impossible to say with certainty whether or not his
somewhat dramatically uninvolved 1910 operatic recordings are representative of
his stage performances of the period.   McCormack himself confessed to feeling
inadequate as an actor on the operatic stage, especally when portraying the
somewhat stilted characters in *bel canto* opera with whom he had difficulty
identifying.   In the latter parts of their careers, both Caruso and Martinelli
were acclaimed as great actors, and it is certain that McCormack never at any
time reached their dramatic heights on the opera stage.   However, McCormack
himself also said that his acting was about on par with Melba's.   No less an
authority than Emilio DeGogorza said that the only Melba recording representative
of her true qualities was another Mapleson cylinder, the priceless fragment of the
Queen's Aria from Meyerbeer's *Les Huguenots* recorded in performance at the
Metropolitan Opera in 1901.   It is not unreasonable to think, therefore, that
McCormack's early studio recordings of operatic excerpts do not tell the whole
story and that his live performances would have been more vividly characterized
than the isolated arias and ensembles on the records.
     In addition to the many operatic sides recorded that year, McCormack's 1910
records also included yet another round of the traditional Irish songs.   In
these remakes his singing has a good deal more nuance and subtlety than in the
excellent Odeons of a few years earlier, not to mention the 1904 versions, and
the sense of the text is given more emphasis.
     McCormack's operatic activities continued unabated even though Oscar
Hammerstein had sold the Manhattan Opera to the Metropolitan in the spring of
1910.   The Philadelphia-Chicago Grand Opera Company was organized as successor
to Hammerstein's company, and McCormack was a member of this troupe as well as of
the Boston Grand Opera Company during the 1910 - 1911 season.   He made his
Metropolitan Opera début on 29 November 1910, in *La Traviata*, partnering Melba
with whom he had sung frequently at Covent Garden.   McCormack and the
incomparable Mary Garden starred in the world première of Victor Herbert's
American Indian opera *Natoma*, presented in Philadelphia on 25 February 1911 by
the Philadelphia-Chicago company.
     After his session with HMV in May 1910, McCormack made no further records
until he visited Victor's New York City studios on 16 March 1911.   He had five
sessions with Victor that spring and two sessions with HMV in July.
Unfortunately, his operatic activity was mainly confined to the opera house that
year.   He recorded but three operatic titles: duets with baritone Mario
Sammarco from Bizet's *I Pescatori de Perle*, Ponchielli's *La Gioconda*, and
Rossini's *Il Barbiere di Siviglia*.   Sammarco and McCormack had become close
friends, but the baritone was not the ideal vocal collaborator, as he lacked
the tenor's vocal suavity.   Two non-operatic *bel canto* novelties were a pair of
duets from Rossini's "Les Soirées Musicales" in which McCormack was partnered by
Sammarco and Emmy Destinn, this being his only recorded collaboration with the
fiery Bohemian soprano.   The remaining 1911 recordings were mostly Irish songs
such as "Macushla," which was sung with a meltingly lovely tone.   Such songs had
evidently proven to be better sellers than the operatic discs.   The evergreen
"I'm Falling in Love With Someone" from Victor Herbert's *Naughty Marietta* was the
first of many popular songs McCormack was to record.   Another notable disc from
1911 was "Ah! Moon of My Delight" from Liza Lehmann's song cycle "In a Persian
Garden" which McCormack had sung at Queen's Hall, London in 1907.
     McCormack cut his 1911 Covent Garden season short in order to tour Australia
as leading tenor with Melba's opera company.   His first extensive concert tour
took place upon his return to the United States in the spring of 1912.   It's
phenomenal success helped to convince McCormack that his true *métier* lay in
concert rather than opera.   Though his operatic career was to continue for
eleven more years, concerts came to occupy a place of ever-increasing importance
in his music making.
     In 1912, McCormack recorded eight operatic titles for Victor and HMV.   Like
the duets recorded in 1911, these records demonstrated the effect of the
tremendous amount of operatic experience he had gained while singing with the
greatest artists of the age.   "Paul's Address" from *Natoma* and the fiery duet
from *La Gioconda* are sung with a dramatic fervor not found in any of the 1910
operatic recordings.   Similarly, the lyrical arias from Boito's *Mefistofele*
reveal a new intensity in McCormack's singing.   Whether his acting upon the

stage had likewise improved may be a moot question, but there can be no doubt
that he had learned to act with his voice.   On 15 July 1912 McCormack made his
last HMV recording until 1924, a duet from Wolf-Ferrari's *I Gioielli della
Madonna*, his only recording with the great contralto Louise Kirkby-Lunn.   The
tenor had been especially pleased with his performances in Gounod's *Roméo et
Juliette* with Melba during the Australian tour, so it is especially disappointing
that his recording of Roméo's aria "Ah! lève-toi soleil" was never published.
Victor issued a Red Seal version of the aria by Charles Dalmorès and a purple
label version by Lambert Murphy.   Another tantalizing unpublished McCormack
recording from this period was "O Souverain, O Juge, O Père!" from Massenet's *Le
Cid*.   Riccardo Martin had recorded this aria for Victor in 1910 and Caruso was
to record his definitive interpretation in 1916.   These two unpublished arias
were the first McCormack recordings to be sung in French.   The operatic arias
recorded in 1912 were not the only music to benefit from the tenor's newly
acquired ability to convey heightened emotion through his singing.   A not
particularly distinguished song, "Nirvana," recorded in December of that year was
sung with an almost ecstatic passion.
     The tenor was again a member of the Boston Grand Opera Company during its
1912 - 1913 season, during which he sang his first United States performance of
Don Ottavio in *Don Giovanni* under the baton of Felix Weingartner.   Mozart's
masterpiece was not performed at the Metropolitan during the years of McCormack's
operatic career, but he did sing the aria "Il mio tesoro" at one of the Met's
Sunday Concerts a couple of years later.   Other Boston Opera performances
included Verdi's *Messa da Requiem* with Elizabeth Amdsen, Maria Gay, and José
Mardones, and Rossini's *Il Barbiere di Siviglia* with the brilliant coloratura
soprano Frieda Hempel who, like McCormack, was able to maintain a career by
virtue of superb musicianship long after her voice had lost its original range
and flexibility.   In addition, McCormack gave sixty-seven United State concerts
during the 1912 - 1913 season.   Melba chose him as her Rodolfo in the gala
performance of *La Boheme* on 22 May 1913 - the twenty-fifth anniversary of her
Covent Garden début.   After the London season, McCormack made a triumphant
concert tour of Australia with accompanist Vincent O'Brien, choirmaster of the
Palestrina Choir in Dublin in which McCormack had sung as a teenager.
     The 1913 recordings consisted mainly of concert songs and sentimental
encores, such as "Silver Threads Among the Gold," and included but four operatic
titles.   The dream aria from Massenet's *Manon* was sung in Italian, but the
Micaëla-Don José duet from Bizet's *Carmen* with concert soprano Lucy Isabelle
Marsh became McCormack's first published recording to be sung in French.   The
date 2 May 1913 marked an important milestone in John McCormack's recording
career: on that day he made his first records with the excellent pianist Edwin
("Teddy") Schneider, who was to remain his regular accompanist for over a quarter
of a century and prove to be the ideal musical partner.
     McCormack's next United States concert tour began in October 1913 and
extended through March 1914.   On 25 March 1914 he recorded Braga's "Angel's
Serenade" with violin obbligato by the immortal Fritz Kreisler, the first of many
recorded collaborations by these two celebrated artists, which included the
"Berceuse" from Godard's *Jocelyn* recorded at the same session.   Most of
McCormack's 1914 operatic recordings were of ensembles, including duets from *La
Traviata* and *La Boheme* as well as the quartet from *Rigoletto* with the greatly
beloved Spanish soprano Lucrezia Bori.   Bori was one of McCormack's favorite
Mimi's, and the gentle quality of their voices blended more satisfactorily on
records than the combination of Melba and McCormack, despite a trace of
shrillness in Bori's top notes.   The smooth voice of Reinald Werrenrath, a much
underrated baritone and the Rigoletto in the quartet, likewise proved to better
match McCormack's voice than Sammarco's rougher *timbre*.   Werrenrath took part in
the background chorus of a number of McCormack's recordings as well as singing
several duets with the tenor.   Lucy Isabelle Marsh was again teamed with
McCormack in a poignantly lyrical version of "O terra addio" from the *Aida* Tomb
Scene.   They were joined by Werrenrath in two takes of the trio from Verdi's
Attila, neither of which was ever issued.
     In June 1914, McCormack sang for the last time with the Boston Grand Opera
Company while it was on tour in Paris, before returning to London for the Royal
Opera season where he appeared in performances of *Mefistofele* with the exciting
Rosa Raisa and the divine Claudia Muzio, his other favorite Mimi.   The aged but
still legendary Lilli Lehmann invited McCormack to appear as Don Ottavio in an
all-star production of *Don Giovanni* at the Salzburg Festival that August with
herself as Donna Anna, Geraldine Farrar as Zerlina, Johanna Gadski as Donna
Elvira, Antonio Scotti as Don Giovanni, and José Mardones as Leporello.   After
giving concerts, McCormack was enroute to Salzburg when Germany declared war on

England and invaded Belgium.   The Salzburg Festival was cancelled and the
McCormacks immediately returned to London and in October sailed for America.
     McCormack's first recording after the beginning of the European war was of
the famous "It's a Long Way to Tipperary," made on 23 November 1914.   "Somewhere
a Voice is Calling" was recorded at the same session.   It was sung with an
exquisite sweetness of tone and a beautifully controlled high ending not found in
the electrically recorded remake of 1927.   By this time, John McCormack had
become the most popular concert singer in the country.   During the 1914 - 1915
season he sang ninety-five concerts.   His recital programs were carefully
planned to please all of his audience at least some of the time.   A typical
McCormack recital would open with a classical group, largely Bach, Handel, and
Mozart with a few classical Italian airs.   Next would come art songs including
German lieder which were sung in translation during the war years,   Suitable
encores would follow each group.   After intermission, a group of traditional
Irish airs and encores would be sung followed by songs of a strictly popular
nature.   At the conclusion of the recital the tenor would be compelled to sing
encore after encore until he had sung a great many of the audience's favorites.
     McCormack developed a gigantic repertoire.   In the 1915 - 1916 season he
gave twelve concerts in New York City alone without repeating a single number,
save encores.   He visited music shops on his tour routes looking for new items
to perform.   He and Teddy Schneider devoted much time and effort to the selection
of new music, aided in no small way by their excellent sight-reading abilities.
     Part of McCormack's widespread popularity derived from his unusually catholic
repertoire which appealed to music lovers of widely divergent tastes.   Another
part was a result of the sheer beauty and individuality of his voice, his
unmatched technical skills, and his inspired musicality.   To these must be added
the unsurpassed eloquence of his singing in the English language, a virtue less
than universal among his lyric brethren.   Most singers adopt a peculiar
flavorless pronunciation when singing in English which they would never use in
speaking.   Richard Crooks, for example, was guilty of this in addition to
invariably using distorted vowel sounds to facilitate the production of his high
notes, giving his otherwise attractive singing an unappealing artificiality that
somehow distanced him from his audience.   McCormack's singing, despite his Irish
accent, was free from such stilted-sounding mannerisms.   He sang as he spoke and
did not alter the pronunciation because of high *tessitura*, thus retaining a
certain naturalness that enhanced his ability to communicate.   Yet the essence
of his art transcended these mere means - deriving instead from his ability to
reach his listeners, to express a wide range of human emotion through song, to
involve his audience and profoundly move them.
     During the period in which McCormack was at the peak of his popularity as a
concert artist, from the early 'teens through the mid-'thirties, it is surely no
mere coincidence that the two other most popular concert artists were pianist
Ignace Jan Paderewski and violinist Fritz Kreisler.   As dissimilar in some ways
as these three musicians might seem, they appear to have shared a power that
accounted for their overwhelming appeal.   Paderewski's playing of his own
"Chant du Voyageur" and "Nocturne in B-flat" as well as some of Chopin's works
evoked the nostalgic sensibilities of his audience.   It was as if they were
hearing music from some long-forgotten age.   Kreisler, especially in his own
charming miniatures, evoked the romantic flavor of Old Vienna.   McCormack was
able to accomplish much the same effect, evoking not merely a mythical Ireland
but also a more universally felt nostalgia.   All three of these supreme artists
were able, as it were, to cast a spell (on records as well as in the concert hall)
that transported the listener from a mundane reality to a somewhat bitter-sweet
never-never-land.   Such an ability is exceedingly rare.   It never seems to
occur in our more sophisticated age and its absence is our loss.   Despite all
the great pianists, violinists, and singers to come along since the heyday of
these three unique musicians, none of them can be truly said to have had a
successor - McCormack least of all.   Other tenors sang and recorded some of the
same repertoire, yet Eugene Conley, Richard Crooks, Theo Karle, Christopher
Lynch, James Melton, Colin O'More, and Walter Scanlan are largely forgotten today
except by collectors of vintage discs.   Their appeal was mainly confined to
their own age whereas McCormack's transcends temporal limitations.
     The Victor Talking Machine Company was ever on the lookout for new talent.
In late 1913 the company added to its roster of stellar tenors, Caruso and
McCormack, another uniquely great artist, Giovanni Martinelli.   Martinelli, a
spinto primarily active in opera, was assigned many arias to record by Victor in
1914 and the years following.   This fact, along with McCormack's decrease in
operatic activity, may explain the paucity of his operatic recordings from this
period.   He made no published recordings of opera in 1915.   Most of his discs

that year were of concert favorites, plus a couple of war songs.   Dix's "The
Trumpeter" recorded on 30 March 1915 well illustrates McCormack's powers.   The
utter depths and sincerity of emotion conveyed by his singing are truly awesome,
especially the poignant tone quality his voice takes on when expressing the
agony of the trumpeter playing his rallying call to dead soldiers "who are lying
around, face down to the ground, and they can't hear me sound the rally."   At
the conclusion of the song when the dead soldiers hear Gabriel play his heavenly
trumpet, McCormack's voice takes on an heroic, exalting quality, perfectly suited
to the lighter Wagnerian roles, which he never was to sing.   Today, the words of
the song may reek of period sentimentality, but the absolute conviction of
McCormack's utterance can be almost frighteningly cathartic when the record is
heard by a modern listener who is even slightly susceptible.   One can only
imagine the effect it must have had on contemporary audiences at a time when
young men were slaughtering each other in the European holocaust.
    On 31 March 1915 McCormack brought his eight year old son, Cyril, to a
Victor recording studio to record "It's a Long Way to Tipperary."   Cyril sang
in piping tones with a clear Irish accent that was delightful and Papa joined in
on the refrain.   He did the same thing two years later on 9 May 1917 when his
eight year old daughter, Gwen, recorded "Poor Butterfly."
    On 14 January 1916 McCormack recorded one take of "M'appari" from Flotow's
Martha, but Victor chose to issue Giovanni Martinelli's 28 March 1916 recording
instead.   McCormack made the most famous of all his recordings, "Il mio tesoro"
from *Don Giovanni* on 9 May of that year.   He had sung the opera in January with
the Chicago Grand Opera Company.   The amazing execution of the intricate
fioritura and the remarkable breath control, not to mention the lovely sound of
his voice and his infallible musical taste, have made the performance on this
recording the touchstone against which all other versions are judged.   It is the
recording that McCormack himself wanted to be remembered by and it would seem
that his wish has been fulfilled, judging by its fifteen microgroove incarnations
to date.   His lilting version of "When Irish Eyes Are Smiling" was recorded on
20 September 1916.   The United States had not yet been drawn into the European
war, so performances and recordings of Wagner's music were not yet proscribed.
Thus McCormack was able to record his lyrically sung "Prize Song" from *Die
Meistersinger*, albeit in English.   Such a recording would not have been allowed
two years later because of the pernicious anti-German hysteria then prevailing.
    By this time, McCormack's operatic appearances had become sporadic indeed,
among them *La Boheme* at the Metropolitan with the sympathetic-voiced Frances
Alda and in Chicago in 1918 with the sensational new soprano Amelita Galli-Curci,
who shortly would rival the tenor in popularity, and *Tosca* and *Madama Butterfly*
at the Metropolitan with the beautiful Geraldine Farrar.   McCormack made an
extensive tour on behalf of the Red Cross.   He sang "The Star Spangled Banner"
at a Fourth of July ceremony at George Washington's tomb.   President Wilson
himself told the tenor that it was the best performance of the National Anthem
he had ever heard - no doubt a sincere compliment, though not the most gallant
thing to say since the president's own daughter Margaret, a soprano, had recently
recorded "The Star Spangled Banner" for Columbia!   McCormack recorded his own
stirring rendition for Victor on 29 March 1917.   Naturally he recorded more war
songs during that fateful year, including "Keep the Home Fires Burning" and "Send
Me Away With a Smile."   In 1918 he recorded "God Be With Our Boys Tonight" and
George M. Cohan's "When You Come Back."   At war bond rallies McCormack would
autograph copies of his records for a certain amount of bond purchases.   His
efforts were reputed to have raised more money than those of any other musician.
    John McCormack was a deeply religious man and, like the later opera singers
Jan Peerce and Jerome Hines, rather publicly ostentatious in his faith.
Religious songs of varying musical quality naturally came to have a place in his
concerts.   One of the best, "The Lord is My Light," Frances Allitsen's setting
of the 27th Psalm, was recorded on 23 October 1917.   It was sung in a manner that
bespoke McCormack's extroverted faith.   A musical rarity, also of a religious
nature, was recorded at the same session, the aria "Champs paternels! Hébron
douce vallée" from *Joseph en Égypte*, Mehul's biblical opera.   The Belgian tenor
Fernand Ansseau recorded it a few years later for HMV.   A comparison of the two
performances confirms McCormack's greatness.   The distinguishing qualities of
McCormack's performance are the tonal equality of his voice throughout its range,
the smooth legato, and the elegant phrasing befitting music of the period.
Ansseau sings the aria in a more heroic manner with grandly ringing high notes,
but with coarse-sounding low notes, poor legato, insensitive phrasing and a
stylistically alien *verismo* intensity.
    The Victor Talking Machine Company had, during its first fifteen years of
existence, achieved unparalleled commercial success and attained tremendous

prestige through its ability to advertise Victor records by most of the famous classical musicians of the time.   During this period Victor's artistic growth had paralleled the growth of its physical and monetary resources.   In its earliest years, when its competitors offered little serious music on their records, Victor began recording a few of the popular operatic arias by competent if uncelebrated singers as well as a few band renditions of overtures and potpourris.   A few years later, following Columbia's short-lived lead, Victor put a few of the great names in opera and concert under exclusive contract. Among these was the elegant concert baritone Emilio De Gogorza, a pioneer recording artist.   De Gogorza not only made excellent records himself, but was also put on the Victor payroll to act as artistic liason between the company and the famous singers it wanted to record.   By 1912, largely through De Gogorza's tactful and solicitous efforts, virtually all the truly stellar names in opera and concert in the United States had become exclusive Victor artists, the only important exceptions being violinist Eugen Ysaye, pianist Josef Hofmann, and sopranos Mary Garden, Lillian Nordica, and Olive Fremstad, who were all under exclusive contract to Columbia.   Victor's recorded operatic repertoire by this time extended far beyond the most popular arias to include important duets, ensembles, and choruses.   Most ambitious was an extensive series of excerpts from *Faust* starring Geraldine Farrar, Enrico Caruso, Antonio Scotti, and Marcel Journet.   Victor established an excellent "house" orchestra which played the accompaniments for operatic items as well as recording overtures and a few abridged movements from the most popular symphonies.   In 1915 extensive recordings of excerpts from *Carmen* featuring Geraldine Farrar, Giovanni Martinelli, and Pasquale Amato were recorded and around 1916 the Victor Concert Orchestra, conducted by Joseph Pasternack, recorded Beethoven's *Fifth Symphony* in its entirety, the first complete symphony to have been recorded in the United States.   At this point Victor's progress in expanding the range of its recorded repertoire came to an abrupt halt.   The company was prospering as never before and the logical development would have been to record complete operas by its unmatched galaxy of stars and additional complete symphonies by established symphony orchestras under celebrated conductors.   In actuality, no such developments took place.   Columbia, which had made recordings of Felix Weingartner conducting the Columbia Symphony as early as 1913, took the lead again by engaging the Chicago Symphony under its excellent conductor Frederick Stock to record a few short pieces in 1916.   More than a year later, Victor followed suit by recording the Boston Symphony under Dr. Karl Muck, the great Wagnerian, and the Philadelphia Orchestra under the magnetic Leopold Stokowski. Complete symphonic works were not recorded by either company until the mid-'twenties.   After 1915, Victor recorded only the most popular opera arias, duets, and a mere handful of ensembles.   Not until 1939 was RCA Victor to again record an extensive series of excerpts from an opera.   Not until 1950 was it to record a complete opera, something Columbia had been doing since 1947 and the European companies since 1907!

During the war years and into the 'twenties the great singers under contract to Victor began to record a larger proportion of lighter works, many of a strictly ephemeral nature.   Evidently it was thought that these would have a wider appeal to a mass market than more serious music.   Less emphasis was placed on preserving great vocal art for the ages.   Maximizing short-term profits now took precedence over investing in recordings of classical masterpieces that could be expected to have a smaller but steady sale over an extended period of years. Because of the spectacular sales of McCormack's recordings of popular music, Victor almost totally ignored the more serious portions of his repertoire during a period when he had begun to include quantities of classical arias and lieder on his programs.   Often the release of the few serious items that were recorded was delayed, some only being issued after McCormack's death over twenty years later, while the popular items were, of course, issued immediately.   During the last five years of the acoustical recording era McCormack recorded almost two hundred matrices.   His only Victor recordings of serious music during this period were "Se il mio nome" from Rossini's *Il Barbiere di Siviglia* recorded in 1919 (never issued), "O Sleep! Why Dost Thou Leave Me?" from Handel's *Semele*, Schumann's "The Singer's Consolation" (issued in a limited edition in the mid-'fifties, but not generally circulated until 1977), and Rachmaninoff's "When Night Descends" and "O Cease Thy Singing Maiden Fair" (both with Kreisler) recorded in 1920; Rachmaninoff's "To the Children" (again with Kreisler and not published until 1984 by an independent label although a 1924 HMV remake was issued in England) recorded in 1922; Lotti's "Pur Dicesti" and Kramer's "Swans" (their issuance delayed until the very end of the acoustical era in 1925), Franz's "O Thank Not Me" (not published until the 1980's by an independent label), Schubert's "Die

Liebe hat gelogen" (issued in a limited edition in the mid-'fifties) and "Der
Jungling an der Quelle" (unpublished) recorded in 1923.   That was all.   Victor
also failed to issue any of McCormack's 1924 HMV recordings of art songs and
lieder to which they had rights.   One would have thought the profits from the
vast sales of McCormack's popular records would have been sufficient to subsidize
the issuance of at least a few of the less commercially viable items.   It is
partly because of this benighted policy on Victor's part that many present day
music lovers consider McCormack *only* a singer of Irish ballads and sentimental
songs.

As previously mentioned, McCormack was the victim of a near-fatal illness, a
streptococcus infection, in April 1922.   Even after his convalescence he did not
try his voice and spent the entire summer of 1922 without singing a note.   It
was not until 15 October 1922 at the Hippodrome in New York City, scene of many
of his previous triumphs, that he gave his first concert following his illness.
Two days later he returned to the recording studio.   Most of the titles recorded
that October, such as the best-selling "Three O'Clock in the Morning," placed few
demands on the voice.   One however, "The Lost Chord," is sung with a noticeable
restraint and the voice fails to ring out at the climax as it would have done
prior to his illness.   It is evident that his voice had lost power; the very top
notes, especially, lacked their former freedom.   From this time through the end
of his recording career twenty years later, McCormack's voice underwent a slow
but perceptible decline.   It became more baritonal and in place of its former
sweetness it took on a dusky quality.   The famous *pianissimo* high notes began to
show slight signs of noticeable effort and occasional insecurity.   The loud
upper tones took on a darker somewhat hollow sound in place of their previous
easy clarion ring and a slight nasality was sometimes apparent.   As the years
passed these changes became more pronounced.

If a classical singer has been properly trained and does not neglect or abuse
his voice, noticeable vocal decline will not take place until around age fifty.
This was the case with the voices of Giovanni Martinelli, Helen Traubel, and Lily
Pons, though Pons' retained an almost miraculous vocal quality at the time of her
final concerts at age seventy-four.   Other singers, such as Kirsten Flagstad,
Joan Sutherland, Florence Easton, Fernando DeLucia, Lauritz Melchior, Jan Peerce,
Richard Tucker, and Feodor Chaliapin, were able to sing almost as well at sixty
as they ever did.   Until his illness in 1922, McCormack's voice showed
absolutely no sign of the exceedingly hard use to which it had been subjected by
the rigors of his career.   From 1914 to 1920 McCormack never sang less than
eighty concerts each season in the United States.   It must be remembered that
concerts of that period were more extended affairs than they are today.
McCormack would sing upwards of two dozen songs and arias.   Thus, each concert
would contain as much actual singing as McCormack would have done in two or three
complete opera performances.   Few if any other singers have done so much singing
over such an extended period of years.   His immense popularity made it necessary
for his recitals to be given in the halls with the greatest seating capacity and
he thus was required to project his voice to fill these hugh spaces, placing
demands on it that singing in more intimate concert rooms would never have done.
Not only did McCormack's voice show no ill effects from this heroic amount of
strenuous singing, it seemed to thrive on such activity.   There can be no doubt
that because of his proper schooling with Sabatini, McCormack's voice would have
remained untouched by the years until he was in his sixties, had his illness not
precipitated its premature decline.

John McCormack's last operatic performances took place in the early
'twenties in Monte Carlo, where he appeared in *Il Barbiere di Siviglia, Madama
Butterfly, Tosca, Martha,* and on 17 March 1923, the world premier of
Moussorgsky's *La Foire de Sorotchintzi.*   His farewell operatic performance, in
the Moussorgsky work, took place on 25 March 1923, bringing his eighteen year
operatic career to a close.

The year 1924 saw McCormack's return to London for recordings and recitals,
his first appearances there since 1914.   Three recording sessions for the
Gramophone Company took place in September, at which were recorded some of the
classics which Victor had for so long neglected: lieder by Schubert, Schumann,
Brahms, Wolf, and Richard Strauss; arias by Handel and Donaudy; and songs by
Mozart and Rachmaninoff.   These revealed the darkening of his voice and the soft
high notes were perhaps less well integrated with the rest of the voice than they
would have been a few years earlier, but the legato as well as the musicianship
remained unimpaired.

Since mid-century a style of lieder singing has become dominant in which the
singer tries to emphasize each minute shade of meaning in the text through vocal
inflections.   As a result, the musical line suffers.   Carried to extreme, this

can cause the song to degenerate into little more than a series of mannered nuances.   It is probable that this peculiar style of lieder singing will one day seem as quaint as a nineteenth century thespian's over-dramatic declamation of Shakespeare's prose would seem to us.   McCormack's lieder singing was in marked contrast to this tortured approach.   He maintained a just balance, emphasizing neither text nor music at the expense of the other.   His German was both intelligible and eloquent.   Though it retained a slight Celtic flavor, it was not nearly as strongly accented as his English.   Like everything he sang, these lieder were carefully prepared in rehearsal, but the effect of spontaneity was never sacrificed nor the communication diminished.   The darker hue his voice had taken on by this time enhanced his range of expressivity.   McCormack's lieder records stand up to frequent rehearings in a way that the overly-precious performances of some later singers do not.

The tenor returned to the United State before the end of 1924 and his last acoustical recording session took place on 17 December of that year. Predictably, after the musical heights of Handel, Mozart, Schubert, and Brahms the Victor repertoire was something of a letdown: Irving Berlin's "All Alone" and Rudolf Friml's "Rose Marie."   This was, however, the golden age of the American popular song.   McCormack sang and recorded some of the best, as well as some that are best forgotten, including songs by Victor Herbert, Jerome Kern, Irving Berlin, Rudolf Friml, Buddy DeSylva, Lew Brown, Ray Henderson, and Sigmund Romberg.   Many of these songs have since become "standards" and are heard to the present day in a variety of arrangements.   On one of his radio broadcasts in the 'thirties McCormack talked about singing lieder at a party with none other than George Gershwin playing the piano accompaniments – quite well, according to the tenor.   It is strange that McCormack never recorded a single Gershwin song.   The singer approached this light-weight material with the same seriousness of purpose that he brought to a Mozart aria or a Wolf lied, totally without condescension and without trying to impose spurious subtleties.   When classically trained singers attempt to perform popular music the results are often less than successful but McCormack belonged to that small group of artists, including Helen Traubel and Elly Ameling, able to sing popular music without sacrificing either its spirit or their own dignity.

John McCormack made his first electrically recorded disc, a pleasant though not especially distinguished popular song, "When You and I Were Seventeen," on 23 April 1925 in Victor's Camden studios.   The early electrical recording process added a slight edge and trace of nasality to the reproduction of his voice.   The accompaniments were much more realistically recorded but the same altered orchestration deemed necessary for acoustical recording, especially the substitution of prominent tuba for string basses, was retained for several years. By the autumn of 1925 the engineers had perfected the new recording process so that the nasality characterizing the very early electrics was eliminated to a great extent and the by now darkened quality of McCormack's voice was recorded with a realism that captured more of its heightened expressiveness than was possible with the earlier recording technique.   It became possible to record a larger supporting chorus and the 1926 remake of "Adeste Fideles" featured the eighteen member Trinity Choir, which included among its tenors the young Richard Crooks, successor to some of McCormack's repertoire.

On 1 September 1927 McCormack made his first electrical recordings for HMV. Again, a more serious repertoire was chosen.   Selections included lieder by Schubert and Richard Strauss as well as art songs by Bantock and Quilter, among others.   Victor sessions in October 1927 yielded some of McCormack's most famous records of lighter pieces. his last and definitive versions of "Kathleen Mavourneen," "Mother Machree," and "I Hear You Calling Me."   Like nearly all the HMV recordings from 1924 until his retirement, these 1927 Victor discs benefitted immeasurably by having Teddy Schneider as piano accompanist rather than the schrammel orchestra usually provided.   However, Victor returned to the orchestral accompaniments in the autumn of 1928, tuba and all.

In 1928 Victor embarked on an ambitious, though artistically misguided, project to commemorate the one hundredth anniversary of Franz Schubert's untimely death, a series of Schubert lieder sung by McCormack in English and accompanied by a large orchestra (with male chorus in some cases) rather than the piano of the composer's original settings.   This expensive project constituted a real period piece, but it is sad that McCormack's sensitive and moving performances had to be marred by such bloated arrangements.   The male chorus heard on some of the Schubert recordings included the very young James Melton who was later to make recordings of some of McCormack's repertoire in the 'forties, including one of the better non-McCormack versions of "Il mio tesoro."

The Schubert monstrosity constituted McCormack's last recordings for the old

Victor Talking Machine Company.   When he again recorded for Victor in April of
1929 it was for the RCA Victor Division, Radio Corporation of America.   Again
only lighter material was chosen.   In October 1929 McCormack recorded some of
the selections featured in the Fox film "Song O' My Heart" in which he made his
auspicious motion picture début.   It was completed in January 1930 and in
February McCormack returned to the RCA Victor studios to record other songs from
the film.   His last regular recordings for RCA Victor were of a more serious
nature, including an excerpt from Beethoven's *Christus am Ölberg* recorded on 27
February 1930, a Hugo Wolf song, and a lyrically poetic "O König" from Wagner's
Tristan und Isolde recorded on 10 March 1930 with a full symphony orchestra.
None of these musically consequential items were published until the 'fifties and
the Wolf song still remains unpublished.   After this date there were but two
further RCA Victor sessions, neither of which yielded recordings published at the
time.   The tenor's last RCA Victor session on 2 November 1931 was devoted wholly
to recording experimental 33-1/3rpm discs, none of which were ever issued.
These included two Wolf lieder and Thomas Moore's "The Last Rose of Summer."
The latter song seemed to be a "jinxed" title for McCormack as far as recordings
went.   He sang it frequently and recorded it four times between 1910 and 1931,
but none of the recordings were ever published, though the 1931 version is
rumored to exist and may yet be issued.

    McCormack's recording contract with RCA Victor was not to end until 1938,
but he made no recordings for them after 1931.   This in no way reflects any
decline in his popularity.   During this period he was singing a great deal on
the radio and receiving unprecedented numbers of fan letters in response to his
broadcasts.   RCA Victor's ceasing to record McCormack was brought about by
economic factors.   When the Radio Corporation of America bought out the Victor
Talking Machine Company in 1929, most of the contracts with famous (and
expensive) classical singers such as Rosa Ponselle, Mary Garden, Giovanni
Martinelli, Giuseppe DeLuca, and Ezio Pinza were terminated or allowed to lapse.
The advent of the depression with its devastating effect on the record business
reinforced this policy.   The Boston Symphony, Chicago Symphony, Detroit
Symphony, Philharmonic-Symphony Orchestra of New York, St. Louis Symphony, and
San Francisco Symphony were dropped from the active RCA Victor recording roster
and the Philadelphia Orchestra was reduced to about half of its concert strength
for recording purposes.   The few records of serious vocal music that were made
during this period were by young artists who could not yet command high fees,
among them Lily Pons, Helen Jepson, Gladys Swarthout, Richard Crooks, and John
Charles Thomas.   It was cheaper for RCA Victor to record Helen Jepson than Rosa
Ponselle; thus Jepson's "Ah! fors' è lui" was committed to disc and Ponselle's
was not.   Likewise, it was cheaper to record Richard Crooks than McCormack and
this fact alone is sufficient to explain why there were no RCA Victor records of
McCormack from this period.

    Fortunately, the European record industry was less affected by the
depression than its United States counterpart.   Thus, even after HMV and English
Columbia merged in 1931 to become Electrical and Musical Industries Limited, many
of their celebrated artists, McCormack among them, remained under contract and
continued to make records.   It is fortunate too that McCormack was making
broadcasts so frequently in the mid-'thirties and that home recording devices
were available with which to preserve them.   Prior to his retirement in 1938
there were recording sessions for EMI in each year through 1936, covering much of
his current repertoire.   A series of Wolf lieder was recorded by EMI under the
auspices of the Hugo Wolf Society.   Understandably, EMI was more interesting in
recording English art songs and traditional sentimental favorites than Tin Pan
Alley tunes.   The two Stephen Foster songs, "Sweetly She Sleeps, My Alice Fair"
and "Jeanie With the Light Brown Hair," are especially attractive and sung with
far greater sensitivity than Richard Crooks' album of Foster songs made about the
same time.   "Terence's Farewell to Kathleen" conjures up the aching feeling of
farewell with such vividness as to almost cause a lump in the throat of the
listener.   "The Kerry Dance" is one of McCormack's finest performances.   The
fact that his voice is no longer that of a young man adds to its verity since the
song is about an older person looking back to the halcyon days of his youth.

    McCormack's voice had continued the slow decline begun after his illness in
1922.   By the mid-'thirties his tone had lost much of its former vigor.   There
was an occasional unsteadiness, the top was becoming thin sounding and
increasingly insecure, and even the breath control was no longer the phenomenon
it had once been.   His musical instincts, though, remained and his personal
magnetism was as potent as ever.   Like Kreisler and Paderewski, both of whom
retained their hold on their audiences' affection long after age, accident, and
illness had robbed them of much of their former technical prowess, McCormack's

magical appeal continued unabated.   The Handel arias and lieder by Wagner and
Wolf recorded 7 April 1936 at McCormack's last HMV session prior to his
retirement remain great musical experiences.

A musician's art is usually derived from a unique combination of two factors:
instinct and learning.   McCormack posessed a particularly felicitous blending
of the intellectual and intuitive in his approach to musical interpretation.   He
was an excellent sight reader and in informal situations read through volumes of
lieder with the likes of Sergei Rachmaninoff and George Gershwin at the piano,
yet everything he sang in public was meticulously prepared.   This enabled him to
adjust to his increasing vocal limitations, eliminating from his repertoire music
to which he felt he could no longer do justic, revising his interpretations and
adding new pieces consonant with his current vocal means.   All the while he
miracuously maintained the unique instinctive spontaneity that had long
distinguished his singing.   Throughout his singing years McCormack continued
his daily vocalization on the excerises Sabatini had given him during his brief
period of study.   When a vocal problem arose in performance, he was usually able
to overcome it, as happened on 13 May 1937 during his singing of "Shannon River"
on a Bing Crosby radio show.   In addition to the pronounced unsteadiness of the
voice, McCormack was in obvious vocal distress.   A soft high note that occurred
several times in the song emerged as a hoarse croak, though he was able to sing
it *forte* without particular difficulty.   Most other singers in such a situation
would just sing the note loudly for safety's sake without regard for the musical
marking.   McCormack sang the note *forte* where appropriate but continued to
attempt the difficult *pianissimo* where called for, but without success.   In his
acute distress, he cut the note short and, usually the most rhythmically precise
of singers, came in a beat late on a phrase.   The listener can imagine the
terror in the singer's mind during this ordeal, being broadcast on live radio,
especially if he knew of McCormack's acute stage fright and the fact that the
song concluded on this same troblesome high note which must be sung softly and
sustained.   Evidently, during his singing of the song, McCormack was able to
make whatever adjustments were necessary in his vocal mechanism without
interrupting the music, for when the note emerged at the end of the song it is
sung with the customary McCormack tone: soft, clear, perfectly focused and
sustained.   It is a triumph of vocal technique over physical incapacity, and the
listener is moved to a renewed admiration of the artist.

McCormack made a cameo appearance in *Wings of the Morning*, filmed in the
summer of 1936.   In that year and the two years following, during which he made
no commercial recordings, he made a number of broadcasts which have been
preserved, thus continuing the unbroken documentation of his career.   His final
public appearance in the United States was in Buffalo, New York on 16 March 1937,
though he sang on broadcasts from Hollywood, California a year later.   His
British tour with a new accompanist, Gerald Moore, during the summer and autumn
of 1938 culminated in his Farewell Performance at the Royal Albert Hall, London
on 27 November.

During his retirement, McCormack took time to relax and travel with his
family.   After England declared war on Germany following the invasion of Poland
in 1939, he came out of retirement to sing for the Red Cross and the armed forces
as he had done in the United States during the previous war.   He also returned
to the HMV studios on 30 November 1939 and, with Gerald Moore at the piano,
recorded a total of 128 matrices in twenty-five wartime sessions between this
date and 10 September 1942.

McCormack had become the victim of a progressive pulmonary disease, yet
despite this, he drove himself unstintingly on behalf of his wartime charity
efforts.   His voice was, of course, affected by his illness.   It lost support
and legato and became more hollow sounding, with audibly effortful breathing.
Yet, it must again be stated that even these handicaps could not wholly impair
the effectiveness of his performances.   Some of his most cherishable recordings
date from this late period, mostly simpler songs which were obviously chosen with
great care.   "The Old House" was written especially for McCormack's Farewell.
"Off to Philadelphia" can bring tears to one's eyes, so convincingly does
McCormack convey the emigrant's desolation: at one point his voice sounds as if
he is choking in an effort to hold back his own tears.   The 1940 recording of
"The Bard of Armagh" was sung with personal feeling not heard in the 1920
version.   "When You Wish Upon a Star" is utterly charming.   Siegfried Och's
"Praise Ye the Lord" was sung with a simple dignity worthy of Handel, to whom it
was attributed at one time.   "Plasir d'amour" demonstrated that though the voice
itself was practically gone, the easy genuine trill remained, a tribute to the
singer's technique and Sabatini's teaching.

Among these last recordings, there are only two real disappointments: "God

Bless America" and "The Battle Hymn of the Republic," recorded shortly after the
bombing of Pearl Harbor.   The tenor altered the words of the Irving Berlin song
so as to stress the bond between England and the United States as allies in the
war, a not very subtle form of propaganda.   The results, despite repeated takes
in two different recording sessions, can only be described as feeble, the voice
having long since lost the clarion quality needed to project such songs with the
necessary vigor and conviction.   McCormack's patriotic feelings no doubt were
responsible for their selection, overriding his usual careful choice of music.
It is significant that neither of these songs was issued in the United States
until re-recorded to microgroove thirty-five years after they were made, as part
of a United States Bi-Centennial tribute album.

Of the three items recorded at the final session on 10 September 1942, two
were by Mozart, providing a suitable close to the recording career of one of the
finest of Mozart singers.   The very last commercial recording of his voice was
a pleasant song, "Waiting For You."   Of course, this was not intended to be the
tenor's last recording session.   He continued to sing for the armed forces and
to broadcast until 28 March 1943.   Because of exposure to the harsh wartime
winter he caught a bad cold that exacerbated his emphysema to the point where
further singing was impossible.

McCormack's adult life may be said to have been wholly dedicated to song.
The sheer amount of singing he did demonstrates this.   It was not an easy life.
Unlike the opera singer usually active for months at a time with an opera company
at its home base, the concert artist was constantly on the road.   The strain of
continual travel in the days before jets and air conditioning can hardly be
appreciated today.   McCormack tried to spend at least two or three months each
year at home with his family and to be with them on important holidays.
Especially after he relinquished his operatic career he spent most of his life
staying in hotels and traveling between a series of seemingly unending one night
stand concerts.   The terrifying stage fright from which he suffered has already
been alluded to: McCormack was haunted by the fear that he would open his mouth
to sing and no sound would come out.   It is hardly surprising that some of his
letters reveal that he occasionally rebelled against the constant strain and this
essentially wearying and lonely lifestyle.   Despite everything, McCormack
endured year after year of this lonely stressful life for the sake of his art.

By the time McCormack had been singing professionally for a decade he was
the highest paid singer before the public and thus he became a wealthy man at an
early age.   He was not compelled to perform because he needed the money.   The
man must simply have enjoyed singing, as Artur Rubinstein must have enjoyed
playing the piano and Andre Segovia, the guitar.   Musical talent and an
overwhelming love of music do not necessarily go hand in hand.   Maria Callas'
great talents brought her a celebrity that provided her entry into high society.
At the peak of her fame, she virtually abandoned her musical career and even
ceased her regular vocalizing.   It would seem that jet set social life meant
more to Callas than her art.   McCormack was fortunately not possessed of such a
fatal flaw.   In spite of his humble origins, he likewise achieved entry into the
upper strata of international society through the celebrity his art brought him.
He enjoyed socializing with other celebrities, musical and otherwise, including
statesmen, writers, artists, athletes, film stars, and members of the
aristocracy.   He owned or leased several palatial home and entertained lavishly,
entered his own horses in the Derby, owned paintings by famous artists, a
Stradivarius violin, and numerous Rolls Royce automobiles, and indulged in many
other extravagances.   Yet his love of music remained steadfast and he was never
seduced by this glittering social life into abandoning his art.

Many musicians after becoming established favorites fall into a rut and just
perform a small group of favorite works over and over.   Pianist Josef Hofmann
and conductor Arturo Toscanini were guilty of this in the latter years of their
careers.   The last one-quarter of the operatic careers of Lily Pons and Maria
Callas were sustained by a handful of performances of but two or three operas.
Soprano Frances Alda, so the story goes, after submitting her proposed programs
for her next concert tour to her manager, received a telegram from him containing
only a biblical citation, "Hebrews 13:8."   She opened the Bible to this verse
and read, "Jesus Christ the same yesterday, and today, and forever."   Madame
Alda took the hint and prepared new songs for her programs!   In striking
contrast to these famous musician's musical "laziness," McCormack enjoyed the
challenge of learning and performing new music and continued to do so until the
end of his lengthy career.

John McCormack's recordings reveal him as a singer for all seasons, from the
enthusiastic very young performer of Irish songs, to the young opera and concert
star revelling in his almost unlimited vocal gifts and technique while becoming a

great artist, to the middle-aged tenor reaching new levels of expressivity with his darkened voice, to the singer in old age with his voice clearly in decline but with his musicality triumphantly whole. His deep love of music was the driving force that enabled him to make such artistic transitions so successfully, to a degree attained by no other singer. McCormack was so ill after age fifty-eight as to be unable to sing at all. Even his speaking voice had become weak and husky. Singing had been his whole reason for living and even in these last years he would attempt to do so upon occasion, but most often he would just wave his hand in time with the music while others sang and played. He often listened to his own recordings, declaring "I was a damn good singer, wasn't I?" When he died in 1945, a life-long love affair with music came to an end.

John McCormack was the last of the line of great musicians, among them Adelina Patti, Ignace Jan Paderewski, Ernestine Schumann-Heink, Enrico Caruso, Fritz Kreisler, and Amelita Galli-Curci, to have been literally beloved by the public at large. Since McCormack, classical musicians, even the most celebrated, have with few exceptions enjoyed their fame within a more limited sphere. These exceptions have most often achieved a wider appeal for non-musical reasons. Texas pianist Van Cliburn no doubt had the most encompassing popularity of any classical musician within recent years, but that was, alas, for political more than musical reasons when he won the Tschaikowsky Competition in Moscow during the Cold War 'fifties. Maria Callas, posthumously, developed a large coterie of worshippers more drawn by her mystique than by her music, and Beverly Sills and Luciano Pavarotti had a few short years of fame outside of operatic circles derived, at least in Sill's case, from appearances on television talk shows. McCormack's appeal was far more universal and lasted for more than a quarter of a century during his lifetime. Since his death, his many recordings have kept his art alive for new generations of music lovers to enjoy. More of his records are available today than were available at any single time in the past. It seems likely that his popularity will continue into the immediate future, for his records preserve a unique voice used with an artistry that communicates through song perhaps more eloquently than any other singer in history. Through his legacy of recordings John McCormack has come as close as any man can to achieving immortality.

Documenting the Extant
Recordings

The McCormack Discography falls logically into five sections: 1) the 1904–1905 recordings of the untrained voice, made before and during his training in Italy; 2) the 1906–1909 recordings, reflecting the beginning of his career as a recitalist and his early success in operatic singing; 3) the acoustic records for Victor and HMV from 1910 through 1924, in which the pinnacle of his vocalism was reached; 4) the early electrical recordings, 1925–1936, for the same companies, showing his continuing development as a musician, though the voice has lost some of its earlier bloom; and 5) the later electrics, 1939 through 1942, in which the vastness of his repertoire and his stylistic finesse easily compensate for the declining voice.

Various figures have been published as the purported total of McCormack's recordings. We have been able to document 1197 commercial disc or cylinder recordings, of which 733 exist as published records, microgroove transfers, or test pressings of unpublished recordings. In addition there are 33 film recordings, of which 17 are extant. There are also 39 broadcast transcriptions known to exist, deriving originally from air or line checks. There may well be other test pressings or extant broadcasts that we have missed.

The significance of John McCormack as an artist transcends the recordings that survive him. The history of his career subsumes his activities in the recording studios. Our intention has been to document the latter and leave biographical matters and extensive criticism to others. We believe the records speak for themselves, but that, though they say a great deal, they do not constitute the sole basis for history's verdict on the art of McCormack. His public life touched innumerable people: listeners, friends, beneficiaries of his generosity, record collectors, and even critics. There is an undeniable consensus among all who knew him that he was a great singer, a generous human being, and a sincerely religious man. If he at times revelled in his life-style, basked in his acclaim, and was proud of his talent and accomplishments, it is understandable. In any event, such matters fall outside the scope and purpose of this discography.

All recordings of McCormack's singing that survive ought to be included in his discography. The fact that some are on film originals, and that others originated as broadcasts, is immaterial. That they exist and may be heard is sufficient. While we have documented all unpublished recordings known to have been made in the recording studios, as well as those known to have been made on film, we have not attempted to list any broadcast performances beyond those known to have survived in some sort of transcription. McCormack made hundreds of broadcasts on both sides of the Atlantic, and a listing of these is a task for others to undertake.

Although purists prefer to listen to McCormack's recordings in the form of the original discs and cylinders, there is no doubt that the transfer of these records to 45 and 33 rpm discs has made it possible for a much larger audience to appreciate his singing. It is impractical, if not impossible, for many afficionados of his singing to hear the original records properly reproduced. In the first place, the RIAA compensation curve is inappropriate for reproducing the acoustic and most of the electrical recordings. An audio equalizer along with flat preamplification is necessary for setting the proper curve, which varies from one group of records to the next, and for eliminating

those frequencies in which those early recordings have no musical sound. In
addition, most turntables today do not have a 78 rpm setting, and most of those
that do usually do not have sufficient range in their pitch control to achieve
the speeds above and below 78 rpm to play many of the McCormack records at the
proper pitch, necessarily an important requirement.   Proper styli for early recordings are manufactured for only a limited number of audio cartridges, and
proper stylus selection is as important as use of the proper curve and pitch.
Even for those collectors who have all the appropriate equipment, it is probable
that many of the rarer items will forever elude them.   Thus, even for these
collectors, microgroove transfers will constitute the only means, other than
tapes made by the more fortunate, of hearing such records.   For most people,
the availability of McCormack's recordings on numerous 33 rpm rerecordings, along
with its convenience, make this format a necessary choice.

McCormack has in fact been well served by long playing discs.   Transfers of
his recordings appeared at the dawn of the LP era and have appeared steadily
since then, both from the original recording companies and from many others.
As of 1984, McCormack's centenary year, nearly 300 discs containing one or more
of his recordings had been issued, with eight in that year alone.

Previous discographies have not documented this extensive series of reissues.
Philip Roden's early effort, of course, was compiled before the onset of long
playing discs.   The two editions of that compiled by Leonard Roe essentially
ignored this format, even though the second edition appeared in the early 1970's,
after more than one hundred EP and LP discs had been issued.   There is no doubt
that Roe's skepticism on this subject was justified in a number of cases where
the reissue had been poorly done and yielded worse sound than originals common-
ly available.   Nevertheless, most music lovers today rely on LP's, and an
accurate listing of their contents should be useful to collectors, librarians,
and casual listeners alike.   These discs have made McCormack's singing available
to a world that for the most part has forgotten the 78 rpm era and to people
who have probably never seen a machine that would play a shellac disc, much less
a cylinder.

In most cases, discography must be a collective enterprise to successfully
achieve the joint goals of accuracy and completeness.   The older the recordings
and the more numerous they are for a given artist, the more this axiom applies.
This discographic effort began with data supplied by the original recording company files and supplemented by previous discographies.   The surviving documentary
evidence of a recording company's activity is always to some extent incomplete,
often ambiguous, and usually less than easy to decipher.   For one set of McCormack's recordings (the Odeons), the original files are missing altogether.   For
the earlier Gramophone and Typewriter discs, the ledger is sketchy at best.   The
files for the Victor and Gramophone Company recordings are more extensive, but
they are fraught with confusing entries, ambiguities, and missing data.   To
overcome these deficiencies, the discographer must turn to outside help.   We have
received the benefit of help from several prominent scholars and discographers in
our efforts to derive the maximum use from the original company files.   Having
thus begun we turned to those collectors who specialize in McCormack's records.
Valuable as is the data from documentary evidence, that which derives from extant
records in the hands of collectors provides a very necessary supplement.   This is
especially true for the very early recordings.

McCormack has been the subject of several previous discographies.   The
first compilation, by Philip F. Roden, was published as an appendix to *I Hear You
Calling Me* (1949), Lily McCormack's biographical memoir of her husband.   This
was followed in 1956 by *John McCormack - The Complete Discography* by Leonard
F. X. McDermott Roe. In 1957 a landmark article and discography by Philip F.
Roden and Robert L. Webster appeared in *The Record Collector* magazine, which
documented in greater detail McCormack's Odeon recordings (1906-1909).   This
work has required little emendation over the years and is still a valuable reference.   Paul Morby published a similar article on the cylinder recordings in
the pages of the same journal in 1968.   In 1972 Roe published a second edition
of his discography, which included matrix and take numbers for most published
recordings and listed alternate takes and extant unpublished recordings which
had been discovered since his earlier work.   Two years later John Ward, Alan
Kelly, and John Perkins in their article, "The Search for John O'Reilly," documented the existence of six hitherto unsuspected G & T matrices of McCormack,
which had been published on the affiliated Zonophone label under the pseudonym
"John O'Reilly."   As of this writing, copies of all six are known to exist.
This article was also published in *The Record Collector*, as was in 1984 a detailed listing of the pre-1910 recordings by Brian Fawcett-Johnston.   John Keveny
published in the early 1970's in *The Newsletter of the John McCormack Society of
America* the results of a study that he and James Sheehan had made of the Edison

Bell cylinders which verified the existence of the alternate takes of these recordings.   We have benefitted from all of these research efforts and many more
besides in our attempt to compile a complete and accurate listing of McCormack's
recordings.

During his career, McCormack recorded for six companies.   There was no
overlap among the groups of records made for each, although he did make records
for the Victor and Gramophone Companies alternately from 1910 on. There are
various problems associated with the records for each company, which it will
be useful to survey briefly.

Most of McCormack's cylinder recordings predate his vocal training in Italy.
Other than the aria from *The Lily of Killarney* (Edison Bell 6447), all of them
were Irish ballads and parlor songs.   The Edisons and Edison Bells were all
recorded within a two month period in the fall of 1904.   The ten published Edison
cylinders were two-minute black wax records in the gold-molded series.   Presumab-
ly there was only one take of each of these.   The first Edison cylinder has the
following information on the edge in raised letters: "[*Title*]. *J. McCormack.
Thomas A. Edison. Pat'd 13124.*"   The remaining nine cylinders have this information incised on the surface of the cylinder, and the word "Patented" is spelled
out in full.   A small Arabic number (1, 2, 3, or 4) is located immediately after
it.   These are most likely manufacturing codes and not indicators of multiple
takes. Spoken announcements are by John McCormack.

The Edison Bell cylinders were also two-minute black wax and were recorded
in sets of four takes per title over a two day period.   The separate takes may
be distinguished (visually) by small Roman numerals following the catalog numbers incised on the surface of the cylinder.   Some examples of a first take omit
the numeral.   The recording date (3 or 10 November 1904) is given following the
take number.   The issue number, title, and artist's name ("*J. F. McCormack*") are
found on the edge of the cylinder in raised block letters.   No date is shown on
the cylinder of "Home to Athlone." This title was recorded later than the others,
either in the summer of 1905 or in 1906.   (In *I Hear You Calling Me*, Lily McCormack states that John came back from Italy in the summer of 1905 and "returned to
Milan at the end of September 1905.)   The voice is much better than on the other
cylinders made by this company, and it was packaged in a newer style container
than the others.   On this cylinder all of the recording and title information
is given on the edge in white letters.   The separate takes for this cylinder are
designated "A," "B," "C," or "D."   Spoken announcements are most likely by J. E.
Hough, who made them for many recordings by this company.   It must be noted
that until copies of all of the actual sets of four takes are located, it is uncertain that four takes of all titles were issued for sale.

In the case of the Sterling cylinders, probably only one take of each was
made.   These were "Special" three-minute black wax cylinders, one half inch
longer than the standard length.   Title, catalog number, and an alphabetical
manufacturing code ("A," "B," "C," or "D") are engraved on the edge of the
cylinder.   All Sterling cylinders were recorded originally on larger master
cylinders, the cylinders offered for sale being dubbings from these masters.
Two of McCormack's Sterling cylinders were also dubbed onto discs and marketed
by Pathé.

McCormack's 24 extant recordings for the Gramophone and Typewriter Company
(G & T) were all recorded within two weeks of the sessions which produced the
Edison Bell cylinders.   There were nine issued from 7 inch matrices and another
nine from 10 inch matrices.   Six further 10 inch recordings were issued on the
Zonophone label.   Discographic details for all G & T recordings derive largely
from extant files in the EMI Archives, supplemented by the research of several
scholars who have studied the activities of this company in its early years, and
from actual discs owned by individual collectors and libraries.   The original
source for the data on these records is a bound, handwritten ledger in the EMI
Archives.   Evidence suggests that it represents a copy made from earlier sheets
whose contents were somewhat hard to decipher.   The ledger is a listing by matrix
number and includes the artist and title of the record, as well as its issue
number (if it was published).   Some entries are marked "*destr.*," which seems to
mean that the wax was discarded on the spot, destroyed, and that no test pressings
were made.   Other matrix numbers have no entry at all regarding either publication or destruction.   A few lines in the ledger have a matrix number but no
other data at all.   In this discography we have followed the contents of this
ledger exactly, guided by the comments and caveats of Alan Kelly and his collaborator, the late John Perkins.   In only one instance, discussed below, does our
listing deviate from that of the original G & T ledger.

The Roe discographies did not list matrix numbers for the G & T records.
In both, however, he indicates that disc 3-2520 is "When Shall the Day Break
in Ireland."   The matrix number was listed in the 1974 article by Ward, Kelly,

and Perkins as 6464a, and extant copies in fact show this number in the wax.
The G & T ledger, though, shows the matrix number for this disc as 6463a.   The
next title, "Believe Me If All Those Endearing Young Charms," is shown with the
6464 serial number in the ledger, but the two entries for this title are given
with the suffixes "Ei" and "WD2."   According to Alan Kelly, these entries represent two separate recordings beyond that represented by 6464a.   Published copies
of disc 3-2519 also show the matrix number 6464a in the wax, but this is apparently an erroneous marking in the light of the ledger entries for this title.   Thus
two different discs bear the matrix number 6464a, but for disc 3-2519 the actual
matrix number is 6464WD2.   No copies of either disc are known to the compilers
to bear the matrix number 6463a in the wax.   This matrix number was in all
probability not used for any artist.   It has not been possible to explain these
departures from the G & T numbering system, other than to be sure that 6464Ei and
6464WD2 represent two separate and distinct takes.   Should disc 3-2519 turn up
bearing 6463a in the wax, it might well be an alternate take of "When Shall the
Day Break in Ireland," but to date this has not happened.

     Our designation of 76 rpm as the proper playing speed for the G & T records
is based on the sound of his voice at that speed and on the fact that it seems
consistent with the playing speeds of other G & T records of this period. Since
for records of this era a change in playing speed of four rpm causes a change
in pitch of a half step, the only other speed possible for McCormack's G & T
records is 72 rpm, one which some collectors prefer. This speed to the present
compilers, however, makes him sound too baritonal, and it is inconsistent with
the speeds for other G & T records of this time.   (For example, Melba's May 1904
recordings definitely play at 76 rpm.)

     Footnotes in our Recording Chronology indicate those matrix numbers for
which the G & T ledger offers only a blank line.   We have listed only those
entries which are undoubtedly by McCormack.   As best as can be determined, those
matrix numbers not listed are not by him.

     One of the most interesting discoveries in research on McCormack since the
second edition of Roe's discography was that of the six G & T matrices published
under the pseudonym "John O'Reilly" on Zonophone.   It was only after their existence was hypothesized by Ward, Kelly, and Perkins that the discs bearing this
name were credited to McCormack.   It was not uncommon for G & T matrices to be
issued on Zonophone in this period (cf. Lauder's discography, for example), as
well as for pseudonyms to be used as label credits.   (Peter Dawson comes to mind
in this regard.)   The intermeshing of the two sets of matrix numbers, along with
the sound of the voice, can only lead to the conclusion that the performances are
sung by the same artist.   All six are now known to exist; four have been transferred to LP.

     Several of the G & T labels list a violin obbligato where in fact none can
be heard.   We have noted this accompaniment only when it is audible on the record.

     Along with many pleasures for listeners, McCormack's recordings for the
Odeon Company present a variety of problems for listeners and discographers.   Of
the 93 matrices known to have been recorded 82 survive in the form of shellac
discs, published (79) and unpublished (3). Most of the former (64) have been reissued numerous times on microgroove.   The 82 extant recordings are often the
subject of controversy and dispute among McCormack's admirers, and it is the
intent here to describe the reasons for this.   Interested readers should also
consult the 1957 article by Roden and Webster.

     Looking down the numerical list of Odeon matrix numbers, one notices in
several places gaps in the series of from one to eleven places.   Since the Odeon
recording ledgers have apparently not survived, these gaps remain a mystery.
They may represent the efforts of other artists, or they may be recordings by
McCormack which were rejected for issue. In some cases they fall between two
recording sessions, and in others in the midst of a session.

     One of these gaps (Lx 1578) has been filled by interpolation based on the
testimony of Lily McCormack in chapter two of *I Hear You Calling Me*. When she
and John returned to England from Milan late in 1906, she writes,

          We found rooms suitable to our purse in Torrington Square,
     London, where many well known stage people were living; and John
     started at once to look for engagements. He was determined that
     we should get along on our own, and before leaving Milan had
     written to Arthur Brooks [manager of the Odeon Company], for
     whom he had made records before. . . . Arthur Brooks, however
     sent word that he would be happy to see John.

The evidence from matrix numbers is relevant here: McCormack's first Odeons are
numbered Lx 1565 through Lx 1582.   Thus the records that he had made "before"

are within only a day or two of those of the second session.   Perhaps Lily's memory is at fault insofar as Brooks might have previously *agreed* to make records with John but had not actually yet done so.   (Or could Brooks have previously worked for one of the companies for which McCormack had already made records?) At any rate there is no evidence of a McCormack recording prior to Lx 1565 for the Odeon Company.   Lily continued:

> Fearing that I would be lonely without him, John took me along, and while we were there I was thrilled to have Mr. Brooks ask us if we would like to record a duet.

Lily was an accomplished singer herself, and, even if her recollection of just when John first recorded for Odeon is faulty, she is not apt to forget making a record with her husband at this point in his career.   In the spring of 1907 McCormack experienced his first major successes in various Ballad Concerts in London, and in the fall of that year made his debut at Covent Garden.   Other than the aria from *The Lily of Killarney*, he had made no operatic recordings up to this point.   What is important to note is that the duet was not recorded until after the first Odeon session.   There is only one blank in the sequence of matrix numbers for the second session (Lx 1578), and it seems logical that this was the wax allotted for the private recording which Lily describes:

> We did "Home to Our Mountains" [Ai nostri monti, from *Il Trovatore*] which we had sung together before, and I recall that I was quite satisfied with myself. But when I heard the record I nearly wept and kept insisting that it wasn't my voice at all - it sounded like a foghorn. This was a turning point for me, and one which I never regretted. I never made another record, and I never sang in public again. I left the singing in the family to John, though I often teased him by accusing him of having me make that record on purpose!

Since Lily describes having heard the record, apparently a test pressing was made. It is not known to have survived, possibly an early victim of McCormack's well known propensity to destroy test pressings of less than perfect recordings.

Dating the Odeon recordings has long been problematic. On only one record (Lx 2844) does what seems to be a recording date appear in the wax (3 October 1908).   Though it has been known in which years the various recordings were made, the dates of the actual sessions were unknown, the files of the Odeon Company having been lost or destroyed.   Neither can McCormack's recordings be accurately dated from Odeon records made by other artists.   We have tentatively adopted the dates given by Brian Fawcett-Johnston in his discography of the early record-ings.   It does seem possible that the longer sessions may in fact represent two sessions, and that some of the dates may be *issue* dates rather than recording dates.   (For example, in January and February of 1908 McCormack was on tour in the north of Britain. Newspaper accounts of this tour show that he was in Sunderland on January 29, and that he sang in Edinburgh on February 1 and again in Aberdeen on February 3, making the January 31 and February 3 Odeon dates highly improbable as *recording* dates.) Ultimate solution of the problem of the Odeon recording dates may not be possible, and in any event must await the results of additional research.

For any given Odeon serial number the first take is indicated by the serial number alone, as we have shown in the Recording Chronology.   For further takes a superscript Arabic number was added to the serial number (e.g., Lx 1577²). For consistency in our format we have adopted the convention of designating any Odeon takes beyond the first with a hyphen and a numeral in the same fashion as the entries for Victor and HMV.   Many of the titles for Odeon exist in more than one take.   In some cases the same matrix number was used, and in others a new one was assigned.   For some pairs of recordings it is apparent that the second (or third) performance was recorded at a later date because of the obvious diff-erences in the singing or in the sound of the accompaniment.   Three of these multiple takes exist as unpublished test pressings (Lx 2559, Lx 2793, and Lx 2491-3) and have hitherto not been generally disseminated.   The first is sched-uled for LP release, and one hopes that the other two will one day be likewise published.

The playing speeds for the Odeons do not follow the widely recognized axiom that recordings made within the same session will play at the same speed.   The reason for this irregularity is not known.   Perhaps more than one recording lathe was used, or variations in speed were introduced as it was switched on and off.   We have given playing speeds for individual recordings in the Odeon section of the Recording Chronology.

Most of the McCormack Odeons have been extensively reissued on microgroove. Many of the early extended play and long play reissues of his recordings, in fact, relied mostly on Odeon originals, perhaps because of uncertain expectations regarding the proprietary behavior of RCA and EMI.   This was unfortunate for two reasons: Not all of the Odeons represent his best singing by any means, and, in addition, many of the transfers were poorly done, incorrect pitch being the most common problem.   It is readily apparent that an indiscriminant 78 rpm playback speed was often used, which yields alarming results in many cases.   Over the last decade we have seen much greater concern for the use of proper pitch, equalization, and stylus on the part of reissue producers.   Recent efforts by EMI (World Records), Pearl, Arabesque, and Rubini, to name a few, have given us transfers as good as we may ever hope to hear.

As Roden pointed out, "the company which made these records was neither continuous in its existence nor consistent in its methods of labelling and numbering. . . ."   There are many anomalies to be found upon examining the original discs.   They were issued according to several numbering systems (see Appendix G). Some were issued in one series and not another.   Some were never doubled, and others were never issued on single face.   Those issued on double face in the 57000 series were not always paired with the same reverse side.   Most records were issued with more than one colored label.   The speeds printed on these labels were usually inaccurate.   Some discs have the matrix number inscribed in the wax, while others do not.

Many of the Odeon recordings were reissued by one or more of six other companies using the original stampers: American Odeon, Columbia-Fonotipia, Ariel, English Columbia, Okeh, and Regal.   Roden and Webster listed the known issue numbers for each of these labels, but several others have come to light since their article was published.   We have corrected two misprints in their lists: AM 30055 was a misprint of 33035; 969 should have been 869 in the English Columbia list.   It is possible that there are other issues in these six series, as is suggested by the gaps in the various numbering sequences.

There were four different series of couplings for McCormack's records on the original Odeon label itself.   The least systematic of these was that which utilized numbers in the 57000 series for each of the two sides but had no catalog number that referred to both.   There was no set pairing of sides, and recordings are often found with different couplings.   The other three series were designated by a single number: an "X" (prefix) series, an "O" series, and an "RO" series.   A few double face numbers have no prefix.

In addition to discs pressed from original stampers, there are four known non-microgroove rerecordings of Odeon originals: Avoca 78-2077, CRS-12, and IRCC 3092 and 3101.   As in the case of all dubbings, these pressings do not necessarily play at the same speed as those made from the original stampers.

During the period for which McCormack recorded for the Victor Talking Machine Company, later the RCA Victor Division, Radio Corporation of America, a simple method was used to assign prefix (size designation), serial number, and take number to a given wax master record.   With few exceptions, a title by a particular artist with a particular accompaniment was assigned a serial number followed by a take number.   This serial number was preceded by a letter indicating the size of the disc, "B" indicating a ten inch disc, and "C" indicating a twelve inch disc.   After electrical recording was introduced, the letters "VE" were placed after these same prefixes.   Recordings made on the west coast had a "P" (for Pacific Coast Studios) preceding the "BVE" or "CVE."

Occasionally it was considered desirable to rerecord a new master. During the acoustical era, these rerecordings were indicated by an "S/8" in the inner land of the pressing.   In the electrical era rerecorded masters were indicated by an "R" following the take number.

In one instance (CVE 49209-1, -1A) an alternate master, indicated by an "A" following the take number, was recorded of a particular take.   This was a common practice during electrical recording sessions, since the recording artists and accompanists were freed from the specific positioning required by the acoustical process.   Since two microphones and two recording lathes were used, two separate masters of the same performance were produced independently of each other.   As far as can be determined, this procedure was used only when a large instrumental ensemble was being recorded, the purpose being to find the best microphone placement.   In some cases, however, both masters were eventually used for pressing recordings which were issued, either because the first one became worn, or through carelessness.   Thus two records of the same performance were published, but each with a slightly different recording balance because of the different microphone placement.   Where these microphone positions differed along a left-right axis the records, when synchronized, yield serendipitous

stereophonic sound. It is not known whether any of the later McCormack electrical recordings with orchestral accompaniment exist in such pairs, but the
possibility exists. To date, recordings by the Philadelphia Orchestra, Paul
Whiteman's Orchestra, Duke Ellington's Orchestra, and some recordings made in
England by Sir Edward Elgar are known to exist in pressings made from paired
masters, and many have been successfully synchronized to produce genuine
stereophonic sound.

RCA Victor introduced the first commercial 33 1/3 rpm long playing records
in 1931 and during the next few years made extensive recordings at this new speed,
but the economic climate prevented their gaining wide acceptance. McCormack's
long playing recordings were made experimentally and not published, though at
least one test pressing is known to exist. These masters were assigned special
two digit serial numbers preceded by the prefix "BRC-HQ" and were followed by
conventional take numbers. RCA did issue one long playing disc containing
electrical recordings by McCormack in the early 1930's, disc L-4509, but these
performances were dubbings from selections made at the 1928-1929 sessions and
issued in the 33 1/3 rpm "Program Transcription" series.

Initially the Gramophone and Typewriter Company, Limited, which became the
Gramophone Company, Limited, and later still Electrical and Musical Industries,
Limited (EMI), did not use take numbers for different takes of the same selection
by the same artist. Rather, each take was assigned a unique number and alphabetical suffix, the latter indicating the diameter of the disc. McCormack's
1904 records for the G & T Company are so designated. By the time he again
recorded for this company, in 1904, a system of serial numbers, prefixes which
indicated disc size, and take numbers had been adopted, although the same serial
number was not used for remakes of the same title in sessions subsequent to the
initial take. Prefixes were changed three times during the electrical era, and
Roman numerals were used for take numbers until July 1940, when Arabic numerals
were adopted for this purpose.

Neither Victor nor the Gramophone Company issued single faced discs after
1923, although the latter continued to assign single face part numbers to their
matrices using the old single face issue numbering system. Test pressings of
recordings by both companies are sometimes found bearing these numbers.

Perhaps no singer of the 78 rpm era has had his recordings so extensively
distributed on long playing transfers as John McCormack. Nearly all of his
recordings made after 1906 may be heard in this form. For those disinclined to
collect 78's or for whom proper playback of them is problematic, there are
numerous microgroove reissues, many in splendid sound and including many rarities.
The centennial year of 1984 saw four discs issued by EMI, two by Pearl, and one
each by RCA and Rubini. McCormack's appeal as a singer easily overarches no
less than three generations of listeners, and it is the LP that has made this
possible. In an age where most vintage recordings, originally "recorded for
posterity" in the years before World War II have vanished utterly, the recorded
legacy of McCormack is more widely available than ever before.

Long play and extended play transfers of his records appeared almost
immediately upon the commercial demise of the 78 rpm disc, although the latter
continued to be the choice of purists during the 1950's, as witnessed by the sets
of recordings issued by the American Gramophone Society, Irish HMV, and RCA
Ireland during this decade. Since many of the early microgroove discs were
poorly produced, the disdain for them in some quarters is understandable. By
1960, however, enough discs had appeared (on Jay, Eterna, Scala, EMI 45 rpm, and
RCA LCT 1036) that purists were then outnumbered by those who bought these
reissues. RCA Camden CAL 407, "John McCormack Sings Irish Songs," became a
best-selling disc, with sales eventually exceeding a million copies. This record,
along with the two in EMI's Great Recordings of the Century series (COLH 123 and
124), though the transfers were far from perfect, probably endeared McCormack's
singing to more listeners than 78 rpm records had in the preceding 50 years.

Over the next fifteen years McCormack's recordings appeared on dozens of
LP's and EP's. His best performances were widely anthologized. Many of his
records have never been out of print for more than a few years since they were
made. The quality of the transfers has continued to improve for the most part.
Reissues have been released not only by the parent companies, RCA and EMI, but
by a host of others as well. In 1978 Pavilion Records (UK) initiated on its
Pearl label what is intended to be the first effort to reissue all of McCormack's
records in a comprehensive set. The series will eventually consist of about
40 LP's in ten volumes. As of June 1984, with the release of Pearl GEMM 274/275,
20 discs had been issued in four volumes. Ten more discs are scheduled to
appear by the end of 1986, at which point virtually all of the recordings made
between 1906 and 1935 will be available. The Pearl transfers are generally well
done. The first four volumes have included many broadcast and film recordings,

notably four of the O'Reilly Zonophones, and some previously unpublished test pressings.

Within the group of nearly 300 microgroove discs containing recordings by McCormack, there are some recurring problems that may be discerned. Chief among these are those of improper pitch (playback speed) and equalization. Improper stylus selection is another, since discs from different periods play best with differently shaped styli. Other engineering problems often encountered are the use of worn and noisy originals, overfiltering of the high frequencies, addition of echo and artificial stereo quality, flutter and wow in originals, and clipped end notes. Fortunately, problems like these have tended to occur with less frequency in recent years. Other problems that seem to beset older and newer reissues alike are short catalog life, limited circulation, repetitious contents, and inaccurate jacket notes. Space does not allow an evaluation of the quality of the many microgroove discs. The best reissues of recent years will be found on EMI EX 2900073 and 2900563, World Records P 69, Arabesque 8124 and 8105-2 (all transfers by Keith Hardwick); World Records SH 306 (transfers by Chris Ellis); all of the Pearl sets (transfers by Brian Fawcett-Johnston); Ember GVC 15, 30, and 51 (transfers by James Sheehan); and on the three Rubini releases. Most of these records are still available as of this writing and are well worth seeking out. We have corrected discographic errors that have been perpetuated by LP liner notes and other sources, though we have not footnoted these corrections. We have verified the contents of as many LP's and EP's possible, paying particular attention to the problem of multiple takes and repeat recordings. Since our listing of reissues will date rapidly, it is hoped that the information in Appendix C will be of use to collectors as future discs are released.

McCormack recorded many selections more than once in his career. In most cases he seems to have done this because he liked the song or because the demand for his rendition of it was so great, or both. In other instances multiple takes of a particular selection from the same recording session have survived. In most cases only one was released officially, and the other(s) exist only as unpublished test pressings. Some items were never officially published at all and exist only in the latter form. In still other cases, separate takes were published under the same issue number. In yet a fourth case, some record- ings were released only after the end of the 78 rpm period as microgroove transfers, and a great many officially unreleased items have been transferred to this medium on independent labels. We have documented these extant test pressings in the Recording Chronology to the extent that we have been able to confirm their existence. Others probably exist. These recordings are an important part of McCormack's recorded legacy, illustrating as they do that even in those performances which he judged unsuitable for publication, his singing is admirable.   With them, however, one faces the necessity of distinguishing between the two (or three) aurally. Particularly in cases where alternate takes were not published in 78 rpm format, it is often not easy to distinguish one from the other when hearing one or the other as a rerecording. Clues in the wax of the shellac discs are often (though not always) decisive, but these are not avail- able to one who is dealing with an LP transfer, as most of us are in the case of variant takes. We have provided the audible clues that we used in our analysis in Appendix C. That list, though, is incomplete, since not all variants were available to us.

As with records made by other artists in the 78 rpm era, determining the correct playing speed for McCormack's recordings is crucial. Rarely do 78's play at precisely that speed before about 1935. Since playing speed determines the pitch of a musical performance on disc, it follows that for any record the choices must perforce be limited to those discrete speeds which actually yield a specific key for the performance, rather than placing it in the cracks.   The choice of which keys are reasonable for a given performance is in turn constrained to those in which the singer's voice sounds like that singer and to the transpos- itions that make sense for the work in question. A second rule of thumb that usually holds true is that recordings made on the same day in the same studio will play at the same speed. At least for the Victor and HMV recordings, this principle discredits the assertion that McCormack never transposed in opera, since in some cases that would require that an operatic performance be played at a different speed from the other recordings in a session in order to achieve score pitch.

Inexplicably, no written record was ever made of the turntable speeds used in early recording studios, as the records were being made. Since there was no standardized speed for "78" rpm records until the mid 1930's, it is a first prin- ciple for their enjoyment that the proper speed be determined. This is done by adjusting the speed of the playback (i.e., the pitch of the performance) such that an appropriate key for the performance is achieved.   One then measures the speed of the turntable, the most common method being the use of a strobe disc on which various gradations in speed are marked.   Where we have given speeds for McCormack's records to two decimal places, we have done so on the basis of this type of measurement.   Should no band on the strobe disc be exactly the speed called for, one can still determine the speed of the turntable by taking the arithmetic average of two bands that seem to be moving in opposite directions at the same speed.

If one had access to all the original records, the appropriate sheet music, an accurate way to measure turntable speed, and access to the records made by other artists in that studio at more or less the same time, it would be a simple matter to determine the correct playing speed for each and every disc, assuming that one had a good enough ear to judge timbre and pitch accurately.   The reality is that very few collectors benefit from all of these assets, the present writers included.   Since determining proper speeds is the empirical process described above, one must rely in an enterprise of this sort on the judgements of others, especially with regard to the early recordings.   Since a short-coming in any one of the above factors can yield an inaccurate speed designation, we tried to consult with as many collectors as possible on this matter.   The most common problem seemed to be the lack of a completely variable turntable, along with the lack of an accurate way to measure speeds decided upon.   In most cases, though, a consensus emerged.   Submitted speeds that were well off the mark were obvious.   In some cases, speeds submitted by different correspondents were discrepant by less than half an rpm.   This was probably due to measurement error, and we made our choice according to which source had the best track record.   The compilers checked as many originals themselves as was possible.

The choice of proper speeds for the Odeon recordings was particularly difficult, and opinion was much more varied for these records than for those on other labels.   In some cases we could locate but a single copy of a disc, so there was no way to gather other opinions regarding its proper speed. In a few cases, knowing the speed at which a record had been taped for us, we were able to determine its proper speed by raising or lowering the pitch using the pitch control on the tape deck, but this would only work if the dubbing was a half step off pitch in one direction or another.   For the Victor and HMV recordings this process was greatly facilitated by speeds supplied or confirmed by William R. Moran (from forthcoming volumes of *The Encyclopedic Discography of Victor Recordings*, to be published by Greenwood Press).   There were no serious disagreements with these speeds from other sources that we consulted.   By the 1930's, playback speeds for electrical recordings were much less variable, and by the last years of that decade there is hardly ever found a divergence from 78.26 rpm as the industry standard in the United States and 77.9 as the standard in the United Kingdom, a difference attributable to the characteristics of electrical power standards in each nation.

We have provided speeds but not keys for each performance.   It was thought that the latter would be useful to comparatively few collectors, though for wrongly pitched microgroove transfers it would have been a guide to correct this problem in playback.   (To do this requires either a turntable or a tape deck with a very sensitive pitch control, since the speed variations necessary to correct less than a half step are minute indeed with these machines.)

We have treated film recordings and broadcast transcriptions like disc and cylinder recordings, entering them in the appropriate places in the Recording Chronology.   Apparently the performances from the films *Song O' My Heart* and *Wings of the Morning* are the only recordings that survive in listenable form from film originals.   These are discussed at length in Appendix E.   Likewise we have listed only those broadcasts known to have been preserved.   For convenience we have summarized these in Appendix F.

Format of This Discography

A chronological listing of all recordings, organized by session, contains the complete information for each recorded performance. Several user's aids include an alphabetical listing of titles, a guide to the contents of long play and extended play reissues, and seven Appendices giving further detail on various aspects of McCormack's recordings.

Recording Chronology

The Recording Chronology is the complete discography. The entries in the other sections contain only enough data to identify an individual performance (title, matrix and take, and date) and allow the user to easily find its place in the chronological listing. Several tables following this section contain the explanatory information for the different entries provided for each recording.

The chronological format was devised to meet the specific needs of a discography on the scale of McCormack's. It also allows one to trace the course of his career over its nearly four decade span. In each session the performances are listed as closely as can be determined in the sequence in which they were recorded. For each session, a two line heading gives details of recording date, recording locale, day of the week, accompaniment, and playing speed. The entry for each recording is arranged in five columns: The first (leftmost) contains the serial and take number, which together comprise the unique matrix number for that performance. Published Takes are underlined. The second column (moving to the right) contains the title, lyricist and composer (always in that order), and other identifying information for the composition. Composer and lyricist have been verified from sheet music whenever possible. The third and fourth columns contain data regarding the publication of the selection during the 78 rpm era. If it was published the issue numbers are given; extant test pressings are footnoted. The designation of these two columns changes as one recording company gives way to the next. The last column (rightmost) contains entries for reissues on microgroove. These entries consist of the release number (usually including an alphabetical prefix) for each disc. The corresponding companies for these prefixes or abbreviations are given in a table following this section.

Speeds are given for pressings from original stampers. Rerecordings (dubbings) on shellac may play at different speeds, and it has not been possible to verify these.

The language in which a given selection is sung is indicated by that in which it is entered in the discography. In the case of operatic recordings this is true for the first line of the aria, but the name of the opera is given in its original language.

Accompanists, conductors, and assisting artists are designated as precisely as possible. For many earlier recordings the conductors of the orchestras are unknown.

Assigned but unreleased issue numbers are given in parentheses for Victor. Single face part numbers for Odeon are likewise indicated. For HMV, numbers in parentheses before 1925 are assigned single face numbers; after that year they are single face part numbers identifying the metal stampers. On the advice of William R. Moran, we have not included any of the many annotations that may be found in the Victor Recording Ledgers.   These notes (indicating recordings to be mastered, held, destroyed, etc.) are often conflicting and inaccurate.   Virtually all recordings were mastered unless there was an obvious fluff in the performance or an accident with the unprocessed wax.   Masters were necessary in order to make a test pressing for audition by the artist and the release committee.   Annotations relevant to the disposition of the recordings that passed the audition refer to the masters that were held in the vaults. often alternate versions were passed and held for substitution or future release. Changes in the status of these masters were often made but not noted in the various files.

The information in the Recording Chronology is as accurate as has been possible to achieve for this edition.   Various persistent uncertainties have been noted.

Alphabetical Guide

The alphabetical guide to titles includes matrix number and date for each recording.   Extant recordings are given in capital letters; unpublished record-ings in lower case letters.   Extant test pressings, cylinders, film recordings, and broadcast recordings are noted.   Operatic selections are given under the title of the opera, and arias are cross-indexed.

Microgroove Reissues

The second major user's aid provided is a detailed guide to the contents of those long play and extended play discs known to the compilers.   The same data is given as in the alphabetical guide, along with the title and release number of the reissue.   Contents of each disc follow the sequence of selections on it.   Unless otherwise noted, all discs are 12 inch, 33 1/3 rpm.   The chapter is divided into five sections: RCA, EMI, EMI Affiliates, Pearl, and miscel-laneous labels.   Within each of these categories the entries are alphabetized by the prefix of the release number.

Appendices, References, and Artist Index

Appendix A is a guide to the contents of 78 rpm albums and sets, given in a format similar to that of the Microgroove guide.   Appendix B lists extant test pressings of recordings not released commercially on 78 rpm discs. Appendix C contains descriptions of aural differences for those alternate takes available to the compilers.   Appendix D is a description of the pirate discs issued in Canada from Victor masters.   Appendix E is a discussion of McCormack's film recordings.   Appendix F is a summary of extant broadcast recordings.   Appendix G is a listing by matrix number of the various issues and reissues on shellac of the Odeon recordings.

The references we have given are for published sources that were consulted in addition to the other sources mentioned in the introductory essays.

The entries in the index are for lyricists, composers, librettists, arrangers, assisting artists, translators, and accompanists.   Numbers refer to page numbers in the Recording Chronology only.

Tables of Codes
and Abbreviations

MATRIX AND ISSUE CODES:
RECORDINGS MADE BEFORE 1910

Edison
(National Phonograph Company, UK)

Original Issue Numbers:	Acoustic Recordings:
13100 series	Two minute black wax cylinders

Edison-Bell
(Edison-Bell Consolidated Phonograph Company, UK)

Original Issue Numbers:	Acoustic Recordings:
6400 series	Two minute black wax cylinders

Sterling
(Russell Hunting Company, UK)

Original Issue Numbers:	Acoustic Recordings:
600 series	Three minute black wax cylinders
77000 series	Rerecordings by Pathé Frères from Sterling originals, discs (sf)*
8000 series	Rerecordings by Pathé Frères from Sterling originals, discs

Odeon
(International Talking Machine Company, UK)

Matrix Number Prefixes:	Acoustic Recordings:
L	7 1/2 inch (19 cm) disc
Lx	10 3/4 inch (27.3 cm) disc
Lxx	12 inch (30.5 cm) disc

Original Issue Numbers:	
40000 series	10 3/4 inch disc (sf)
66000 series	10 3/4 inch disc (sf)
84000 series	12 inch disc (sf)
57000 series	10 3/4 inch sf side number**
C(70000), R(70000)	Sf part (stamper) numbers
2800 series	7 1/2 inch disc (sf)***
0200 through 0900 series	10 3/4 inch disc
600, 900 series	10 3/4 inch disc
X 10, X 100 series	12 inch disc
Ro 200 series	12 inch disc

Reissues on Non-Odeon Labels:
(From original stampers)

Ariel 5000, 6000 series	Ariel, 10 3/4 inch disc
Ariel 8000 series	Ariel, 12 inch disc
G 5000 series	Regal, 10 3/4 inch disc
AM 30000 series	American Odeon, 10 3/4 inch disc (sf)
70000 series	Okeh, 10 3/4 inch disc (sf)
50000 series	Okeh, 10 3/4 inch disc (sf)
800 series	English Columbia, 12 inch disc
F 110, F 120, F 130 series	Columbia Fonotipia, 10 3/4 inch disc

Rerecordings (non-microgroove):

78-2077	Avoca****
12	CRS (Collectors' Record Shop)
3000 series	IRCC (International Record Collectors Club)

---

* Single face numbers are denoted "sf." All other numbers are for double face.
** Different numbers used on each side of a double face disc.
*** Single face numbers used on either side of a double face disc.
**** Diameter of dubbing is not necessarily that of the original recording.

MATRIX AND ISSUE CODES:

THE GRAMOPHONE (AND TYPEWRITER) COMPANY, UK

Matrix Number Prefixes:

Acoustic Recordings:

6000a, 6000Ei, 6000WD2	7 inch (17.9 cm) disc (G & T)
5000b	10 inch (25 cm) disc (G & T)*
4000f	12 inch (30.5 cm) disc
5100f, 5200f	12 inch disc
Bb 5000, Bb 5100	10 inch disc
Cc 5000	12 inch disc
HO 201 af	12 inch

Electrical Recordings:

Bb 11000, Bb 21000	10 inch disc
Cc 11000	12 inch disc
CR 1400	12 inch disc
2B 2200, 2B 3400	12 inch disc
OB 3800, OB 5300	10 inch disc
OEA 400, OEA 2100, OEA 2700	10 inch disc
OEA 8300, OEA 8500	10 inch disc
OEA 8600, OEA 8800	10 inch disc
OEA 9000 through 9400	10 inch disc
OEA 9600, OEA 9800	10 inch disc
2EA 2700	12 inch disc

Original Issue Numbers:

Acoustic Recordings:

3-2500 series	7 inch disc (sf) (G & T)
3-2100, 3-2200 series	10 inch disc (sf) (G & T)
X-40000 series	10 inch disc (sf) (Zonophone record from G & T masters)
2-030000 series	12 inch disc (sf)
2-040000 series	12 inch disc (sf)
2-050000 series	12 inch disc (sf)
02000 series	12 inch disc (sf)
3-4000 series	10 inch disc (sf)
4-2000 series	10 inch disc (sf)
5-2000 series	10 inch disc (sf)
7-30000 series	10 inch disc (sf)
7-40000 series	10 inch disc (sf)
7-50000 series	10 inch disc (sf)

(Prefixes):

Acoustic and Electrical Recordings:

DA	10 inch disc
DB	12 inch disc
DM	12 inch disc
DK	12 inch disc
GSS	12 inch disc (sf)
IR, IRX	10 and 12 inch discs, Irish HMV
VA	10 inch disc
VB	12 inch disc
AGSA	10 inch disc (American Gramophone Society special pressing)
AGSB	12 inch disc (American Gramophone Society special pressing

Foreign Reissues:
(From original stampers)

Opera Disc (label)	Repressings of pre-1914 matrices for release in United States.**
Musica (label)	Repressings of pre-1914 matrices for release in Europe.**
IRCC (label)	International Record Collectors Club

* Entries for Gramophone and Typewriter Co. issues are designated; others are for The Gramophone Company.
** Illicit reissues by Deutsche Grammophon after its break with The Gramophone Co.

MATRIX AND ISSUE CODES:

THE VICTOR TALKING MACHINE COMPANY / RCA VICTOR

Matrix Number Prefixes:

B	
C	

Acoustic Recordings:

10 inch (25 cm) disc
12 inch (30.5 cm) disc

BVE, PBVE	
CVE	
BRC-HQ	

Electrical Recordings:

10 inch disc
12 inch disc
10 inch disc (High Fidelity test
  recordings, unissued)

Original Issue Numbers:

64000 series
66000 series
74000 series
87000 series
88000 series
89000 series

Acoustic Recordings:

10 inch disc (sf)
10 inch disc (sf)
12 inch disc (sf)
10 inch disc (sf)
12 inch disc (sf)
12 inch disc (sf)

700 through 1700 series
2100, 2200 series
3000 series
6000 series
8000 series
10000 series
12000 series
14000 series
26000 series

Acoustic and Electrical Recordings:

10 inch disc
10 inch disc (Canada)
10 inch disc
12 inch disc
12 inch disc
12 inch disc
12 inch disc
12 inch disc (HMV masters)
10 inch disc

10-0040 through 10-0042
10-1434 through 10-1439
15-1000 series
16-0000 series
16-5000 series
42-0000 series
410-0000 series

10 inch discs (3)(in album DM 1358)
10 inch discs (6)(in album MO 1228)
12 inch disc (red vinyl, Heritage series)
10 inch disc
12 inch disc
10 inch disc
12 inch disc

Foreign Reissues:
(From original stampers)

AGSA (prefix) series

AGSB (prefix) series

ERC (prefix) series
IRCC (label)
Opera Disc (label)

Musica (label)

10 inch disc (American Gramophone
  Society special pressing)
12 inch disc (American Gramophone
  Society special pressing)
10 inch disc (RCA Ireland)
International Record Collectors Club
Repressings of pre-1914 matrices for
  release in United States.*
Repressings of pre-1914 matrices for
  release in United States.*

* Illicit reissues by Deutsche Grammophon after its break with The Gramophone Co.
Note: All entries in this table and the preceding two tables are for shellac
  disc, unless otherwise noted.

ISSUE NUMBER PREFIXES: MICROGROOVE RERECORDINGS

A (34)	Rondo-Lette	HQM	HMV (EMI) (UK)
A (110)	Asco	Hud.	Hudson
AB	Belcantodisc (UK)**	IDLP	ID Records (UK)
AK	International Award Series	ISLE	HMV (EMI)(Ireland)
All.	Allegro	Jay	Jay Records
All.R.	Allegro Royale	JM*	JM Records
ANNA*	Anna Record Corp.	JMcC.*	John McCormack Society of
Arab.	Arabesque (EMI)		Ireland (Ireland)
A.R.C.	Associated Record Corp. (UK)	J.M.A.*	John McCormack Association
ARM	RCA		of Greater Kansas City
ATL	Delta, Fidelio, Leonore (UK)	L (4509)	RCA "Program Transcription"
AU*	AU Records (UK)		(long-playing, 1931)
AV	Avoca Records	LCT	RCA
BC	Belcantodisc (UK)	LEG	Allegro
BDL	Bulldog (UK)	LM	RCA
BLP	HMV (EMI) (UK)	LP*	Pelican
Boul.	Boulevard (UK)	LPA	Audio Rarities
CAL	RCA Camden	LSE	Summit
Cant.	Cantilena (Rococo)(Canada)	M.H.	Murray Hill
CCS	Collectors' Records (Ireland)	MFP	Music For Pleasure (EMI)(UK)
CDM	Pickwick (UK)	MKER	Tralee (EMI)(UK)
CDN	RCA Camden (UK)	MRF*	MRF Records
CEN	Connoisseur Records (UK)	NP	Angel (EMI)
CM	RCA	NW*	New World Records
CO	Court Opera Classics (Austria)	OASI*	OASI Records
COLH	Angel (EMI)	OL	Columbia (Japan)
CRE	Collectors' Records (Ireland)	OXLP	HMV (EMI)(Australia)
CRM	RCA	7 P	HMV (EMI) (UK)
CSLP	HMV (EMI) (UK)	P (69)	World Records (EMI) (UK)
DLP	Design	PPR	Pearl (UK)
DOLB	Dolphin (Ireland)	RB	RCA (UK)
DOLM	Dolphin (Ireland)	RD	Readers' Digest
DRLP	Demesne (Ireland)	RDM	Readers' Digest
7 EB	HMV (EMI) (UK)	RCA 45	RCA (45 rpm)
EB	Belcantodisc (UK)	RCX	RCA (UK)
EGM	Egmont (UK)	RHA	Rhapsody (UK)
EJS*	Golden Age of Opera	RL	RCA (UK)
Emb.	Ember (UK)	RLS	HMV (EMI) (UK)
EP	Royale	RM	Radiex
7 ER	HMV (EMI) (UK)	RO	Smithsonian Records
ERAT	RCA	Roc.	Rococo
Et.	Eterna	Roy.	Royale
EX	HMV (EMI) (UK)	RVC	RCA (Japan)
Ev.	Everest	S*	Murray Hill
F	RCA	Sera.	Seraphim (EMI)
FB	Belcantodisc (UK)	SP	RCA
FDY	Associated Record Corp. (UK)	Saga	Saga Records
FLPS	Fiesta (EMI)	SC	Scala, Scala-Everest
FRP	Famous Records of the Past	SH	World Records (EMI) (UK)
Gal.	Galaxy	STAL	Talisman (EMI) (UK)
GEMM	Pearl (UK)	SU	Sutton Records
GD	Tapestry	T	TAP (Top Artists Platters)
G.J.R.*	Golden Jubilee Record	TQD	Delta (UK)
GM	Treasury	UORC*	Unique Opera Records Co.
GV*	Rubini (UK)	VIC	RCA Victrola
GVC	Ember (UK)	Voce	Voce Records
Halo	Halo Records (UK)	VRCS*	Vocal Records Collectors Society
HER	Heritage (UK)	WCT	RCA
HLM	HMV (EMI) (UK)	West.*	Westwood
HPE	Pickwick (UK)	XTRA	Xtra Records (UK)

Note: Prefixes in capitals with no periods are part of the microgroove record
number. Others are abbreviations of the label name.
* - Privately distributed, sold in limited quantities, or sold mostly by mail.
** - Countries of origin for discs not manufactured in the United States.

JOHN McCORMACK

Recording Chronology

NATIONAL PHONOGRAPH COMPANY

take	title	Edison	microgroove

12 SEPTEMBER 1904, MONDAY (25-29 Banner Street, London)
w. orchestra conducted by HUBERT BATH (?)(160rpm)
w. spoken announcement by McCormack

take	title	Edison	microgroove
take 1	The Snowy Breasted Pearl (Sir Stephen Edward De Vere/Old Irish Air: "Pearl of the White Breast, arr. Joseph Robinson)	13124	
take 1	The Meeting of the Waters (Thomas Moore/ Old Irish Air: "Old Head of Denis")	13142	
take 1	When Shall the Day Break in Ireland (D. J. Downing/C. Milligan(?) Fox)	13143	
take 1	Molly Bawn (Samuel Lover/Old Irish Air, arr. MacMurrough)	13144	
take 1	The Irish Emigrant (Helen Selina, later Lady Dufferin/G. A. Barker)	13145	
take 1	Avourneen (E. Cecilia Fitzpatrick/Wilton King)	13146	
take 1	Killarney (Edmund O'Rourke, writing as Edmund Falconer/Michael William Balfe)	13152	
take 1	The Green Isle of Erin (C. Clifton Bingham/ Joseph L. Roeckel)*	13153	
take 1	Love Thee Dearest, Love Thee (Thomas Moore/ Old Irish Air)	13154	
take 1	Believe Me If All Those Endearing Young Charms (Thomas Moore/Old Irish Air: "My Lodging is on the Cold Ground")	13191	

THE GRAMOPHONE AND TYPEWRITER COMPANY, LIMITED

matrix	title	G & T	Zonophone**	microgroove

19 SEPTEMBER 1904, MONDAY (21 City Road, London)
w. FRED GAISBERG (?), piano

* - On Cylinder Phonograph Division, Thomas A. Edison, Incorporated memo dated 15 August 1929 listing moulds to be preserved "for historical reasons."
** - Issued under the pseudonym of "John O'Reilly."

| 5882b | Believe Me If All Those Endearing Young Charms (Thomas Moore/Old Irish Air: "My Lodging is on the Cold Ground") | UNPUBLISHED |
| 6453[a] | Believe Me If All Those Endearing Young Charms (Thomas Moore/Old Irish Air: "My Lodging is on the Cold Ground") | UNPUBLISHED |

<u>23 SEPTEMBER 1904, FRIDAY (21 City Road, London)</u>*
w. FRED GAISBERG(?), piano (76.00rpm)

<u>6462a</u>	Love Thee Dearest, Love Thee (Thomas Moore/Old Irish Air)	3-2513
<u>6464a</u>	When Shall the Day Break in Ireland (D. J. Downing/C. Milligan(?) Fox)	3-2520
6464Ei	Believe Me If All Those Endearing Young Charms (Thomas Moore/Old Irish Air: "My Lodging is on the Cold Ground")	UNPUBLISHED
<u>6464WD2</u>	Believe Me If All Those Endearing Young Charms (Thomas Moore/Old Irish Air: "My Lodging is on the Cold Ground") w. violin obbligato	3-2519
<u>6466a</u>	Killarney (Edmund O'Rourke, writing as Edmund Falconer/Michael William Balfe) w. violin obbligato	3-2514
<u>6467a</u>	Norah, the Pride of Kildare (?/John Parry)	3-2515
<u>6468a</u>	Come Back to Erin (John William Cherry/Charlotte Alington Barnard, writing as Claribel)	3-2516
<u>6469a</u>	Eileen Allanah (E. S. Marble/J. R. Thomas)	3-2521
<u>6470a</u>	The Irish Emigrant (Helen Selina, later Lady Dufferin/G. A. Barker)	3-2525
<u>6471a</u>	The Minstrel Boy (Thomas Moore/Old Irish Air: "The Moreen," also "The Moirin," also "The Greenwoods of Trnigha")	3-2522
6472a	The Harp That Once Through Tara's Halls (Thomas Moore/Old Irish Air: "Gramachree")	UNPUBLISHED

<u>24 SEPTEMBER 1904, SATURDAY (21 City Road, London)</u>**
w. FRED GAISBERG(?), piano (76.00rpm)

| 5923b | Avourneen (E. Cecilia Fitzpatrick/Wilton King) | X-42258 |

* - There is no entry in the G & T Recording Ledger for matrices 6461a, 6465a, and 6473a and there is no evidence that matrix 6463a was actually used.
** - There is no entry in the G & T Recording Ledger for matrix 5929b. Matrices 5936b, 5936b, and 5937b are of unpublished violin records by an unknown artist.

<u>5924b</u>	The Snowy Breasted Pearl (Sir Stephen Edward De Vere/Old Irish Air: "Pearl of the White Breast," arr. Joseph Robinson)	3-2168	
<u>5925b</u>	The Meeting of the Waters (Thomas Moore/Old Irish Air: Old Head of Denis," arr. Thomas Moore)	3-2163	
5926b	The Green Isle of Erin (C. Clifton Bingham/Joseph L. Roeckel)	UNPUBLISHED	
<u>5927b</u>	The Green Isle of Erin (C. Clifton Bingham/Joseph L. Roeckel)	X-42310	GEMM 275
<u>5928b</u>	Molly Bawn (Samuel Lover/Old Irish Air)	3-2164	
<u>5930b</u>	Killarney (Edmund O'Rourke, writing as Edmund Falconer/ Michael William Balfe) w. violin obbligato	3-2216 DA 552	CEN 1003 GEMM 245
<u>5931b</u>	Believe Me If All Those Endearing Young Charms (Thomas Moore/Old Irish Air: "My Lodging is on the Cold Ground") w. violin obbligato	X-42208	GEMM 160 GEMM 176e
<u>5932b</u>	Believe Me if All Those Endearing Young Charms (Thomas Moore/Old Irish Air: "My Lodging is on the Cold Ground") w. violin obbligato	3-2217	GEMM 245
<u>5933b</u>	Killarney (Edmund O'Rourke, writing as Edmund Falconer/ Michael William Balfe) w. violin obbligato	3-2169	
<u>5934b</u>	Come Back to Erin (John William Cherry/Charlotte Alington Barnard, writing as Claribel) w. violin obbligato	3-2170 DA 552	CEN 1003 GEMM 183

26 SEPTEMBER 1904, MONDAY (21 City Road, London)*
w. FRED GAISBERG(?), piano (76.00rpm)

<u>5938b</u>	Eileen Allanah (E. S. Marble/J. R. Thomas)	X-42318	GEMM 275
5939b	Eileen Allanah (E. S. Marble/J. R. Thomas)	UNPUBLISHED	
<u>5940b</u>	Hath Sorrow Thy Young Days Shaded (Thomas Moore/Old Irish Air: "Sly Patrick," a variant of "Old Head of Denis")	X-42210	
5941b	The West's Awake (Thomas Davis/ Old Irish Air)	UNPUBLISHED	
5942b	The West's Awake (Thomas Davis/ Old Irish Air)	UNPUBLISHED	

* - There is no entry in the G & T Recording Ledger for matrices 5948b and 5949b. Matrix 5950b is of the Coldstream Guard Band.

5943b	The Irish Emigrant (Helen Selina, later Lady Dufferin/ G. A. Barker)	UNPUBLISHED		
5944b	The Foggy Dew (Alfred Perceval Graves/Old Irish Air, arr. Charles Villiers Stanford)	3-2171		
5945b	The Minstrel Boy (Thomas Moore/ Old Irish Air: "The Moreen," also "The Moirin," also "The Greenwoods of Trnigha")		X-42209	GEMM-275
5946b	Kathleen Mavourneen (Annie Barry Crawford/Frederick Nicholls Williams Crouch)	UNPUBLISHED		
5947b	Kathleen Mavourneen (Annie Barry Crawford/Frederick Nicholls Williams Crouch)	3-2139		

EDISON-BELL CONSOLIDATED PHONOGRAPH COMPANY*

take	title	Edison-Bell	microgroove
3 NOVEMBER 1904, THURSDAY (39 Charing Cross Road, London)			
w. orchestra (160.00rpm)			
w. spoken announcements by J. E. Hough(?)			
take I	The Dear Little Shamrock (Andrew Cherry/ John W. Cherry, arr. W. Jackson)	6442	GJR-7** ***
take I	The Green Isle of Erin (C. Clifton Bingham/ Joseph L. Roeckel)	6443	
take II	The Green Isle of Erin (C. Clifton Bingham/ Joseph L. Roeckel)	6443	
take I	Eileen Allanah (E. S. Marble/J. R. Thomas)	6444	
take II	Eileen Allanah (E. S. Marble/J. R. Thomas)	6444	
take I	Killarney (Edmund O'Rourke, writing as Edmund Falconer/Michael William Balfe)	6445	
take II	Killarney (Edmund O'Rourke, writing as Edmund Falconer/Michael William Balfe)	6445	
take I	Kathleen Mavourneen (Annie Barry Crawford/ Frederick Nicholls Williams Crouch)	6446	GJR-7** ***
take II	Kathleen Mavourneen (Annie Barry Crawford/ Frederick Nicholls Williams Crouch)	6446	GJR-7** ***
take I	THE LILY OF KILLARNEY (John Oxenford, after Dion Boucicault/Sir Julius Benedict): Eily Mavourneen, I See Thee Before Me	6447	
take II	THE LILY OF KILLARNEY (John Oxenford, after Dion Boucicault/Sir Julius Benedict): Eily Mavourneen, I See Thee Before Me	6447	
take I	The Minstrel Boy (Thomas Moore/Old Irish Air: "The Moreen," also "The Moirin," also "The Greenwoods of Trnigha")	6448	cass.III***

* – It is not certain that all four takes of each title were actually issued.
** – Spoken announcement not included in this re-recording.
*** – It is not known which take was used for re-recording.

take II	The Minstrel Boy (Thomas Moore/Old Irish Air: "The Moreen," also "The Moirin," also "The Greenwoods of Trnigha")	6448	cass. III*
take I	Once Again (?/Sir Arthur Sullivan)	6449	GJR-7* **
take I	Come Back to Erin (John William Cherry/ Charlotte Alington Barnard, writing as Claribel)	6450	cass. IV*

10 NOVEMBER 1904, THURSDAY (39 Charing Cross Road, London)
w. orchestra (160.00rpm)
w. spoken announcements by J. E. Hough(?)

take II	The Dear Little Shamrock (Andrew Cherry/ John W. Cherry, arr. W. Jackson)	6442	GJR-7* **
take III	The Dear Little Shamrock (Andrew Cherry/ John W. Cherry, arr. W. Jackson)	6442	GJR-7* **
take IV	The Dear Little Shamrock (Andrew Cherry/ John W. Cherry, arr. W. Jackson)	6442	GJR-7* **
take III	The Green Isle of Erin (C. Clifton Bingham/ Joseph L. Roeckel)	6443	
take IV	The Green Isle of Erin (C. Clifton Bingham/ Joseph L. Roeckel)	6443	
take III	Eileen Allanah (E. S. Marble/J. R. Thomas)	6444	
take IV	Eileen Allanah (E. S. Marble/J. R. Thomas)	6444	
take III	Killarney (Edmund O'Rourke, writing as Edmund Falconer/Michael William Balfe)	6445	
take IV	Killarney (Edmund O'Rourke, writing as Edmund Falconer/Michael William Balfe)	6445	
take III	Kathleen Mavourneen (Annie Barry Crawford/ Frederick Nicholls Williams Crouch)	6446	GJR-7* **
take IV	Kathleen Mavourneen (Annie Barry Crawford/ Frederick Nicholls Williams Crouch)	6446	GJR-7* **
take III	THE LILY OF KILLARNEY (John Oxenford, after Dion Boucicault/Sir Julius Benedict): Eily Mavourneen, I See Thee Before Me	6447	
take IV	THE LILY OF KILLARNEY (John Oxenford, after Dion Boucicault/Sir Julius Benedict): Eily Mavourneen, I See Thee Before Me	6447	
take III	The Minstrel Boy (Thomas Moore/Old Irish Air: "The Moreen," also "The Moirin," also "The Greenwoods of Trnigha")	6448	cass. III*
take IV	The Minstrel Boy (Thomas Moore/Old Irish Air: "The Moreen," also "The Moirin," also "The Greenwoods of Trnigha")	6448	cass. III*
take II	Once Again (?/Sir Arthur Sullivan)	6449	GJR-7* **
take III	Once Again (?/Sir Arthur Sullivan)	6449	GJR-7* **
take IV	Once Again (?/Sir Arthur Sullivan)	6449	GJR-7* **

* - It is not known which take was used for re-recording.
** - Spoken announcement not included in this re-recording.

take	title		
take II	Come Back to Erin (John Willam Cherry/ Charlotte Alington Barnard, writing as Claribel)	6450	cass. IV*
take III	Come Back to Erin (John William Cherry/ Charlotte Alington Barnard, writing as Claribel)	6450	cass. IV*
take IV	Come Back to Erin (John William Cherry/ Charlotte Alington Barnard, writing as Claribel)	6450	cass. IV*
take I	The Wearing of the Green (Dion Boucicault/ Old Scottish Air: "The Tulip," arr. Oswald James)	6451	
take II	The Wearing of the Green (Dion Boucicault/ Old Scottish Air: "The Tulip," arr. Oswald James)	6451	
take III	The Wearing of the Green (Dion Boucicault/ Old Scottish Air: "The Tulip," arr. Oswald James)	6451	
take IV	The Wearing of the Green (Dion Boucicault/ Old Scottish Air: "The Tulip," arr. Oswald James)	6451	

1905 or 1906, (39 Charing Cross Road, London)
w. orchestra (160.00rpm)
w. spoken announcements by J. E. Hough(?)

take	title	
take A	Home to Athlone (Blue are the Skies Above) (C. Clifton Bingham/Edwin Greene)	10085
take B	Home to Athlone (Blue are the Skies Above) (C. Clifton Bingham/Edwin Greene)	10085
take C	Home to Athlone (Blue are the Skies Above) (C. Clifton Bingham/Edwin Greene)	10085
take D	Home to Athlone (Blue are the Skies Above) (C. Clifton Bingham/Edwin Greene)	10085

RUSSELL HUNTING COMPANY, LIMITED

take	title	Sterling	Pathe**	microgroove

5 JULY(?) 1906, THURSDAY(?) (81 City Road, London)
w. orchestra (160.00rpm)
w. spoken announcement by Russell Hunting

take	title	Sterling	Pathe**	microgroove
take 1	God Save Ireland (Timothy D. Sullivan/"Tramp, Tramp, Tramp" by George F. Root)	612		GJR-7***
take 1	The Boys of Wexford (Robert Dwyer Joyce/Old Irish Air, arr. J. J. Johnson)	613		GJR-7***
take 1	A Nation Once Again (Thomas Davis/Old Irish Air)	614		
take 1	The Croppy Boy (William McBurney/Old Irish Air)	615		

* – It is not known which take was used for re-recording.
** – Pathe discs were re-recorded from cylinder masters at various speeds.
*** – Spoken announcement not included in this re-recording.

| take <u>1</u> | Come Back to Erin (John William 682 Cherry/Charlotte Alington Barnard, writing as Claribel) | 77686* ** GJR-7* 8028-B* |
| take <u>1</u> | The Dear Little Shamrock (Andrew 683 Cherry/John W. Cherry, arr. W. Jackson) | 77687* *** cass.IV**** 8028-B* |

INTERNATIONAL TALKING MACHINE COMPANY

matrix or matrix and take	title	Odeon	other than Odeon	microgroove
4 DECEMBER 1906, TUESDAY (14 Hemsell Street, London)				
w. orchestra				
<u>Lx 1565</u>	A Nation Once Again (Thomas Davis/Old Irish Air) (71.29rpm)	0214 634 44364 57556 AM 33017 (R(71563))	70002 G 5002	GV 532 S-4359 SC 853 SH 306
<u>Lx 1566</u>	God Save Ireland (Timothy D. Sullivan/"Tramp, Tramp, Tramp," by George F. Root) (72.00rpm)	0213 44365 57554 AM 33016 (R(71561))	G 5002	ATL 4085 ATL 4088 EGM 7015 GV 532 HPE 669 LSE 2019 RHA 6001 S-4359 SC 853 SH 306
<u>Lx 1567</u>	The Boys of Wexford (Robert Dwyer Joyce/Old Irish Air) (72.00rpm)	0213 44366 57555 (R(71562))	G 5003	ATL 4085 EGM 7015 GV 532 HPE 669 LSE 2019 RHA 6001 SH 306
<u>Lx 1568</u>	The Croppy Boy (William McBurney/Old Irish Air) (72.00rpm)	0212 44367 57552 AM 33014 (R(71559))	70006 G 5003	All. 1718 ATL 4085 EGM 7015 GV 532 Halo 50324 HPE 669 Jay 3002 LEG 9022 RHA 6001 S-4359 SC 853 SH 306 SU-272

* - Spoken announcement not included in this re-recording.
** - Re-recorded matrix 33511 M.S. (86.00rpm) used.
*** - Re-recorded matrix 33517 M.S. (81.80rpm) used.
**** - Re-recorded from Pathe 77687.

Lx 1569	The Dear Little Shamrock (Andrew Cherry/John W. Cherry, arr. W. Jackson)(72.73rpm)	0215 635 44368 57558 AM 33018 (R(71565))	70001 G 5004	All. 1718 GEMM 183 Halo 50324 Hud. 225 Jay 3002 LEG 9022 S-4359 S 853 SH 306 SU-272
Lx 1570	The Snowy Breasted Pearl (Sir Stephen Edward De Vere/Old Irish Air: "Pearl of the White Breast," arr. Joseph Robinson)(72.00rpm)	0212 44369 57553 AM 33015 (R(71560))	6231 G 5001	EGM 7015 SH 306

5 DECEMBER 1906, WEDNESDAY (14 Hemsell Street, London)
w. orchestra

Lx 1576	The Green Isle of Erin (C. Clifton Bingham/Joseph L. Roeckel)(72.73rpm)	0214 634 44374 57557 (R(71564))	G 5004	SH 306
Lx 1577	Kathleen Mavourneen (Annie Barry Crawford/Frederick Nicholls Williams Crouch)	UNPUBLISHED		
-2	(73.47rpm)	0215 635 44375 57559 (R(71566))	6229 G 5005	CEN 1003 SH 306
Lx 1578	IL TROVATORE (Salvatore Cammarano, after Antonio Garcia Guiterrez/Giuseppe Verdi): Ai nostri monti w. LILY MC CORMACK, contralto	UNPUBLISHED		
Lx 1579	Come Back to Erin (John William Cherry/Charlotte Alington Barnard, writing as Claribel) (72.73rpm)	0216 44376 57560 AM 33019 (R(71567))	78-2077* F 119 G 5005	Arab. 8124 GV 532 SH 306
L 1580	Come Back to Erin (John William Cherry/Charlotte Alington Barnard, writing as Claribel) (71.00rpm)	2896 2896/5		
L 1581	The Dear Little Shamrock (Andrew Cherry/John W. Cherry, arr. W. Jackson)(71.00rpm)	2895 2895/6		
Lx 1582	Killarney (Edmund O'Rourke, writing as Edmund Falconer/ Michael William Balfe) (72.73rpm)	0216 44377 57561 (R(71568))	F 119 G 5006	Arab. 8124 GV 532 SH 306

1 JUNE 1907, SATURDAY (14 Hemsell Street, London)**
w. orchestra (81.00rpm)

---

* - 78rpm re-recording.
** - McCormack Odeon records of 1907 and later all have "Fonotipia circles."

Lx 2132	My Dark Rosaleen (words from the Irish by James Clarence Mangan/Alicia Adélaïde Needham-Morgan)	0382 44889 57510 (R(71556))	G 5000	GEMM 183 HPE 670 RHA 6005 S-4359 SC 853 SH 306 TQD 3023
Lx 2133	Savourneen Deelish (My Sweet Love)(Anonymous Irish poem, trans. George Colman/Old Irish Air)	0220 44852 57550	F 120	GEMM 183
Lx 2134	Terence's Farewell to Kathleen (Helen Selina, later Lady Dufferin/Old Irish Air: "The Pretty Girl Milking Her Cow")	0220 44853 57551 AM 33013 (R(71558))	G 5001	Arab. 8124 GEMM 183 SH 306
Lx 2135	Oft in the Stilly Night (Thomas Moore/Old Scottish Air, arr. Sir John Stevenson)	44854 57512		CRE 2 EB 12 GEMM 183

28 NOVEMBER 1907, THURSDAY (14 Hemsell Street, London)
w. orchestra (79.00rpm)

Lx 2430	Absent ("Sometimes, between long shadows on the grass") (Catherine Glen/John W. Metcalf)	0382 57511 66066 AM 33011	70003 F 130	GV 532 S-4359 SC 843
Lx 2431	A Farewell (My Fairest Child) (Charles Kingsley/Samuel Liddle)	57548 66067		
-2		0219 57548² 66067	F 131	S-4359 SC 843
Lx 2432	Love's Golden Treasury (?/J. M. Capel)	0219 57549 AM 33012		
-2		0219 57549² 66068		S-4359 SC 843

31 JANUARY 1908, FRIDAY (14 Hemsell Street, London)
w. orchestra

Lx 2487	Like Stars Above (J. A. McDonald/William Henry Squire)(81.82rpm)	0410 57507 66267 AM 33008	F 121	CRE 2 EB 12 GV 532 S-4359 SC 843
Lx 2488	CAVALLERIA RUSTICANA (Guido Menasci and Giovanni Targioni-Tozzetti, after Giovanni Verga/Pietro Mascagni): Oh Lola, pretty one (Siciliana) (81.82rpm)	57523 66180 RO 217	5049 F 177	All.R. 1555 Arab.8105-2 Et. 469 Et. 731 S-4359 SC 820 SH 399
Lx 2489	PAGLIACCI (libretto and music by Ruggiero Leoncavallo): To act! With my heart bowed down with sorrow...On with the motley ("Vesti la giubba")	57524 66215 RO 217	5049	All.R. 1555 Roy. 18119 S-4359 SC 820 SH 399

Lx 2490	The Awakening of a Perfect Spring (words and music by Harold Fraser Simpson) (81.82rpm)	0390 998* 57504 66208*	6231	CRE 5 EB 22
Lx 2491	RIGOLETTO (Francesco Maria Piave, after Victor Hugo/ Giuseppe Verdi): La donna e mobile (76.60rpm)	57508 66201 RO 276		A-110 BC 231 EB 36 FDY 2068 GEMM 155 Roy. 18119 S-4359 SC 820
-2		UNPUBLISHED		

3 FEBRUARY 1908, MONDAY (14 Hemsell Street, London)
w. orchestra (78.00rpm)

Lx 2500	Thora (Frederic Edward Weatherley/Stephen Adams)	0919 66190		CRE 2 EB 12 GEMM 160 GEMM 176e
Lx 2501	TOSCA (Luigi Illica and Giuseppe Giacosa, after Victorien Sardou/Giacomo Puccini): E lucevan le stelle	942 57525** 66191		
Lx 2502	A Child's Song (from "A Masque") (Thomas Moore/Charles Marshall)	0390 57503 66177 AM 33006		All. 1718 GV 532 Halo 50324 LEG 9022 S-4359 SC 820

29 FEBRUARY 1908, SATURDAY (14 Hemsell Street, London)
w. orchestra (80.00rpm)

Lx 2545	I Sent My Love Two Roses (words and music by Harold Fraser Simpson)	0381 57506 66254	F 130	All. 1718 GV 532 Halo 50234 Jay 3007 LEG 9022 S-4359 SC 853

2 MARCH 1908, MONDAY (14 Hemsell Street, London)
w. orchestra (76.60rpm)

Lx 2558	The Lord is My Light (Psalm 27/ Frances Allitsen)	0410 57505 AM 33007		CRE 2 EB 12 GV 532
Lx 2559	RIGOLETTO (Frances Maria Piave, after Victor Hugo/ Giuseppe Verdi): Questa o quella	UNPUBLISHED***		
-2		UNPUBLISHED		

31 MARCH 1908, MONDAY (14 Hemsell Street, London)
w. orchestra (79.13rpm)

Lx 2619	THE BOHEMIAN GIRL (Alfred Bunn, after Jules H. Vernoy de Saint-Georges/Michael William Balfe): When other lips and other hearts (Then You'll Remember Me)	0381 0741 939 57522 66256	F 118	A 34 All. 1721 BC 231 Gal. 4834 S-4359 SC 843

* - Label gives title as "The Perfect Spring."
** - Mislabelled "E lucian..."
*** - Extant test pressing.

29 AUGUST 1908, SATURDAY (14 Hemsell Street, London)
w. orchestra (78.00rpm at score pitch; 74.00rpm if transposed one-half step below
score pitch as is common)*

Lxx 2791	LA BOHEME (Giuseppe Giacosa and Luigi Illica, after Henri Murger/Giacomo Puccini): Che gelida manina (Racconto di Rodolfo)	84205^2** X 3	8645***	All. 1555 ANNA 1058 Arab.8105-2 Roy. 18119 S-4359 SC 853 SH 399
-2		84205 X 3	8645***	A-110 Et. 731

31 AUGUST 1908, MONDAY (14 Hemsell Street)****
w. orchestra

Lx 2793	Mattinata (words and music by Ruggiero Leoncavallo) (76.60rpm)	UNPUBLISHED*****		
-2	(78.26rpm)******	57633 AM 33028 RO 586 RO 658	IRCC No. 3101-B *******	A 34 All. 1721 Gal. 4834 S-4359 SC 820
Lx 2795	CARMEN (Henri Meilhac and Ludovic Halevy, after Prosper Merimée/Georges Bizet): See here the flower (Air de la Fleur)(75.00rpm)	57582 RO 454		A 34 All. 1721 Arab.8105-2 Et. 469 Gal. 4834
Lx 2796	I'll Sing Thee Songs of Araby (William Gormon Wills/ Frederic Clay)	UNPUBLISHED		
-2	(80.00rpm)	0455 57583 AM 33021	6234 F 118	ALL. 1718 GV 532 Halo 50324 LEG 9022 S-4359 SC 843
Lx 2797	MIGNON (Jules Barbier and Michel Carré, after Johann Wolfgang von Goethe/Ambroise Thomas): In her simplicity (78.26rpm)	0503 57581		A 34 All. 1721 Arab.8105-2 BC 231 EB 36 FDY 2068 Gal. 4834 RLS 743 S-4359 SC 820 SH 399
Lx 2798	Roses (Frederic Edward Weatherley/Stephen Adams)	0455 57580 AM 33020	70004 F 121	S-4359 SC 843

* - McCormack's 1910 Victor recording is transposed down one-half step.
** - The superscript "2" refers to sequence of issue, not recording sequence;
thus the first take was published later than the second take.
*** - Probably only the first take was issued with this number.
**** - There is no information available on matrix Lx 2794.
***** - Extant test pressing.
****** - May have been recorded at later session, on basis of speed probably that
of 5 September 1909.
******* - 78rpm re-recording.

Lxx 2799	Pianto del Core (?/Ciro Pinsuti) (78.26rpm)	84206* X 3		A11.R. 1555 Et. 469 Et. 731 S-4359 SC 853
Lx 2491-3**	RIGOLETTO (Francesco Maria Piave, after Victor Hugo/ Giuseppe Verdi): La donna è mobile	UNPUBLISHED***		
-4**	(76.60rpm)	0218 57508² AM 33009	IRCC No. 3101-A ****	A-110 A11.R. 1555 Arab.8105-2 ATL 4088 EP 324 Et. 469 Et. 731 FRP-1 GM 132 RHA 6015 S-4359 SC 820 SH 399 TQD 3009

<u>3 OCTOBER 1908, SATURDAY (14 Hemsell Street, London)</u>*****
w. orchestra (84.00rpm)

Lx 2133-<u>2</u>******	Savourneen Deelish (My Sweet Love)(Anonymous Irish poem, trans. George Colman/Old Irish Air)	0538 57550² (R(71557))	6229 G 5000	A11. 1718 CEN 1003 EGM 7015 Halo 50324 HPE 669 Hud. 225 Jay 3002 LEG 9022 RHA 6001 SC 853 SH 306 SU-272
Lx 2840	Has Sorrow Thy Young Days Shaded? (Thomas Moore/Old Irish Air: "Sly Patrick," arr. Thomas Moore)	0468 57587 AM 33022		A11. 1718 Halo 50324 Hud. 225 Jay 3002 LEG 9022 S-4359 SC 843 SU-272
Lx 2841	Avenging and Bright (Thomas Moore/Old Irish Air: "Mount of the Fenlands")	0468 57590		A11. 1718 ATL 4085 EGM 7015 Halo 50324 HPE 669 Hud. 225 Jay 3002 LEG 9022 RHA 6001 S-4359 SC 853 SU-272

* - Some copies have matrix mistakenly inscribed as "Lxx 2719."
** - May have been recorded at a later session.
*** - Extant test pressing.
**** - 78rpm re-recording.
***** - There is no available information on matrices Lx 2846 - Lx 2849 and Lx 2851.
****** - Additional takes have been reported but remain unconfirmed.

Lx 2842	The Foggy Dew ("Oh, a wane cloud was drawn o'er the dim weeping dawn")(An Ode to the River Shannon)(Alfred Perceval Graves/Old Irish Air, arr. Sir Charles Villiers Stanford)	0469 57593		SH 306
Lx 2843	Trotting to the Fair (Alfred Perceval Graves/Old Irish Air, arr. Sir Charles Villiers Stanford)	0469 57594		FLPS 1840 GEMM 183 JMcC. 1 SH 306 STAL 1057
Lx 2844*	MARITANA (Edward Fitzball/ William Vincent Wallace): There is a Flower That Bloometh	0503 57588		A 34 All. 1721 FDY 2068 Gal. 4834 S-4359 SC 820
Lx 2845	I Know of Two Bright Eyes ("Myrra")(No. 4 from "Songs of the Turkish Hills")(Abdul Mejid/George H. Clutsam)	0513 57591	F 131	
Lx 2850**	Mary of Allendale (Anonymous Scottish Poem/James Hook, arr. H. Lane Wilson)	0513 57602	F 120	All. 1718 Halo 50324 Jay 3007 LEG 9022 S-4359 SC 853

w. CHARLES MARSHALL, piano

Lxx 2852**	I Hear You Calling Me (Harold Lake, writing as Harold Harford/Charles Marshall)	84207 (C(74290)) X 100	864	All. 1718 Halo 50324 HPE 670 LEG 9022 P 69 RHA 6005 S-4359 SC 843 TQD 3023
Lxx 2853**	When Shadows Gather (Frederic Edward Weatherley/Charles Marshall)	84210 X 100	50008	GV 532 Halo 50324 LEG 9022 S-4359 SC 843

w. orchestra conducted by CHARLES MARSHALL(?)

Lxx 2854**	I Hear You Calling Me (Harold Lake, writing as Harold Harford/Charles Marshall)	84208 X 11	50001	

5 DECEMBER 1908, SATURDAY (14 Hemsell Street, London)***
w. CHARLES MARSHALL, piano (79.13rpm)

Lxx 2962	Lolita (Serenata Espagnol)(words and music by Antonio Buzzi-Peccia)	84217 (C(74289)) X 11	864	A 34 All. 1721 Gal. 4834 GEMM 160 GEMM 176e GV 532 Jay 3007 P 69

* - Only known Odeon with date inscribed in master and visible under label.
** - May have been recorded at later session.
*** - There is no information on matrix Lx 2964.

Lx 2963   Parted (words and music by   0336   A 34
                    Alicia Scott)   57608   All. 1721
                                                                Gal. 4834
                                                                Jay 3007
                                                                S-4359
                                                                SC 820
                                                                SU-272

Lx 2965   Love's Philosophy (Poem by Percy 0816
                    Bysshe Shelley/Roger Quilter, 57704
                    Op. 3, No. 1)

5 SEPTEMBER 1909, SUNDAY (14 Hemsell Street, London)
w. orchestra
Lx 2501-2   TOSCA (Luigi Illica and Giuseppe 0218   C.R.S. No. A-110
                    Giacosa, after Victorien   57525^2 12-B*   AK-168
                    Sardou/Giacomo Puccini): E   RO 454   F 117   All.R. 1555
                    lucevan le stelle (76.00rpm)   All.R. 1595
                                                                       Arab.8105-2
                                                                       DLP 121
                                                                       Et. 469
                                                                       Et. 731
                                                                       LPA 2340
                                                                       S-4359
                                                                       SC 820
                                                                       SH 399
                                                                       T 303

Lx 2559-3   RIGOLETTO (Francesco Maria   0218   A 34
                    Piave, after Victor Hugo/   57631   All. 1721
                    Giuseppe Verdi): Questa o   AM 33026   All.R. 1555
                    quella (76.00rpm)   RO 276   All.R. 1902
                                                                 All.R.EP(?)
                                                                 Arab.8105-2
                                                                 BC 231
                                                                 Gal. 4834
                                                                 S-4359
                                                                 SC 853
                                                                 SH 399
                                                                 T 325

Lxx 3134-1   A Southern Song (words and music UNPUBLISHED
                    by Robert Batten)
        -2   (78.26rpm)   84233   50007   cass.IV
                                                 X 41

Lxx 3135   Mountain Lovers (Frederic   84226   880   Et. 469
                    Edward Weatherley/William   (C(74329))   Et. 731
                    Henry Squire)(76.00 or   X 75**   S-4359
                    80.00rpm)   SC 853

Lx 3136   When Shadows Gather (Frederic   UNPUBLISHED
                    Edward Weatherley/Charles
                    Marshall)
        -2   (78.26rpm)   57632
                                                 AM 33027
                                                 RO 317

Lx 3137   Take, Oh Take Those Lips Away   57630   All. 1718
                    (William Shakespeare/Sir   AM 33025   Halo 50324
                    William Sterndale Bennett)   RO 317   Jay 3007
                    (78.26rpm)   LEG 9022
                                                                 S-4359
                                                                 SC 853

* - 76.60rpm re-recording.
** - Some pressings are known to have labels reversed.

Lxx 3138

CARMEN (Henri Meilhac and   84225   863   A-110
Ludovic Halevy, after Prosper (C(74288)) 50002   All.R. 1555
Merimée/Georges Bizet): I1   X 75*   Arab.8105-2
fior che avevi a me(Air de la   A.R.C. 53
Fleur)(78.26rpm)   BC 231
                                                      Et. 496
                                                      Et. 731
                                                      FDY 2068
                                                      GM 132
                                                      Roy. 18119
                                                      S-4359
                                                      SC 820
                                                      SH 399

7 SEPTEMBER 1909, TUESDAY (14 Hemsell Road, London)**
w. orchestra
Lx 3150

Lolita (Serenata Espagnol)(words UNPUBLISHED
and music by Antonio
Buzzi-Peccia)

-2   (78.26rpm)   57640   IRCC No.   S-4359
                                    AM 33029   3092-B   SC 820
                                    (C(74289))   ***
                                    RO 658

Lxx 3151

My Dark Rosaleen (Words from   UNPUBLISHED
the Irish by James Clarence
Mangan/Alicia Adélaïde
Needham-Morgan)

-2   (81.82rpm)   84240   50006   All. 1718
                                    X 44   Halo 50324
                                                          Hud. 225
                                                          Jay 3002
                                                          LEG 9022
                                                          SU-272

Lxx 3152

LA FAVORITA (Alphonse Royer and UNPUBLISHED
Gustave Waez, Baculard
Darnaud/Gaetano Donizetti):
Spir'to gentil

-2   (81.00rpm)   84230   869   A-110
                                    (C(74331)) 8647   All.R. 1555
                                    X 65   Arab.8105-2
                                                          BC 231
                                                          CCS 1004
                                                          EB 36
                                                          Et. 469
                                                          Et. 731
                                                          GEMM 155
                                                          S-4359
                                                          SC 853
                                                          SH 399

Lxx 3153

Voi dormite, Signora! (Rocco   UNPUBLISHED
Pagliara/Sir Francesco Paolo
Tosti)

-2   (81.00rpm)   57643   IRCC No.   A 34
                                    AM 33031   3092-A   All. 1721
                                    RO 586   ***   Gal. 4834
                                                          Jay 3007
                                                          S-4359
                                                          SC 820

* - Some pressings are known to have labels reversed.
** - There is no available information on matrices Lx 3154, Lx 3159, Lx 3161,
Lx 3165, and Lx 3170 - Lx 3172.
*** - 78rpm re-recording.

Lx 3155	The Fairy Glen (words(?) and music by Charles Marshall) (81.00rpm)	0716 57644		FLPS 1840 JMcC-1 STAL 1057
Lx 3156	Eileen Aroon (Thomas Davis/Old Irish Air, arr. Dermot MacMurrough)(81.00rpm)	0538 57641 AM 33030 (R(71569))	G 5006	All. 1718 GV 532 Halo 50324 Hud. 225 Jay 3002 LEG 9022 S-4359 SC 853 SH 306 SU-272
Lx 3157	Ideale (Errica/Sir Francesco Paolo Tosti)(81.00rpm)	0336 57642		All.R. 1555 CRE 5 EB 22 EP-324 Et. 496 Et. 731 S-4359 SC 820
Lxx 3158	O Lovely Night (from song cycle, "Summertime")(Margaret Teschemacher/Sir Landon Ronald)(81.00rpm)	84229 (C(74330)) X 41	869 50003	All. 1718 Halo 50324 HPE 670 Jay 3007 LEG 9022 RHA 6005 S-4359 SC 843 TQD 3023
Lxx 3160	The Green Isle of Erin (C. Clifton Bingham/Joseph L. Roeckel)(81.00rpm)	84234 (C(74332)) X 44	880 50004	GEMM 183 S-4359 SC 843
Lx 3162	L'Ultima Canzone (Francisco Cimmino/Sir Francesco Paolo Tosti)(81.00rpm)	0741 57645 AM 33033		All.R. 1555 CRE 5 EB 22 Et. 469 Et. 731 S-4359 SC 853
Lxx 3163	My Queen (words(?) and music by Joseph Blumenthal)(81.00rpm)	84231 X 62		
Lxx 3164	The Last Watch (words(?) and music by Ciro Pinsuti) (81.00rpm)	84239 X 62		
Lx 3166	Oft in the Stilly Night (Thomas Moore/Old Scottish Air, arr. Sir John Stevenson)(81.00rpm)	0716 57646	6234	

matrix or matrix and take	title	Victor	HMV	microgroove
Lx 3167	The Ould Plaid Shawl (Francis A. Fahy/Old Irish Air, arr. Battison Haynes)(81.00rpm)	0633 57647 AM 33035	70005 78-2077*	All. 1718 ATL 4085 Halo 50324 HPE 669 Hud. 225 Jay 3002 LEG 9022 RHA 6001 S-4359 SC 820 SU-272
Lx 3168	The Bay of Biscay (words and music by Waldeck, Cherry, and Davey)(81.00rpm)	0633 57648 AM 33036		All. 1718 GV 532 Halo 50324 Jay 3007 LEG 9022 S-4359 SC 820 SU-272
Lx 3169	Goodbye, Sweetheart, Goodbye (F. Williams/John L. Hatton) (81.00rpm)	0816 57705 AM 33037		
Lxx 3173**	AIDA (Antonio Ghislanzoni, after Camille du Locle and Auguste Mariette Bey/Giuseppe Verdi): Celeste Aida (80.00rpm)	84236 (C(74287)) X 65	863 8647 50005 C.R.S. No. 12-A***	A-110 All.R. 1555 Arab.8105-2 ATL 4088 BC 231 CCS 1004 EB 36 EP-324 Et. 469 Et. 731 FDY 2068 GEMM 155 LPA-2304 RHA 6015 Roy. 18119 S-4359 SC 820 SH 399 TQD 3009

Victor/RCA/HMV/EMI

matrix or
matrix and take title   Victor   HMV   microgroove

VICTOR TALKING MACHINE COMPANY

3 JANUARY 1910, MONDAY (Camden)****
w. orchestra

* – 78rpm re-recording.
** – May have been recorded on 8 September 1909.
*** – 76.60rpm re-recording.
**** – The Victor Recording Book shows that both the LUCIA aria and "Killarney" were recorded on this date, the latter being identified as a "Test." Both were probably intended as test recordings but were so successful that they were later assigned regular matrix and take numbers and issued, hence the out of sequence matrices.

C 8535-1*   LUCIA DI LAMMERMOOR (Salvatore   6196-B**   2-052023   17-0346-A
                   Cammerano, after Sir Walter   74223***   DB 345   in WCT-53
                   Scott/Gaetano Donizetti): Fra   88215   IRX 1003** A.R.C. 53
                   poco a me ricovero (76.60rpm)   CO 383
                                                                            ERAT 17
                                                                            FDY 2068
                                                                            GEMM 155
                                                                            GM 132
                                                                            HER 509
                                                                            LCT-1036
                                                                            RHA 6015
                                                                            Roc. 5274
                                                                            TQD 3009
                                                                            VIC-1393

C 8594-1****   Killarney (Edmund O'Rourke,   6199-A   02246   ATL 4085
                   writing as Edmund Falconer/   74157   DB 342   EMB 3400
                   Michael William Balfe)   IRX 67   GVC 11
                   (76.00rpm)   HPE 669
                                                                            M.H. 920344
                                                                            RHA 6001
                                                                            S-4359
                                                                            SC 873

7 JANUARY 1910, FRIDAY (Camden)
w. orchestra (76.60rpm)
C 8536-1   L'ELISIR D'AMORE (Felice Romani, UNPUBLISHED
                   after Eugène Scribe/Gaetano
                   Donizetti): Una furtiva
                   lagrima
B 8537-1   Believe Me If All Those   UNPUBLISHED
                   Endearing Young Charms
                   (Thomas Moore/Old Irish Air:
                   "My Lodging is on the Cold
                   Ground")
C 8538-1   CARMEN (Henri Meilhac and   6200-A   2-052027   ATL 4088
                   Ludovic Halevy, after Prosper   74218   DB 343   CAL-512
                   Merimée/Georges Bizet): Il   88216   IRX 1011   CDM 1057
                   fior che avevi a me (Air de   CDN 1023
                   la Fleur)   CDN 1057
                                                                            CO 382
                                                                            GEMM 156
                                                                            HER 509
                                                                            RHA 6015
                                                                            TQD 3009
                                                                            VIC-1472

1 FEBRUARY 1910, TUESDAY (Camden)
w. orchestra (76.00rpm)
C 8587-1   Drink to Me Only With Thine Eyes UNPUBLISHED
     -2   (Ben Jonson/Old English Air,   UNPUBLISHED
                   setting by Calcott)
C 8588-1   Come Back to Erin (John William   6201-A   02244   ATL 4085
                   Cherry/Charlotte Alington   74158   DB 344   GEMM 183
                   Barnard, writing as Claribel)   IRX 82   HPE 669
                                                                            RHA 6001
                                                                            S-4359
                                                                            SC 843

C 8589-1   LA BOHEME (Giuseppe Giacosa and   UNPUBLISHED
                   Luigi Illica, after Henri
                   Murger/Giacomo Puccini): Che
                   gelida manina (Racconto di
                   Rodolfo)

* - Possibly recorded on 7 January 1910.
** - Re-recording.
*** - Later pressings are re-recordings identified by "S/8" in inner land.
**** - Possibly recorded on 1 February 1910.

C 8589-2	LA BOHEME (Giuseppe Giacosa and Luigi Illica, after Henri Murger/Giacomo Puccini): Che gelida manina (Racconto di Rodolfo)*	6200-B 74222 88218	2-052021 DB 343 IRX 1002	CAL-512 CDN-1023 GEMM 156 VIC-1472
C 8536-2	L'ELISIR D'AMORE (Felice Romani, after Eugène Scribe/Gaetano Donizetti): Una furtiva lagrima	6204-B 74219 88217	2-052022 DB 324 IRX 59	17-0348-B in WCT-53 A.R.C. 53 CO 382 Et. 739 FDY 2068 GEMM 155 HER 509 LCT-1036 RHA 6015 Roc. 5274 TQD 3009 VIC-1393
B 8590-1	The Minstrel Boy (Thomas Moore/ Old Irish Air: "The Moreen," also "The Moirin," also "The Greenwoods of Trnigha")	763-A 64117	4-2071 DA 295	ARM1-4997 GEMM 245

4 MARCH 1910, FRIDAY (Camden)
w. orchestra (76.60rpm)

C 8587-3	Drink to Me Only With Thine Eyes (Ben Jonson/Old English Air, setting by Calcott)	6197-A 74204	02245 DB 340 (IRX 1019)	GEMM 160 HPE 670 OASI-624 RHA 6005 S-4359 SC 882 TQD 3023 XTRA 1107
B 8537-2	Believe Me If All Those Endearing Young Charms (Thomas Moore/Old Irish Air: "My Lodging is on the Cold Ground")	UNPUBLISHED		
B 8683-1	Annie Laurie (Douglas of Fingland/Anne, Lady John Scott)	740-A 64138	4-2072 DA 302	Boul. 4074 Emb. 3400 FLPS 1840 GEMM 241 GVC 11 JMcC. 2 M.H. 920344 S-4359 SC 873 STAL 1057
B 8684-1	The Last Rose of Summer (Thomas Moore/Old Irish Air: "The Groves of Blarney," also "The Young Man's Dream," arr. Thomas Moore)	UNPUBLISHED		

10 MARCH 1910, THURSDAY (Camden)
w. orchestra (76.60rpm)

* - Transposed down one-half step below score pitch.

C 8693-1   LA TRAVIATA (Francesco Maria   (74328)   2-052025   A-110
            Piave, after Alexandre Dumas/ IRCC No.   AGSB 3   CO 382
            Giuseppe Verdi): Lunge da lei   96-A   DB 631   CRM8-5177
            per me non v'ha diletto!...   IRX 1001   ERAT-45
            De' miei bollenti spiriti   GEMM 155
                                                                   RHA 6015
                                                                   Roc. 5274
                                                                   TQD 3009
                                                                   VIC-1393

C 8694-1   FAUST (Jules Barbier and Michel 6203-A   2-052028   ATL 4052
            Carré, after Johann Wolfgang   74220   DB 634   CAL-512
            von Goethe/Charles Gounod):   88230   IRX 1006*   CDM 1057
            Salve dimora, casta e pura**   Opera Disc CDN-1023
                                                          77732   CDN-1057
                                                                   FDY 2064
                                                                   FDY 2068
                                                                   GEMM 156
                                                                   GM 132
                                                                   RHA 6015
                                                                   TQD 3009
                                                                   VIC-1472

B 8695-1   I Hear You Calling Me (Harold   64120*** 4-2076
            Lake, writing as Harold
            Harford/Charles Marshall)

B 8696-1   When Shadows Gather (Frederic   64127   4-2070   GEMM 160
            Edward Weatherley/Charles   DA 497
            Marshall)

23 MARCH 1910, WEDNESDAY (Camden)
w. orchestra (76.60rpm)
C 8737-1   LA BOHEME (Giuseppe Giacosa and 89044   2-054011   ATL 4050
            Luigi Illica, after Henri   15-1009-A DB 630   CO 382
            Murger/Giacomo Puccini): Ah   IRX 1007   GEMM 156
            Mimi, tu piu non torni w.   LM-20115
            GEORGES MARIO SAMMARCO,   RHA 6012
            baritone   Roc. 5274
                                                                   VIC-1393

C 8738-1   LES PÊCHEURS DE PERLES (Eugene   UNPUBLISHED
            Cormon and Michel Carré/
            Georges Bizet): Del tempio
            al limitar w. GEORGES MARIO
            SAMMARCO, baritone

C 8739-1   LA FILLE DU REGIMENT   6203-B*   2-052026   BC 231
            (Jules-Henri Vernoy de   74221**** DB 631   CO 382
            Saint-Georges and   88245   IRX 1014   CRM1-2472
            Jean-Francois-Alfred   15-1015-B Opera Disc FDY 2064
            Bayard, Italian translation   72607   FDY 2068
            of the aria by McCormack/   GEMM 155
            Gaetano Donizetti): Per viver   LM-20114
            vicino a Maria   RHA 6015
                                                                   Roc. 5274
                                                                   RL 12472
                                                                   TQD 3009
                                                                   VIC-1393

---

* - Re-recording.
** - Transposed down one-half step below score pitch.
*** - Takes 2 and 3 were also issued under this number. Take 1 may be recognized
by its having the Victor "patents" label with the record number not underlined and
no "R" in inner land.
**** - Later pressings are re-recordings identified by "S/8" in inner land.

C 8740-1	LUCIA DI LAMMERMOOR (Salvatore Cammerano, after Sir Walter Scott/Gaetano Donizetti): Tu che a Dio spiegasti l'ali	6196-B 74224 88249	2-052024 DB 345 IRX 1003 Opera Disc 72605	A.R.C. 53 CO 382 FDY 2068 GEMM 155 HER 509 RHA 6015 Roc. 5274 TQD 3009 VIC-1393
C 8741-1	The Snowy Breasted Pearl (Sir Stephen Edward De Vere/Old Irish Air: "Pearl of the White Breast," arr. Joseph Robinson)	6201-B* 74166**	02247 DB 344 IRX 82	ATL 4085 ATL 4088 GEMM 183 HPE 669 LSE 2019 RHA 6001 Roc. 5301 S-4359 SC 843

25 MARCH 1910, FRIDAY (New York City)
w. orchestra (76.60rpm)

B 8750-1	LAKME (Edmond Gondinet and Philippe Gille, after Pierre Loti/Léo Delibes): Immenso vienteso...A vien al boscaglia (Cantilena)***	775-A 3029-B 64171 87063 10-1438-A in MI-1228	7-52016 DA 379 (IR 1049)	AB 11 CAL-512 CDN-1023 CDN-1057 CO 382 FB 1 FDY 2064 FDY 2068 GEMM 156 RHA 6015 TQD 3009 VIC-1472
B 8751-1	My Lagan Love (Joseph Campbell, writing as Seosamh MacCathmhaoil/Old Irish Air, arr. Sir Hamilton Harty as one of "Three Traditional Ulster Airs")	64154 ERC 6008-	4-2073 IR 1027 VA 24	GEMM 184 HPE 670 JM-201 RCX 210 RHA 210 TQD 3023
C 8752-1	Molly Bawn (Samuel Lover/Old Irish Air, arr. MacMurrough)	74157****	02286	GEMM 245
C 8753-1	Has Sorrow Thy Young Days Shaded? (Thomas Moore/Old Irish Air: "Sly Patrick")	6206-A 74184	02306 DB 326 IRX 1017	ARM1-4997 ATL 4085 Boul. 4074 GEMM 245 HPE 669 RHA 6001

8 APRIL 1910, FRIDAY (Camden)
w. orchestra (76.60rpm)

B 8818-1	TOSCA (Luigi Illica and Giuseppe Giacosa, after Victorien Sardou/Giacomo Puccini): Recondita armonia	UNPUBLISHED		
B 8819-1	The Dear Little Shamrock (Andrew Cherry/John W. Cherry, arr. W. Jackson)	64153 753-A ERC 6006-	4-2074 DA 287 ***** IR 1035	GEMM 184 LM-2755 RB-6632 VIC-1622

* - Re-recording.
** - Later pressings are re-recordings identified by "S/8" in inner land.
*** - Recitative begins at score pitch but modulates down one-half step below score pitch. Aria transposed down one-half step below score pitch.
**** - Take 2 was also issued under this number. Take 1 may be recognized by its having neither "R" nor "S/8" in inner land.
***** - Some pressings are re-recordings.

THE GRAMOPHONE COMPANY, LIMITED

11 MAY 1910, WEDNESDAY or 12 MAY 1910, THURSDAY (21 City Road, London)*
w. New Symphony Orchestra conducted by SIR LANDON RONALD

4187f	LA TRAVIATA (Francesco Maria Piave, after Alexandre Dumas/ Giuseppe Verdi): Duet w. DAME NELLIE MELBA, soprano**	UNPUBLISHED	
4188f	FAUST (Jules Barbier and Michel Carré, after Johann Wolfgang von Goethe/Charles Gounod): All'erta! All'erta! O tempo piu non é (Final Trio) w. DAME NELLIE MELBA, soprano and GEORGES MARIO SAMMARCO, baritone (76.00rpm)		Cant. 6207 GEMM 245 HLM 7086 RLS 719 SH 399
4189f	RIGOLETTO (Francesco Maria Piave, after Victor Hugo/ Giuseppe Verdi): Bella figlia dell'amore (Quartet) w. DAME NELLIE MELBA, soprano; EDNA THORNTON, contralto; and GEORGES MARIO SAMMARCO, baritone (77.43rpm)	2-054025 DM 118 IRX 1007	A-110 Arab.8105-2 BC 233 GEMM 155 P 69 RLS 719 Saga 7029 SH 399
4190f	FAUST (Jules Barbier and Michel Carré, after Johann Wolfgang von Goethe/Charles Gounod): All'erta! All'erta! O tempo piu non é (Final Trio) w. DAME NELLIE MELBA, soprano; and GEORGES MARIO SAMMARCO, baritone (76.00rpm)	15-1019-B IRCC No. 7-B IRX 1006	A-110 ATL 4052 BC 233 GEMM 156 RLS 719

VICTOR TALKING MACHINE COMPANY

16 MARCH 1911, THURSDAY (New York City)
w. orchestra (75.00rpm)

C 10060-1	The Irish Emigrant (Helen Selina, later Lady Dufferin/ G. A. Barker)	6207-A 74237	02326 DB 327 IRX 1017	ATL 4085 GEMM 184 HPE 669 RHA 6001
C 10061-1	Kathleen Mavourneen (Annie Barry Crawford/Frederick Nicholls Williams Crouch)	6199-B 74236	02325 DB 342 IRX 67	ATL 4085 ERAT-18 GEMM 184 HPE 669 LSE 2019 RHA 6001 S-4359 SC 843
C 10062-1	I'm Falling in Love With Someone (from "Naughty Marietta") (Rida Johnson Young/Victor Herbert)	UNPUBLISHED		
B 8695-2	I Hear You Calling Me (Harold Lake, writing as Harold Harford/Charles Marshall)	64120***	4-2076	GEMM 160

* - Authoritative sources of information disagree about the date of this session.
** - No additional information is available and the duet may even have been by Melba and Sammarco rather than by Melba and McCormack. If by Melba and McCormack it was probably not the "Brindisi" which requires chorus as it is known that no chorus was present, so would have to be either "Un dì felice" or "Parigi, o cara."
*** - Takes 1 and 3 were also issued under this number. Take 2 may be recognized by its having "R" in inner land.

B 8537-<u>3</u>	Believe Me If All Those Endearing Young Charms (Thomas Moore/Old Irish Air: "My Lodging is on the Cold Ground)	746-A 64180	(4-2141) 5-2107 DA 306	GEMM 184
C 10063-<u>1</u>	Ah! Moon of My Delight (from "In a Persian Garden")(Omar Khayyam, trans. Edward Fitzgerald/Elizabetta Nina Mary Frederika Lehmann)	6197-B 74232	02327 DB 340 IRX 1005	CRM1-2472 GEMM 244 HPE 670 RHA 6005 RL-12472 Roc. 5343 S-4359 SC 882 TQD 3023 XTRA 1107

<u>17 MARCH 1911, FRIDAY (New York City)</u>
w. orchestra (75.00rpm)

C 8752-<u>2</u>	Molly Bawn (Samuel Lover/Old Irish Air, arr. MacMurrough)	6206-B* 74175**	02286 DB 326	CAL-407 CAS-407(e) CDM 1024 CDN-1001 DRLP 007 GEMM 184
B 10069-<u>1</u>	Mother Machree (from "Barry of Ballymore")(Rida Johnson Young/Chauncey Olcott and Ernest R. Ball)	768-A 64181	4-2142 DA 304	EMB 3400 GEMM 184 GVC-11 OASI-624 S-4359 SC 873
B 10062-<u>1</u>	I'm Falling in Love With Someone (from "Naughty Marietta") (Rida Johnson Young/Victor Herbert)	765-B 64174	(4-2140)	GEMM 186 IDLP 2005 LP-110 RO 17 Roc. 5301

<u>30 MARCH 1911, THURSDAY (New York City)</u>
w. orchestra (75.00rpm)

B 10134-<u>1</u>	Macushla (Josephine V. Rowe/ Dermot MacMurrough)	759-A 64205 10-1436-A in MO-1228 ERC 6001-	4-2144 DA 293 IR 386	CAL-407 CAS-407(e) CDM-1024 CDN-1002 DRLP 007 EMB 3400 GEMM 184 GVC-11 LM-2627 LM-6705 RB-6506 RCX-208 S-4359 SC 873
C 10135-<u>1</u>	An Evening Song ("Good Night, Love, Good Night, Love")(F. A. Butler/Joseph Blumenthal)	6205-A 74243	02323 DB 325 IRX 1004	GEMM 186 R 5301 S-4359 SC 882 XTRA 1107

* - Re-recording.
**- Take 1 was also issued under this number. Take 2 was issued both as an original recording distinguished by an "R" in inner land and as a re-recording indicated by "S/8" in inner land.

B 10136-1   The Happy Morning Waits (L'Alba   UNPUBLISHED
                   Nascente)(words and music by
                   Attilio Parelli)

31 MARCH 1911, FRIDAY (New York City)
w. orchestra (75.00rpm)

C 10138-<u>1</u>	She is Far from the Land (Thomas Moore/Old Irish Air: "Open the Door," arr. Frank Lambert)	6207-B 74242	02324 DB 327	GEMM 184
B 10136-<u>2</u>	The Happy Morning Waits (L'Alba Nascente)(words and music by Attilio Parelli)	64250	4-2143	GEMM 241 JM-201 OASI-624
B 10137-1	Li Marinari (No. 12 from "Les Soirées Musicales")(Count Carlo Pepoli/Gioacchino Rossini) w. GEORGES MARIO SAMMARCO, baritone	UNPUBLISHED		
C 8738-<u>2</u>	LES PÊCHEURS DE PERLES (Eugene Cormon and Michel Carré/ Georges Bizet): Del tempio al limitar w. GEORGES MARIO SAMMARCO, baritone		2-054018	A-110 GEMM 240 OASI-624
B 8738-1	LES PÊCHEURS DE PERLES (Eugene Corman and Michel Carré/ Georges Bizet): Del tempio al limitar w. GEORGES MARIO SAMMARCO, baritone	UNPUBLISHED		

4 APRIL 1911, TUESDAY (New York City)
w. orchestra (75.00rpm)

B 10137-2 -<u>3</u>	Li Marinari (No. 12 from "Les Soirées Musicales") (Count Carlo Pepoli/Gioacchino Rossini) w. GEORGES MARIO SAMMARCO, baritone e	UNPUBLISHED 87078 87563*	7-54002*	BC 231 GEMM 155 HPE 670 RHA 6005 Roc. 5301 TQD 3023
B 8738-<u>2</u>	LES PÊCHEURS DE PERLES (Eugene Corman and Michel Carré/ Georges Bizet): Del tempio al limitar w. GEORGES MARIO SAMMARCO, baritone	87082 87553 10-1439-B in MO-1228	7-54001* IR 1026	CO 382 FDY 2064 FDY 2068 GEMM 156 Roc. 5274 VIC-1393

THE GRAMOPHONE COMPANY, LIMITED

3 JULY 1911, MONDAY (21 City Road, London)
w. "The Symphony Orchestra" conducted by PERCY PITT

5130f	Mira la bianca luna (La Serenata)(No. 11 from "Les Soirées Musicales")(Count Carlo Pepoli/Gioacchino Rossini) w. EMMY DESTINN, soprano	UNPUBLISHED
5131f	Mira la bianca luna (La Serenata)(No. 11 from "Les Soirées Musicales")(Count Carlo Pepoli/Gioacchino Rossini) w. EMMY DESTINN, soprano	UNPUBLISHED

* - Possibly unissued.

18 JULY 1911, TUESDAY (21 City Road, London)
w. "The Symphony Orchestra" conducted by PERCY PITT (80.00rpm)

5203f	Mira la bianca luna (La Serenata)(No. 11 from "Les Soirées Musicales")(Count Carlo Pepoli/Gioacchino Rossini) w. EMMY DESTINN, soprano		2-054019 DK 123 (IRX 1015)	A-110 GEMM 155 OASI-603 SH 399
5204f	LA GIOCONDA (Arrigo Boïto, writing as Tobia Gorrio, after Victor Hugo/Amilcare Ponchielli): Badoer questa notte...O grido di quest'anima w. GEORGES MARIO SAMMARCO, baritone	UNPUBLISHED		
5205f	IL BARBIERE DI SIVIGLIA (Cesare Sterbini, after Pierre-Augustin Beaumarchais/ Gioacchino Rossini): O il meglio mi scordavo...Numero quindici w. GEORGES MARIO SAMMARCO, baritone	IRCC No. 96-B	2-054021 DB 608 IRX 1013 VB 33	A-110 A-114 Arab.8105-2 FDY 2068 GEMM 155 RHA 6015 SH 399 TQD 3009
5206f	LA GIOCONDA (Arrigo Boïto, writing as Tobia Gorrio, after Victor Hugo/Amilcare Ponchielli): Badoer questa notte...O grido di quest'anima w. GEORGES MARIO SAMMARCO, baritone		2-054022 DB 608 IRX 1013 VB 33 Opera Disc 77512	A-110 Arab.8105-2 BC 231 CO 348 GEMM 156 RHA 6015 SH 399 TQD 3009

VICTOR TALKING MACHINE COMPANY

2 APRIL 1912, TUESDAY (Camden)
w. orchestra (76.60rpm)

C 11813-1	Maire, My Girl (John Keegan Casey/George Aitken)	74298	02400 DB 632 IRX 1010	GEMM 160 GEMM 176e JM-202
C 11814-1	Like Stars Above (J. A. McDonald/William Henry Squire)	74296	02402 DB 633 (IRX 1022)	GEMM 242 HPE 670 RHA 6005 TQD 3023
B 11815-1	Take, O Take Those Lips Away (William Shakespeare/William Sterndale Bennett)	749-B 64252	4-2220 DA 308 IR 1006	GEMM 160 HPE 670 LM-2755 RB 6632 RHA 6005 Roc. 5301 TQD 3023 VIC-1622
B 11816-1	A Child's Song (from "A Masque") (Thomas Moore/Charles Marshall)	64253 ERC 6001-	4-2217 IR 1034 VA 24	GEMM 242 HPE 670 IDLP 2005 JM-201 RHA 6005 Roc. 5301 TQD 3023

C 11817-1	Asthore (C. Clifton Bingham/ Henry Trotère)	6198-A 74299	02410 DB 341	Boul. 4074 GEMM 160 GEMM 176e JM-202 Roc. 5301
C 11818-1	Green Isle of Erin (C. Clifton Bingham/Joseph L. Roeckel)	UNPUBLISHED		
B 11819-1	A Farewell (Charles Kingsley/ Samuel Liddle)	64254	4-2218 DA 501	DOLM 5023 GEMM 242 HPE 670 JM-201 RHA 6005 TQD 3023

3 APRIL 1912, WEDNESDAY (Camden)*
w. orchestra conducted by VICTOR HERBERT (76.00rpm)

C 11822-1	NATOMA (Joseph D. Redding/Victor Herbert): My Commander as Envoy Bids Me Come...No Country Can My Own Outvie (Paul's Address)	74295	AGSB 3 IRX 1002	CAL-512 CDN-1023 GEMM 160 NW 241 RO 17 VIC-1472
B 11823-1	I Know of Two Bright Eyes ("Myrra")(No. 4 from "Songs of the Turkish Hills")(Abdul Mejid/George H. Clutsam)	64225	4-2219 DA 499	Boul. 4074 GEMM 244
B 11824-1 -2	Eileen Aroon (Thomas Davis/Old Irish Air, arr. Dermot MacMurrough)	UNPUBLISHED 64256 ERC 6005-	4-2214 DA 500 IR 1007	Boul. 4074 GEMM 184 JM-201
B 11825-1	The Rosary (Robert Cameron Rogers/Ethelbert W. Nevin)	UNPUBLISHED		
B 11826-1	The Wearing of the Green (Dion Boucicault/Old Scottish Air: "The Tulip," arr. Oswald James)	788-A 64258	4-2213 DA 322	EMB 3400 GVC 11 HPE 670 M.H. 920344 RHA 6005 S-4359 SC 873 TQD 3023

5 APRIL 1912, FRIDAY (Camden)
w. orchestra (76.00rpm)

C 11814-2	Like Stars Above (J. A. McDonald/William Henry Squire)	UNPUBLISHED		
C 11818-2	Green Isle of Erin (C. Clifton Bingham/Joseph L. Roeckel)	UNPUBLISHED		
B 11825-2	The Rosary (Robert Cameron Rogers/Ethelbert W. Nevin)	64257**	4-2221 DA 314***	GEMM 244

* - The soprano and and baritone arias from NATOMA were also recorded under their
composer's baton at this session: Three unpublished takes (C 11820-1,2,3) of "I
List the Trill of Golden Throat" (Spring Song) sung by Agnes Kimball and one take
(B 11821-3) of "When the Sunlight Dies" (Serenade) sung by Reinald Werrenrath and
issued on 60072.
** - Take 3 was also issued under this number. Take 2 may be recognized by its
having the Victor "patents" label and no take number in inner land or later Victor
acoustic label with take number in inner land, neither having "R" in inner land.
*** - Take 3 also published under this number though less common than take 2.

C 11831-1   LE CID (Adolphe d'Ennery, Louis UNPUBLISHED
             Gallet, and Edouard Blau,
             after Pierre Corneille/Jules
             Massenet): O Souverain, O
             Juge, O Pere!*

C 11832-1   ROMEO ET JULIETTE (Jules Barbier UNPUBLISHED
             and Michel Carré, after
             William Shakespeare/Charles
             Gounod): Ah! leve toi soleil*

| B 11833-<u>1</u> | The Harp That Once Through Tara's Halls (Thomas Moore/ Old Irish Air, "Gramachree") | 746-B 64259 | 4-2216 DA 306 | GEMM 184 HPE 670 RHA 6005 |
| B 11834-<u>1</u> | Silver Threads Among the Gold (Ebenezer B. Rexford/Hart Pease Danks)** | 64260 | 4-2215 | FLPS 1840 GEMM 244 JM-201 JMcC. 1 STAL 1057 |

        -2   UNPUBLISHED

THE GRAMOPHONE COMPANY, LIMITED

<u>15 JULY 1912, MONDAY (21 City Road, London)</u>
w. "The Symphony Orchestra" conducted by PERCY PITT (80.40rpm)

| Ho201af | I GIOIELLI DELLA MADONNA (C. Zangarini and E. Golisciani/ Ermanno Wolf-Ferrari): T'eri un giorna ammalato w. LOUISE KIRKBY-LUNN, contralto | 2-054040 DK 123 (IRX 1015) | A-110 Arab.8105-2 CO 374 GEMM 159 SH 399 T-321 |

VICTOR TALKING MACHINE COMPANY

<u>11 DECEMBER 1912, WEDNESDAY (Camden)</u>
w. orchestra (77.43rpm)

B 12704-<u>1</u>	At Dawning (Nelle Richmond Eberhart/Charles Wakefield Cadman, Op. 29, No. 1)	742-A*** 64302	4-2326 DA 303	BDL 2019 GEMM 244 GVC-51 LM-2755 RB 6632 SC 889 VIC-1622
B 12705-<u>1</u>	MEFISTOFELE (Arrigo Boïto, after Johann Wolfgang von Goethe/ Arrigo Boïto): Dai campi, dai prati	64303 10-1438-B in MO-1228	7-52033 DA 498 IR 1004	AB 11 CAL-512 CDM 1057 CDN-1023 CDN-1057 CO 382 FB 1 GEMM 156 VIC-1472
B 12706-<u>1</u>	MEFISTOFELE (Arrigo Boïto, after Johann Wolfgang von Goethe/ Arrigo Boïto): Giunto sul passo	923-A 64304	7-52034	CAL-512 CDM 1057 CDN-1023 CDN-1057 GEMM 156 VIC-1472

* - It is not known whether or not the recitative preceeding the aria was
included in this recording.
** - Take 3 was also issued under this number. Take 1 may be recognized by its
having the Victor "patents" label and no "R" in inner land.
*** - Included in Music Arts Library of Victor Records Album 3, "Concert Songs."

B 12707-<u>1</u>	LES PÊCHEURS DE PERLES (Eugene Corman and Michel Carré, trans. Zauardini/Georges Bizet): Mi par d'udir ancora*	923–B 64305	7–52032 DA 502 VA 21 (IR 1055)	CAL–512 CDM 1057 CDN–1023 CDN–1057 CO 382 CRM1–2472 GEMM 156 JM–202 LM–6705 RL–12472 VIC–1472
C 12708-<u>1</u>	Nirvana (Frederic Edward Weatherley/Stephen Adams)	74329	02847 DB 633 (IRX 1022)	GEMM 244 JM–202
B 12709-1	The Holy City (Frederic Edward Weatherley/Stephen Adams)	UNPUBLISHED		
B 12710-1	MARITANA (Edward Fitzball/ William Vincent Wallace): There is a Flower That Blommeth	UNPUBLISHED 775–B 64307 10–1437–A in MO–1228	4–2328 DA 336 DA 484 IR 1005	CAL–407 CAS–407(e) CDM 1024 CDN–1002 DRLP 007 GEMM 156 Roc. 5274 VIC–1472

2 JANUARY 1913, THURSDAY (Camden)
w. orchestra (77.43rpm)

B 12758-<u>1</u>	My Dreams (Frederic Edward Weatherley/Sir Francesco Paolo Tosti)	745–B 64310	4–2349 DA 305	Boul. 4074 GEMM 241 S–4359 SC 882 XTRA 1107
B 12759-1 -<u>2</u>	Sweet Genevieve (George Cooper/ Henry Tucker)	UNPUBLISHED 780–B 64309	4–2378 DA 317	BDL 2019 FLPS 1840 GEMM 244 GVC 15 JMcC. 1 S–4359 SC 882 STAL 1057 XTRA 1107
B 12760-<u>1</u>	I'll Sing Thee Songs of Araby (William Gormon Wills/ Frederic Clay)	760–B 64375	4–2437 DA 294 (IR 1059)	Boul. 4074 GEMM 244 Roc. 5301
B 12761-1 -<u>2</u>	Where the River Shannon Flows (words and music by James I. Russell)	UNPUBLISHED 758–A 64311	4–2395 DA 292	CAL–407 CAS–407(e) CDM 1024 CDN 1002 DRLP 007 Emb. 3400 GEMM 184 GVC 11 M.H. 920344 S–4359 SC 873

3 JANUARY 1913, FRIDAY (Camden)
w. orchestra (77.43rpm)

* – Transposed down one half step from score pitch.

B 12762-<u>1</u>	Within the Garden of My Heart (Marshall Roberts/Alicia Scott)	764-B 64317	4-2380 DA 296	GEMM 243 LM-2755 RB-6632 VIC-1622
B 12763-<u>1</u>	Dear Love, Remember Me (Harold Lake, writing as Harold Harford/Charles Marshall)	754-A 64318	4-2396 DA 288	GEMM 242
B 12764-1 -<u>2</u>	MANON (Henri Meilhac and Philippe Gille, after Abbé Prévost/Jules Massenet): Chiudo gli occhi (Il Sogno)	UNPUBLISHED 767-A 64312	7-52047 DA 297 VA 21	CAL-512 CDM 1057 CDN-1023 CDN-1057 CO 382 Et. 731 GEMM 156 LM-6705 VIC-1472
B 11834-<u>3</u>	Silver Threads Among the Gold (Ebenezer B. Rexford/Hart Pease Danks)	781-B 64260*	4-2215 DA 322	BDL 2019 GVC 51 OASI-624 SC 889

w. SPENCER CLAY, piano

B 12765-<u>1</u>	Molly Brannigan (Traditional/Old Irish Air, arr. Sir Charles Villiers Stanford)	743-B 64316	4-2379 DA 304 IR 1001	CAL-407 CAS-407(e) CDM 1024 CDN-1002 DRLP 007 Emb. 3400 GEMM 184 GVC 11 M.H. 920344 RCX 210 S-4359 SC 873
B 12766-1 -2	Mattinata (words and music by Ruggiero Leoncavallo)	UNPUBLISHED UNPUBLISHED		
B 12767-<u>1</u>	The Foggy Dew ("A' down the hill I went one morn...")(E. Milligan/C. Milligan Fox, arr. Spencer Clay)	763-B 64326	4-2381 DA 295	CAL-407 CAS-407(e) CDM 1024 CDN-1002 DRLP 007 GEMM 184
-2		UNPUBLISHED		

19 MARCH 1913, WEDNESDAY (Camden)
w. orchestra

B 13003-1	Pleading (Arthur L. Salmon/Sir Edward Elgar, Op. 48, No. 1)	UNPUBLISHED

28 MARCH 1913, FRIDAY (Camden)
w. orchestra (76.60rpm)

C 13028-1 -2	CARMEN (Henri Meilhac and Ludovic Halevy, after Prosper Merimée/Georges Bizet): Votre mère avec moi sortait de la chapelle...Ma mere je la vois w. LUCY ISABELLE MARSH, soprano**	UNPUBLISHED UNPUBLISHED

* - Take 1 was also issued under this number. Take 3 may be recognized by its having an "R" in inner land.
** - Victor files list as "Parlé moi de ma mere" even though this is not included on the recording.

B 13031-1	The Low Backed Car (Samuel Lover/Old Irish Air: "The Jolly Ploughboy," arr. Samuel Lover)	753-B 64329 ERC 6009-	4-2366 DA 287 IR 1035	Boul. 4074 Emb. 3400 GEMM 184 GVC 11 LM-2755 M.H. 920344 RB-6632 S-4359 SC 873 VIC-1622
-2		UNPUBLISHED		
B 13032-1	Sospiri miei, andate ove vi mando (words and music by Alberto Bimboni)	64333 IRCC No. 217-A	7-52041 DA 297 IR 1011 VA 20	CAL-512 CDM 1057 CDN-1023 CDN-1057 CRM1-2472 GEMM 241 GVC-51 Roc. 5301 RL-12472
B 13033-1	Say "Au Revoir," but not "Goodbye" (words and music by Harry Kennedy)	780-A 64328	4-2382 DA 317	GEMM 186 GVC-51
B 13034-1	Mother O'Mine (Rudyard Kipling/ Frank Berthold Tours)	776-B 64332	4-2368 DA 314	Emb. 3400 GEMM 244 GVC 11 LM-2755 M.H. 920344 RB-6632 S-4359 SC 873 VIC-1622
B 13035-1	Down in the Forest (Spring, No. 2 from "A Cycle of Life") (Harold Simpson/Sir Landon Ronald)	64331	4-2367 DA 501	ARM1-4997 BDL 2019 Boul. 4074 GEMM 244 GVC 15 Roc. 5301

1 MAY 1913, THURSDAY (Camden)
w. orchestra (76.60rpm)

B 13218-1	I Hear a Thrush At Eve (Serenade)(Nelle Richmond Eberhart/Charles Wakefield Cadman)	UNPUBLISHED		
-2		742-B* 64340	4-2370 DA 303	GEMM 242 S-4359 SC 882 XTRA 1107
C 13219-1	Goodbye (G. J. Whyte-Melville/ Sir Francesco Paolo Tosti)	6198-B 74346	02481 DB 341	BC 231 Boul. 4074 EP 324 GEMM 241 OASI-624 Roy. 18119
B 13220-1	A Little Love, A Little Kiss (English words by Adrian Ross, after French words by A. Nilsson Fysher/Lao Silésu)	UNPUBLISHED		
-2		771-A 64343	4-2373 DA 300	Boul. 4074 GEMM 186 JM-202 OASI-624 S-4359 SC 882 XTRA-1107

* - Included in Music Arts Library of Victor Records Album 3, "Concert Songs."

B 13222-1	RIGOLETTO (Francesco Maria Piave, after Victor Hugo/ Giuseppe Verdi): La donna è mobile	UNPUBLISHED		
B 13223-1	RIGOLETTO (Francesco Maria Piave, after Victor Hugo/ Giuseppe Verdi): Quest o quella	767-B 64344	7-52044 DA 498 IR 1004	CO 382 GEMM 155 Roc. 5274 VIC-1393
C 13224-1	O Dry Those Tears (words and music by Teresa del Riego)	UNPUBLISHED		
B 13225-1	Nearer, My God to Thee (Sarah Frances Adams/Lowell Mason) (verses 1,2, and 5)	773-A 64345	4-2374 DA 312	CAL-635 CDN-1029 DRLP 008 GEMM 275
C 13028-3	CARMEN (Henri Meilhac and Ludovic Halevy, after Prosper Mérimée/Georges Bizet): Votre mère avec moi sortait de la chapelle...Ma mère je le vois	8034-B 74345	2-034019 DB 579	CSLP 501 GEMM 156 LCT-6701 OASI-624
-4	w. LUCY ISABELLE MARSH, soprano*	UNPUBLISHED		

2 MAY 1913, FRIDAY (Camden)
w. orchestra (76.60rpm)

B 13231-1	Eileen Allanah (E. S. Marble/J. R. Thomas)	758-B 64341 ERC 6002-	4-2371 DA 292 IR 1027	Emb. 3400 GEMM 184 GVC 11 JM-201 S-4359 SC 873
B 13232-1	From the Land of Sky Blue Water (No. 1 from "Four American Indian Songs, Op. 45)(Nelle Richmond Eberhart/Charles Wakefield Cadman)	UNPUBLISHED		
B 13233-1	Goodbye, Sweetheart, Goodbye (F. Williams/John L. Hatton)	764-A 64342 10-1437-B in MO-1228 ERC 6004-	4-2372 DA 296 IR 1005	GEMM 244 LM-2755 RB-6632 S-4359 SC 843 VIC-1622

w. EDWIN SCHNEIDER, piano

C 13234-1	Ave Maria (Traditional/Charles Gounod, after Johann Sebastian Bach, BWV 846) w. ROSARIO BOURDON, 'cello obbligato	UNPUBLISHED		
B 13235-1	Le Portrait (words and music by Beatrice Parkyns)	64374	7-32005 DA 502 VA 20	CRM1-2472 GEMM 245 JM-202 RL-12472 Roc. 5301

25 MARCH 1914, WEDNESDAY (New York City)
w. VINCENT O'BRIEN, piano

C 14623-1	Angel's Serenade (words and music by Gaetano Braga)w. FRITZ KREISLER, violin obbligato	8033-B 88479 89103	02540 DB 578 (IRX 1019)	17-0035-A in WCT-8 GEMM 157 GEMM 219 LCT-1005 OASI-624 RVC-1578

* - Label shows title as "Parlé moi de ma mere" even though this is not included on the recording.

C 14624-1   Ave Maria (Traditional/Charles   UNPUBLISHED
                 Gounod, after Johann
                 Sebastian Bach,BWV 846) w.
                 FRITZ KREISLER, violin
                 obbligato

C 14625-1   Le Nil (Armand Renaud/Xavier   88482   2-032016   GEMM 157
                 Leroux) w. FRITZ KREISLER,   89105   IRX 1012   Roc. 5301
                 violin obbligato   RVC-1578

C 14626-1   JOCELYN (S. J. O'Reilly/Benjamin 8032-B   02542   17-0349-B
                 Godard): Beneath the   88483   DB 577   in WCT-53
                 Quivering Leaves...Awake Not   89106   IRX 68   449-0016-
                 Yet from thy Repose (Angels   in WCT-1121
                 Guard Thee)(Berceuse) w.   CSLP 508
                 FRITZ KREISLER, violin   Ev. 3258
                 obbligato   GEMM 157
                                                                          GVC 51
                                                                          LCT-1036
                                                                          LCT-1121
                                                                          LM-6099
                                                                          OL 5003
                                                                          RB-6525
                                                                          RVC-1578
                                                                          S-4359
                                                                          SC 882
                                                                          XTRA 1107

C 14633-1   Ave Maria (Sir Walter Scott/   8033-A   02543   449-0015-
                 Franz Schubert, D. 839) w.   88484   DB 578   in WCT-1121
                 FRITZ KREISLER, violin   89107   CAL-635
                 obbligato   CDN-1029
                                                                          CSLP 508
                                                                          DRLP 008
                                                                          GEMM 157
                                                                          LCT-1121
                                                                          RCX-1042
                                                                          RVC-1578

31 MARCH 1914, TUESDAY (New York City)
w. VINCENT O'BRIEN, piano (78.26rpm)
B 14651-1   Serenade (Softly Through the   3021-A   4-2470   GEMM 132
                 Night is Calling)   87191   DA 458   GEMM 157
                 ("Ständchen")(Ludwig   87545   IR 387   RVC-1578
                 Rellstab, trans. Alice   SC 889
                 Mattullath/Franz Schubert,
                 D. 957, No. 4) w, FRITZ
                 KREISLER, violin obbligato

C 14624-2   Ave Maria (Traditional/Charles   8032-A   02541   CAL-635
                 Gounod, after Johann   88481   DB 577   CDN-1029
                 Sebastian Bach, BWV 846) w.   89104   IRX 68   DRLP 008
                 FRITZ KREISLER, violin   GEMM 132
                 obbligato   GEMM 157
                                                                          RDA-57
                                                                          RDM 2301-4
                                                                          RVC-1578

B 14652-1   Ave Maria (Frederic Edward   3021-B   4-2471   GEMM 157
                 Weatherley/after "Intermezzo"   87192   DA 458   RVC-1578
                 from CAVALLERIA RUSTICANA by   87546   IR 387   SC 889
                 Pietro Mascagni) w. FRITZ
                 KREISLER, violin obbligato

2 APRIL 1914, THURSDAY (New York City)
w. orchestra

C 14657-1	RIGOLETTO (Francesco Maria	UNPUBLISHED		
-2	Piave, after Victor Hugo/	UNPUBLISHED		
-3	Giuseppe Verdi): Bella figlia	UNPUBLISHED		
	dell'amore (Quartet) w.			
	LUCREZIA BORI, soprano;			
	JOSEPHINE JACOBY, contralto;			
	and REINALD WERRENRATH,			
	baritone			
B 14658-1	LA BOHEME (Giuseppe Giacosa and	UNPUBLISHED		
-2	Luigi Illica, after Henri	UNPUBLISHED		
-3	Murger/Giacomo Puccini): O	UNPUBLISHED		
	soave fanciulla w. LUCREZIA			
	BORI, soprano			

6 APRIL 1914, MONDAY (Camden)
w. orchestra (76.00rpm)

B 14665-**1**	Who Knows? (Paul Laurence	789-A	4-2473	GVC 30
	Dunbar/Ernest R. Ball) w.	64424	DA 323	
	Francis J. Lapitino, harp			
-2		UNPUBLISHED		
B 14666-1		UNPUBLISHED		
-**2**	The Little Grey Home in the West			
	(from "The Marriage Market")	770-A	5-2111	BDL 2019
	(D. Eardley-Wilmot/Hermann	64425	DA 299	GEMM 244
	Löhr) w. ROSARIO BOURDON,			GVC 51
	'cello obbligato			
B 14667-**1**	My Wild Irish Rose (from "The	895-A	4-2481	Emb. 3400
	Romance of Athlone")(Chauncey	64426	DA 474	GEMM 243
	Olcott/Ernest R. Ball)			GEMM 184
				GVC 11
				M.H. 920344
				S-4359
				SC 873
B 14668-1	Bonnie Wee Thing (Robert Burns/	UNPUBLISHED		
-**2**	Elizabetta Nina Mary Lehmann)	895-B	4-2482	CRM1-2472
	w. Francis J. Lapitino, harp	64427	DA 474	GEMM 241
			IR 1034	GVC 30
				RL-12472
B 14669-**1**	Beautiful Isle of Somewhere	744-A	4-2483	GEMM 244
	(Jessie B. Pounds/John S.	64428	DA 497	GVC 51
	Fearis)			IDLP 2005
B 13220-3	A Little Love, A Little Kiss	UNPUBLISHED		
	(English words by Adrian			
	Ross, After French words by			
	A. Nilsson Fysher/Lao Silésu)			

7 APRIL 1914, TUESDAY (Camden)
w. orchestra (76.00rpm)

B 14670-**1**	Golden Love (Mary Mark Lemon/	64429	4-2484	GEMM 242
	Milton Wellings)		DA 499	JM-201
B 14671-**1**	Because (English words by	745-A	4-2579	Boul. 4074
	Edward Teschemacher, after	64430	DA 305	GEMM 244
	French words by Helen Guy		IR 1048	LM-2755
	Rhodes, writing as Guy			RB 6632
	d'Hardelot/Helen Guy Rhodes,			Roc. 5301
	writing as Guy dIHardelot)			S-4359
				SC 882
				VIC-1622
				XTRA 1107
B 14672-1	Absent (Catherine Young Glen/	UNPUBLISHED		
	John W. Metcalf)			

B 14673-1   Avournéen (E. Cecilia   64431   4-2485   GEMM 184
               Fitzpatrick/Wilton King)   ERC 6010- DA 500   JM-201
                                                        IR 1007

B 14674-1   Mary of Argyle (Charles   740-B   4-2486   Boul. 4074
               Jeffreys/S. Nelson)   64432   DA 302   GEMM 241
                                                                  GVC 30
                                                                  LM-2755
                                                                  RB-6632
                                                                  VIC-1622

      -2   UNPUBLISHED
B 14675-1   Ben Bolt (Thomas Dunn English/ UNPUBLISHED
      -2   Nelson Kneass)   747-B   4-2487   BDL 2019
                                              64433   DA 307   FLPS 1840
                                                         IR 208   GEMM 241
                                                                   GVC 15
                                                                   OASI-624
                                                                   SC 889
                                                                   STAL 1057

B 14676-1   A Dream (Charles B. Cory/J. C. UNPUBLISHED
      -2   Bartlett)   759-B   4-2489   BDL 2019
                                              64434   DA 293   CRM1-2472
                                                         IR 386   GEMM 186
                                                                   GVC 15
                                                                   OASI-624
                                                                   RL-12472

B 14677-1   THE BOHEMIAN GIRL (Alfred Bunn (64599)   4-2488
               after Jules H. Vernoy de
               Saint-Georges/Michael William
               Balfe): When other lips and other
               hearts (Then You'll Remember Me)

8 APRIL 1914, WEDNESDAY (Camden)
w. orchestra (76.00rpm)
B 14678-1   Come Where My Love Lies Dreaming UNPUBLISHED
      -2   (words and music by Stephen   751-A   4-2472   GEMM 245
               Foster) w. male chorus (Harry 64423   DA 310   LM-2755
               Macdonough and Lambert   RB-6632
               Murphy, tenors; Reinald   VIC-1622
               Werrenrath, baritone)

B 14679-1   Funiculi, Funicula (words and   751-B   7-52061   BDL 2019
               music by Luigi Denza) w. male 64437   DA 310   GEMM 219
               chorus (Harry Macdonough and   (IR 1050) GVC 15
               Lambert Murphy, tenors;
               Reinald Werrenrath, baritone)

C 14657-4   RIGOLETTO (Francesco Maria   UNPUBLISHED
      -5   Piave, after Victor Hugo/   10006-A   2-054061 FLPS 1840
               Giuseppe Verdi): Bella figlia 89080   DM 104   GEMM 155
               del'amore (Quartet) w.   (IRX 1018) JMcC. 2
               LUCREZIA BORI, soprano;   Roc. 5724
               JOSEPHINE JACOBY, contralto;   STAL 1057
               and REINALD WERRENRATH,
               baritone

B 14658-4   LA BOHEME (Giuseppe Giacosa and 3029-A   7-54003   CO 382
               Luigi Illica, after Henri   87512   DA 379   ERAT-17
               Murger/Giacomo Puccini): O   10-1439-A (IR 1049) GEMM 156
               soave fanciulla w. LUCREZIA   in MO-1228   LCT-1004
               BORI, soprano   LM-2628
                                                                  RB-6516
                                                                  Roc. 5274

      -5   UNPUBLISHED

| C 14686-<u>1</u> | LA TRAVIATA (Francesco Maria Piave, after Alexandre Dumas/ Giuseppe Verdi): Parigi, O cara w. LUCREZIA BORI, soprano | 10006-B 88453 89126 15-1009-B | 2-054055 DM 104 IRX 1001 | 17-   -B in WCT-57 CO 382 CSLP 518 ERAT-17 FLPS 1840 GEMM 155 LCT-1037 Roc. 5321 STAL 1057 |
| -2 | | | | UNPUBLISHED |

9 APRIL 1914, THURSDAY (Camden)
w. orchestra (76.00rpm)

B 14692-1 -2	ATTILA (Temistocle Solera/ Giuseppe Verdi): Te sol quest'anima w. LUCY ISABELLE MARSH, soprano; REINALD WERRENRATH, baritone	UNPUBLISHED UNPUBLISHED		
B 14693-<u>1</u>	LILY OF KILLARNEY (John Oxenford, after Dion Boucicault/Sir Julius Benedict): The Moon hath Raised Her Lamp Above w. REINALD WERRENRATH, baritone	3024-A 64440	2-4205 DA 172 IR 1001	Emb. 3400 FLPS 1840 GEMM 156 GVC 11 JMcC. 2 Roc. 5274 S-4359 SC 873 STAL 1057
-2		UNPUBLISHED		
C 14694-<u>1</u> -2	AIDA (Antonio Ghislanzoni, after Camille du Locle and Auguste Mariette Bey/Giuseppe Verdi): Tutto è finito...O terra addio (Tomb Scene) w. LUCY ISABELLE MARSH, soprano	8034-A 74398 UNPUBLISHED	2-054059 DB 579	GEMM 155 Roc. 5274 VIC-1393
B 14695-1 -2	I Need Thee Every Hour (Annie S. Hawkes/Robert Lowry)	UNPUBLISHED UNPUBLISHED		

23 NOVEMBER 1914, MONDAY (New York City)
w. orchestra conducted by WALTER B. ROGERS (76.00rpm)

B 15415-<u>1</u>	It's a Long Way to Tipperary (Jack Judge/Harry Williams) w. male chorus (Harry Macdonough, tenor; Reinald	896-A 64476	4-2513 DA 475 IR 1041	GEMM 160 LP 101 West. 504
-2	Werrenrath, baritone; William F. Hooley, bass)	UNPUBLISHED		
B 15416-1 -2	Tenting on the Old Camp Ground (words and music by Walter Kitteredge) w. male chorus (Harry Macdonough, tenor; Reinald Werrenrath, baritone; William F. Hooley, bass) and celeste	UNPUBLISHED UNPUBLISHED		
B 15417-1	The Vacant Chair (George F. Root/H. S. Washburn) w. male chorus (Harry Macdonough, tenor; Reinald Werrenrath, baritone; William F. Hooley, bass) and celeste	UNPUBLISHED		
B 15418-1	Forward Belgium (Belgium Forever)(Yvonne Townsend/ Natalie Townsend)	UNPUBLISHED		

B 15419-<u>1</u>	Somewhere a Voice is Calling (Eileen Newton/Arthur F. Tate)	783-A 64405	5-2115 DA 319	ARM1-4997 CAL-407 CAS-407(e) CDM 1024 CDN-1002 DRLP 007 GEMM 244 GVC-51 RCX-209 SC 889
B 15420-1 -<u>2</u>	Mavis (L. A. Lefevre/Harold Craxton)	UNPUBLISHED 770-B 64407	4-2601 DA 299 (IR 1052)	BDL 2019 GEMM 242 GVC 15

w. EDWIN SCHNEIDER, piano

B 15421-1	The Bard of Armagh (Traditional/ Old Irish Air, arr. Herbert Hughes)	UNPUBLISHED	

29 MARCH 1915, MONDAY (Camden)
w. orchestra conducted by WALTER B. ROGERS (75.00rpm)

B 15838-1 -2	The Evening Song (Sidney Lanier/ Henry Kimball Hadley, Op. 53, No. 7) w. Francis J. Lapitino, harp	UNPUBLISHED UNPUBLISHED		
C 15839-1 -<u>2</u>	When My Ship Comes Sailing Home (Reginald Stewart/Francis Dorel)	UNPUBLISHED 6205-B 74428	02610 DB 325 (IRX 1016)	BDL 2019 GEMM 186 GVC 15 JM-202
B 15840-1	The Hour of Love (R. H. Elkins/ R. Barthelmy)	UNPUBLISHED		

30 MARCH 1915, TUESDAY (Camden)
w. orchestra conducted by WALTER B. ROGERS (75.00rpm)

B 15844-1 -<u>2</u>	Until (Edward Teschemacher/ Wilfrid Sanderson)	UNPUBLISHED 750-A 64495	4-2645 DA 309	BDL 2019 GEMM 245 GVC 15 JM-201
C 15845-<u>1</u>	The Trumpeter (J. Francis Barron/J. Airlie Dix) w. Emil Keneke(?), trumpet	6209-A 74432	02630 DB 329	BDL 2019 GEMM 244 GVC 15 JM-202 LP 110
C 15846-<u>1</u>	Come Into the Garden, Maud (Alfred Tennyson/Michael William Balfe) w. Francis J. Lapitino, harp	6202-A 74434	02629 DB 421 IRX 1005	BDL 2019 CRM1-2472 GEMM 184 GVC 15 JM-202 RL-12472
B 15838-<u>3</u>	The Evening Song (Sidney Lanier/ Henry Kimball Hadley, Op. 53, No. 7) w. Francis J. Lapitino, harp	760-A 64496	4-2621 DA 294	BDL 2019 GEMM 242 GVC 15 JM-201
B 15847-<u>1</u>	Morning (Frank L. Stanton/Oley Speaks)	64498	4-2643	ARM1-4997 BDL 2019 GEMM 242 GVC 15 JM-201 OASI-624

B 15847-2	Morning (Frank L. Stanton/Oley Speaks)	UNPUBLISHED		
C 15848-<u>1</u>	Turn Ye to Me (from "Songs of the North")(Christopher North, writing as John Wilson/Old Scottish Air)	74435	02611 DB 632 IRX 1010	BDL 2019 FLPS 1840 GEMM 241 GVC 15 JM-202 JMcC. 2 STAL 1057
B 11825-<u>3</u>	The Rosary (Robert Cameron Rogers/Ethelbert W. Nevin)	776-A 64257	4-2221 DA 314**	GEMM 275 GVC 30 S-4359 SC 882 XTRA 1107

31 MARCH 1915, WEDNESDAY (Camden)
w. orchestra conducted by WALTER B. ROGERS (75.00rpm)

C 15849-<u>1</u>	Adeste Fideles (Traditional/ Marcus Portugal, arr. F. J. Wade) w. male chorus (Harry Macdonough, tenor; Reinald Werrenrath, baritone; William F. Hooley, bass) and William H. Reitz, chimes	6208-A 74436	2-052169 DB 328	GEMM 159 GEMM 176e OASI-624
B 15416-3	Tenting on the Old Camp Ground (words and music by Walter Kitteredge) w. male chorus (Harry Macdonough, tenor; Reinald Werrenrath, baritone; William F. Hooley, bass), celeste and extra cornet	UNPUBLISHED		
B 15417-2 　-<u>3</u>	The Vacant Chair (George F. Root/H. S. Washburn) w. male chorus (Harry Macdonough, tenor; Reinald Werrenrath, baritone; William F. Hooley, bass) and celeste***	UNPUBLISHED 896-B 64499	5-2117 DA 475 IR 1041	GEMM 244 LM-2755 RB-6632 VIC-1622
B 15850-1 　-<u>2</u>	When the Dew is Falling (Fiona McCleod/Edwin Schneider)	UNPUBLISHED 789-B 64497	4-2644 DA 323	GEMM 242 GVC 15

private recording by CYRIL MC CORMACK, treble (age 8)
w. EDWIN SCHNEIDER, piano

-1	It's a Long Way to Tipperary (Jack Judge/Harry Williams) w. JOHN MC CORMACK joining in refrain and announcing date at end and Howard Rattay, violin obbligato			cass.IV

10 JUNE 1915, THURSDAY (New York City)
w. orchestra conducted by WALTER B. ROGERS (76.00rpm)

C 16089-1 　-2	DIE MEISTERSINGER VON NÜRENBERG (libretto and music by Richard Wagner): Morning was gleaming (Prize Song) w. FRITZ KREISLER, violin obbligato	UNPUBLISHED UNPUBLISHED		

* - Take 2 was also issued under this number.　Take 3 may be recognized by its having an "R" in inner land.
** - Take 2 was also issued under this number.　Take 3 less common.
*** - The last note McCormack sings is D-flat above high C, the highest note he recorded.

B 16090-1   Serenata (English words by   3018-B   4-2700   GEMM 157
                    Nathan Haskell Dole/Moriz   87230   DA 455   GVC 51
                    Moszkowski) w. FRITZ   87547   RVC-1578
                    KREISLER, violin obbligato

      -2   UNPUBLISHED
B 16091-1   Carmé (Canto Sorrentino)   UNPUBLISHED
      -2   (Traditional, arr. G. B.   3018-A   7-52075   Et. 731
                    de Curtis) w. FRITZ KREISLER, 87231   DA 455   EV. 3258
                    violin obbligato   87548   IR 1006   GEMM 57
                                                                      JM-202
                                                                      OASI-624
                                                                      OL 5003
                                                                      RVC-1578

w. LUDWIG SCHWAT, piano
B 16092-1   Flirtation ("Des Fensterin")   3022-B   4-2730   GEMM 233
                    (English words by Alice   87232   DA 459   GEMM 240
                    Mattullath/Erik   87549
                    Meyer-Helmund) w. FRITZ
                    KREISLER, violin obbligato

B 16093-1   Still as the Night ("Still wie UNPUBLISHED
      -2   die Nacht")(English words by 3023-A   4-2699   Ev. 3258
                    Alice Mattullath/Carl Böhm, 87233   DA 460   GEMM 157
                    Op. 326, No. 27) w. FRITZ   87550   OL 5003
                    KREISLER, violin obbligato   RVC-1578
                                                                      SC 889

10 NOVEMBER 1915, WEDNESDAY (Camden)
w. orchestra conducted by WALTER B. ROGERS (75.00rpm)
B 16760-1   Forgotten (A Love Song of   761-A   GEMM 242
                    Poland)(Kavahaff/Eugene   64546   GVC 30
                    Cowles)   JM-202

B 16762-1   Sing, Sing, Birds on the Wing   UNPUBLISHED
      -2   (Leslie Cooke/Godfrey   782-A   4-2798   GEMM 186
                    Nutting) w. Francis J.   64532   DA 318   GVC 30
                    Lapitino, harp   JM-201

      -3   UNPUBLISHED
B 16763-1   God's Hand (Edward W. Bok/Old   UNPUBLISHED
      -2   Dutch Air, arr. Josef   (64548)*
                    Hoffmann) w. celeste
B 16764-1   A Little Bit of Heaven (from   768-B   GEMM 242
                    "The Heart of Paddy Whack") 64543   OASI-624
                    (Joseph Keirn Brennan/Ernest
                    R. Ball)

B 16765-1   Venetian Song (B. C. Stephenson/ UNPUBLISHED
      -2   Sir Francesco Paolo Tosti)   786-B   4-2824   CRM1-2472
                                                 64549   DA 324   GEMM 241
                                                            (IR 1050) RL-12472
                                                                      Roc. 5301

14 JANUARY 1916, FRIDAY (Camden)
w. orchestra conducted by WALTER B. ROGERS (76.00rpm)
B 17008-1   The Old Refrain (English words UNPUBLISHED
      -2   by Alice Mattullath/Fritz   752-A   5-2114   GEMM 243
                    Kreisler)   64559   DA 286   GVC 30

      -3   UNPUBLISHED
B 17009-1   MARTHA (Friedrich Wilhelm Riese, UNPUBLISHED
                    writing as W. Friedrich,
                    after Jules H. Vernoy de
                    Saint-Georges/Friedrich von
                    Flotow): M'appari

* - Extant test pressing.

B 17010-<u>1</u>

Parted (Frederic Edward Weatherley/Sir Francesco Paolo Tosti)

757-A
64578

5-2056
DA 291

GEMM 241
GVC 30
OASI-624
SU 272

9 MAY 1916, TUESDAY (Camden)
w. orchestra conducted by WALTER B. ROGERS (76.00rpm)

B 17645-1

Ora pro nobis (Horspool/Nicolo Piccolomini)

UNPUBLISHED

B 17646-<u>1</u>

Dreams (Baroness Porteous/Anton Strelezki)

761-B
64603

4-2950
DA 291

GEMM 30
GVC 186

C 17647-<u>1</u>

DON GIOVANNI (Lorenzo da Ponte/ Wolfgang Amadeus Mozart, K. 527): Il mio tesoro

6204-A
74484
15-1015-A

2-052110
DB 324
IRX 59

17-0042-B
  in WCT-10
  −   −B
in WDM-1626
CRM1-2472
FLPS 1840
GEMM 158
GEMM 164
LCT-1006
LM-1202
LM-2631
LM-6705
RB-6515
RL-12472
Roc. 5274
STAL 1057
VIC-1472

C 17648-<u>1</u>

The Kerry Dance (words and music by James Lyman Molloy)

6202-B
74485

02823
DB 421

GEMM 160
GEMM 176e

B 17649-1
      -<u>2</u>

Your Eyes (Elizabeth K. Reynolds/Edwin Schneider)

UNPUBLISHED
777-B
64604

DA 520

GEMM 242

B 17650-1
      -<u>2</u>

Little Boy Blue (Eugene Field/ Ethelbert W. Nevin, Op. 12, No. 4) w. Emil Keneke, trumpet

UNPUBLISHED
769-A
64605

4-2952
DA 298

GEMM 275

C 17651-<u>1</u>

Non é ver (words and music by Tito Mattei)

74486

2-052111
DB 630
IRX 1011

CAL-512
CDM 1057
CDN-1023
CDN-1057
GEMM 241
Roc. 5301

10 MAY 1916, WEDNESDAY (Camden)
w. EDWIN SCHNEIDER, piano (77.43rpm)

B 17653-1

For All Eternity (Mazzoni/A. Mascheroni) w. FRITZ KREISLER, violin obbligato

UNPUBLISHED

B 17654-1
      -<u>2</u>

Serenade (Sternan, trans. F. W. Rosier/Joachim Raff) w. FRITZ KREISLER, violin obbligato

UNPUBLISHED
3019-B
87258
87552

4-2953
DA 456

GEMM 157
SC 889

B 17655-<u>1</u>

LES CONTES D'HOFFMANN (Jules Barbier/Jacques Offenbach): Beauteous night, O night of love (Barcarolle) w. FRITZ KREISLER, violin

3019-A
87245
87551

5-2153
DA 456

GEMM 132
GEMM 157
SC 889
RVC-1578

w. orchestra conducted by WALTER B. ROGERS (76.00rpm)

C 17656-1   DIE MEISTERSINGER VON NÜRENBERG   6209-B   02846   Et. 731
             (libretto and music by   74479   DB 329   GEMM 160
             Richard Wagner): Morning was   VB 7   Roc. 5274
             gleaming (Prize Song) w.   VIC-1393
             Francis J. Lapitino, harp

11 MAY 1916, THURSDAY (Camden)
w. orchestra conducted by WALTER B. ROGERS
B 17672-1   Cradle Song 1915 (adapted from   UNPUBLISHED
      -2   "Caprice Viennois")(Alice   752-B   5-2109   GEMM 243
             Mattullath/Fritz Kreisler)   64606   DA 286   GVC 51
             w. harp and bells
B 14677-2   THE BOHEMIAN GIRL (Alfred Bunn,   747-A   4-2488   CAL-407
             after Jules H. Vernoy de   64599   DA 307   CAS-407(e)
             Saint-Georges/Michael William   ERC 6009- IR 208   CDM 1024
             Balfe): When Other lips and   CDN-1002
             other hearts (Then You'll   DRLP 007
             Remember Me)   GEMM 156
                                                                   Roc. 5274
                                                                   SC 889
                                                                   VIC-1472

20 SEPTEMBER 1916, WEDNESDAY (Camden)
w. orchestra conducted by ROSARIO BOURDON (78.26rpm)
B 18383-1   The Sunshine of Your Smile   783-B   BDL 2019
             (Leonard Cooke/Lilian Ray)   64622   GEMM 244
                                                                   GVC 15
                                                                   IDLP 2005

      -2   UNPUBLISHED
B 18384-1   Love, Here is My Heart (Adrian   UNPUBLISHED
      -2   Ross/Lao Silésu)   771-B   4-2870   DOLM 5023
                                                64623   DA 300   GEMM 186

B 18385-1   Tommy Lad (Edward Teschemacher/   769-B   4-2865   GEMM 243
             E. J. Margetson)   64630   DA 298   GEMM 252/6
                                                                   GVC 51

B 18386-1   In an Old Fashioned Town (A. L.   UNPUBLISHED
      -2   Harris/William Henry Squire)   UNPUBLISHED
B 18387-1   When Irish Eyes Are Smiling   UNPUBLISHED
      -2   (from "The Isle O'Dreams")   788-B   4-2866   449-0172-
             (Chauncey Olcott and George   64631   DA 321   7 ER 5066
             Graff/Ernest R. Ball)   410-0172* IR 1036   CAL-407
                                                ERC 6007-A   CAS-407(e)
                                                                   CDM 1024
                                                                   CDN-1002
                                                                   DRLP 007
                                                                   ERAT-18
                                                                   GEMM 185
                                                                   LM-6705
                                                                   RCX-208

B 18388-1   Love Bells (Charleton/Francis   UNPUBLISHED
      -2   Dorel)   UNPUBLISHED
B 18389-1   In Old Madrid (C. Clifton   UNPUBLISHED
             Bingham/Henry Trotère)

21 SEPTEMBER 1916, THURSDAY (Camden)
w. orchestra conducted by ROSARIO BOURDON (78.26rpm)
C 18390-1   Flow Gently, Deva (words and   UNPUBLISHED
      -2   music by Joseph Parry) w.   UNPUBLISHED
             REINALD WERRENRATH, baritone
B 18391-1   Crucifix (F. W. Rosier/Jean   UNPUBLISHED**
             Baptiste Faure) w. REINALD
             WERRENRATH, baritone

 * - Re-recording
** - Extant test pressing.

```
B 18392-1        Larboard Watch (words and music  UNPUBLISHED
     -2             by T. Williams)                UNPUBLISHED
```

29 MARCH 1917, THURSDAY (Camden)
w. orchestra conducted by JOSEF A. PASTERNACK (76.00rpm)

```
B 19534-1        The Star Spangled Banner         UNPUBLISHED
     -2             (Francis Scott Key/Old         UNPUBLISHED
     -3             English Air) w. male chorus    64664     4-2886     GEMM 244
                   (Harry Macdonough and Lambert
                   Murphy, tenors; Reinald
                   Werrenrath, baritone; William
                   F. Hooley, bass)
```

5 APRIL 1917, THURSDAY (New York City)
w. orchestra conducted by VICTOR HERBERT (76.00rpm)

```
B 19447-1        Ireland, My Sireland (from       756-A     4-2885     ARM1-4997
                   "Eileen")(Henry Blossom/        64665     DA 290     GEMM 243
                   Victor Herbert) w. Dominic                           JM-201
                   Melillo, harp

     -2                                            UNPUBLISHED
B 19448-1        Eileen (Alanna Asthore)(from     UNPUBLISHED
     -2             "Eileen")(Henry Blossom/        756-B     4-2884     BDL 2019
                   Victor Herbert) w. Dominic      64666     DA 290     GEMM 185
                   Melillo, harp                                        GVC 15
                                                                        JM-201
```

9 MAY 1917, WEDNESDAY (?)
w. piano
private recording by CYRIL MC CORMACK (age 10)

```
     -1             If I Knock the "L" Out of Kelly  UNPUBLISHED*
                   (Sam M. Lewis and Joe Young/
                   Bert Grant)
```

private recording by GWEN MC CORMACK (age 8)

```
     -1             Poor Butterfly (John Golden/    UNPUBLISHED*
                   Raymond Hubbell) w. JOHN
                   MC CORMACK briefly joining in
                   refrain and announcing date
                   at end
```

7 JUNE 1917, THURSDAY (Camden)
w. orchestra conducted by JOSEF A. PASTERNACK (75.00rpm)

```
B 20016-1        The Trumpet Call (P. J.          UNPUBLISHED
     -2             O'Reilly/Wilfred Sanderson)    64733     5-2067     GEMM 245
                                                             DA 336

B 20017-1        Keep the Homes Fires Burning     UNPUBLISHED
     -2             (Lena Guilbert Ford/Ivor        766-A                GEMM 160
                   Novello)                        64696                LP 101
                                                                        West. 504

B 20018-1        There's a Long, Long Trail       766-B                GVC 30
                   (Stoddard King/Zo Elliot)       64694                LP 101
                                                                        West. 504

     -2                                            UNPUBLISHED
B 20019-1        Any Place is Heaven if You Are   UNPUBLISHED
     -2             Near Me (Edward Lockton/        741-A     5-2055     GEMM 242
                   Hermann Löhr)                   64699     IR 1037    LM-2755
                                                   ERC 6003-            RB-6632
                                                                        VIC-1622
```

8 JUNE 1917, FRIDAY (Camden)
w. orchestra conducted by JOSEF A. PASTERNACK (75.00rpm)

```
B 20021-1        The Rainbow of Love (William F.  UNPUBLISHED
     -2             Kirk/Gustav Ferrari) w.         778-A     5-2054**
                   Rosario Bourdon, celeste        64732     DA 315**
```

* - Extant test pressing.
** - HMV discs show title as "The Light in Your Eyes."

B 20027-1	Three Shadows (Dante Gabriel	UNPUBLISHED		
-2	Rossetti/Henry Thacker Burleigh)	UNPUBLISHED		
B 20028-1	The Girl I Left Behind Me	UNPUBLISHED		
-2	(Samuel Lover/Old English Air, harmonized by Max Vogerich)	UNPUBLISHED		
C 18390-3	Flow Gently, Deva (words and	UNPUBLISHED		
-4	music by Joseph Parry) w. REINALD WERRENRATH, baritone	(74544)		
B 18391-2	Crucifix (F. W. Rosier/Jean	UNPUBLISHED		
-3	Baptiste Faure) w. REINALD WERRENRATH, baritone	3024-B 64712	3-4048 DA 172 (IR 1047)	GEMM 159 GEMM 176e

7 SEPTEMBER 1917, FRIDAY (New York City)
w. orchestra conducted by EDWARD KING* (76.00rpm)

B 20546-1	Send Me Away With a Smile (Louis Weslyn/A. Piantidosi)	64741**		GEMM 275
-2		UNPUBLISHED		

23 OCTOBER 1917, SUNDAY (Camden)
w. orchestra conducted by JOSEF A. PASTERNACK (76.60rpm)

C 20898-1	JOSEPH EN ÉGYPTE (A. Duval/ Etienne-Nicolas Méhul): Champs paternels! Hébron douce vallée	74564	2-032032 DB 634 IRX 1012 VB 7	CAL-512 CDM 1057 CDN-1023 CDN-1057 CO 382 CSLP 501 GEMM 156 LCT-6701 LM-2372 LM-6705 RB-16198 VIC-1472
-2		UNPUBLISHED		
B 20546-3	Send Me Away With a Smile (Louis Weslyn/A. Piantidosi)	64741***	5-2035 DA 491	LP 119
-4		UNPUBLISHED		
B 20899-1	The Lord is My Light (after Psalm 27/Frances Allitsen)	744-B 64726	5-2116 DA 324	CAL-635 CDN-1029 DRLP 008 GEMM 159 GEMM 176e

5 APRIL 1918, FRIDAY (114 North 5th Street, Camden)
w. orchestra conducted by JOSEF A. PASTERNACK (76.60rpm)

B 21663-1	God Be With Our Boys Tonight (Fred G. Bowles/Wilfrid Sanderson)	64773 ****		GEMM 275 JM-202

30 APRIL 1918, TUESDAY (New York City)
w. orchestra conducted by JOSEF A. PASTERNACK (76.60rpm)

B 21808-1	Calling Me Home to You (Edward	UNPUBLISHED		
-2	Teschemacher/Francis Dorel)	750-B 64803	5-2108 DA 309	DOLM 5023 GEMM 186
B 21809-1	My Irish Song of Songs (Alfred Dubin/Daniel J. Sullivan)	772-B 64796	5-2113 DA 311	GEMM 185 IDLP 2005

* - Victor files show orchestra as "King's Orchestra", which was Victor's New York studio orchestra of the period, conducted by King, Rogers, Bourdon, etc. and augmented for some operatic sessions by extra musicians brought from Camden.
** - Take 3 also issued under this number.
*** - Take 1 also issued under this number.
**** - Takes 2 and 3 also issued under this number.

B 21809-2	My Irish Song of Songs (Alfred Dubin/Daniel J. Sullivan)	UNPUBLISHED			
B 21810-1	Little Mother of Mine (George S.	UNPUBLISHED			
-2	Brengle*/Henry Thacker Burleigh)	755-B	5-2112	GEMM 242	
		64778	DA 289	GVC 51	
B 21663-2	God Be With Our Boys Tonight (Fred G. Bowles/Wilfrid Sanderson)	64773**			

1 MAY 1918, WEDNESDAY (New York City)
w. orchestra conducted by JOSEF A. PASTERNACK (76.60rpm)

B 21811-1	Dear Old Pal of Mine (Harold	UNPUBLISHED			
-2	Robé/Gitz Rice)	755-A	5-2110	GEMM 243	
		64785	DA 289		
B 21812-1	Love's Garden of Roses (Ruth	774-A	5-2094	ARM1-4997	
	Rutherford/Haydn Wood)	64787	DA 319	GEMM 242	
				GVC 30	
-2		UNPUBLISHED			
B 21813-1	Ideale (Errica/Sir Francesco	UNPUBLISHED			
-2	Paolo Tosti)	UNPUBLISHED			
B 21814-1	Sometime You'll Remember Me (Raymond Wallace/Mauricel Head)	918-A (66163)	(5-2938) DA 576		
B 21663-3	God Be With Our Boys Tonight (Fred G. Bowles/Wilfrid Sanderson)	64773***			

24 SEPTEMBER 1918, TUESDAY (Camden)
w. orchestra conducted by JOSEF A. PASTERNACK (76.00rpm)

B 22253-1	Dream On, Little Soldier Boy (from "Yip! Yip! Yaphank")		AGSA 51	ANNA-1026	
-2	(Jean Havez/Irving Berlin)	UNPUBLISHED		GEMM 186	
B 22254-1	In Flanders Fields (Lieutenant Colonel John McCrae/Frank Tours)	UNPUBLISHED			
B 22255-1	Smiles (J. Will Callahan/Lee M.	UNPUBLISHED			
-2	Roberts)	UNPUBLISHED			
B 22256-1	When You Come (words and music by George M. Cohan)	UNPUBLISHED			

25 SEPTEMBER 1918, WEDNESDAY (Camden)
w. orchestra conducted by JOSEF A. PASTERNACK (76.00rpm)

B 22256-2	When You Come Back (words and	64791		GEMM 275	
	music by George M. Cohan)				
-3		UNPUBLISHED			

16 APRIL 1919, WEDNESDAY (Camden)
w. orchestra conducted by JOSEF A. PASTERNACK (76.00rpm)

B 22690-1	When You Look in the Heart of a	UNPUBLISHED			
-2	Rose (from "The Better Ole")	778-B	5-2118	GEMM 186	
	(Marian Gillespie/Florence Methven)	64814	DA 315	IDLP 2005	
B 22691-1	Roses of Picardy (Frederic	748-B	(IR 1054)	GEMM 244	
	Edward Weatherley/Haydn Wood)	64825	****	GVC 30	
				LP 101	
				West. 504	

* - Originally published with words attributed to Walter H. Brown, a friend of Brengle's. See letter from Brengle in Chapter 5 of I Hear You Calling Me by Lily McCormack. Early pressings show Brown as lyricst, later pressings, Brengle.
** - Takes 1 and 3 were also issued under this number.
*** - Takes 1 and 2 were also issued under this number.
**** - Possibly the electrical recording was schuduled for this number.

B 22691-2   Roses of Picardy (Frederic   UNPUBLISHED
                 Edward Weatherley/Haydn Wood)
B 22692-1   The First Rose of Summer (from   UNPUBLISHED
     -2   "She's a Good Fellow")(Anne   762-A   GEMM 245
                 Caldwell/Jerome Kern)   64818

B 22693-1   Only You (Elizabeth K. Reynolds/   UNPUBLISHED
     -2   Edwin Schneider)   777-A   GEMM 242
                                                      64838   GVC 30
                                                                                    JM-201

1 JULY 1919, TUESDAY (Camden)
w. orchestra conducted by JOSEF A. PASTERNACK (75.00rpm)
B 23042-1   Rose of My Heart (D.   UNPUBLISHED
     -2   Eardley-Wilmot/Hermann Löhr)   779-A   (5-2939)   GEMM 275
                 w. Howard Rattay, violin   66012   DA 316

B 23043-1   The Road That Brought You to Me   UNPUBLISHED
     -2   (words and music by Bernard   779-B   (5-2940)   GEMM 243
                 Hamblen) w. Howard Rattay,   66024   DA 316
                 violin

B 23044-1   When Ireland Comes into Her Own   UNPUBLISHED
                 (Jeff Branen/Jack Stanley)

5 NOVEMBER 1919, WEDNESDAY (Camden)*
w. EDWIN SCHNEIDER, piano
B 23454-1   Christ in Flanders (Gordon   UNPUBLISHED
     -2   Johnstone/Ward Stephens)   UNPUBLISHED
B 23455-1   Your Eyes Have Told Me So   UNPUBLISHED
     -2   (Gustave Kahn and Egbert Van   UNPUBLISHED
                 Alstyne/Walter Blaufuss)
B 23456-1   That Tumble Down Shack in   UNPUBLISHED
     -2   Athlone (Richard W. Pascoe   UNPUBLISHED
     -3   and Monte Carlo/Alma M.   UNPUBLISHED
                 Sanders)

w. JOSEF A. PASTERNACK, piano**
B   -1   IL BARBIERE DI SIVIGLIA (Cesare   UNPUBLISHED
                 Sterbini, after
                 Pierre-Augustin Beaumarchais/
                 Gioacchino Rossini): Se il
                 mio nome

10 DECEMBER 1919, WEDNESDAY (Camden)
w. orchestra conducted by JOSEF A. PASTERNACK (75.00rpm)
B 23456-4   That Tumble Down Shack in   UNPUBLISHED
     -5   Athlone (Richard W. Pascoe   785-A   5-2203   GEMM 185
                 and Monte Carlo/Alma M.   64837   DA 320   IDLP 2005
                 Sanders) w. Howard Rattay,
                 violin

C 23522-1   The Victor (George F. O'Connell/   UNPUBLISHED
     -2   Henry Thacker Burleigh) w.   UNPUBLISHED
                 Rosario Bourdon, celeste
B 23523-1   Somewhere (words and music by   UNPUBLISHED
                 Alton Waters) w. Howard
                 Rattay, violin

* - McCormack brought his brother James to make trial recordings at the beginning
of this session:
JAMES MC CORMACK w. EDWIN SCHNEIDER, piano
B   -1   Smilin' Thro' (words and music   UNPUBLISHED
                 by Arthur A. Penn)
B   -1   'Tis the Hour of Farewell (words   UNPUBLISHED
                 and music by Elizabetta Nina
                 Mary Frederika Lehmann)
** - Private recording for Josef A. Pasternack, date uncertain.

<u>11 DECEMBER 1919, THURSDAY</u> (Camden)
w. orchestra conducted by JOSEF A. PASTERNACK (75.00rpm)

B 23524-1	Thank God for a Garden (words	UNPUBLISHED			
-2	and music by Teresa	786-A	5-2036	GEMM 242	
	Del Riego) w. Francis J.	64900	DA 320	GVC 51	
	Lapitino, harp and Rosario				
-3	Bourdon, celeste	UNPUBLISHED			
B 23525-1	When You and I Were Young,	UNPUBLISHED			
-2	Maggie (George W. Johnson/	781-A		BDL 2019	
	James A. Butterfield)	64913		GVC 51	
				LM-2755	
				RB-6632	
				VIC-1622	

B 23523-2	Somewhere (words and music by	782-B	5-2577	GEMM 242	
	Alton Waters) w. Howard	64976	DA 318	GVC 30	
	Rattay, violin		IR 1025*		

B 23455-3	Your Eyes Have Told Me So	UNPUBLISHED			
-4	(Gustave Kahn and Egbert Van	787-B	5-2202	JM-202	
	Alstyne/Walter Blaufuss)	64860	DA 520		
	w. Rosario Bourdon, celeste				
-5		UNPUBLISHED			

<u>4 MARCH 1920, THURSDAY</u> (Camden)
w. orchestra conducted by JOSEF A. PASTERNACK (75.00rpm)

B 23755-1	'Tis an Irish Girl I Love and	UNPUBLISHED			
-2	She's Just Like You (from	784-B	5-2331		
	"Macushla")(J. Keirn Brennan	64925	DA 491		
	and Alfred Dubin/Ernest R.				
	Ball) w. Howard Rattay,				
	violin				

B 23756-1	Honour and Love (from "Monsieur	765-A	5-2286	GEMM 245	
	Beaucaire")(Adrian Ross/André	64901	DA 109		
	Messager)				
-2		UNPUBLISHED			
B 23758-1	Beneath the Moon of Lombardy	UNPUBLISHED			
-2	(Edward Lockton/Harold	748-B	5-2432	GEMM 242	
	Craxton) w. Howard Rattay and	64962	DA 308	LM-2755	
	Witzmann, violins			RB-6632	
				VIC-1622	

<u>30 MARCH 1920, TUESDAY</u> (Camden)
w. orchestra conducted by JOSEF A. PASTERNACK (75.00rpm)

B 23791-1	Sweet Peggy O'Neill (Joseph P.	UNPUBLISHED			
-2	Redding/Uda Waldrop)	784-A	5-2544	GEMM 185	
		66028	DA 490	GVC 51	

B 23792-1	The Bard of Armagh (Traditional/	UNPUBLISHED			
-2	Old Irish Air, arr. Herbert	983-A	(5-2890)	CRM1-2472	
	Hughes) w. Rosario Bourdon,	(66155)	DA 624	GEMM 185	
	piano			RL-12472	

B 23793-1	A Song of Thanksgiving (James	UNPUBLISHED			
-2	Thomson/Frances Allitsen)	UNPUBLISHED			
B 23794-1	Wonderful World of Romance	UNPUBLISHED			
-2	(Harold Simpson/Haydn Wood)	UNPUBLISHED			
	w. Howard Rattay, violin;				
	Francis J. Lapitino, harp;				
	and William H. Reitz, bells				

<u>1 APRIL 1920, THURSDAY</u> (Camden)
w. orchestra conducted by JOSEF A. PASTERNACK (75.00rpm)

B 23794-3	Wonderful World of Romance	774-B		GEMM 243
	(Harold Simpson/Haydn Wood)	66080		
-4		UNPUBLISHED		

* – Label incorrectly credits Kreisler as assisting artist.

B 23793-3	A Song of Thanksgiving (James	UNPUBLISHED		
-4	Thomson/Frances Allitsen) w.	UNPUBLISHED		
	Rosario Bourdon and Selzer			
B 23901-1	The Barefoot Trail (Marion	741-B	5-2259	GEMM 242
	Phelps/Alvin S. Wiggers) w.	64878	DA 109	LM-2755
	Howard Rattay, violin			RB-6632
				VIC-1622
-2		UNPUBLISHED		
B 23902-1	SEMELE (William Congreve/George	749-A	5-2622	AB 11
	Frederic Handel): O Sleep!	66096	DA 484	CRM1-2472
	Why Dost Thou Leave Me?			ERAT-17
				FB 1
				GD 7377
				GEMM 159
				GEMM 252 -
				256
				JM-201
				RL-12472
				VIC-1393
-2		UNPUBLISHED		
B 23903-1	When (words and music by Earl	UNPUBLISHED		
-2	Benham) w. Rosario Bourdon,	UNPUBLISHED		
	piano and Francis J.			
	Lapitino, harp			

2 APRIL 1920, FRIDAY (Camden)*
w. EDWIN SCHNEIDER, piano (75.00rpm)

B 23799-1	The Singer's Consolation	UNPUBLISHED		
-2	("Sängers Trost")(Kerner,		AGSA 47	ANNA-1026
	trans. Alice Mattullath/		(IR 1059)	CRM1-2472
	Robert Schumann, Op. 127,			GEMM 160
	No. 1			GEMM 176e
				RL-12472
B 23900-1	When Pershing's Men Go Marching	UNPUBLISHED		
-2	Into Picardy (Dana Burnett/	UNPUBLISHED		
	James H. Rogers)			
B 23904-1	The Next Market Day	743-B	5-2369	CRM1-2472
	(Traditional/Old Irish Air,	64926	DA 490	GEMM 185
	arr. Herbert Hughes);			IDLP 2005
	A Ballynure Ballad (Traditional/			RL-12472
	Old Irish Air, arr. Herbert			
	Hughes)			
B 23905-1	When Night Descends (Fet, trans.	3020-A	5-2263	CRM1-2472
	Schneider and McCormack/	87571	DA 457	Ev. 3258
	Sergei Rachmaninoff, Op. 4,	ERC 6011-	IR 1009	GEMM 157
	No. 3) w. FRITZ KREISLER,			LM-6099
	violin obbligato			OL 5003
				RB-6525
				RL-12472
				Roc. 5343
				RVC-1578
-2		UNPUBLISHED		
-3		UNPUBLISHED		

* - McCormack brought 'cellist Lauri Kennedy and a Gerald McCormack (relationship
to John McCormack, if any, unknown) to this session to make trial recordings:
LAURI KENNEDY, 'cello w. GEORGE O'HARA, piano
      -1   title unknown
GERALD MC CORMACK w. GEORGE O'HARA, piano
      -1   I'm Just an Old Fashioned Girl
      -1   Live and Love

B 23906-<u>1</u>   O Cease Thy Singing, Maiden Fair   3020-B   5-2377   GEMM 157
                    (Aleksander Sergeyevich   87574   DA 457   GVC 30
                    Pushkin, trans. McCormack and   ERC 6006-   IR 1009   LCT-1158
                    Schneider/Sergei   LM-6099
                    Rachmaninoff, Op. 4, No. 4)   RB-6525
                    w. FRITZ KREISLER, violin   Roc. 5343
                    obbligato   RVC-1578

      -2   UNPUBLISHED
      -3   UNPUBLISHED

<u>5 MAY 1920, WEDNESDAY (New York City)</u>
w. EDWIN SCHNEIDER, piano (76.00rpm)
B 24034-1   O Dry Those Tears (words and   UNPUBLISHED
      -2   music by Teresa Del Riego) w.   UNPUBLISHED
                    FRITZ KREISLER, violin
                    obbligato
B 24035-1   Where Blooms the Rose (Arlo   UNPUBLISHED
      -2   Bates/Clayton Johns) w. FRITZ   UNPUBLISHED
                    KREISLER, violin obbligato
B 24036-<u>1</u>   The Last Hour (Jessie Christian   3023-B   (5-2505)   GEMM 157
                    Brown/A. Walter Kramer, Op.   87576   DA 460   RVC-1578
                    34, No. 6) w. FRITZ KREISLER,
      -2   violin obbligato   UNPUBLISHED
B 24037-1   Since You Went Away ("Seems Lak'   UNPUBLISHED
      -<u>2</u>   to Me")(James Weldon Johnson/   3022-A   5-2318   GEMM 233
                    J. Rosamond Johnson) w. FRITZ   87573   DA 459   GEMM 240
                    KREISLER, violin obbligato   DA 520

<u>16 JUNE 1921, THURSDAY (Camden)</u>
w. orchestra conducted by JOSEF A. PASTERNACK (76.00rpm)
B 25351-1   Learn to Smile (from "The   UNPUBLISHED
      -2   O'Brien Girl")(Otto Harbach*/   UNPUBLISHED
                    Louis A. Hirsch)
B 25352-1   When You Gave Your Heart to Me   UNPUBLISHED
      -2   (words and music by Arthur R.   UNPUBLISHED
                    Grant)
B 8695-<u>3</u>   I Hear You Calling Me (Harold   754-A   4-2076   GEMM 275
                    Lake, writing as Harold   64120**   DA 288
                    Harford/Charles Marshall)   10-1436-B
                                                       in MO-1228

      -4   UNPUBLISHED

<u>17 JUNE 1921, FRIDAY (Camden)</u>
w. orchestra conducted by JOSEF A. PASTERNACK (76.00rpm)
B 25351-3   Learn to Smile (from "The   UNPUBLISHED***
      -<u>4</u>   O'Brien Girl")(Otto Harbach*/   762-B   GEMM 186
                    Louis A. Hirsch)   64982

B 25353-1   Little Town in the Ould County   UNPUBLISHED***
      -<u>2</u>   Down (Richard W. Pascoe and   772-A   5-2484   CAL-407
                    Monte Carlo/Alma Sanders)   64994   DA 311   CAS-407(e)
                                                                               CDM 1024
                                                                               CDN-1002
                                                                               DRLP 007
                                                                               GEMM 185
                                                                               RCX-208

<u>17 OCTOBER 1922, TUESDAY (Camden)****</u>
w. orchestra conducted by JOSEF A. PASTERNACK (75.00rpm)

* - Book lyrics by Otto Harbach and Frank Mandel; Mandel not credited on this song.
** - Takes 1 and 2 also published under this number.
*** - Extant test pressing.
**** - McCormack's first recordings after his near fatal illness of April 1922.

B 27029-1	Three O'Clock in the Morning	UNPUBLISHED		
-2	(Dorothy Teriss/Julian	UNPUBLISHED		
-3	Robledo) w. Rosario Bourdon,	787-A	(5-2679)	GEMM 186
	celeste	66109	DA 321	IDLP 2005
				LP-110
				OASI-539

B 27030-1	Mother in Ireland (Gerald	UNPUBLISHED		
-2	Griffin/Gustave Kahn and Abe	785-B		
	Lyman)	66112		

-3		UNPUBLISHED		
B 27031-1	Jesus, My Lord, My God, My All	UNPUBLISHED		
-2	(Reverend Faber/Sir Joseph	UNPUBLISHED		
	Barnby)			
B 27032-1	Remember the Rose (from "Her	918-B	(5-2798)	GEMM 275
	Family Tree")(Sidney D.	(66162)	DA 576	
	Mitchell/Seymour S. Simons)			
-2		UNPUBLISHED		
-3		UNPUBLISHED		

20 OCTOBER 1922, FRIDAY (Camden)
w. orchestra conducted by JOSEF A. PASTERNACK (76.00rpm)

C 27043-1	The Lost Chord (Adelaide A.	6208-B	02992	GEMM 159
	Proctor/Sir Arthur Sullivan)	74791	DB 328	GEMM 176e
			(IRX 1016)	LM-2755
				VIC-1622
				RB-6632

-2		UNPUBLISHED		
B 27031-3	Jesus, My Lord, My God, My All	UNPUBLISHED		
-4	(Reverend Faber/Sir Joseph	773-B	(5-2719)	GEMM 185
	Barnby)	66122	DA 312	

w. orchestra conducted by ROSARIO BOURDON (76.00rpm)

B 27044-1	The Kingdom With Your Eyes	UNPUBLISHED		
-2	(Worton David/Horatio	757-B		GEMM 275
	Nicholls)	66146		

w. EDWIN SCHNEIDER, piano (76.00rpm)

B 27045-1	A Fairy Story By the Fire (from		cass.IV
	"Songs of Finland")(Angela		
-2	Campbell-MacInnes/Oscar	UNPUBLISHED	
	Merikanto)		
B 27047-1	To the Children (A. Khomyakoff,	UNPUBLISHED	
	trans. Rosa Newmarch/Sergei		
	Rachmaninoff, Op. 26, No. 7)		

20 NOVEMBER 1922, MONDAY (Camden)
w. orchestra conducted by JOSEF A. PASTERNACK (76.00rpm)

B 27084-1	The Land of Might Have Been	UNPUBLISHED	
-2	(Edward Moore/Ivor Novello)	UNPUBLISHED	
-3	w. Francis J. Lapitino, harp	UNPUBLISHED	
B 27085-1	To the Children (A. Khomyakoff,	UNPUBLISHED	
-2	trans. Rosa Newmarch/Sergei		VOCE-88
	Rachmaninoff, Op. 26, No. 7)		

24 SEPTEMBER 1923, MONDAY (Camden)*
w. orchestra conducted by ROSARIO BOURDON (75.00rpm)

B 28600-1	Wonderful One (Dorothy Teriss/	UNPUBLISHED		
-2	Paul Whiteman and Ferde	UNPUBLISHED		
-3	Grofé) w. Charles Linton,	961-B	(5-2821)	GEMM 245
	celeste	(66190)	DA 538	OASI-539

B 28601-1	Love Sends a Little Gift of	UNPUBLISHED		
-2	Roses (Leslie Cooke/John	961-A	(5-2820)	GEM 245
	Openshaw)	(66189)	DA 538	

* - Date shown on alphabetical cards.   Recording book shows 22 September 1923.

```
B 28602-1        Where the Rainbow Ends (Clifford  UNPUBLISHED
     -2             Grey/Nathaniel D. Ayer)        968-B      (5-2853)    GEMM 275
                                                   (66199)    DA 592

B 28603-1        Somewhere in the World (words     968-A      (5-2852)
                   and music by Nathaniel D.        (66198)   DA 592
                   Ayer) w. Alexander Schmidt,
     -2             violin; Charles Linton,         UNPUBLISHED
                   celeste
```

25 SEPTEMBER 1923, TUESDAY (Camden)
w. orchestra conducted by ROSARIO BOURDON (75.00rpm)

```
B 28604-1        Take a Look at Molly (Hazel M.    UNPUBLISHED
     -2             Lockwood/Lee W. Lookwood)       1003-B
                                                    (66242)

B 28605-1        Dream Once Again (P. J.           UNPUBLISHED
     -2             O'Reilly/William Henry          1059-B     (6-2097)    GEMM 243
                   Squire)                          DA 682

B 28606-1        Thanks Be to God (P. J.           UNPUBLISHED
     -2             O'Reilly/Stanley Dickson)       1059-A     (6-2096)    CAL-635
                                                    DA 682                 CDN-1029
                                                                           DRLP 008
                                                                           GEMM 243

B 28607-1        Sometime (I'll Hear Your Sweet    UNPUBLISHED
     -2             Voice Calling)(Hazel M.         1003-A     5-2950
                   Lockwood/Lee W. Lockwood) w.     (66243)    AGSA 51
                   Alexander Schmidt, violin;
                   Lennartz, 'cello
```

26 SEPTEMBER 1923, WEDNESDAY (Camden)
w. orchestra conducted by ROSARIO BOURDON (75.00rpm)

```
B 28608-1        Would God I Were the Tender       UNPUBLISHED
     -2             Apple Blossom (Katherine        983-B      (5-2891)    GEMM 185
                   Tynan-Hinkson/Old Irish Air:     (66215)    DA 624      GVC 30
                   "Londonderry Air," arr. N.
                   Clifford Page)
```

w. EDWIN SCHNEIDER, piano (75.00rpm)

```
B 28609-1        Pur Dicesti (Pero/Antonio Lotti)                          GEMM 275

     -2                                             1081-A     (7-52293)   BC 231
                                                    10-1435-A  DA 716      GEMM 160
                                                    in MO-1228 IR 1003     VIC-1393

B 28610-1        Die Liebe hat gelogen (A. von                 AGSA 47     ANNA-1026
                   Platen Hallermunde/Franz                                GEMM 158
                   Schubert, D. 751)                                       VIC-1393

B 28611-1        Der Jungling an der Quelle (J.    UNPUBLISHED
                   G. von Salis-Seewis/Franz
                   Schubert, D. 300)
B 28612-1        O Thank Not Me ("Widmung")                                GEMM 160
                   (Wolfgang Müller/Robert                                 GEMM 176e
                   Franz, Op. 14, No. 1)

B 28613-1        Swans (from "Rivers to the Sea")  1081-B      (6-2182)    ARM1-4997
                   (Sara Teasdale/A. Walter                    DA 716      BC 231
                   Kramer, Op. 44, No. 4)                      IR 1003     GEMM 160
                                                                           NW-247
                                                                           VIC-1393
```

8 APRIL 1924, TUESDAY (Camden)
w. orchestra conducted by ROSARIO BOURDON (76.00rpm)

```
B 29864-1        Indiana Moon (Benny Davis/Isham   UNPUBLISHED
     -2             Jones)                          1011-B     (5-2980)    GEMM 186
                                                    (66253)    DA 606
```

B 29865-1	Marchéta (A Love Song of Old	UNPUBLISHED			
-2	Mexico)(words and music by	1011-A	(5-2979)	GEMM 186	
	Victor L. Schertzinger)	(66252)	DA 606	OASI-539	
B 29866-1	A Love Song (from "The Magic	1020-A	(5-2993)	GEMM 243	
	Ring")(Zelda Sears/Harold	(66267)	DA 664		
	Levey)				
-2		UNPUBLISHED			
B 29867-1	Little Yvette (Frederic Edward	1020-B	(5-2994)	GEMM 243	
	Weatherley/Haydn Wood)	(66268)	DA 664		
-2		UNPUBLISHED			

9 APRIL 1924, WEDNESDAY (Camden)
w. orchestra conducted by ROSARIO BOURDON (76.6Orpm)

B 29870-1	Holy God We Praise Thy Name ("Te	UNPUBLISHED		
-2	Deum laudamus")(Traditional/		AGSA 46	ANNA-1026
	Clarence A. Walworth) w.		(IR 1058)	CAL-635
	ALEXANDER SCHMIDT, violin			CDN-1029
	obbligato			DRLP 008
				GEMM 185
B 29871-1	Onward Christian Soldiers	UNPUBLISHED		
-2	(Reverend Sabine			GEMM 160
	Baring-Gould/Sir Arthur S.			GEMM 176e
	Sullivan)			
B 29872-1	When (words and music by Earl	1040-A	(6-2042)	GEMM 243
	Benham)		DA 642	
-2		UNPUBLISHED		
B 29873-1	Bridal Dawn (from "High Days and	UNPUBLISHED		
-2	Holidays")(Helen Taylor/	UNPUBLISHED		
-3	Easthope Martin) w. Alexander	1040-B	(6-2043)	GEMM 243
	Schmidt, violin; Bruno		DA 642	
	Reibold, celeste			

THE GRAMOPHONE COMPANY, LIMITED

4 SEPTEMBER 1924, THURSDAY (Room No. 1, Hayes, Middlesex)*
w. EDWIN SCHNEIDER, piano (76.6Orpm)

Cc 5029-I**	Wo find ich Trost (Eduard	(2-042022)	Arab.8105-2
	Mörike/Hugo Wolf)	DB 766	EX 2900563
		VB 32	GEMM 158
			HLM-7037
			HQM-1176
			Roc. 5343
-II		(IRX 1021)	
		***	
Cc 5030-I	Du bist die Ruh (Friedrich	UNPUBLISHED	
-II	Rückert/Franz Schubert,	(2-042023)	Arab.8105-2
	D. 776)	DB 766	GEMM 158
		(IRX 1021)	HLM-7037
		VB 32	HQM-1176
			RLS 766
			Roc. 5343

* – McCormack brought his daughter Gwen to this session to make a private recording:
GWEN MC CORMACK, soprano w. EDWIN SCHNEIDER, piano
Bb 5036-I   When Love is Kind (Thomas Moore)
** – Roman numbers were used to designate takes of recordings made at McCormack HMV
sessions from this date through 19 June 1940. Some later pressings of these
recordings substitute arabic numerals.
*** – Extant test pressing.

Bb 5031-I	Die Mainacht (Ludwig Hölty and	UNPUBLISHED		
-II	Voss/Johannes Brahms, Op. 43,		(7-42085)	Arab.8105-2
	No. 2)		AGSA 48	COLH 123
			DA 628	EX 2900563
			IR 1008	GEMM 158
				SH-110

Bb 5032-I	In Waldeseinsamkeit (Lemcke/	UNPUBLISHED		
-II	Johannes Brahms, Op. 85,		(7-42086)	Arab.8105-2
	No. 6)		AGSA 48	COLH 123
			DA 628	GEMM 158
			IR 1008	RLS 1547003
				SH-110

Bb 5033-I	Luoghi sereni e cari (words and	UNPUBLISHED*		
-II	music by Stefano Donaudy)		(7-52275)	COLH 123
			AGSA 49	EX 2900563
			DA 627	GEMM 159
			IR 1000	SH-110

-II		UNPUBLISHED*			
Bb 5034-I	ATALANTA (Valeriani, adapted by	10-1434-A	(6-2032)	COLH 123	
	Mrs. Rudolf Lehmann, writing	in MO-1228	DA 645	EX 2900563	
	as A. L./George Frederic	IRCC No.	IR 1002	GEMM 159	
	Handel): Come My Beloved	60-A		GEMM 252 -	
				256	
				HLM-7004	
				Sera. 60206	
				SH-110	

Bb 5035-I	O del mio amato ben (words and	IRCC No.	(7-52276)	COLH 123	
	music by Stefano Donaudy)	217-B	AGSA 49	EX 2900563	
			DA 627	GEMM 159	
			IR 1000	SH-110	

Bb 5037-I	The Last Rose of Summer (Thomas	UNPUBLISHED	
-II	Moore/Old Irish Air: "The	UNPUBLISHED	
	Groves of Blarney," also "The		
	Young Man's Dream," arr.		
	Thomas Moore)		

19 SEPTEMBER 1924, FRIDAY (Room No. 1, Hayes, Middlesex)**
w. EDWIN SCHNEIDER, piano (76.60rpm)

Bb 5094-I	Komm Bald (Klaus Groth/Johannes			GEMM 275
	Brahms, Op. 97, No. 5)			
-II		IRCC No.	(7-42087)	GEMM 158
		62-	AGSA 50	HLM-7037
			DA 635	HQM-1176
			IR 1024	RLS 1547003
				Roc. 5343

Bb 5095-I	Feldeinsamkeit (Hermann Almers/	10-1435-B	(7-42088)	EX 2900563
	Johannes Brahms, Op. 86,	in MO-1228	AGSA 50	GEMM 158
	No. 2)	IRCC No.	DA 635	HLM-7037
		62-	IR 1011	HQM-1176

-II		UNPUBLISHED	
Bb 5096-I	Ridente la calma (?/Wolfgang	UNPUBLISHED*	
	Amadeus Mozart, K. 152)		

---

* - Extant test pressing.
** - McCormack brought his son Cyril to this session to make a private recording:
CYRIL MC CORMACK, ? w. EDWIN SCHNEIDER, piano
Bb 5098-I   A Brown Bird Singing (Royden Barrie/Haydn Wood)

Bb 5096-<u>II</u>   Ridente la calma (?/Wolfgang   10-1434-B (7-52278)   COLH 123
                    Amadeus Mozart, K. 152)   in MO-1228 DA 645   EX 2900563
                                                 IRCC No.   IR 1002   GEMM 158
                                                 60-B   SH-110

Bb 5097-I   Duet w. GWEN MC CORMACK, soprano UNPUBLISHED
Bb 5099-I   The Soldier's Execution ("Der   UNPUBLISHED
                    Soldat")(Albert Chamisso/
                    Robert Schumann, Op. 40,
                    No. 3)
Bb 5100-I   Oh! That It Were So! (words and UNPUBLISHED*
                    music by Frank Bridge)
Bb 5101-<u>I</u>   How Fair This Spot (G. Galina,   (6-2038)   GEMM 158
                    trans. Rosa Newmarch/Sergei   DA 680   HLM-7037
                    Rachmaninoff, Op. 21, No. 7)   (IR 1051) HQM-1176

     -II   UNPUBLISHED

---

24 SEPTEMBER 1924, WEDNESDAY (Room No. 1, Hayes, Middlesex)
w. EDWIN SCHNEIDER, piano (76.60rpm)
Bb 5115-I   Morgen (John Henry MacKay/   UNPUBLISHED
     -II   Richard Strauss, Op. 27,   UNPUBLISHED
     -<u>III</u>   No. 4) w. FRITZ KREISLER,   (7-42089) Arab.8105-2
                    violin obbligato   DA 644   EX 2900563
                                                                      GEMM 157
                                                                      Roc. 5343

Bb 5116-<u>I</u>   Before My Window (The Cherry   VOCE-88
                    Tree)(G. Galina, trans. Henry
     -<u>II</u>   G. Chapman/Sergei   (6-2039)   EX 2900563
                    Rachmaninoff, Op. 26, No. 10)   DA 644   GEMM 157
                    w. FRITZ KREISLER, violin   RLS 743
                    obbligato   Roc. 5343

     -III   UNPUBLISHED*
Bb 5117-I   To the Children (A. Khomyakov,   UNPUBLISHED
     -<u>II</u>   trans. Rosa Newmarch/Sergei   (6-2114)   BLP 1107
                    Rachmaninoff, Op. 26, No. 7)   DA 680   EX 2900563
                    w. FRITZ KREISLER, violin   GEMM 157
                    obbligato   HLM-7037
                                                                      HQM-1176
                                                                      P 69

Bb 5118-I   Padraic the Fiddler (Padraic   UNPUBLISHED
     -<u>II</u>   Gregory/John F. Larchet) w.   (6-2040)   GEMM 157
                    FRITZ KREISLER, violin   DA 636
                    obbligato   IR 1010

     -III   UNPUBLISHED*
Bb 5119-<u>I</u>   I Saw From the Beach (Thomas   (6-2041)   GEMM 157
                    Moore/Old Irish Air: "Miss   AGSA 46
                    Molly," arr. Herbert Hughes)   DA 636
                    w. FRITZ KREISLER, violin   IR 1010
                    obbligato
     -II   UNPUBLISHED
     -III   UNPUBLISHED*
     -IV   UNPUBLISHED

VICTOR TALKING MACHINE COMPANY

17 DECEMBER 1924, WEDNESDAY (New York City)**
w. orchestra (2 violins, viola, 'cello, flute, 2 cornets, trombone, tuba, piano,
traps) conducted by NATHANIEL SHILKRET (76.00rpm)
B 31523-1   All Alone (from "Primrose")   UNPUBLISHED*
     -<u>2</u>   (words and music by Irving   1067-A   (6-2188)   GEMM 186
                    Berlin)   DA 707   OASI-539

* - Extant test pressing.
** - McCormack's last acoustic recording session.

```
B 31526-1         Rose Marie (from "Rose Marie")   UNPUBLISHED
      -2          (Otto Harbach and Oscar          UNPUBLISHED
      -3          Hammerstein/Rudolf Friml)        1067-B      (6-2119)   GEMM 186
                                                   DA 707      LP 110
```

23 APRIL 1925, THURSDAY (Camden)*
w. orchestra conducted by ROSARIO BOURDON (75.00rpm)

```
BVE 32534-1       When You and I Were Seventeen    UNPUBLISHED
      -2          (Gustave Kahn/Charles Rosoff)    UNPUBLISHED
      -3                                           UNPUBLISHED
      -4                                           1086-A      (6-2203)   GEMM 186
                                                   DA 693      IDLP 2005
                                                               OASI-539

BVE 32535-1       Moonlight and Roses (words and   UNPUBLISHED
      -2          music by Ben Black, Neil         1092-A      (6-2200)   GEMM 187
                  Morét, and Edwin H. Lemare,                  DA 741     LP 110
                  after "Andantino in D-flat"                  IR 1028    OASI-539
                  by Edwin H. Lemare)
      -3                                           UNPUBLISHED
BVE 32536-1       June Brought the Roses (Ralph    1086-B      (6-2204)   DOLM 5023
                  Stanley/John Openshaw)                       IR 1028    GEMM 187

      -2                                           UNPUBLISHED**
BVE 32537-1       The Sweetest Call (Alma Troon/   UNPUBLISHED
      -2          John Morrow)                     1092-B      (6-2212)   DOLM 5023
                                                   DA 692      GEMM 187
                                                   DA 741
```

24 APRIL 1925, FRIDAY (Camden)
w. orchestra conducted by ROSARIO BOURDON (75.00rpm)

```
BVE 32538-1       Schlafendes Jesuskind (Eduard    UNPUBLISHED
      -2          Mörike/Hugo Wolf)                1272-B      (7-42093)  GEMM 158
                                                   DA 953

BVE 32539-1       I Look Into Your Garden (Charles UNPUBLISHED
      -2          Wilmott/Haydn Wood)              1147-B      (6-2202)   DOLM 5023
                                                   DA 693      GEMM 185

BVE 32540-1       What a Wonderful World It Would  UNPUBLISHED
      -2          Be (D. Eardley-Wilmot/           UNPUBLISHED
                  Hermann Löhr)
BVE 32541-1       Devotion (Wenda/Haydn Wood)      UNPUBLISHED
      -2                                           1147-A      (6-2201)   GEMM 275
                                                   DA 692
```

14 OCTOBER 1925, WEDNESDAY (Camden)
w. orchestra conducted by NATHANIEL SHILKRET (75.00rpm)

```
BVE 33464-1       You Forgot to Remember (words    1121-A      (6-2346)   GEMM 187
                  and music by Irving Berlin)                  DA 760     IDLP 2005
                                                                          LP 110
                                                                          OASI-539

      -2                                           UNPUBLISHED
      -3                                           UNPUBLISHED
BVE 33465-1       Oh, How I Miss You Tonight       1121-B      (6-2347)   GEM 187
                  (Benny Davis and Mark Fisher/               DA 760     OASI-539
                  Joe Burke)
      -2                                           UNPUBLISHED
```

27 OCTOBER 1925, TUESDAY (New York City)
w. Victor Salon Orchestra (3 violins, 'cello, flute, cornet, tuba, piano, traps)
conducted by NATHANIEL SHILKRET (75.00rpm)

```
BVE 33819-1       Just a Cottage Small (Buddy G.   UNPUBLISHED
      -2          De Sylva/James. F. Hanley)       UNPUBLISHED
      -3                                           1133-A      (6-2350)   GEMM 187
                                                   DA 765      IDLP 2005
```

* - McCormack's first electric recording session.
** - Extant test pressing.

BVE 33820-1	Through All the Days to Be	UNPUBLISHED*		
-2	(Royden Barrie/Barbara	UNPUBLISHED		
-3	Melville-Hope)	1133-B	(6-2377)	GEMM 187
			DA 780	
BVE 33821-1	Mother My Dear (Katherine Nolen/	1137-A	(6-2351)	DOLM 5023
	Bryceson Treharne)		DA 765	GEMM 187
-2		UNPUBLISHED		
-3		UNPUBLISHED		

17 DECEMBER 1925, THURSDAY (New York City)
w. orchestra (3 violins, viola, 'cello, flute, clarinet, 2 cornets, trombone, tuba, piano, traps) conducted by NATHANIEL SHILKRET (75.00rpm)

BVE 34159-1	Love Me and I'll Live Forever	1594-B**	(6-2765)	LP 110
	(Alfred Bryan/Ted Snyder)		DA 893	OASI-624
-2		UNPUBLISHED		
-3		ERC 6007-B IR 1029		GEMM 275
BVE 23525-3	When You and I Were Young,	UNPUBLISHED		
-4	Maggie (George W. Johnson/	1173-B	(6-2606)	GEMM 187
	James A. Butterfield)		DA 823	GV 901
			IR 265	

w. EDWIN SCHNEIDER, piano (75.00rpm)

BVE 34160-1	Luoghi sereni e cari (words and	UNPUBLISHED		
-2	music by Stefano Donaudy)	1288-B	(7-52331)	GEMM 159
			IR 1025	GV 523
				VIC-1393
BVE 27085-3***	To the Children (A. Khomyakoff,	UNPUBLISHED		
-4	trans. Rosa Newmarch/Sergei	1288-A	(6-2764)	GEMM 158
	Rachmaninoff, Op. 26, No. 7)		DA 1112	GV 523
			IR 368	VIC-1393

18 DECEMBER 1925, FRIDAY (New York City)
w. orchestra (3 violins, viola, 'cello, flute, clarinet, 2 cornets, trombone, tuba, piano, traps) conducted by NATHANIEL SHILKRET

BVE 34166-1	Night Hymn at Sea (Felicia D.	UNPUBLISHED		
-2	Hemans/Arthur Goring-Thomas)	UNPUBLISHED		
-3	w. LUCREZIA BORI, soprano	UNPUBLISHED		
BVE 34167-1	Underneath the Window ("Unter'm	UNPUBLISHED		
-2	Fenster")(Nathan Haskell	(3039-B)****		RLS 1547003
	Dole, based on German text,			
-3	after Robert Burns/Robert	UNPUBLISHED		
-4	Schumann, Op. 34, No. 3) w.	UNPUBLISHED		
	LUCREZIA BORI, soprano			
	(76.60rpm)*****			

23 DECEMBER 1925, WEDNESDAY (New York City)
w. orchestra (3 violins, viola, 'cello, flute, clarinet, oboe, 2 cornets, trombone, tuba, piano, traps) conducted by NATHANIEL SHILKRET (75.00rpm)

BVE 34176-1	A Brown Bird Singing (Royden	UNPUBLISHED		
-2	Barrie/Haydn Wood)	1137-B	(6-2430)	GEMM 187
			DA 780	
			IR 258	
BVE 11834-4	Silver Threads Among the Gold	1173-A	(6-2605)	GEM 187
	(Ebenezer B. Rexford/Hart		DA 823	
	Pease Danks)		IR 261	

* - Extant test pressing.
** - In addition to original pressings, a few later white label vinyl pressings are also known to exist.
*** - This matrix number, also used for the acoustically recorded takes, was substituted for matrix number 34161 originally assigned to the electrical remake.
**** - Extant single face vinyl test pressings bear this number.
***** - Victor files erroneously list as "In the Woods."

BVE 11834-5   Silver Threads Among the Gold   UNPUBLISHED
        (Ebenezer B. Rexford/Hart
        Pease Danks)

BVE 14677-3   THE BOHEMIAN GIRL (Alfred Bunn, UNPUBLISHED
        after Jules H. Vernoy de
        Saint-Georges/Michael William
        Balfe): When other lips and
        other hearts (Then You'll
        Remember Me)

24 DECEMBER 1925, THURSDAY (New York City)
w. orchestra conducted by NATHANIEL SHILKRET

BVE 34166-4   Night Hymn at Sea (Felicia D.   UNPUBLISHED*
    -5   Hemans/Arthur Goring-Thomas) (3039-A)**   GEMM 245
        w. LUCREZIA BORI, soprano

    -6   UNPUBLISHED

BROADCAST (WJZ)

1 JANUARY 1926, FRIDAY (New York City)
w. Victor Salon Orchestra conducted by NATHANIEL SHILKRET
When You and I Were Young, Maggie (George W.   UNPUBLISHED
   Johnson/James A Butterfield)

w. Victor Salon Orchestra conducted by JOSEF A. PASTERNACK or NATHANIEL SHILKRET
Night Hymn at Sea (Felicia D. Hemans/Arthur   UNPUBLISHED
   Goring Thomas) w. LUCREZIA BORI, soprano

VICTOR TALKING MACHINE COMPANY

28 SEPTEMBER 1926, TUESDAY (New York City)
w. orchestra (2 violins, viola, 'cello, flute, 2 clarinets, 2 cornets, trombone)
conducted by NATHANIEL SHILKRET (75.00rpm)

BVE 36361-1   The Far Away Bells (Douglas   1215-B   (6-2712)   DOLM 5023
        Furber/Westfell Gordon)   ERC 6008- DA 858   GEMM 187
                                    DA 914   GV 901
                                    IR 1030

    -2   UNPUBLISHED*
BVE 36362-1   When Twilight Comes, I'm   UNPUBLISHED*
    -2   Thinking of You (H. J.   UNPUBLISHED*
    -3   Tandler/Harold Horne)   1197-B   (6-2675)   DOLM 5023
                                    DA 840   GEMM 185

BVE 36363-1   Just for Today (Sybil F.   1281-A   (6-2766)   CAL-635
        Partridge/Blanche Ebert   DA 929   CDN-1029
        Seaver)   IR 201   DRLP 008
                                            GEMM 159
                                          GEMM 176e

    -2   UNPUBLISHED

30 SEPTEMBER 1926, THURSDAY (New York City)
w. orchestra (3 violins, 'cello, flute, 2 clarinets, 2 cornets, trombone, tuba,
piano, traps) conducted by NATHANIEL SHILKRET (75.00rpm)

BVE 36374-1   Lillies of Lorraine (Clifford 1229-A   (6-2755)   DOLM 5023
        Grey/Pierre Connor)   DA 881   GEMM 187

    -2   UNPUBLISHED
BVE 36375-1   A Rose for Every Heart (Nelle UNPUBLISHED
    -2   R. Eberhart/Charles Wakefield 1229-B   (6-2756)   DOLM 5023
        Cadman)   DA 881   GEMM 187

    -3   UNPUBLISHED*

* - Extant test pressing.
** - Extant single face vinyl test pressings bear this number.

BVE 36376-1   Calling Me Back to You (words   UNPUBLISHED
       -2   and music by Blanche Ebert   1197-A   (6-2676)   GEMM 187
                       Seaver)   DA 840

1 OCTOBER 1926, FRIDAY (Camden)
w. orchestra conducted by ROSARIO BOURDON
CVE 36606-1   Adeste Fideles (Traditional/   6607-A   (2-052318) 17-0346-B
                  Marcus Portugal, arr. F. J.   V-Disc No. DB 984   in WCT-53
                  Wade) w. Trinity Choir (Olive   49-A*   IRX 18   449-0015-
                  Kline, Lucy Isabelle Marsh,   in WCT-1121
                  Helen Clark, Mina Hager,   CSLP 508
                  Giles, Lambert Murphy,   DRLP 008
                  Charles Hart, Paul Parks,   GEMM 245
                  Fred Patton, Mary Allen, Ruth   LCT-1036
                  Rogers, Elsie Baker, Margaret   LCT-1121
                  Dunlap, Richard Crooks, J.   RCX-1042
                  Kinsey, Charles Harrison,   RDA 57
                  Royal Dadmun, Frank Croxton)   RDM 2301/4
                  (74.23rpm)   VIC-1682

       -2   UNPUBLISHED

w. EDWIN SCHNEIDER, piano (75.00rpm)
BVE 35891-1   She Rested by the Broken Brook   Voce 88
                  (Robert Louis Stevenson/
                  Samuel Coleridge-Taylor)

BVE 35892-1   A Prayer to Our Lady (from   UNPUBLISHED**
                  ("Skylark and Swallow")
                  (Reverend R. L. Gates/Donald
                  Ford) w. Alexander Schmidt,
                  violin; Lennartz, 'cello
BVE 35893-1   Love's Secret (William Blake/   17-0059-B
                  Granville Bantock)   in WCT-12
                                                                                GEMM 159
                                                                                LCT-1008
                                                                                VIC-1393

4 OCTOBER 1926, MONDAY (New York City)
w. orchestra (3 violins, 'cello, flute, 2 clarinets, cornet, trombone, tuba, piano,
organ, traps) conducted by NATHANIEL SHILKRET (75.00rpm)
CVE 36384-1   The Palms ("Les Rameaux")(Jean   6607-B   (2-02202)   GEMM 159
                  Baptist Faure)   DB 984   GEMM 176e
                                                               IRX 18

       -2   UNPUBLISHED

17 DECEMBER 1926, FRIDAY (New York City)
w. orchestra (3 violins, 'cello, flute, 2 clarinets, cornet, trombone, tuba, piano,
traps and L. Shilkret, organ) conducted by NATHANIEL SHILKRET (77.43rpm)
BVE 37147-1   The Holy Child (Traditional/   1281-B   (6-2767)   449-0015-
                  Easthope Martin)   DA 929   in WCT-1121
                                                               IR 201   CAL-635
                                                                           CDN-1029
                                                                           CSLP 508
                                                                           DRLP 008
                                                                           GEMM 159
                                                                           GEMM 176e
                                                                           LCT-1121
                                                                           RCX-1042
                                                                           VIC-1682

       -2   UNPUBLISHED**

* - Re-recording, matrix ND3-MC-3371-1.   Reverse side not by McCormack.
** - Extant test pressing.

BVE 37148-1   Because I Love You (words and   UNPUBLISHED
     -2   music by Irving Berlin)   1215-A   (6-2711)   GEMM 187
                                                         DA 858   OASI-539
                                                         DA 893
                                                          IR 1029

w. EDWIN SCHNEIDER, piano (77.43rpm)
BVE 37149-1   All'mein Gedanken ("Minnelied") 1272-A   (7-42105) GEMM 159
             (Traditional/Old German, arr.   DA 953   VIC-1393
             Sigfried Karg-Elert)   DA 1675
                                              IR 1024

BROADCAST (WJZ and WEAF joint Red and Blue Networks)

1 JANUARY 1927, SATURDAY (New York City (?))
w. orchestra
Calling Me Back to You (Blanche Ebert Seaver)   UNPUBLISHED

w. EDWIN SCHNEIDER, piano
On Wings of Song ("Auf Flügeln des Gesänges")   UNPUBLISHED
   (Heinrich Heine/Felix Mendelssohn, Op. 34,
   No. 2)

w. orchestra
The Holy Child (Traditional/Easthope Martin)   UNPUBLISHED

VICTOR TALKING MACHINE COMPANY

12 APRIL 1927, TUESDAY (Liederkranz Hall, New York City)
w. orchestra (3 violins, viola, 'cello, string bass, 2 clarinets, oboe, bassoon,
2 cornets, trombone, piano, traps) conducted by NATHANIEL SHILKRET
BVE 15419-2   Somewhere a Voice is Calling   UNPUBLISHED
     -3   (Eileen Newton/Arthur F.   1247-A   (6-2840)   GEMM 187
             Tate)   ERC 6011- DA 914   GV 901
                                              IR 261

BVE 29865-3   Marchéta (A Love Song of Old   1247-B   LP 110
             Mexico)(words and music by
             Victor L. Schertzinger)

14 APRIL 1927, THURSDAY (Liederkranz Hall, New York City)
w. orchestra (3 violins, viola, 'cello, string bass, flute, 2 clarinets, oboe,
bassoon, 2 cornets, trombone, piano, traps) conducted by NATHANIEL SHILKRET*

4 MAY 1927, WEDNESDAY (Liederkranz Hall, New York City)
w. orchestra (3 violins, viola, 'cello, string bass, flute, 2 clarinets, oboe,
bassoon, 2 cornets, trombone, piano, traps) conducted by NATHANIEL SHILKRET
(77.43rpm)
BVE 38386-1   Under the Spell of the Rose   UNPUBLISHED
     -2   (Wild Rose Lane)(from "Songs   DOLM 5023
             of the Hedgerow")(Helen   GEMM 275
             Taylor/Easthope Martin)

BVE 38387-1   The Fallen Leaf (An Indian Love UNPUBLISHED
     -2   Song)(Virginia K. Logan/   UNPUBLISHED
     -3   Frederick Knight Logan)   AGSA 63** ANNA 1026
                                                    GEMM 187

CVE 38388-1   Christ Went Up Into the Hills   6708-B   (2-02243) CAL-635
             Alone (Katherine Adams/   IRX 1004   CDN-1029
             Richard Hageman)   DRLP 008
                                                      GEMM 159
                                                      GEMM 176e

* - Victor files note, "Mr. McCormack voice poorly - could not record.   Orchestra
called 2:00 - dismissed 2:45."
** - Re-recording, matrix BVE 38387-5R.

6 MAY 1927, FRIDAY (New York City)
w. orchestra (4 violins, viola, 'cello, string bass, flute, 2 clarinets, oboe,
bassoon, 2 cornets, trombone, piano, traps) conducted by NATHANIEL SHILKRET
(77.43rpm)

BVE 38731-1	When You're in Love (Walter	UNPUBLISHED		
-2	Donaldson/Walter Blaufuss)		AGSA 63*	GEMM 187
BVE 38732-1	Tick, Tick, Tock (words and	1594-A**		GEMM 243
	music by Bernard Hamblen)			GV 523
				JM 202
				LP-110
				OASI-624
-2		UNPUBLISHED		

w. orchestra (4 violins, viola, 'cello, string bass, piano, organ) conducted by
NATHANIEL SHILKRET (77.43rpm)

CVE 38733-1	Panis Angelicus (from Mass in a,	UNPUBLISHED		
-2	M. 61)(Thomas Aquinas/	6708-A		17-0034-A
	César-Auguste Franck)			in WCT-8
				449-0016-
				in WCT-1121
				CAL-635
				CDN-1029
				CSLP 508
				DRLP 008
				GEMM 275
				LCT-1005
				LCT-1121
				RCX-1042
				RDA 57
				RDM 2301/4

THE GRAMOPHONE COMPANY, LIMITED

1 SEPTEMBER 1927, THURSDAY ("C" Studio, Small Queen's Hall, London)
w. EDWIN SCHNEIDER, piano (77.43rpm)

Cc 11335-I	La Procession ("Dieu s'avance	UNPUBLISHED		
-II	à travers les champs!")		(2-032118)	EX 2900563
	Charles Brizeaux/		DB 1095	GEMM 159
	César-Auguste Franck)		IRX 26	GEMM 176e
				P 69
Bb 11336-I	Desolation (from "Songs of the		(6-2904)	GEMM 159
	Chinese Poets")("Kao-Shih,"		DA 917	GV 523
	A.D. 1700/Sir Granville		IR 1018	Roc. 5343
	Bantock, Op. 2, No. 3)		VA 59	
-II		UNPUBLISHED***		
Bb 11337-I	A Dream of Spring (from "Songs		(6-2905)	GEMM 159
	of the Chinese Poets")("Tsen		DA 917	GV 523
	Ts'an," A.D. 750/Sir Granville		IR 1018	Roc. 5343
	Bantock, Op. 2, No. 2)		VA 59	
-II		UNPUBLISHED		
Bb 11338-I	Du meines Herzens Krönelein	UNPUBLISHED***		
-II	(Dahn/Richard Strauss,		(7-42106)	Arab.8105-2
	Op. 21, No. 2)		DA 932	EX 2900563
				GEMM 158
				GV 523
				VRCS-1968

* - Re-recording, matrix BVE 38731-5R.
** - 76.00rpm re-recording. In addition to original pressings, a few later white
label vinyl pressings are also known to exist.
*** - Extant test pressing.

Bb 11339-I	Allerseelen (Hermann von Gilm/	UNPUBLISHED*		
-II	Richard Strauss, Op. 10,	1660-A	(7-42107)	Arab.8105-2
	No. 8)		DA 932	COLH 123
			IR 1019	EX 2900563
			VA 72	GEMM 158
				SH-110

2 SEPTEMBER 1927, FRIDAY ("C" Studio, Small Queen's Hall, London)
w. EDWIN SCHNEIDER, piano (77.43rpm)

Bb 11340-I	Since First I Saw Your Face	UNPUBLISHED		
-II	(from "Musicke of Sundrie		(6-2908)	GEMM 159
	Kindes")(Thomas Ford/Old		DA 946	
	English Air, arr. Arthur			
	Somervell)			
Bb 11341-I	FORTUNIO (G. A. de Caillavet and		(7-32121)	GEMM 156
	Robert de Flers, after Alfred		DA 946	GV 523
	de Musset/André Messager:			
-II	J'amais la vielle maison	1660-B		GEMM 275
	grise (La Maison grise)			
Bb 11342-I	Who is Sylvia? (William	UNPUBLISHED*		
-II	Shakespeare/Franz Schubert,	1306-B	(6-2893)	Arab.8105-2
	D. 891)		DA 933	EX 2900563
			IR 1012	GEMM 158
				P 69
				Roc. 5343
Bb 11343-I	Die Liebe hat gelogen (A. von	UNPUBLISHED		
-II	Platen Hallermunde/Franz		(7-42108)	Arab.8105-2
	Schubert, D. 751)		DA 933	COLH 123
			IR 1012	GEMM 158
				RLS 766
				SH-110
Bb 11344-I	A Fairy Story By the Fire	UNPUBLISHED		
-II	(Angela Campbell-MacInnes/	1307-A	(6-2906)	AU 4792
	Oscar Merikanto)		DA 942	BLP 1107
			DA 1111	FLPS 1840
			IR 303	GEMM 160
				GEMM 176e
				MRF 5
				STAL 1057
Bb 11345-I	The Silver Ring ("L'Anneau	1303-B**	(6-2607)	DOLM 5023
	D'Argent")(Eugene Oudin,		DA 942	EX 2900073
	after Rosemonde Gérard/Cécile		DA 973	GEMM 160
	Chaminade)		IR 259	GEMM 176e
			(IR 1051)	GV 523
				GV 901
				P 69
Bb 11346-I	Now Sleeps the Crimson Petal		(6-2894)	ARM1-4997
	(Alfred, Lord Tennyson/Roger		DA 1111	COLH 124
	Quilter, Op. 3, No. 2)		IR 304	EX 2900563
				GEMM 160
				GEMM 176e
				MKER 2002
				P 69
-II		1307-B		
Bb 11347-I	The Cloths of Heaven (from "The		(6-2895)	Arab. 8124
	Wind Among the Reeds")			
	(William Butler Yeats/Thomas			
	F. Dunhill)			

* - Extant test pressing.
** - Title shown as "The Little Silver Ring."

<u>5 SEPTEMBER 1927, MONDAY ("D" Studio, Small Queen's Hall, London)</u>
w. EDWIN SCHNEIDER, piano and R. GOSS-CUSTARD, organ (77.43rpm)

CR 1497-<u>I</u>	Panis Angelicus (from Mass in a,	(2-052348)	GEMM 159
	M. 61)(Thomas Aquinas/	DB 1095	GEMM 176e
	César-Auguste Franck) w.	IRX 26	P 69
	LAURI KENNEDY, 'cello		
-II	obbligato	UNPUBLISHED	
-III		UNPUBLISHED	

VICTOR TALKING MACHINE COMPANY

<u>11 OCTOBER 1927, TUESDAY (New York City)</u>
w. EDWIN SCHNEIDER, piano

CVE 39889-1	Kathleen Mavourneen (Annie Barry	UNPUBLISHED		
-2	Crawford/Frederick Williams	UNPUBLISHED		
<u>-3</u>	Nicholls Crouch)	6776-A	(2-02277)	7ER 5066
		DB 1200		CAL-407
		IRX 9		CAS-407(e)
				CDM 1024
				CDN-1002
				DRLP 007
				GEMM 185
				RCX-209

CVE 40165-1	Love's Old Sweet Song (C.	UNPUBLISHED		
<u>-2</u>	Clifton Bingham/James Lyman	6776-B	(2-02271)	BLP 1084
	Molloy)	DB 1200		GEMM 185
		DB 2454*		OASI-624
		IRX 9		

BVE 40166-1	Bird Song at Eventide (Royden	UNPUBLISHED**		
<u>-2</u>	Barrie/Eric Coates)	1303-A	(7-2006)	ARM1-4997
		DA 973		AU 4792
		DA 1712		DOLM 5023
		IR 205		GEMM 185
				GV 523
				MRF 5
				OASI-624

BVE 40167-1	Beloved, I am Lonely (May	UNPUBLISHED**		
<u>-2</u>	Aldington/Harold Craxton)			DOLM 5023
				GEMM 185

<u>12 OCTOBER 1927, WEDNESDAY (New York City)</u>
w. EDWIN SCHNEIDER, piano (76.00rpm)

BVE 40170-1	None But a Lonely Heart (Johann	UNPUBLISHED**		
<u>-2</u>	Wolfgang von Goethe/Piotr	1306-A	(7-2083)	GEMM 158
	Ilyich Tchaikovsky, Op. 6,	DA 1112***		
	No. 6) w. LAURI KENNEDY,	IR 265		
	'cello obbligato			

BVE 40171-1	The Rosary (Robert Cameron	UNPUBLISHED		
<u>-2</u>	Rogers/Ethelbert W. Nevin) w.	1458-A	(40-2031)	CAL-635
	LAURI KENNEDY, 'cello	ERC 6010-	DA 1116	CDN-1029
	obbligato	IR 263		DRLP 008
				GEMM 187
				RCX-210

* - King George V Silver Jubilee disc containing partial re-recording.
** - Extant test pressing.
*** - Title shown as "None But the Weary Heart."

BVE 40172-1	I Hear You Calling Me (Harold Lake, writing as Harold Harford/Charles Marshall)	1293-A ERC 6012-	(6-2966) DA 958 IR 256	17-0347- B in WCT-53 ARM1-4997 BLP 1084 CAL-407 CAS-407(e) CDM 1024 CDN-1002 DRLP 007 LCT-1036 RCX-210 TR1S-9457 inRD4-49
-2		UNPUBLISHED*		
BVE 40173-1 -2	Mother Machree (from "Barry of Ballymore")(Rida Johnson Young/Chauncey Olcott and Ernest R. Ball)	UNPUBLISHED 1293-B 410-0172- ** ERC 6003-	(6-2965) DA 958 IR 264	7ER 5066 CAL-407 CAS-407(e) CDM 1024 CDN-1002 CM-0700 DRLP 007 ERAT-18 GEMM 243 LM-6705 RCA449-0172 RCX-209

13 OCTOBER 1927, THURSDAY (New York City)
w. EDWIN SCHNEIDER, piano (76.00rpm)

BVE 40177-1 -2	Annie Laurie (Douglas of Fingland/Anne, Lady John Scott)	UNPUBLISHED* 1305-A	(7-2036) DA 966 IR 260	GEMM 241
BVE 40178-1 -2	The Auld Scotch Sangs (O Sing to Me the Auld Scotch Sangs) (Reverend Dr. Bethune/J. F. Leeson)	UNPUBLISHED 1305-B	(7-2037) DA 966 (IR 1052)	ARM1-4997 GEMM 241

13 JANUARY 1928, FRIDAY (New York City)
w. EDWIN SCHNEIDER, piano (77.43rpm)

BVE 41543-1 -2	Dear Old Pal of Mine (Harold Robé/Lieutenant Gitz Rice)	UNPUBLISHED 1321-A	(7-2042) DA 965	GEMM 187 GV 901
-3 BVE 41544-1 -2	The Irish Emigrant (Helen Selina, later Lady Dufferin/ G. A. Barker)	UNPUBLISHED* ERC-6004- ** 1528-A	(40-3994) DA 1234 IR 210	GEMM 185
BVE 41545-1 -2	Roses of Picardy (Frederic E. Weatherley/Haydn Wood)	UNPUBLISHED 1321-B	(7-2043) DA 965 (IR 1054)	GEMM 187 GV 901 LP 110
BVE 41546-1	By the Short Cut to the Rosses (Nora Hopper/Old Irish Air, arr. C. Milligan Fox)	10-0041-B in DM-1358 42-0003		GEMM 185

* - Extant test pressing.
** - Re-recording.

BVE 41546-<u>2</u>   By the Short Cut to the Rosses   1528-B   (40-3995) ARM1-4997
                  (Nora Hopper/Old Irish Air,   DA 1234   AU 4792
                  arr. C. Milligan Fox)   IR 210   GEMM 245
                                                                           MRF 5
                                                                   VIC-1393

17 JANUARY 1928, TUESDAY (New York City)
w. EDWIN SCHNEIDER, piano
BVE 41561-1   A Song Remembered (Royden   UNPUBLISHED
                  Barrie/Eric Coates)

19 NOVEMBER 1928, MONDAY (New York City)
w. orchestra (4 violins, viola, 'cello, flute, 2 clarinets, oboe, 2 cornets,
trombone, tuba, piano, traps) conducted by NATHANIEL SHILKRET (77.43rpm)
BVE 48178-1   Sonny Boy (from "The Singing   UNPUBLISHED
      -2   Fool")(words and music by   UNPUBLISHED
      <u>-3</u>   Buddy G. DeSylva, Lew Brown, 1360-A   (7-2279)   GEMM 188
                  and Ray Henderson)   DA 1027   LP-110
                                                                   OASI-539

BVE 48179-<u>1</u>   Jeannine, I Dream of Lilac Time 1360-B   (7-2286)   GEMM 188
                  (from "Lilac Time")(L. Wolfe   DA 1027   OASI-539
                  Gilbert/Nathaniel Shilkret)
      -2   UNPUBLISHED
      -3   UNPUBLISHED
BVE 48180-<u>1</u>   Song of the Night (Rida Johnson 1463-A   (40-2268) GEMM 188
                  Young/Uda Waldrop)   DA 1135

      -2   UNPUBLISHED
BVE 48181-<u>1</u>   The Gateway of Dreams (J. Will 1463-B   (40-2269) GEMM 188
                  Callahan/Granville English)   DA 1135

      -2   UNPUBLISHED

21 NOVEMBER 1928, WEDNESDAY (New York City)
w. orchestra (4 violins, viola, 'cello, flute, 2 clarinets, oboe, 2 cornets,
trombone, tuba, piano, traps) conducted by NATHANIEL SHILKRET
BVE 48191-1   Crossroads (from "Show People") UNPUBLISHED
      -2   (words and music by Raymond UNPUBLISHED
                  Klagen, William Axt, and
                  David Mendoza)

27 NOVEMBER 1928, TUESDAY (New York City)
w. Victor Orchestra (8 violins, 2 violas, 2 'celli, string bass, flute,
2 clarinets, oboe, bassoon, 2 trumpets, 2 french horns, trombone, tuba, harp,
piano, organ, traps) conducted by NATHANIEL SHILKRET (77.43rpm)
CVE 49209-1, <u>1A</u> Ave Maria (Sir Walter Scott/   (2-02310) GEMM 158
                  Franz Schubert, D. 839) w.   DB 1297   GV 523
                  Victor Salon Group (James   IRX 100*
                  Melton and Lewis James,
      -<u>2</u>   tenors; Elliot Shaw,   6927-B   (2-02310) GEMM 275
                  baritone; Wilfred Glenn,   in C-3** DB 1297   L-4509***
                  bass)
      -<u>3</u>   6927-B
                                      in C-3****

* - Re-recording.
** - Original issue.
*** - Re-recording for early RCA 33 1/3rpm Program Transcription, matrix
LBVE 69735-1.
**** - Later issue.

CVE 49210-_1_*	Serenade (Softly Through the Night is Calling) ("Ständchen")(Ludwig	6927-A in C-3**		GEMM 275
-_2_	Rellstab, trans. Alice Mattullath/Franz Schubert, D. 957, No. 4) w. Victor Salon Group (James Melton and Lewis James, tenors; Elliott Shaw, baritone; Wilfred Glenn, bass)	6927-A in C-3***	(2-02308) DB 1297 IRX 100	GEMM 158 GV 523 L-4509****

28 NOVEMBER 1928, WEDNESDAY (New York City)
w. Victor Orchestra (8 violins, 2 violas, 2 'celli, string bass, flute,
2 clarinets, bassoon, 2 trumpets, 2 french horns, trombone, tuba, harp, piano,
harmonium, traps) conducted by NATHANIEL SHILKRET (77.43rpm)

CVE 49213-1	The Organ Grinder (The Hurdy	UNPUBLISHED	
-_2_	Gurdy Man)("Der Leiermann")	UNPUBLISHED	
-_3_	(from (Wilhelm Müller/Franz Schubert, D. 911, No. 24); Farewell ("Abschied")(from "Schwanengesang")(Ludwig Rellstab/Franz Schubert, D. 957, No. 7)******	6928-A in C-3	GEMM 158 GV 523 L-4509*****

CVE-49214-1	Hark, Hark, the Lark! ("Horch,	UNPUBLISHED*******
-2	horch, die Lerch!" (William Shakespeare/Franz Schubert, D. 889); Who is Sylvia? ("Was ist Sylvia")(William Shakespeare/ Franz Schubert, D. 891)********	UNPUBLISHED

6 DECEMBER 1928, THURSDAY (New York City)
w. Victor Orchestra (8 violins, 2 violas, 2 'celli, string bass, flute,
2 clarinets, oboe, bassoon, 2 cornets, 2 french horns, trombone, tuba, harp,
2 pianos, traps) conducted by NATHANIEL SHILKRET (77.43rpm)

CVE 49237-1	Holy Night ("Nacht und Träume")	UNPUBLISHED		
-_2_	(Matthäus von Collin/Franz	UNPUBLISHED		
-_3_	Schubert, D. 827);********* To the Lyre ("An die Leier") (Franz Seraph von Bruchmann, after Anacreon/Franz Schubert, D. 737) w. Victor Salon Group (James Melton and Lewis James, tenors; Elliott Shaw, baritone; Wilfred Glenn, bass)**********	6926-B	(42-725) DB 1383 (IRX 1020)	GEMM 158 GV 523

* - Re-recorded onto 10" matrix for test.
** - Later issue.
*** - Original issue.
**** - Re-recorded for early RCA 33 1/3rpm Program Transcription, matrix
LBVE 69735-1.
***** - Re-recorded for early RCA 33 1/3rpm Program Transcription, matrix
LBVE 69736-1.
****** - In addition to the two songs sung by McCormack, an orchestral transcription
of "Ungeduld" (from "Die schöne Müllerin," D. 795) is also on this record.
******* - Extant test pressing.
******** - In addition to the two songs sung by McCormack, an orchestral
transcription of "Heidenröslein," D. 257 is also on this record.
********* - Abridged. Label attributes words to Schiller.
********** - In addition to the two songs sung by McCormack, orchestral
transcriptions of "Die Forelle," D. 550 and Impromptu in A-flat, D. 935, No. 2
are also included on this record.

| CVE 49214-3 | Hark, Hark, the Lark! ("Horch, horch, die Lerch!" (William Shakespeare/Franz Schubert, D. 889); Who is Sylvia? ("Was ist Sylvia")(William Shakespeare/ Franz Schubert, D. 891)* | UNPUBLISHED | | |

7 DECEMBER 1928, FRIDAY (New York City)
w. Victor Orchestra (8 violins, 2 violas, 2 'celli, string bass, flute,
2 clarinets, oboe, bassoon, 2 cornets, 2 french horns, trombone, tuba, harp,
2 pianos, traps) conducted by NATHANIEL SHILKRET (77.43rpm)

BVE 49240-1	Under the Spell of the Rose (Wild Rose Lane)(from "Songs of the Hedgerow")(Helen		AGSA 62	ANNA-1026 GEMM 188
-2	Taylor/Easthope Martin)	UNPUBLISHED		
-3		UNPUBLISHED		
CVE 49214-4	Hark, Hark, the Lark! ("Horch horch, die Lerch!")(William Shakespeare/Franz Schubert, D. 889);	6926-A	(42-700) DB 1383 (IRX 1020)	GEMM 158 GV 523
-5	Who is Sylvia? ("Was ist Sylvia")(William Shakespeare/ Franz Schubert, D. 891) w. Victor Salon Group (Charles Harrison and Lewis James, tenors; Elliott Shaw, baritone; Wilfred Glenn, bass)*	UNPUBLISHED		

RCA VICTOR DIVISION, RADIO CORPORATION OF AMERICA

10 APRIL 1929, WEDNESDAY (44th Street Laboratory, New York City)
w. orchestra (4 violins, viola, 'cello, flute, 2 clarinets, oboe, 2 cornets,
trombone, tuba, piano, traps) conducted by NATHANIEL SHILKRET (77.43rpm)

| BVE 51613-1 | I Love to Hear You Singing (Glanville/Haydn Wood) | UNPUBLISHED | | |
| -2 | | 1425-A | (40-632) DA 1059 DA 1077 | GEMM 188 |

| BVE 51614-1 | Lady Divine (from "The Divine Lady")(Richard Kountz/ Nathaniel Shilkret) | UNPUBLISHED | | |
| -2 | | UNPUBLISHED | | |

12 APRIL 1929, FRIDAY (44th Street Laboratory, New York City)
w. orchestra (4 violins, viola, 'cello, flute, 2 clarinets, oboe, 2 cornets,
trombone, tuba, piano, traps) conducted by NATHANIEL SHILKRET (77.43rpm)

BVE 51620-1	Little Pal (from "Say It With	UNPUBLISHED		
-2	Song")(words and music by Buddy G. De Sylva, Lew Brown, and Ray Henderson)	1425-B	(40-631 or 40-632) DA 1059 IR 1037	LP-110 OASI-539
-3		UNPUBLISHED		
BVE 51621-1	A Garden in the Rain (James	UNPUBLISHED		
-2	Dyrenforth/Carroll Gibbons)	1400-A ERC 6012-	(7-2443) DA 1050 IR 1030	GEMM 188 OASI-539

| BVE 51622-1 | Lover Come Back to Me (from "The | UNPUBLISHED | | |
| -2 | New Moon")(Oscar Hammerstein, II/Sigmund Romberg) | 1400-B | (7-2444) DA 1050 DA 1077 | GEMM 188 LP-110 |

FOX FILM CORPORATION

* - In addition to the two songs sung by McCormack, an orchestral transcription of
"Heidenröslein," D. 257 is also on this record.

Song O' My Heart film soundtrack (Fox Movietone Sound on Film process)*

? AUGUST 1929 (vicinity of Moore Abbey, County Kildare, Ireland)
w. EDWIN SCHNEIDER, piano
(70mm)   A Fairy Story by the Fire (Angela Campbell-MacInnes/   UNPUBLISHED
(35mm)   Oscar Merikanto)   GEMM 188
                                                                           J.M.A. LP
                                                                           UORC-107

? AUGUST 1929 (unidentified church, County Kildare, Ireland)
w. EDWIN SCHNEIDER, organ
(70mm)   Just for Today (Sybil F. Partridge/Blanche Ebert   UNPUBLISHED
(35mm)   Seaver)   GEMM 188
                                                                           J.M.A. LP
                                                                           UORC-107

RCA VICTOR DIVISION, RADIO CORPORATION OF AMERICA

15 OCTOBER 1929, TUESDAY (44th Street Laboratory, New York City)
w. EDWIN SCHNEIDER, piano
BVE TEST 426-1   TRISTAN UND ISOLDE (libretto and   GEMM 275
                     music by Richard Wagner): O   VOCE-88
                     König**

16 OCTOBER 1929, WEDNESDAY (44th Street Laboratory, New York City)
w. orchestra (5 violins, viola, 'cello, flute, 2 clarinets, oboe, bassoon,
2 cornets, trombone, tuba, harp (Francis J. Lapitino), piano, traps) conducted by
NATHANIEL SHILKRET
BVE 56188-1   O Mary Dear (John McCormack/Old   UNPUBLISHED***
                     Irish Air: "Londonderry
                     Air," arr. Edwin Schneider)
BVE 56198-1   Just a Corner of Heaven to Me   UNPUBLISHED***
     -2   (Ballard MacDonald and Karl   EB 22
                     Stark/James F. Hanley)   GEMM 243

BVE 56190-1   FORTUNIO (G. A. de Caillavet and UNPUBLISHED
     -2   Robert de Flers, after Alfred   UNPUBLISHED
                     de Musset/André Messager):
                     J'amais la vielle maison
                     grise (La Maison grise)

17 OCTOBER 1929, THURSDAY (44th Street Laboratory, New York City)
w. orchestra (5 violins, viola, 'cello, string bass, flute, 2 clarinets, oboe,
bassoon, 2 cornets, trombone, piano, traps) conducted by NATHANIEL SHILKRET
BVE 56192-1   Ireland, Mother Ireland (P. J.   UNPUBLISHED
     -2   O'Reilly/Raymond   UNPUBLISHED***
                     Loughborough) w. Francis J.
                     Lapitino, harp
BVE 56193-1   Bantry Bay (Traditional/Old   UNPUBLISHED
     -2   Irish Air, arr. James L.   UNPUBLISHED
                     Molloy)

* - Entire soundtrack of U.S. version (9 reels) re-recorded to disc for use in
theatres lacking sound-on-film equipment:
MVE 62870-1A, 2, 2A   Reel No. 1
MVE 62871-1A, 2, 2A   Reel No. 2
MVE 62872-1A, 2, 2A   Reel No. 3
MVE 62873-1A, 2, 2A   Reel No. 4
MVE 62874-1, 1A, 2A   Reel No. 5
MVE 62875-1A, 2, 2A   Reel No. 6
MVE 62876-1, 1A, 2, 2A   Reel No. 7
MVE 62877-1A, 2, 2A   Reel No. 8
MVE 62878-1A, 2, 2A   Reel No. 9
It is not known whether the two additional reels of the foreign versions were
transferred to disc.
** - Incomplete, ends in mid-phrase before end of aria. Victor files note, "For
Mr. McCormack to hear." Test pressings exist of 45rpm re-recording.
*** - Extant test pressing.

18 OCTOBER 1929, FRIDAY (44th Street Laboratory, New York City)
w. orchestra (5 violins, viola, 'cello, string bass, flute, 2 clarinets, oboe,
bassoon, 2 cornets, french horn, trombone, harp (Francis J. Lapitino), piano,
traps) conducted by NATHANIEL SHILKRET (77.43rpm)

BVE 56197-1	When Night Descends (Fet, trans	UNPUBLISHED
-2	Schneider and McCormack/	UNPUBLISHED
	Sergei Rachmaninoff, Op. 4,	
	No. 3)	
BVE 56188-2	O Mary Dear (John McCormack/Old	UNPUBLISHED
	Irish Air: "Londonderry	
	Air," arr. Edwin Schneider)	
BVE 56198-1	Norah O'Neale (Traditional/Old	UNPUBLISHED
-2	Irish Air, arr. Herbert	17-0059-A
	Hughes)	in WCT-12
		GEMM 185
		IDLP 2005
		LCT-1008

FOX FILM CORPORATION

Song O' My Heart film soundtrack (Fox Movietone Sound on Film Process)

25 NOVEMBER 1929 THROUGH 16 JANUARY 1930
(Fox Studios, Hollywood, California)
w. EDWIN SCHNEIDER, piano

(70mm)	THE BOHEMIAN GIRL (Alfred Bunn, after Jules H. Vernoy	UNPUBLISHED
(35mm)	de Saint-Georges/Michael William Balfe): When	GEMM 188
	coldness or deceit (Then You'll Remember Me)	J.M.A. LP
		UORC-107
(70mm)	I Feel You Near Me (Joseph McCarthy/James F. Hanley)	UNPUBLISHED
(35mm)		GEMM 188
		J.M.A LP
		UORC-107
(70mm)	Kitty, My Love, Will You Marry Me? (Traditional/	UNPUBLISHED
(35mm)	Old Irish Air, arr. Herbert Hughes)	GEMM 160
		GEMM 176e
		GEMM 188
		J.M.A. LP
		UORC-107
(70mm)	The Rose of Tralee (C. Mordaunt Spencer/Charles W.	UNPUBLISHED
(35mm)	Glover)	GEMM 188
		J.M.A. LP
		UORC-107
(70mm)	O Mary Dear (John McCormack/Old Irish Air:	UNPUBLISHED
(35mm)	"Londonderry Air, arr. Edwin Schneider)*	UNPUBLISHED

w. Fox Studio Orchestra conducted by ARTHUR KAY (?)

(70mm)	A Pair of Blue Eyes (words and music by William	UNPUBLISHED
(35mm)	Kernell)	GEMM 188
		J.M.A. LP
		UORC-107

unaccompanied:

(70mm)	The Magpie's Nest (Traditional/Old Irish Air, arr.	UNPUBLISHED
(35mm)	Herbert Hughes)	GEMM 188
		J.M.A. LP

(Los Angeles Philharmonic Auditorium, 5th and Grand, Los Angeles California)
w. EDWIN SCHNEIDER, piano

(70mm)	Luoghi sereni e cari (words and music by Stefano	UNPUBLISHED
	Donaudy)	

* - Used in Spanish intertitled synchronized version only.

(35mm)	Luoghi sereni e cari (words and music by Stefano Donaudy)	GEMM 188 J.M.A. LP UORC-107
(70mm) (35mm)	Little Boy Blue (Eugene Field/Ethelbert W. Nevin, Op. 12, No. 4)	UNPUBLISHED GEMM 188 J.M.A. LP UORC-107
(70mm) (35mm)	Plasir d'Amour (J. P. Claris de Florian/Giovanni Martini)*	UNPUBLISHED GEMM 188 J.M.A. LP UORC-107
(70mm) (35mm)	All'mein Gedanken ("Minnelied")(Traditional/Old German, arr. Sigfrid Karg-Elert)*	UNPUBLISHED GEMM 188 J.M.A. LP UORC-107
(70mm) (35mm)	Ireland, Mother Ireland (P. J. O'Reilly/Raymond Loughborough)	UNPUBLISHED GEMM 188 J.M.A. LP UORC-107
(70mm) (35mm)	I Hear You Calling Me (Harold Lake, writing as Harold Harford/Charles Marshall)	UNPUBLISHED GEMM 188 J.M.A. LP UORC-107

RCA VICTOR DIVISION, RADIO CORPORATION OF AMERICA

19 FEBRUARY 1930, WEDNESDAY (44th Street Laboratory, New York City)
w. orchestra (4 violins, viola, 'cello, string bass, flute, 2 clarinets, oboe, bassoon, 2 cornets, french horn, trombone, tuba, harp, traps) conducted by NATHANIEL SHILKRET (77.43rpm)

BVE 58586-1 -2	The Rose of Tralee (C. Mordaunt Spencer/Charles W. Glover)	UNPUBLISHED 1452-A (40-2194) 10-0040-A DA 119 in DM-1358 IR 202 ** 42-0002- ERC 6005-		ARM1-4997 BLP 1084 CAL-407 CAS-407(e) CAS-535 CDM 1024 CDN-1002 DRLP 007 GEMM 245 GV 901 LM-6705 RCX-209 SP-33-22
BVE 58587-1 -2	I Feel You Near Me (from "Song O' My Heart")(Joseph McCarthy/James F. Hanley)	UNPUBLISHED UNPUBLISHED		
BVE 58588-1	A Pair of Blue Eyes (from "Song O' My Heart")(words and music by William Kernell)	1453-B (40-1795) DA 1113		BLP 1084
-2		UNPUBLISHED***		

21 FEBRUARY 1930, FRIDAY (44th Street Laboratory, New York City)
w. orchestra (4 violins, viola, 'cello, string bass, flute, 2 clarinets, oboe bassoon, 2 cornets, french horn, trombone, tuba, harp, piano, traps) conducted by NATHANIEL SHILKRET (77.43rpm)

BVE 58595-1	Little Boy Blue (Eugene Field/ Ethelbert W. Nevin, Op. 12, No. 4)	UNPUBLISHED

* - Not included in U.S. version.
** - Re-recording.
*** - Extant test pressing.

BVE 58595-<u>2</u>	Little Boy Blue (Eugene Field/ Ethelbert W. Nevin, Op. 12, No. 4)	1458-B	(40-2032) DA 1116 IR 259	FLPS 1840 GEMM 243 LP-110 STAL 1057

BVE 58596-1	A Fairy Story by the Fire (Angela Campbell-McInnes/Oscar Merikanto)	(1307-A)*		

BVE 56192-3 -<u>4</u>	Ireland, Mother Ireland (P. J. O'Reilly/Raymond Loughborough)	UNPUBLISHED 1452-B 10-0040-B in DM-1358 ** ERC 6002-	(40-2195) DA 1119 IR 202	ARM1-4997 GEMM 245 RCX-208

BVE 58587-<u>3</u>	I Feel You Near Me (from "Song O' My Heart")(Joseph McCarthy/James F. Hanley)	1453-A	(40-1829) DA 1113	

<u>27 FEBRUARY 1930, FRIDAY (Liederkranz Hall, New York City)</u>***
w. RCA Victor Symphony Orchestra (7 1st violins, 4 2nd violins, 4 violas, 4 'celli, 3 string basses, 2 flutes, 2 clarinets, 2 oboes, 2 bassoons, 2 trumpets, 4 french horns, 3 trombones, tuba, harp, piano, traps) conducted by NATHANIEL SHILKRET

CVE 58684-<u>1</u>	CHRISTUS AM ÖLBERG ("Christ on the Mount of Olives")(Franz Xaver Huber/Ludwig von Beethoven, Op. 85): Jehovah, Hear Me (Recitative)	AB 11 CAL-635 CDN-1029 F7-OH-7606/ 7**** FB 1 GEMM 240

CVE 58684-<u>2</u>	CHRISTUS AM ÖLBERG (Franz Xaver Huber/Ludwig von Beethoven, Op. 85): Jehova! Du mein Vater! (Recitative)	GEMM 240

CVE 58685-<u>1</u>	CHRISTUS AM ÖLBERG ("Christ on the Mount of Olives")(Franz Xaver Huber/Ludwig von Beethoven, Op. 85): My Heart is Sore Within Me (Aria)	AB 11 CAL-635 CDN-1029 F7-OH-7607/ 6**** FB 1 GEMM 240

<u>10 MARCH 1930, MONDAY (Liederkranz Hall, New York City)</u>
w. RCA Victor Symphony Orchestra (4 1st violins, 4 2nd violins, 2 violas, 2 'celli, 2 string basses, flute, 2 clarinets, oboe, bassoon, 2 trumpets, 2 french horns, trombone, tuba, harp, piano, traps) conducted by NATHANIEL SHILKRET

BVE 58690-<u>1</u>	Song O' My Heart (Joseph McCarthy/James F. Hanley)	AGSA 62	ANNA-1026 GEMM 243

w. RCA Victor Symphony Orchestra (9 1st violins, 8 2nd violins, 4 violas, 5 'celli, 3 string basses, 2 flutes, 3 clarinets, 2 oboes, English horn, 2 bassoons, 2 trumpets, 4 french horns, 3 trombones, tuba, harp, piano, traps) conducted by NATHANIEL SHILKRET

BVE 58691-1 -2	Wo find' ich Trost (Eduard Mörike/Hugo Wolf)	UNPUBLISHED UNPUBLISHED*

* – Extant test pressing.
** – Re-recording.
*** – Date on test pressings of CVE 58684-1 and CVE 58685-1. RCA files give date as 28 February 1930.
**** – Label states, "RCA Victor limited edition. John McCormack Commemorative Record to Reviewers on the 10th Anniversary of his death September 16, 1955 – Not for Sale."

CVE 58692-1*   TRISTAN UND ISOLDE (libretto and DSRB 0980**   17-0347-A
                music by Richard Wagner): O   in WCT-53
                König   GEMM 240
                                                  LCT-1036
                                                  VIC-1472

THE GRAMOPHONE COMPANY, LIMITED

3 DECEMBER 1930, WEDNESDAY ("C" Studio, Small Queen's Hall, London)
w. EDWIN SCHNEIDER, piano (77.72rpm)

Matrix	Title			
Bb 21026-I	There (from "English Lyrics, Set	UNPUBLISHED***		
-II	9")(Mary Coleridge/Sir		(30-5304)	ARM1-4997
	Charles Hubert Hastings		DA 1172	GEMM 240
	Parry, Op. 176, No. 7)			HQM 1228
Bb 21027-I	The Fairy Tree (Temple Lane/	UNPUBLISHED		
-II	Vincent O'Brien)	UNPUBLISHED		
-III			(30-5305)	17-0349-A
			DA 1178	in WCT-53
			IR 266	ARM1-4997
				AU 4792
				GEMM 240
				LCT-1036
				MRF 5
Bb 21028-I	Far Apart (Faith Van	1554-B	(30-5306)	ARM1-4997
	Falkenburgh-Vilas/Edwin		DA 1178	AU 4792
	Schneider)		IR 303	GEMM 240
				MRF 5
Bb 21029-I	Three Aspects (from "English	UNPUBLISHED		
-II	Lyrics, Set 9")(Mary		(30-5307)	ARM1-4997
	Coleridge/Sir Charles Hubert		AGSA 21	GEMM 240
	Hastings Parry, Op. 176,		DA 1172	HQM 1228
	No. 1)			Roc. 5343
Bb 21030-I	Anakreons Grab (Johann Wolfgang	UNPUBLISHED***		
-II	von Goethe/Hugo Wolf)	1568-B	(30-5308)	EX 2900563
			DA 1170	GEMM 240
			IR 1019	HLM 7037
				HQM 1176
				Roc. 5343
Bb 21031-I	Schlafendes Jesuskind (Eduard		(30-5309)	Arab.8105-2
	Mörike/Hugo Wolf)		DA 1170	EX 2900563
			IR 1026	GEMM 240
Bb 21032-I	Love's Secret (William Blake/		(30-5391)	ARM1-4997
	Sir Granville Bantock)		DA 1175	AU 4792
			IR 1013	GEMM 240
				MRF 5
				Roc. 5343

4 DECEMBER 1930, THURSDAY ("C" Studio, Small Queen's Hall, London)
w. EDWIN SCHNEIDER, piano (76.00rpm)

Matrix	Title			
Bb 21036-I	The Garden Where the Praties	UNPUBLISHED		
-II	Grow (Johnny Patterson/	1553-A	(30-5310)	7EB 6029
	Old Irish Air, arr. Samuel		DA 1171	7ER 5188
	Liddle)		IR 209	Arab. 8124
				COLH 124
				EX 2900073
				GEMM 240
				GV 901
				MKER 2002
				P 69

* – Re-recorded to unpublished 10" matrix EO-RC-1263.
** – Christmas gift for some RCA dealers.
*** – Extant test pressing.

Bb 21037-I	The Harp That Once Thro' Tara's Halls (Thomas Moore/Old Irish Air: "Gramachree")	1553-B 10-0042-A in DM-1358	(30-5311) DA 1171 IR 209	7EB 6029 7ER 5188 Arab. 8124 EX 2900073 GEMM 240 GV 901 P 69
Bb 21040-I -II	The Bitterness of Love (Shaemas O'Sheel/James Philip Dunn)	UNPUBLISHED 1568-A	(30-5312) AGSA 21 DA 1175 IR 1013	ARM1-4997 AU 4792 GEMM 240 GV 901 MRF 5 NW-247 Roc. 5343

5 DECEMBER 1930, FRIDAY (Kingsway Hall, London)
w. HERBERT DAWSON, organ (76.00rpm)

Bb 20690-I -II	Ave Maria (Traditional/Peter C. Cornelius) w. string quintet (1st violin, 2nd violin, viola, 'cello, string bass)	UNPUBLISHED	(30-5313) DA 1177 IR 266	EX 2900563 GEMM 240 HLM 7037 HQM 1176
Bb 20691-I -II	The Prayer Perfect (James Whitcomb Riley/Oley Speaks)	UNPUBLISHED 1554-A	(30-5314) DA 1177 IR 304	GEMM 240 GV 901

RCA VICTOR DIVISION, RADIO CORPORATION OF AMERICA

6 JULY 1931, MONDAY (Hollywood)
w. orchestra (2 violins, viola, 'cello, flute, 2 clarinets, bassoon, piano) conducted by ROY SHIELDS*

w. EDWIN SCHNEIDER, piano

PBVE 61097-1 -2	God Gave Me Flowers (M. Ashworth-Hope/Ernest Torrance)	UNPUBLISHED	DRLP 008 GEMM 245

2 NOVEMBER 1931, MONDAY
w. unknown accompaniment (33 1/3rpm)**

BRC-HQ-31-1	Two Brown Eyes (Frederic Edward Weatherley/Stephen Adams)	UNPUBLISHED
BRC-HQ-32-1	The Last Rose of Summer (Thomas Moore/Old Irish Air: "The Groves of Blarney," also "The Young Man's Dream," arr. Thomas Moore)	UNPUBLISHED
BRC-HQ-33-1	Und willst du deinen Liebsten sterben sehen (No. 17 from "Italienisches Liederbuch I") (Anonymous Italian, trans. Paul Heyse/Hugo Wolf)	UNPUBLISHED***
BRC-HQ-34-1 -2	Herr, was trägt der Boden hier (No. 9 from "Spanisches Liederbuch I")(Anonymous Spanish, trans. Paul Heyse/ Hugo Wolf)	UNPUBLISHED UNPUBLISHED

ELECTRIC & MUSICAL INDUSTRIES LIMITED

* - RCA files note, "Orchestra cancelled.   Continued with piano, Schneider. After making several tests, Mr. McCormack decided selection was not suited to his voice."
** - Made with RCA cutting head and high quality amplifier.
*** - Extant test pressing.

27 MAY 1932, FRIDAY (Kingsway Hall, London)
w. HERBERT DAWSON, organ (77.50rpm)

2B 3419-I	Hymn to Christ the King (F. P.	UNPUBLISHED		
-II	Donelly/Vincent O'Brien) w.		(32-2868)	GEMM 274
	male octet		GSS 1*	

31 MAY 1932, TUESDAY (Studio 3, Abbey Road, London)
w. EDWIN SCHNEIDER, piano (77.50rpm)

2B 2276-I	Beherzignung (Johann Wolfgang	UNPUBLISHED		
-II	von Goethe/Hugo Wolf, No. 18)	UNPUBLISHED**		
-III			(32-2883)	COLH 123
			DB 1830***	GEMM 274
			IRX 1008	RLS 759
				SH-110

2B 2277-I	Ganymed (Johann Wolfgang von	UNPUBLISHED		
-II	Goethe/Hugo Wolf, No. 50)		(32-2884)	COLH 123
			DB 1830***	GEMM 274
			IRX 1008	RLS 759
				SH-110

BROADCAST (BBC National Program)

26 JUNE 1932, SUNDAY (Phoenix Park, Dublin)
w. organ (?)
Panis Angelicus (from Mass in a, M. 61)(Thomas   UNPUBLISHED****
   Aquinas/César-Auguste Franck) w. choir of 500
   men and boys

ELECTRIC & MUSICAL INDUSTRIES LIMITED

16 SEPTEMBER 1932, FRIDAY (Studio 3, Abbey Road, London)
w. EDWIN SCHNEIDER, piano (77.50rpm)

OB 3850-I	Bless This House (Helen Taylor/	1625-A	(30-9364)	BLP 1084
	May H. Brahe)		DA 1285	EX 2900073
			DA 1712	GEMM 274
			IR 205	GV 901
				P 69

-II		UNPUBLISHED		
OB 3851-I	Once in a Blue Moon (Emily	UNPUBLISHED		
-II	Westrup/Howard Fisher)		(30-9365)	GEMM 274
			DA 1285	GV 901
				P 69

OB 3852-I	L'Automne (Armand Silvestre/		(30-9366)	EX 2900563
	Gabriel Urbain Fauré, Op. 18,		DA 1286	GEMM 274
	No. 3)		(IR 1047)	
			VA 72	

OB 3853-I	Is She Not Passing Fair	1649-A	(30-9367)	EX 2900563
	(Charles, Duke of Orleans,		DA 1286	GEMM 274
	trans. Louisa Stuart		IR 1036	HLM 7037
	Costello/Sir Edward Elgar)			HQM 1176

OB 3854-I	A Prayer to Our Lady (from	UNPUBLISHED		
-II	"Skylark and Swallow")	1625-B	(30-9368)	GEMM 274
	(Reverend R. L. Gates/Donald		DA 1287	
	Ford)		IR 1014	

* - Single-face disc issued to benefit the building fund of Liverpool Cathedral.
Blank side contains photographs of the Archbishop of Liverpool and of McCormack
as Rodolfo, his favorite photograph.
** - Extant test pressing.
*** - Recorded under the auspices of the Hugo Wolf Society and included in album 2
of Wolf songs.
**** - Only one complete verse known to be extant.   Also included in Pathé
newsreel.

OB 3855-<u>I</u>	Charm Me Asleep (Robert Herrick/	1649-B	(30-9369)	GEMM 274
	Wilfrid Sanderson)		AGSA 57	GV 901
			DA 1287	
			IR 1014	
OB 3856-<u>I</u>	I Know of Two Bright Eyes		(30-9370)	GEMM 274
	("Myrra")(No. 4 from "Songs			
	of the Turkish Hills")(Abdul			
	Mejid/George H. Clutsam)			

BROADCAST

<u>4 APRIL 1933 (Radio City Music Hall, New York City)</u>
w. piano
Panis Angelicus (from Mass in a, M. 61)(Thomas   UNPUBLISHED*
  Aquinas/César-Auguste Franck) w. cello
  obbligato

ELECTRICAL & MUSICAL INDUSTRIES LIMITED

<u>7 SEPTEMBER 1933, THURSDAY (Studio 3, Abbey Road, London)</u>
w. PERCY KAHN, piano (77.92rpm)

OB 5305-I	As I Sit Here (Dena Tempest/	UNPUBLISHED	
-II	Wilfrid Sanderson)**	UNPUBLISHED	
-III		UNPUBLISHED	
-<u>IV</u>		(30-11068)	GEMM 274
		DA 1342	
		IR 302	
OB 5306-<u>I</u>	Vespers (words and music by	(30-11069)	GEMM 274
	Howard Fisher)	DA 1343	
-II		UNPUBLISHED	

w. MARTIN BROONES, piano (77.92rpm)

OB 5307-I	Love's Roses (Frances Ring/	UNPUBLISHED	
-<u>II</u>	Martin Broones)	(30-11070)	GEMM 274
		DA 1341	GV 901
			P 69

w. PERCY KAHN, piano (77.92rpm)

OB 5308-<u>I</u>	South Winds (words and music by		GEMM 274
	Percy Kahn)		
-<u>II</u>		(30-11071)	GEMM 274
		DA 1343	P 69
OB 5309-<u>I</u>	My Moonlight Madonna (words and	(30-11072)	GEMM 274
	music by Zdenka Fibich)	DA 1341	
		IR 258	

<u>13 SEPTEMBER 1933, WEDNESDAY (Studio 3, Abbey Road, London)</u>
w. PERCY KAHN, piano (77.92rpm)

OB 5310-I	I Know of Two Bright Eyes	UNPUBLISHED	
-<u>II</u>	("Myrra")(No. 4 from "Songs	(30-11115)	EX 2900073
	of the Turkish Hills")(Abdul	DA 1342	GEMM 274
	Mejid/George H. Clutsam)	IR 262	P 69
-III		UNPUBLISHED	
-IV		UNPUBLISHED	

BROADCAST (WJZ)

<u>18 OCTOBER 1933, WEDNESDAY (New York City)</u>
w. unknown accompaniment
The Heavy Hours Are Almost Past (words and music UNPUBLISHED
  by Lord Lyttleton)

* - Extant test pressing
** - Sheet music gives title as "Remembering You."

ELECTRICAL & MUSICAL INDUSTRIES LIMITED

24 AUGUST 1934, FRIDAY (Studio 3, Abbey Road, London)
w. EDWIN SCHNEIDER, piano (77.92rpm)

OEA 404-I	Music of the Night (Phyllis	UNPUBLISHED*		
-II	Black/Eric Coates)		DA 1390	
			IR 1015	
OEA 405-I	A Song Remembered (Royden		DA 1390	
	Barrie/Eric Coates)		IR 1015	
-II		UNPUBLISHED		
OEA 406-I	Candle Light (S. Shippey/Charles		DA 1404	
	Wakefield Cadman)**		IR 1039	
OEA 407-I	An Old Sacred Lullaby (Paul		DA 1404	P 69
	England, after German/D.		IR 1039	
	Corner, arr. Samuel Liddle)			
OEA 408-I	Ein neues andachtiges		DA 1675	
	Kindelwiegen (Traditional/		(IR 1055)	
	D. Corner, arr. Samuel			
	Liddle)			
OEA 409-I	Friend O' Mine (Frederic Edward		DA 1391	P 69
	Weatherley/Wilfrid Sanderson)			
OEA 410-I	Poor Man's Garden (Royden	1695-A	DA 1391	P 69
	Barrie/Kennedy Russell)			

OEA 411-I	Sweetly She Sleeps, My Alice	1700-B	DA 1405	7EB 6034
	Fair (George Eastman/Stephen		IR 1016	7ER 5181
	Foster)			COLH 124
				EX 2900563
				MKER 2002
				P 69

OEA 412-I	Jeanie With the Light Brown Hair	UNPUBLISHED		
-II	(words and music by Stephen	1700-A	DA 1405	7EB 6034
	Foster)		IR 1016	7ER 5181
				BLP 1084
				COLH 124
				EX 2900073
				MKER 2002
				P 69

29 AUGUST 1934, WEDNESDAY (Studio 3, Abbey Road, London)
w. EDWIN SCHNEIDER, piano (77.92rpm)

OEA 419-I	Green Pastures (Helen Taylor/	UNPUBLISHED		
-II	Wilfrid Sanderson)	1695-B	DA 1392	P 69
OEA 420-I	A Little Prayer for Me (Frederic	UNPUBLISHED		
-II	Edward Weatherley/Kennedy		DA 1392	BLP 1107
	Russell)			P 69
OEA 421-I	A Life Lesson (James Whitcomb	UNPUBLISHED		
-II	Riley/Ethelbert W. Nevin)	1711-A	DA 1406	BLP 1107
			IR 1020	
OEA 422-I	A Necklace of Love (from "Songs	1711-B	DA 1406	BLP 1107
	of Vine Acre")(Frank L.		IR 1020	P 69
	Stanton/Ethelbert W. Nevin)			

* - Extant test pressing.
** - Label states, "Dedicated by both author and composer to everybody's mother."

OEA 423-I	Terence's Farewell to Kathleen (Helen Selina, later Lady Dufferin/Old Irish Air: "The Pretty Girl Milking Her Cow")	DA 1396 IR 212	7EB 6029 7ER 5188 COLH 124 EX 2900073 MKER 2002 P 69
OEA 424-I -II	The Dawning of the Day (P. W. Joyce/Old Irish Air, arr. N. Clifford Page)	UNPUBLISHED DA 1396 IR 212	AU 4792 MRF 5
OEA 425-I	A House Love Made for You and Me (Gordon Johnstone/Eric Coates)	DA 1393	
OEA 426-I	The Quietest Things (Wymer/Haydn Wood)	DA 1393	HLM 7037 HQM 1176 P 69

BROADCAST (WJZ)

18 SEPTEMBER 1934, TUESDAY (New York City)
FLORIDANTE (George Frederic Handel): Alma mia   UNPUBLISHED

ELECTRICAL & MUSICAL INDUSTRIES LIMITED

27 JUNE 1935, THURSDAY (Studio 3, Abbey Road, London)
w. EDWIN SCHNEIDER, piano (77.92rpm)

OEA 2121-I	Oh Gathering Clouds (Traditional, arr. Bain)	26772-B	DA 1427 DA 1533 IR 1023 IR 1040	
OEA 2122-I	Little Child of Mary (from Negro Spiritual "De New Born Baby")(Henry Thacker Burleigh)	26772-A	DA 1427 DA 1534 IR 1040	
-II			UNPUBLISHED	
OEA 2123-I	When the Children Say Their Prayers (Arthur Stanley/ Kennedy Russell)		DA 1425	BLP 1107
OEA 2124-I	Baby Aroon (words and music by Vincent and M. O'Brien)		DA 1425 IR 1048	BLP 1107
-II			UNPUBLISHED*	
OEA 2125-I	When I Have Sung My Songs (words and music by Ernest Charles)		DA 1446 IR 1017	P 69
OEA 2126-I	Song to the Seals (from "Songs of the Western Isles")(Harold Boulton/Sir Granville Bantock) w. spoken introduction by McCormack		DA 1444 DA 1534 DA 1851 IR 326	Arab. 8124 AU 4792 EX 2900073 FLPS 1856 ISLE 3001 MFP 1090 MFP 50331 MRF 5 OXLP 7644 P 69 Roc. 5343
OEA 2127-I	Earl Bristol's Farewell (Traditional, arr. Lidgey)		DA 1446 IR 1017	P 69

28 JUNE 1935, FRIDAY (Studio 3, Abbey Road, London)
w. EDWIN SCHNEIDER, piano (77.92rpm)

* - Extant test pressing.

OEA 2128-I	O Mary Dear (John McCormack/Old	UNPUBLISHED*		
-II	Irish Air, "Londonderry	10-0042-B	DA 1432	7P 276
	Air," arr. Edwin Schneider)	in DM-1358	IR 368	AV-133
				EX 2900073
				P 69
OEA 2129-I	Believe Me If All Those	26569-A	DA 1432	Arab. 8124
	Endearing Young Charms		IR 257	BLP 1084
	(Thomas Moore/Old Irish Air:			COLH 124
	"My Lodging is on the Cold			EX 2900073
	Ground," arr. Edwin			MKER 2002
	Schneider)			P 69
-II		UNPUBLISHED		
OEA 2130-I	Shannon River (Kathleen Egan/	26569-B	DA 1426	7P 276
	Reginald Morgan)		IR 264	
-II		UNPUBLISHED*		
OEA 2131-I	I Met an Angel (Sievier/Reginald	UNPUBLISHED		
-II	Morgan)		DA 1426	
			IR 301	
OEA 2132-I	Little House I Planned (Parr/		DA 1428	
	Oliver)			
OEA 2133-I	Rise, Dawn of Love (Edward		DA 1428	
	Lockton/Campton)			
OEA 2134-I	Herr, was trägt der Boden hier	1739-B	DA 1441	COLH 123
	(from "Spanisches		IR 1022	EX 2900563
	Liederbuch")(Anonymous			SH-110
	Spanish, trans Paul Heyse/			
	Hugo Wolf)			
OEA 2135-I	Auch kleine Dinge (No. 1 from	1739-A	DA 1441	Arab.8105-2
	"Italienisches Liederbuch I")		IR 1022	COLH 123
	(Anonymous Italian, trans.			EX 2900563
	Paul Heyse/Hugo Wolf)			SH-110

23 JULY 1935, TUESDAY (Studio 3, Abbey Road, London)
w. EDWIN SCHNEIDER, piano (77.92rpm)

OEA 2180-I	Love's Secret (William Blake/Sir		DA 1444	HLM 7037
	Granville Bantock)**		DA 1533	HQM 1176
-II		UNPUBLISHED		
OEA 2181-I	She Rested By the Broken Brook		IR 1060	HLM 7037
	(Robert Louis Stevenson/			HQM 1176
	Samuel Coleridge-Taylor)			
-II		UNPUBLISHED		
OEA 2182-I	The Cloths of Heaven (from "The	26705-A	DA 1445	EX 2900073
	Wind Among the Reeds")		DA 1851	HLM 7093
	(William Butler Yeats/Thomas		IR 326	P 69
	F. Dunhill)			
OEA 2183-I	O Men from the Fields (from	26705-B	DA 1445	BLP 1107
	"Songs of Connacht")(Padraic			HLM 7037
	Colum/Old Irish Air, arr.			HQM 1176
	Herbert Hughes)***			

BROADCAST (NBC)

20 AUGUST 1935, TUESDAY (New York City)****
w. EDWIN SCHNEIDER (?), piano

* - Extant test pressing.
** - Sung in key one-half step lower than in previous recordings.
*** - Label gives title as "Cradle Song" and attributes music to Hamilton Harty.
**** - Possibly 21 August 1935.

Love's Roses (Frances Ring/Martin Broones)   EJS-295
                                                                              GEMM 274

Believe Me If All Those Endearing Young Charms   EJS-295
   (Thomas Moore/ Old Irish Air: "My Lodging is   GEMM 274
   on the Cold Ground," arr. Edwin Schneider)

ELECTRICAL & MUSICAL INDUSTRIES LIMITED

31 MARCH 1936, TUESDAY
(Studio 3, Abbey Road, London)
w. PERCY KAHN, piano (77.40rpm)
OEA 2746-I   In Sweet Content (Louise   DA 1478
                   MacDermaid/Wilfrid Sanderson)
        -II   UNPUBLISHED
OEA 2747-I   Ever In My Mind (Helen Taylor/   DA 1478
                   Kennedy Russell)

(Studio 1, Abbey Road, London)
w. orchestra conducted by LAWRANCE COLLINGWOOD (77.40rpm)
2EA 2748-I, IA   Green Isle of Erin (C. Clifton   DB 2848   Arab. 8124
                   Bingham/Joseph L. Roeckel)   IRX 72   EX 2900073
                                                                         P 69

2EA 2749-I, IA   The Kerry Dance (words and music UNPUBLISHED
        -II   by James Lyman Molloy)   14611-A   DB 2848   7ER 5066
                                                            IRX 72   Arab. 8124
                                                                         ERAT-18
                                                                         EX 2900073
                                                                         FLPS 1856
                                                                         ISLE 3001
                                                                         MFP 1090
                                                                         MFP 50331
                                                                         OXLP 7644
                                                                         P 69

2EA 2750-I, IA   She is Far from the Land   14611-B   DB 2849   7EB 6034
                   (Thomas Moore/Old Irish Air: IRX 1009   EX 2900073
                   "Open the Door," arr. Frank   P 69
                   Lambert)

2EA 2751-I, IA   Drink to Me Only With Thine Eyes   DB 2849   7EB 6034
                   (Ben Jonson/Old English Air,   IRX 1009   7ER 5181
                   arr. Calcott)   EX 2900073
                                                                         P 69

        -IIA   UNPUBLISHED

7 APRIL 1936, TUESDAY (Studio 1, Abbey Road, London)
w. orchestra conducted by WALTER GOEHR (77.40rpm)
2EA 2764-I, IA   IL PASTOR FIDO (Giacomo Rossi/ 14305-B   DB 2867   Arab.8105-2
                   George Frederic Handel): Caro   IRX 95   COLH 123
                   Amor*   EX 2900563
                                                                         P 69
                                                                         SH-110

2EA 2765-I, IA   SEMELE (William Congreve/George 14305-A   DB 2867   Arab.8105-2
                   Frederic Handel): Wher'er You   IRX 95   COLH 123
                   Walk   EX 2900563
                                                                         NP-4
                                                                         Sera. 60113
                                                                         SH-110

* - Some pressings erroneously show this aria as being from FLORIDANTE.

2EA 2766-I, <u>IA</u>	Träume (No. 5 from "Wesendonck Lieder")(Mathilde Wesendonck/ Richard Wagner)		DB 2868 (IRX 1018)	17-0348-A in WCT-53 EX 2900563 HLM 7037 HQM 1176 LCT-1036

-II   UNPUBLISHED

2EA 2767-<u>I</u>	Schlafendes Jesuskind (Eduard Mörike/Hugo Wolf)	DB 2868 IRX 1014	COLH 123 SH-110

TWENTIETH CENTURY FOX

Wings of the Morning film soundtrack

<u>SUMMER 1936 (Elstree, Hertfordshire, England)</u>
w. orchestra

Believe Me If All Those Endearing Young Charms (Thomas Moore/Old Irish Air: "My Lodging is on the Cold Ground")		AU 4792 MRF 5
Killarney (Edmund O'Rourke writing as Edmund Falconer/Michael William Balfe)	Regal Records V.S. 4*	AU 4792 MRF 5
The Dawning of the Day (P. W. Joyce/Old Irish Air, arr. N. Clifford Page)**		AU 4792 MRF 5

BROADCAST (NYBC)

<u>11 OCTOBER 1936, SUNDAY (Nashville)</u>
w. EDWIN SCHNEIDER, piano
w. spoken introductions and close by McCormack

Just for Today (Sybil F. Partridge/Blanche Ebert Seaver)	AU 4792 GEMM 183 MRF 5
The Ould Turf Fire (Traditional/Old Irish Air, arr. Herbert Hughes)***	AU 4792 DOLB 7020 GEMM 183 MRF 5
The Star of the County Down (Traditional/Old English Air, arr. Herbert Hughes)***	A-110 AU 4792 AV-112 DOLB 7020 GEMM 183 MRF 5 UORC-107

<u>19 NOVEMBER 1936, THURSDAY (New York City)</u>
w. orchestra and EDWIN SCHNEIDER, piano
w. spoken introductions by McCormack

O Mary Dear (John McCormack/Old Irish Air: "Londonderry Air," arr. Edwin Schneider)	A-110 AV 112 DOLB 7020 GEMM 183 UORC-107
Ever In My Mind (Helen Taylor/Kennedy Russell)	GEMM 183

<u>27 DECEMBER 1936, SUNDAY (New York City)</u>
w. RCA Orchestra conducted by FRANK BLACK

* - Portion re-recorded to matrix CA 16287-2 and issued as part of Voices of the Stars "in aid of the Cinematograph Benevolent Fund," circa 1938.
** - Most of singing obscured by film dialogue.
*** - World premier of this arrangement.

w. spoken introduction by McCormack
Oh! What Bitter Grief is Mine ("Wie unglücklich   A-110
    bin ich")(Anonymous, trans. and arr.   AU 4792
    McCormack/Wolfgang Amadeus Mozart, K. 147)   AV-112
                                                                  DOLB 7020
                                                                  GEMM 183
                                                                  MRF 5
                                                                  UORC-107

w. EDWIN SCHNEIDER, piano
The Star of the County Down (Traditional/Old   A-110
    English Air, arr. Herbert Hughes)   AU 4792
                                                                  AV-112
                                                                  DOLB 7020
                                                                  GEMM 183
                                                                  MRF 5
                                                                  UORC-107

w. RCA Orchestra conducted by FRANK BLACK
The Silent Hour of Prayer (Helen Boardman Knox/   A-110
    Charles Wakefield Cadman)**   AU 4792
                                                                  AV-112*
                                                                  DOLB 7020
                                                                  ***
                                                                  GEMM 183
                                                                  MRF 5

BROADCAST (?)

2 JANUARY 1937, SATURDAY (Hollywood)
w. Ferde Grofé Orchestra conducted by FERDE GROFÉ
w. spoken introductions to his own and others' performances by McCormack
One Summer Morn (words and music by Sidney   UNPUBLISHED
    Richfield)

w. piano****
The Ould Turf Fire (Traditional/Old Irish Air,   UNPUBLISHED
    arr. Herbert Hughes)

w. Ferde Grofé Orchestra conducted by FERDE GROFÉ
THE TRIUMPH OF TIME AND TRUTH (George Frederic   UNPUBLISHED
    Handel): Dryads and Sylvans w. chorus
Come in, and Welcome (words and music by Kennedy UNPUBLISHED
    Russell)*****

BROADCAST (?)

1 FEBRUARY 1937, MONDAY (?)
w. piano
Just for Today (Sybil F. Partridge/Blanche Ebert   UNPUBLISHED
    Seaver)

BROADCAST (?)

13 MAY 1937, THURSDAY (Hollywood)
w. EDWIN SCHNEIDER, piano
w. spoken introduction by Bing Crosby
conversation with McCormack and Crosby with one   A-110
    remark by Edwin Schneider

* - In an attempt to disguise transcription source, producer of LP spliced in word
"me" in place of McCormack's "this broadcast."
** - Actual title, "Blessed Hour of Prayer," sometimes known as "The Silent Hour."
World premier.
*** - Spoken introduction omitted.
**** - McCormack says that this is his first time on the air without Schneider and
that pianist is friend of his and Schneider's.
***** - World premier.

So Do I Love You (words and music by Kennedy   A-110
   Russell)

Shannon River (Kathleen Egan/Reginald Morgan)   A-110

BROADCAST (NBC)

17 MARCH 1938, THURSDAY (ST. PATRICK'S DAY)(Hollywood)
w. EDWIN SCHNEIDER, piano
w. spoken introductions by McCormack
conversation with McCormack and Rudy Vallee   UNPUBLISHED
The Garden Where the Praties Grow (Johnny   A-110
   Patterson/Old Irish Air, arr. Samuel Liddle)*   AV-112
                                                               DOLB 7020
                                                               PPR-1
                                                               UORC-107

Hail, Glorious Saint Patrick (attrib. Sister   PPR-1
   Agnes)

BROADCAST (?)

17 APRIL 1938, SUNDAY (Hollywood)
accompaniment unknown
Maureen (words and music by Hugh S. Roberton)   UNPUBLISHED

BROADCAST (NBC Red Network)

25 APRIL 1938, MONDAY (Hollywood)
w. EDWIN SCHNEIDER, piano
w. spoken introductions by McCormack
The Bard of Armagh (Traditional/Old Irish Air,   PPR-1
   arr. Herbert Hughes)

The Star of the County Down (Traditional/Old   PPR-1
   English Air, arr. Herbert Hughes)

BROADCAST (BBC)

6 DECEMBER 1938, WEDNESDAY (London)
Scrapbook for 1903 w. Gertie Miller, Countess of UNPUBLISHED
   Dudley

8 DECEMBER 1938, FRIDAY (London)
w. GERALD MOORE, piano
Scrapbook for 1938 w. Patrick Kirwen   UNPUBLISHED
The Snowy Breasted Pearl (Sir Stephen Edward De UNPUBLISHED
   Vere/Old Irish Air: "Pearl of the White
   Breast," arr. Joseph Robinson)

ELECTRICAL & MUSICAL INDUSTRIES LIMITED

30 NOVEMBER 1939, THURSDAY (Studio 3, Abbey Road, London)
w. GERALD MOORE, piano (78.00rpm)
OEA 8320-I   The Old House (words and music   DA 1715   7P 211
              by Sir Frederick O'Connor)**   IR 206   COLH 124
                                                                EX 2900073
                                                                MKER 2002
                                                                P 69

     -II   UNPUBLISHED
OEA 8321-I   A Child's Prayer (Laura   DA 1715   7P 211
              Leycester/Pat Thayer)   IR 206

     -II   UNPUBLISHED

* - Rebroadcast on NBC's "Recollections at 30" show in 1958.
** - Written for McCormack's Albert Hall Farewell Performance and dedicated to him.

OEA 8322-I	The Star of the County Down (Traditional/Old English Air, arr. Herbert Hughes)	DA 1718 IR 200	7EB 6029 7ER 5188 7P 211 Arab. 8124 AV-133 COLH 124 EX 2900073 MKER 2002 P 69
-II		UNPUBLISHED	
OEA 8323-I	I'll Walk Beside You (Edward Lockton/Alan Murray)	DA 1718 IR 200	7P 211 BLP 1084 EX 2900073 P 69
-II		UNPUBLISHED	

12 APRIL 1940, FRIDAY (Studio 3, Abbey Road, London)
w. orchestra conducted by LAWRANCE A. COLLINGWOOD (78.00rpm)

OEA 8525-I	When You Wish Upon a Star (from "Pinocchio")(Ned Washington/ Leigh Harline)	DA 1729 IR 1033	EX 2900073 OASI-539 P 69
-II		UNPUBLISHED	
OEA 8526-I	Little Wooden Head (from "Pinocchio")(Ned Washington/ Leigh Harline)	DA 1729 IR 1033	BLP 1107 EX 2900073 P 69
-II		UNPUBLISHED	
OEA 8574-I	The Magic of Your Love (from "Gypsy Love")(Gustave Kahn and Clifford Grey/Franz Lehar, adapted by Herbert S. Stothart)	DA 1730 IR 207	P 69

2 MAY 1940, THURSDAY (Studio 3, Abbey Road, London)
w. orchestra conducted by WALTER GOEHR (78.00rpm)

OEA 8399-I	So Deep is the Night ("Tristesse")(Sonny Miller, after French/Viaud, after Chopin, Op. 10, No. 3)	DA 1730 IR 207	EX 2900073 FLPS 1856 ISLE 3001 MFP 1090 MFP 50331 OXLP-7644 P 69
-II		UNPUBLISHED	
OEA 8604-I	Mighty Lak' a Rose (Frank L. Stanton/Ethelbert W. Nevin)	DA 1740 (IR 1054)	BLP 1107 FLPS 1856 ISLE 3001 MFP 1090 MFP 50331 OXLP-7644 P 69
-II		UNPUBLISHED	
OEA 8605-I	My Treasure (Joan T. Barr/Joan Trevalsa)	DA 1740 IR 256	BLP 1107

19 JUNE 1940, WEDNESDAY (Studio 3, Abbey Road, London)
w. GERALD MOORE, piano (78.00rpm)

OEA 8806-I	Plasir d'amour (J. P. Claris de Florian/Giovanni Martini, arr. Fevrier)	DA 1829 IR 1042	EX 2900563 FLPS 1856 ISLE 3001 MFP 1090 MFP 50331 OXLP 7644 P 69

OEA 8806-II	Plasir d'amour (J. P. Claris de Florian/Giovanni Martini, arr. Fevrier)	UNPUBLISHED		
OEA 8807-I	Nina ("Tre giorni son che Nina") (Legrenzio Vincenzo Ciampi) (interpolated into Resta's LI TRE CICISBEI RIDICOLI)*		AGSA 61 (IR 1045)	COLH 123 EX 2900563 SH-110
OEA 8808-I	Echo Christina R. Rosetti/Lord Henry Somerset)		DA 1741 IR 305	
-II		UNPUBLISHED		
OEA 8809-I	Trees (Joyce Kilmer/Otto H. Rasbach)		DA 1741 IR 257	FLPS 1856 ISLE 3001 MFP 1090 MFP 50331 OXLP 7644 P 69
-II		UNPUBLISHED		

11 JULY 1940, THURSDAY (Studio 3, Abbey Road, London)
w. GERALD MOORE, piano (78.00rpm)

OEA 8820-1	Kashmiri Song (No. 3 of "Four Indian Love Lyrics" from "The Garden of Kama")(Lawrence Hope/Amy Woodforde-Finden)	2169-A	DA 1746	FLPS 1856 ISLE 3001 MFP 1090 MFP 50331 OXLP 7644 P 69
OEA 8821-1	Till I Wake (No. 4 of "Four Indian Love Lyrics" from "The Garden of Kama")(Lawrence Hope/Amy Woodforde-Finden)	2169-B	DA 1746 (IR 1053)	P 69
-2		UNPUBLISHED		
OEA 8822-1	The Lass With the Delicate Air (words and music by Michael Arne, arr. Lehmann)		AGSA 52	7ER 5054 Arab.8105-2 EX 2900563 P 69
OEA 8823-1	The Blind Ploughman (Margaret Radclyffe-Hall/Robert Coningsby Clark)	UNPUBLISHED**		
OEA 8824-1	Passing By (Anonymous/Edward Purcell-Cockram, writing as E. Purcell)		AGSA 57	7ER 5054 Arab.8105-2 COLH 124 EX 2900073 MKER 2002 P 69
OEA 8825-1	The Sweetest Flower that Blows (C. B. Hawley/Frederic Peterson)	UNPUBLISHED**		
-2		UNPUBLISHED		

9 AUGUST 1940, FRIDAY (Studio 3, Abbey Road, London)
w. GERALD MOORE, piano (78.00rpm)

OEA 8849-1	Oft in the Stilly Night (Thomas Moore/Old Scottish Air, arr. Edwin Schneider)		AGSA 56 (DA 1760) IR 1043	A-110 ANNA-1026 Avoc. 112 COLH 124 DOLB 7020 EX 2900073 MKER 2002 P 69
-2		UNPUBLISHED		

* - Formerly attributed to G. B. Pergolesi.
** - Extant test pressing.

OEA 8850-1	The Meeting of the Waters (Thomas Moore/Old Irish Air: "Old Head of Denis," arr. Edwin Schneider)	10-0041-A in DM-1358	DA 1752 IR 216	COLH 124 EX 2900073 MKER 2002 P 69
OEA 8851-1	The Gentle Maiden (from "Songs of Four Nations")(Harold Boulton, after Irish/Old Irish Air, arr. Arthur Somervell)		AGSA 55 (DA 1760) IR 1043 Pigott Company unnumbered *	A-110 ANNA-1026 AV-112 COLH 124 DOLB 7020 MKER 2002 UORC-107
-2		UNPUBLISHED		
OEA 8852-1	The Bard of Armagh (Traditional/ Old Irish Air, arr. Herbert Hughes)		DA 1752 IR 216	COLH 124 EX 2900073 MKER 2002 P 69
-2		UNPUBLISHED		

25 OCTOBER 1940, FRIDAY (Studio 3, Abbey Road, London)
w. GERALD MOORE, piano (78.00rpm)

OEA 8887-1	Silent Night (Joseph Mohr, trans. Douglas/Franz Gruber, arr. Woodgate)		DA 1755 IR 263	EX 2900073 P 69
-2		UNPUBLISHED		
OEA 8888-1	A Legend (Christ in His Garden) (No. 5 from "Songs for Young People")(Pleshtcheyev, trans. Hazel M. Lockwood/Piotr Ilyich Tchaikovsky, Op. 54)		DA 1755	EX 2900563
OEA 8889-1	Faith (Mainwaring/Gerald Carne)	2205-A	DA 1803 IR 297	
OEA 8890-1	All Through the Night ("Ar hyd y nos")(Walter Maynard, after Welsh/Old Welsh Air: "Poor Mary Ann")		DA 1756 IR 262	
OEA 8891-1	See Amid the Winter Snow (Reverend Edward Caswall/ Old English Air, arr. Goss (?))		DA 1756 IR 302	

17 DECEMBER 1940, TUESDAY (Studio 3, Abbey Road, London)
w. GERALD MOORE, piano (78.00rpm)

OEA 9062-1	There is a Green Hill ("Le Calvaire")(Francis Alexander, after French/Charles Gounod)		DA 1773 IR 1032	
OEA 9063-1	The Blind Ploughman (Marguerite Radclyffe-Hall/Robert Coningsby Clarke)		AGSA 59	ANNA-1026 Arab. 8124 P 69
-2		UNPUBLISHED		
OEA 9064-1	Oh! What Bitter Grief is Mine ("Wie unglücklich bin ich") (Anonymous, trans. and arr.		DA 1828 IR 1038	EX 2900563 P 69
-2	McCormack/Wolfgang Amadeus Mozart, K. 147)	UNPUBLISHED		
OEA 9065-1	Oh, Could I But Express in Song My Sorrow (Grigori Lishin, trans. Rosa Newmarch/Leonid Malashkin)		DA 1829 IR 1042	EX 2900073 P 69

* - Pirated 78rpm disc, probably re-recorded.

OEA 9066-1   Since First I Saw Your Face   IR 1060
                     (from "Musicke of Sundrie
                     Kindes")(Thomas Ford/Old
                     English Air, arr. Arthur
                     Somervell)

OEA 9067-1   Ye Banks and Braes o' Bonnie   DA 1762   COLH 124
                     Doon (Robert Burns/James   IR 260   MKER 2002
                     Miller, arr. Gerald Moore)

OEA 9068-1   Maiden of Morven (Traditional,   DA 1762
                     trans. Harold Boulton/Old   IR 1023
                     Scottish Air, arr. Malcolm
                     Lawson)

OEA 9069-1   Light of the Sunset Glow (from   UNPUBLISHED
      -2   "Evensong")(Curzon/   DA 1770   P 69
                     Easthope Martin, arr. Leslie   (IR 1054)
                     Taylor)

BROADCAST (BBC)
1940 (Drury Lane Theatre, London)
w. GERALD MOORE, piano
SEMELE (William Congreve/George Frederic Handel):   A-110
  Wher'er You Walk   ANNA-1026
                                                                      UORC-107

The Star of the County Down (Traditional/Old   ANNA-1026
  English Air, arr. Herbert Hughes)

I'll Walk Beside You (Edward Lockton/Alan Murray)   ANNA-1026

w. orchestra
If I Should Fall in Love Again (words and music   ANNA-1026
  by J. C. Poppwell) w. EVELYN LAYE, soprano

ELECTRICAL & MUSICAL INDUSTRIES LIMITED

28 JANUARY 1941, TUESDAY (Studio 3, Abbey Road, London)
w. GERALD MOORE, piano (78.00rpm)
OEA 9082-1   "God Keep You" Is My Prayer   DA 1770   FLPS 1856
                     (David Arale/Lilian Ray)   (IR 1058)   ISLE 3001
                                                                        MFP 1090
                                                                        MFP 50331
                                                                        OXLP 7644
                                                                        P 69

OEA 9083-1   At the Mid Hour of the Night   AGSA 60   A-110
                     (Thomas Moore/Old Irish Air: IR 1044   AV-112
                     "Molly My Dear," arr. Sir   DOLB 7020
                     Charles V. Stanford)   UORC-107

OEA 9084-1   When I Awake (Anonymous/Ellen   AGSA 58   ANNA-1026
                     Wright)   (IR 1046)   Arab. 8124

      -2   UNPUBLISHED
OEA 9085-1   Down By the Sally Gardens   DA 1778   EX 2900073
                     (William Butler Yeats/Old   IR 300   FLPS 1856
                     Irish Air: "The Maid of   ISLE 3001
                     Mourne Shore," arr. Herbert   MFP 1090
                     Hughes)   MFP 50331
                                                                        OXLP 7644
                                                                        P 69

OEA 9086-1   She Rested By the Broken Brook   DA 1778
                     (Robert Louis Stevenson/
                     Samuel Coleridge-Taylor)

6 MARCH 1941, THURSDAY (Studio 3, Abbey Road, London)
w. GERALD MOORE, piano (78.00rpm)

OEA 9099-1	Jesus Christ, the Son of God (from Cantata BWV 4, "Christ lag in Todesbanden")(trans.		DA 1773 IR 1032	AU 4792 MRF 5
-2	Paul England/Johann Sebastian Bach, edited West)	UNPUBLISHED		
OEA 9100-1	Jesus, Joy of Man's Desiring (from Cantata BWV 147, "Herz und Mund und Tat und Leben") (trans. ?/Johann Sebastian Bach, arr. Dame Myra Hess)		DA 1786 IR 388	AU 4792 EX 2900563 FLPS 1856 ISLE 3001 MFP 1090 MFP 50331 MRF 5 OXLP 7644 P 69
OEA 9201-1	The Street Sounds to the Soldiers' Tread (No. 5 from "A Shropshire Lad")(A. E. Housman/Arthur Somervell)		DA 1834	Roc. 5343
OEA 9202-1	Silent Noon (Dante Gabriel Rossetti/Ralph Vaughn Williams)		DA 1776 IR 305	COLH 124 EX 2900073 MKER 2002 P 69
OEA 9203-1	Loveliest of Trees (No. 1 from "A Shropshire Lad")(A. E. Housman/Arthur Somervell)		DA 1776 IR 301	EX 2900073 P 69
OEA 9204-1	White in the Moon the Long Road Lies (No. 7 from "A Shropshire Lad")(A. E. Housman/Arthur Somervell)		DA 1834	Roc. 5343

29 MAY 1941, THURSDAY (Studio 3, Abbey Road, London)
w. GERALD MOORE, piano (78.00rpm)

OEA 9314-1	The Dawn Will Break (Glanville/ Haydn Wood)		AGSA 55 (IR 1057)	ANNA-1026 Arab. 8124
-2		UNPUBLISHED		
OEA 9315-1	The Village That Nobody Knows (Harold Simpson/Haydn Wood)		AGSA 59	7ER 5054
OEA 9316-1	Praise Ye the Lord (from	UNPUBLISHED		
-2	"Cantata con Stromenti") (trans. McCormack/Siegfried Ochs, arr. F. W. Franke)*		DA 1786 IR 388	EX 2900563 HLM-7037 HQM-1176

25 JUNE 1941, WEDNESDAY (Studio 3, Abbey Road, London)
w. GERALD MOORE, piano (78.00rpm)

OEA 9326-1	Linden Lea (A Dorset Song) (William Barnes/Ralph Vaughn Williams)		DA 1791 IR 300	AU 4792 EX 2900073 HLM-7037 HQM-1176 MRF 5 P 69
OEA 9327-1	The White Peace (Fiona McCleod/ Arnold Box)		DA 1791 IR 299	HLM-7037 HQM-1176 P 69
-2		UNPUBLISHED		
OEA 9328-1	The Little Boats (Harold Boulton/Old Irish Air, arr. Herbert Hughes)		AGSA 52 (IR 1057)	ANNA-1026 Arab. 8124

* - Formerly attributed to George Frederic Handel.

OEA 9328-2	The Little Boats (Harold Boulton/Old Irish Air, arr. Herbert Hughes)	UNPUBLISHED	
OEA 9329-1	She Moved Through the Fair (Traditional, adapted by Padraic Colum/Old Irish Air, arr. Herbert Hughes)	DA 1813 IR 231	COLH 124 EX 2900073 MKER 2002 P 69
OEA 9330-1	No, Not More Welcome (Thomas Moore/Old Irish Air: "Erin to Gratton, " also "Luggelaw," arr. Frederick Keel)		cass.IV

26 AUGUST 1941, TUESDAY (Studio 3, Abbey Road, London)
w. GERALD MOORE, piano (78.00rpm)

OEA 9458-1	The Green Bushes (Traditional/ Old Irish Air, arr. P. J. Ryan)	AGSA 53 Pigott Company unnumbered *	7ER 5054 COLH 124 EX 2900073 MKER 2002 P 69
OEA 9459-1	Bantry Bay (Traditional/Old Irish Air, arr. James Lyman Molloy)	DA 1813 IR 231	EX 2900073 FLPS 1856 ISLE 3001 MFP 1090 MFP 50331 OXLP 7644 P 69
OEA 9460-1	Our Finest Hour (Heaton and John McCormack/Gerald Moore)	UNPUBLISHED	
OEA 9461-1	Maureen (words and music by Hugh S. Roberton)	AGSA 54	7ER 5054

17 SEPTEMBER 1941, WEDNESDAY (Studio 3, London)
w. GERALD MOORE, piano (78.00rpm)

OEA 9460-2 -3	Our Finest Hour (Heaton and John McCormack/Gerald Moore)	UNPUBLISHED 2205-B	DA 1803 IR 299
-4		UNPUBLISHED	

6 OCTOBER 1941, MONDAY (Studio 3, Abbey Road, London)
w. GERALD MOORE, piano (78.00rpm)

OEA 9478-1	Smilin' Thro (words and music by Arthur A. Penn)	DA 1805 IR 228	AU 4792 FLPS 1856 ISLE 3001 MFP 1090 MFP 50331 MRF 5 OXLP 7644
-2		UNPUBLISHED	
OEA 9479-1	The Devout Lover (Walter Herries Pollock/Maude Valerie White)	DA 1805 IR 228	
-2		UNPUBLISHED	
OEA 9487-1	O Promise Me (interpolated into "Robin Hood")(Clement Scott/ Reginald DeKoven)	AGSA 56 (IR 1053)	ANNA-1026 Arab. 8124
OEA 9488-1 -2	Will You Go With Me (Henry Brandon and Phil Park/Alan Murray)	UNPUBLISHED UNPUBLISHED	
OEA 9489-1	A Rose Still Blooms in Picardy Fred G. Bowles/Haydn Wood)	UNPUBLISHED	

* - Pirated 78rpm disc, probably re-recorded.

6 NOVEMBER 1941, THURSDAY (Studio 3, Abbey Road, London)
w. GERALD MOORE, piano (78.00rpm).
OEA 9497-1   Jerusalem (William Blake/Sir   DA 1817   P 69
                   Charles Hubert Hastings Parry)   IR 1031

OEA 9489-2   A Rose Still Blooms in Picardy   DA 1806
                   (Fred G. Bowles/Haydn Wood)
         -3   UNPUBLISHED

8 NOVEMBER 1941, SATURDAY (Studio 3, Abbey Road, London)
w. GERALD MOORE, piano (78.00rpm)
OEA 9488-3   Will You Go With Me (Henry   DA 1806
                   Brandon and Phil Park/Alan   IR 298
                   Murray)

25 NOVEMBER 1941, TUESDAY 1941 (Studio 3, Abbey Road, London)
w. GERALD MOORE, piano (78.00rpm)
2EA 9651-1   Night Hymn at Sea (Felicia D.   UNPUBLISHED
         -2   Hemans/Arthur Goring-Thomas)   MRF 5
                   w. MAGGIE TEYTE, soprano   RLS-716

2EA 9652-1*   Still as the Night (English words   Arab. 8124
                   by Mrs. J. P. Morgan/Alma   EJS-478
                   Goetze) w. MAGGIE TEYTE,   RLS-716
                   soprano   Roc. 5319

3 DECEMBER 1941, WEDNESDAY (Studio 3, Abbey Road, London)
w. GERALD MOORE, piano (78.00rpm)
OEA 9655-1   Off to Philadelphia (My Name is   AGSA 54   A-110
                   Paddy Leary)(Traditional,   IR 1056   AV-112
                   edited and revised by Stephen   COLH 124
                   Temple/Old Irish Air, arr.   DOLB 7020
                   Battison Haynes)   EX 2900073
                                                                  MKER 2002
                                                                  P 69
                                                                  UORC-107

OEA 9656-1   Come Back My Love (Since First I   DA 1809   OASI-624
                   Met Thee)(Sonny Miller/Grün,   IR 298
                   after "Romance in E-flat" by
                   Anton Rubinstein)

OEA 9657-1   Here in the Quiet Hills (P. J.   DA 1809
                   O'Reilly/Gerald Carne)   IR 297

         -2   UNPUBLISHED

16 DECEMBER 1941, TUESDAY (Studio 3, Abbey Road, London)
w. GERALD MOORE, piano (78.00rpm)
OEA 9666-1   God Bless America (Irving   UNPUBLISHED
         -2   Berlin, revised by McCormack/ UNPUBLISHED
                   Irving Berlin)
OEA 9667-1   The Battle Hymn of the Republic UNPUBLISHED
         -2   (Julia Ward Howe/William   UNPUBLISHED
                   Steffe, arr. Noel Johnson)

23 DECEMBER 1941, TUESDAY (Studio 3, Abbey Road, London)
w. GERALD MOORE, pianist (78.00rpm)
OEA 9666-3   God Bless America (Irving   DA 1808   OASI-619
                   Berlin, revised by McCormack/   IR 1021
         -4   Irving Berlin)   UNPUBLISHED
OEA 9667-3   The Battle Hymn of the Republic   DA 1808   OASI-619
                   (Julia Ward Howe/William   IR 1021
                   Steffe, arr. Noel Johnson)

BROADCAST (BBC)

* - Re-recorded on 24 December 1947 to matrices 2EA 9652-1T1, 1T2, 1T3.

2 JANUARY 1942, FRIDAY (house of Dame Irene Vanbrughn)*
w. GERALD MOORE, piano
w. spoken introduction by McCormack
I'll Walk Beside You (Edward Lockton/Alan Murray)   UORC-151

The Gentle Maiden (from "Songs of Four Nations") UNPUBLISHED
   (Harold Boulton, after Irish/Old Irish Air,
   arr. Arthur Somervell)

ELECTRICAL & MUSICAL INDUSTRIES LIMITED

26 MAY 1942, TUESDAY (Studio 3, Abbey Road, London)
w. GERALD MOORE, piano (78.00rpm)

OEA 9868-1	By the Lakes of Killarney	AGSA 60	A-110
	(Alfred P. Graves/Case)**	IR 1044	AV-112
			DOLB 7020
			UORC-107
OEA 9869-1	Love Thee Dearest, Love Thee	AGSA 53	A-110
	(Thomas Moore/Old Irish Air)	IR 1056	AV-112
			COLH 124
			DOLB 7020
			MKER 2002
			UORC-107
-2		UNPUBLISHED	
OEA 9870-1	Children's Prayer in Wartime	DA 1817	
	(Joseph McCarthy/Wolfe)	IR 1031	
-2		UNPUBLISHED	

10 AUGUST 1942, MONDAY (Studio 3, Abbey Road, London)
w. GERALD MOORE, piano (78.00rpm)

OEA 9887-1	One Love Forever (James	DA 1820	
	Dyrenforth/Kenneth		
-2	Leslie-Smith)	UNPUBLISHED	
OEA 9888-1	Say a Little Prayer (words and	DA 1820	P 69
	music by Daniel Gregory		
-2	Mason)	UNPUBLISHED	

10 SEPTEMBER 1942, THURSDAY (Studio 3, Abbey Road, London)
w. GERALD MOORE, piano (78.00rpm)

OEA 9276-1	Ave Verum Corpus (Traditional/	DA 1828	
	Wolfgang Amadeus Mozart,	IR 1038	
	K. 618, arr. Schmidt)		
-2		UNPUBLISHED	
OEA 9277-1	To Chloe (An Chloë)("Wenn die	AGSA 61	Arab.8105-2
	Lieb")(J. G. Jacobi, trans.	(IR 1045)	COLH 123
	McCormack (?)/Wolfgang		EX 2900563
	Amadeus Mozart, K, 524)		SH-110
OEA 9278-1	Waiting for You (Royden Barrie/	AGSA 58	ANNA-1026
	Montague Philips)	IR 1046	Arab. 8124

* - Rebroadcast 5 August 1942.
** - Label credits words to Fitzgerald.

Alphabetical Listing

Abschied, see The Farewell

ABSENT, Lx 2430	28 November	1907
Absent, B 14672-1	7 April	1914

ADESTE FIDELES, C 15849-1	31 March	1915
ADESTE FIDELES, CVE 36606-1	1 October	1926

Ah! lève toi, soleil, see ROMEO ET JULIETTE
Ah Mimi, tu piu non torni, see LA BOHEME

AH, MOON OF MY DELIGHT, C 10063-1	16 March	1911

Ai nostri monti, see IL TROVATORE

AIDA: CELESTE AIDA, Lxx 3173	7 September	1909

AIDA: TUTTO È FINITO...O TERRA ADDIO, C 14694-1	9 April	1914
AIDA: Tutto è finito...O terra addio, C 14694-2	9 April	1914

Alba Nascente, see The Happy morning waits

ALL ALONE, B 31523-1, (extant test pressing)	17 December	1924
ALL ALONE, B 31523-2	17 December	1924
All Alone, B 31523-3	17 December	1924

ALL'MEIN GEDANKEN (MINNELIED), BVE 37149-1	17 December	1926
ALL'MEIN GEDANKEN (MINNELIED), Song O' My Heart (35mm)		1929
All'mein Gedanken (Minnelied), Song O' My Heart (70mm)		1929

ALL THROUGH THE NIGHT, OEA 8890-1	25 October	1940

ALLERSEELEN, Bb 11339-1, (extant test pressing)	1 September	1927
ALLERSEELEN, Bb 11339-2	1 September	1927

All'erta! All'erta! O tempio piu non, see FAUST (Trio)
Alma mia, see FLORIDANTE
An die Leier, see To the Lyre

ANAKREONS GRAB, Bb 21030-1, (extant test pressing)	3 December	1930
ANAKREONS GRAB, Bb 21030-2	3 December	1930

Angel's Guard Thee, see JOCELYN

ANGEL'S SERENADE (LA LEGGENDA VOLACCA), C 14623-1	25 March	1914

ANNIE LAURIE, B 8683-1	4 March	1910
ANNIE LAURIE, BVE 40177-1, (extant test pressing)	13 October	1927
ANNIE LAURIE, BVE 40177-2	13 October	1927

Any Place is Heaven if You Are Near Me, B 20019-1	7 June	1917
ANY PLACE IS HEAVEN IF YOU ARE NEAR ME, B 20019-2	7 June	1917

Ar Hyd e Nos, see All Through the Night

As I Sit Here, OB 5305-1	7 September	1933
As I Sit Here, OB 5305-2	7 September	1933
As I Sit Here, OB 5305-3	7 September	1933
AS I SIT HERE, OB 5305-4	7 September	1933

ASTHORE, C 11817-1	2 April	1912
AT DAWNING, B 12704-1	11 December	1912
AT THE MID HOUR OF THE NIGHT, OEA 9083-1	28 January	1941
ATALANTA: COME MY BELOVED, Bb 5034-1	4 September	1924
ATTILA: Te sol quest'anima (Trio), B 14692-1	9 April	1914
ATTILA: Te sol quest'anima (Trio), B 14692-2	9 April	1914
AUCH KLEINE DINGE, OEA 2135-1	28 June	1935
Auf Flügeln des Gesanges, see On Wings of Song		
Auld Scotch Sangs, BVE 40178-1	13 October	1927
AULD SCOTCH SANGS, BVE 40178-2	13 October	1927
AUTOMNE, OB 3852-1	16 September	1932
Ave Maria (Bach-Gounod), C 13234-1	2 May	1913
Ave Maria (Bach-Gounod), C 14624-1	25 March	1914
AVE MARIA (BACH-GOUNOD), C 14624-2	31 March	1914
Ave Maria (Cornelius), Bb 20690-1	5 December	1930
AVE MARIA (CORNELIUS), Bb 20690-2	5 December	1930
AVE MARIA (MASCAGNI), B 14652-1	31 March	1914
AVE MARIA (SCHUBERT), C 14633-1	25 March	1914
AVE MARIA (SCHUBERT), CVE 49209-1	27 November	1928
AVE MARIA (SCHUBERT), CVE 49209-2	27 November	1928
AVE MARIA (SCHUBERT), CVE 49209-3	27 November	1928
AVE VERUM CORPUS, OEA 9276-1	10 September	1942
Ave Verum Corpus, OEA 9276-2	10 September	1942
AVENGING AND BRIGHT, Lx 2841	3 October	1908
AVOURNEEN, Edison 13146, (cylinder)	12 September	1904
AVOURNEEN, 5923b,	24 September	1904
AVOURNEEN, B 14673-1	7 April	1914
AWAKENING OF A PERFECT SPRING, Lx 2490	31 January	1908
BABY AROON, OEA 2124-1	27 June	1935
BABY AROON, OEA 2124-2, (extant test pressing)	27 June	1935
Badoer questa notte...O grido di quest'anima, see LA GIOCONDA		
BALLYNURE BALLAD, part of B 23904-1	2 April	1920
Bantry Bay, BVE 56193-1	17 October	1929
Bantry Bay, BVE 56193-2	17 October	1929
BANTRY BAY, OEA 9459-1	26 August	1941
BARBIERE DI SIVIGLIA: O il meglio mi...Numero quindici, 5205f	18 July	1911
BARBIERE DI SIVIGLIA: Se il mio nome, no matrix, (private)	5 November	1919
Bard of Armagh, B 15421-1	23 November	1914
Bard of Armagh, B 23792-1	30 March	1920
BARD OF ARMAGH, B 23792-2	30 March	1920
BARD OF ARMAGH, extant broadcast transcription	25 April	1938
BARD OF ARMAGH, OEA 8852-1	9 August	1940
Bard of Armagh, OEA 8852-2	9 August	1940
BAREFOOT TRAIL, B 23901-1	1 April	1920
Barefoot Trail, B 23901-2	1 April	1920
Battle Hymn of the Republic, OEA 9667-1	16 December	1941
Battle Hymn of the Republic, OEA 9667-2	16 December	1941
BATTLE HYMN OF THE REPUBLIC, OEA 9667-3	23 December	1941
BAY OF BISCAY, Lx 3168	7 September	1909
Beauteous Night, O Night of Love, see CONTES D'HOFFMAN		
BEAUTIFUL ISLE OF SOMEWHERE, B 14669-1	6 April	1914
BECAUSE, B 14671-1	7 April	1914
Because I Love You, BVE 37148-1	17 December	1926

BECAUSE I LOVE YOU, BVE 37148-2   17 December   1926

BEFORE MY WINDOW (THE CHERRY TREE), Bb 5116-1, (extant test)   24 September 1924
BEFORE MY WINDOW (THE CHERRY TREE), Bb 5116-2   24 September 1924
BEFORE MY WINDOW (THE CHERRY TREE), Bb 5116-3, (extant test)   24 September 1924

Beherzigung, 2B 2276-1   31 May   1932
BEHERZIGUNG, 2B 2276-2, (extant test pressing)   31 May   1932
BEHERZIGUNG, 2B 2276-3   31 May   1932

Belgium Forever, see Forward Belgium

BELIEVE ME IF ALL THOSE ENDEARING YOUNG CHARMS, Edison 13191   12 September 1904
Believe Me If All Those Endearing Young Charms, 5882b   19 September 1904
Believe Me If All Those Endearing Young Charms, 6453a   19 September 1904
Believe Me If All Those Endearing Young Charms, 6464Ei   23 September 1904
BELIEVE ME IF ALL THOSE ENDEARING YOUNG CHARMS, 6464WD2   23 September 1904
BELIEVE ME IF ALL THOSE ENDEARING YOUNG CHARMS, 5931b   24 September 1904
BELIEVE ME IF ALL THOSE ENDEARING YOUNG CHARMS, 5932b   24 September 1904
Believe Me If All Those Endearing Young Charms, B 8537-1   7 January   1910
Believe Me If All Those Endearing Young Charms, B 8537-2   4 March   1910
BELIEVE ME IF ALL THOSE ENDEARING YOUNG CHARMS, B 8537-3   16 March   1911
BELIEVE ME IF ALL THOSE ENDEARING YOUNG CHARMS, OEA 2129-1   28 June   1935
Believe Me If All Those Endearing Young Charms, OEA 2129-2   28 June   1935
BELIEVE ME IF ALL THOSE ENDEARING YOUNG CHARMS, extant broadcast   20 August   1935
BELIEVE ME IF ALL THOSE ENDEARING YOUNG CHARMS, film   1936

Bella figlia dell'amore (quartet), see RIGOLETTO

BELOVED I AM LONELY, BVE 40167-1, (extant test pressing)   11 October   1927
BELOVED I AM LONELY, BVE 40167-2, (extant test pressing)   11 October   1927

Ben Bolt, B 14675-1   7 April   1914
BEN BOLT, B 14675-2   7 April   1914

Beneath the Moon of Lombardy, B 23758-1   4 March   1920
BENEATH THE MOON OF LOMBARDY, B 23758-2   4 March   1920

Beneath the Quivering Leaves, see JOCELYN
Berceuse, see JOCELYN

BIRD SONGS AT EVENTIDE, BVE 40166-1, (extant test pressing)   11 October   1927
BIRD SONGS AT EVENTIDE, BVE 40166-2   11 October   1927

Bitterness of Love, Bb 21040-1   4 December   1930
BITTERNESS OF LOVE, Bb 21040-2   4 December   1930

BLESS THIS HOUSE, OB 3850-1   16 September   1932
Bless This House, OB 3850-2   16 September   1932

Blessed Hour of Prayer, see Silent Hour of Prayer

BLIND PLOUGHMAN, OEA 8823-1, (extant test pressing)   11 July   1940
BLIND PLOUGHMAN, OEA 9063-1   17 December   1940
Blind Ploughman, OEA 9063-2   17 December   1940

BOHEME, LA: AH MIMI, TU PIU NON TORNI, C 8737-1   23 March   1910

BOHEME, LA: CHE GELIDA MANINA, Lxx 2791   29 August   1908
BOHEME, LA: CHE GELIDA MANINA, Lxx 2791-2   29 August   1908
BOHEME, LA: Che gelida manina, C 8589-1   1 February   1910
BOHEME, LA: CHE GELIDA MANINA, C 8589-2   1 February   1910

BOHEME, LA: O Soave Fanciulla, B 14658-1   2 April   1914
BOHEME, LA: O soave fanciulla, B 14658-2   2 April   1914
BOHEME, LA: O soave fanciulla, B 14658-3   2 April   1914
BOHEME, LA: O SOAVE FANCIULLA, B 14658-4   8 April   1914
BOHEME, LA: O soave fanciulla, B 14658-5   8 April   1914

BOHEMIAN GIRL, THE: WHEN OTHER LIPS, Lx 2619   30 March   1908
BOHEMIAN GIRL, THE: WHEN OTHER LIPS, B 14677-1   7 April   1914
BOHEMIAN GIRL, THE: WHEN OTHER LIPS, B 14677-2   11 May   1916
BOHEMIAN GIRL, THE: When other lips, BVE 14677-3   23 December   1925
BOHEMIAN GIRL, THE: WHEN COLDNESS OR DECEIT, Song O' My Heart (35mm)   1929
BOHEMIAN GIRL, THE: When coldness or deceit, Song O' My Heart (70mm)   1929

Bonny Wee Thing, B 14668-1   6 April   1914
BONNY WEE THING, B 14668-2   6 April   1914

BOYS OF WEXFORD, Sterling 613 (cylinder)	5 July	1906
BOYS OF WEXFORD, Lx 1567	4 December	1906
Bridal Dawn, B 29873-1	9 April	1924
Bridal Dawn, B 29873-2	9 April	1924
BRIDAL DAWN, B 29873-3	9 April	1924
Brown Bird Singing, BVE 34176-1	23 December	1925
BROWN BIRD SINGING, BVE 34176-2	23 December	1925
BY THE LAKES OF KILLARNEY, OEA 9868-1	26 May	1942
BY THE SHORT CUT TO THE ROSSES, BVE 41546-1	13 January	1928
BY THE SHORT CUT TO THE ROSSES, BVE 41546-2	13 January	1928
Calling Me Back to You, BVE 36376-1	30 September	1926
CALLING ME BACK TO YOU, BVE 36376-2	30 September	1926
CALLING ME BACK TO YOU, extant broadcast transcription	1 January	1927
Calling Me Home to You, B 21808-1	30 April	1918
CALLING ME HOME TO YOU, B 21808-2	30 April	1918

Calm as the Night, see Still As the Night

CANDLE LIGHT, OEA 406-1	24 August	1934

Cantata BWV 4 (Bach), see Jesus Christ, the Son of God
Cantata BWV 147 (Bach), see Jesu, Joy of Man's Desiring
Cantata con Stromenti, see Praise Ye the Lord

Carmé, B 16091-1	10 June	1915
CARMÉ, B 16091-2	10 June	1915
CARMEN: See here thy flower, Lx 2795-1	31 August	1908
CARMEN: Il fior che avevi a me, Lxx 3138	5 September	1909
CARMEN: Il fior che avevi a me, C 8538-1	7 January	1910

CARMEN: Parle moi de ma mère, see CARMEN: Votre mère...

CARMEN: Votre mère avec moi...Ma mère je la vois, C 13028-1	28 March	1913
CARMEN: Votre mère avec moi...Ma mère je la vois, C 13028-2	28 March	1913
CARMEN: VOTRE MÈRE AVEC MOI...MA MÈRE JE LA VOIS, C 13028-3	1 May	1913
CARMEN: Votre mère avec moi...Ma mère je la vois, C 13028-4	1 May	1913

Caro amor, see IL PASTOR FIDO

CAVALLERIA RUSTICANA: O LOLA, Lx 2488	31 January	1908

Champs paternels! Hébron douce vallée, see JOSEPH EN ÉGYPTE

CHARM ME ASLEEP, OB 3855-1	16 September	1932

Celeste Aida, see AIDA
Che gelida manina, see LA BOHEME
Cherry Tree, see Before My Window

CHILDREN'S PRAYER IN WARTIME, OEA 9870-1	26 May	1942
Children's Prayer in Wartime, OEA 9870-2	26 May	1942
CHILD'S PRAYER, OEA 8321-1	30 November	1939
Child's Prayer, OEA 8321-2	30 November	1939
CHILD'S SONG, Lx 2502	3 February	1908
CHILD'S SONG, B 11816-1	2 April	1912

Chiudo gli occhi, see MANON

Christ in Flanders, B 23454-1	5 November	1919
Christ in Flanders, B 23454-2	5 November	1919

Christ in His Garden, see Legend: Christ in His Garden

CHRIST ON THE MOUNT OF OLIVES: JEHOVAH, HEAR ME, CVE 58684-1	27 February	1930
CHRIST ON THE MOUNT OF OLIVES: JEHOVA, DU MEIN VATER, CVE 58684-2	27 February	1930
CHRIST ON THE MOUNT OF OLIVES: MY HEART IS SORE, CVE 58685-1	27 February	1930
CHRIST WENT UP INTO THE HILLS ALONE, CVE 38388-1	4 May	1927

CHRISTUS AM ÖLBERG, see CHRIST ON THE MOUNT OF OLIVES

CID, LE: O Souverain, O Juge, O Pere, C 11831-1	5 April	1912

CLOTHS OF HEAVEN, Bb 11347-1   2 September 1927
CLOTHS OF HEAVEN, OEA 2182-1   23 July   1935

COME BACK MY LOVE, OEA 9656-1   3 December 1941

COME BACK TO ERIN, 6468a   23 September 1904
COME BACK TO ERIN, 5934b   24 September 1904
COME BACK TO ERIN, Edison Bell 6450-I (cylinder)   3 November 1904
COME BACK TO ERIN, Edison Bell 6450-II (cylinder)   10 November 1904
COME BACK TO ERIN, Edison Bell 6450-III (cylinder)   10 November 1904
COME BACK TO ERIN, Edison Bell 6450-IV (cylinder)   10 November 1904
COME BACK TO ERIN, Sterling 682 (cylinder)   5 July   1906
COME BACK TO ERIN, Lx 1579   5 December 1906
COME BACK TO ERIN, L 1580   5 December 1906
COME BACK TO ERIN, B 8588-1   1 February 1910

COME IN AND WELCOME, extant broadcast transcription   2 January   1938

COME INTO THE GARDEN, MAUDE, C 15846-1   30 March   1915

Come My Beloved, see ATALANTA

Come Where My Love Lies Dreaming, B 14678-1   8 April   1914
COME WHERE MY LOVE LIES DREAMING, B 14678-2   8 April   1914

CONTES D'HOFFMAN: BEAUTEOUS NIGHT, B 17655-1   10 May   1916

Cradle Song 1915, B 17672-1   11 May   1916
CRADLE SONG 1915, B 17672-2   11 May   1916

Cradle Song, see O Men From the Fields

CROPPY BOY, Sterling 615 (cylinder)   5 July   1906
CROPPY BOY, Lx 1568   4 December 1906

Crossroads, BVE 48191-1   21 November 1928
Crossroads, BVE 48191-2   21 November 1928

CRUCIFIX, B 18391-1, (extant test pressing)   21 September 1916
Crucifix, B 18391-2   8 June   1917
CRUCIFIX, B 18391-3   8 June   1917

Dai campi, dai prati, see MEFISTOFELE

DAWN WILL BREAK, OEA 9414-1   29 May   1941
Dawn Will Break, OEA 9414-2   29 May   1941

Dawning of the Day, OEA 424-1   29 August   1934
DAWNING OF THE DAY, OEA 424-2   29 August   1934
DAWNING OF THE DAY, film (Wings of the Morning)   1936

DEAR LITTLE SHAMROCK, Edison Bell 6442-I (cylinder)   3 November 1904
DEAR LITTLE SHAMROCK, Edison Bell 6442-II (cylinder)   10 November 1904
DEAR LITTLE SHAMROCK, Edison Bell 6442-III (cylinder)   10 November 1904
DEAR LITTLE SHAMROCK, Edison Bell 6442-IV (cylinder)   10 November 1904
DEAR LITTLE SHAMROCK, Sterling 683 (cylinder)   5 July   1906
DEAR LITTLE SHAMROCK, Lx 1569   4 December 1906
DEAR LITTLE SHAMROCK, L 1581   5 December 1906
DEAR LITTLE SHAMROCK, B 8819-1   8 April   1910

DEAR LOVE, REMEMBER ME, B 12763-1   3 January   1913

Dear Old Pal of Mine, B 21811-1   1 May   1918
DEAR OLD PAL OF MINE, B 21811-2   1 May   1918
Dear Old Pal of Mine, BVE 41543-1   13 January   1928
DEAR OLD PAL OF MINE, BVE 41543-2   13 January   1928
DEAR OLD PAL OF MINE, BVE 41543-3, (extant test pressing)   13 January   1928

Del tempio al limitar, see LA PÊCHEURS DE PERLES

DESOLATION, Bb 11336-1   1 September 1927
DESOLATION, Bb 11336-2   1 September 1927

Devotion, BVE 32541-1   24 April   1924
DEVOTION, BVE 32541-2   24 April   1925

DEVOUT LOVER, OEA 9479-1   6 October   1941
Devout Lover, OEA 9479-2   6 October   1941

DON GIOVANNI: IL MIO TESORO, C 17647-1	9 May	1916

Donna e mobile, La, see RIGOLETTO
Down by the Green Bushes, see The Green Bushes

DOWN BY THE SALLY GARDENS, OEA 9085-1	28 January	1941
Down by the Sally Gardens, OEA 9085-2	28 January	1941
DOWN IN THE FOREST, B 13035-1	28 March	1913
Dream, B 14676-1	7 April	1914
DREAM, B 14675-2	7 April	1914
DREAM OF SPRING, Bb 11337-1	1 September	1927
Dream of Spring, Bb 11337-2	1 September	1927
DREAM ON LITTLE SOLDIER BOY, B 22253-1	24 September	1924
Dream On Little Soldier Boy, B 22253-2	24 September	1924
Dream Once Again, B 28605-1	25 September	1923
DREAM ONCE AGAIN, B 28605-2	25 September	1923
DREAMS, B 17646-1	9 May	1916
Drink to Me Only With Thine Eyes, C 8587-1	1 February	1910
Drink to Me Only With Thine Eyes, C 8587-2	1 February	1910
DRINK TO ME ONLY WITH THINE EYES, C 8587-3	4 March	1910
DRINK TO ME ONLY WITH THINE EYES, 2EA 2751-1	31 March	1936
Drink to Me Only With Thine Eyes, 2EA 2751-2	31 March	1936

Dryads and Sylvans, see THE TRIUMPH OF TIME AND TRUTH

Du Bist die Ruh', Cc 5030-1	4 September	1924
DU BIST DIE RUH', Cc 5030-2	4 September	1924
DU MEINES HERZENS KRÖNELEIN, Bb 11338-1, (extant test pressing)	1 September	1927
DU MEINES HERZENS KRÖNELEIN, Bb 11338-2	1 September	1927

E lucevan le stelle, see TOSCA

EARL BRISTOL'S FAREWELL, OEA 2127-1	27 June	1935
ECHO, OEA 8808-1	19 June	1940
Echo, OEA 8808-2	19 June	1940
Eileen, B 19448-1	5 April	1917
EILEEN, B 19448-2	5 April	1917
EILEEN ALLANAH, 6469a	23 September	1904
EILEEN ALLANAH, 5938b	26 September	1904
Eileen Allanah, 5939b	26 September	1904
EILEEN ALLANAH, Edison Bell 6444-I (cylinder)	3 November	1904
EILEEN ALLANAH, Edison Bell 6444-II (cylinder)	3 November	1904
EILEEN ALLANAH, Edison Bell 6444-III (cylinder)	10 November	1904
EILEEN ALLANAH, Edison Bell 6444-IV (cylinder)	10 November	1904
EILEEN ALLANAH, B 13231-1	2 May	1913
EILEEN AROON, Lx 3156	7 September	1909
Eileen Aroon, B 11824-1	3 April	1912
EILEEN AROON, B 11824-2	3 April	1912

Eily Mavourneen, see THE LILY OF KILLARNEY

ELISIR D'AMORE: Una furtiva lagrima, C 8536-1	7 January	1910
ELISIR D'AMORE: UNA FURTIVA LAGRIMA, C 8536-2	7 January	1910
EVENING SONG, AN, C 10135-1, (Blumenthal)	30 March	1911
Evening Song, The, B 15838-1, (Hadley)	29 March	1915
Evening Song, The, B 15838-2	29 March	1915
EVENING SONG, THE, B 15838-3	30 March	1915
EVER IN MY MIND, OEA 2747-1	31 March	1936
EVER IN MY MIND, extant broadcast transcription	19 November	1936
FAIRY GLEN, Lx 3155	7 September	1909
FAIRY STORY BY THE FIRE, B 27045-1, (extant test pressing)	20 October	1922
Fairy Story By the Fire, Bb 11344-1	2 September	1927
FAIRY STORY BY THE FIRE, Bb 11344-2	2 September	1927

FAIRY STORY BY THE FIRE, Song O' My Heart (35mm)	August	1929
Fairy Story By the Fire, Song O' My Heart (70mm)	August	1929
FAIRY STORY BY THE FIRE, BVE 58596-1, (extant test pressing)	21 February	1930
Fairy Tree, Bb 21027-1	3 December	1930
Fairy Tree, Bb 21027-2	3 December	1930
FAIRY TREE, Bb 21027-3	3 December	1930
FAITH, OEA 8889-1	25 October	1940
Fallen Leaf, BVE 38387-1	4 May	1927
Fallen Leaf, BVE 38387-2	4 May	1927
FALLEN LEAF, BVE 38387-3	4 May	1927
FAR APART, Bb 21028-1	3 December	1930
FAR AWAY BELLS, BVE 36361-1	28 September	1926
FAR AWAY BELLS, BVE 36361-2, (extant test pressing)	28 September	1926
FAREWELL, Lx 2431, (Liddle)	28 November	1907
FAREWELL, Lx 2431-2	28 November	1907
FAREWELL, B 11819-1	2 April	1912
Farewell, part of CVE 49213-1, (Schubert)	28 November	1928
Farewell, part of CVE 49213-2	28 November	1928
FAREWELL, part of CVE 49213-3	28 November	1928
FAUST: ALL'ERTA! ALL'ERTA! (Trio), 4188f	12 May	1910
FAUST: ALL'ERTA! ALL'ERTA! (Trio), 4190f	12 May	1910
FAUST: SALVE DIMORA CASTA E PURA, C 8694-1	10 March	1910
FAVORITA, LA: Spir'to gentil, Lxx 3152	7 September	1909
FAVORITA, LA: SPIR'TO GENTIL, Lxx 3152-2	7 September	1909
FELDEINSAMKEIT, Bb 5095-1	19 September	1924
Feldeinsamkeit, Bb 5095-2	19 September	1924
FILLE DU REGIMENT, LA: PER VIVER VICINO A MARIA	23 March	1910
First Rose of Summer, B 22692-1	16 April	1919
FIRST ROSE OF SUMMER, B 22692-2	16 April	1919
FLIRTATION, B 16092-1	10 June	1915
FLORIDANTE: Alma mia, extant broadcast transcription	18 September	1934
Flow Gently, Deva, C 18390-1	21 September	1916
Flow Gently, Deva, C 18390-2	21 September	1916
Flow Gently, Deva, C 18390-3	8 June	1917
Flow Gently, Deva, C 18390-4	8 June	1917
FOGGY DEW, 5944b, (Graves)	26 September	1904
FOGGY DEW, Lx 2842 (Graves)	3 October	1908
FOGGY DEW, B 12767-1 (Milligan)	3 January	1913
For All Eternity, B 17653-1	10 May	1916
FORGOTTEN, B 16760-1	10 November	1915
FORTUNIO: J'AMAIS LA VIEILLE MAISON GRISE, Bb 11341-1	2 September	1927
FORTUNIO: J'AMAIS LA VIEILLE MAISON GRISE, Bb 11341-2	2 September	1927
FORTUNIO: J'amais la vieille maison grise, BVE 56190-1	16 October	1929
FORTUNIO: J'AMAIS LA VIEILLE MAISON GRISE, BVE 56190-2, (test)	16 October	1929
Forward Belgium (Belgium Forever), B 15418-1	23 November	1914
Fra poco a me ricovero, see LUCIA DI LAMMERMOOR		
FRIEND O' MINE, OEA 409-1	24 August	1934
From the Land of Sky Blue Waters, B 13232-1	2 May	1913
FUNICULI, FUNICULA, B 14679-1	8 April	1914
Ganymed, 2B 2277-1	31 May	1932
GANYMED, 2B 2277-2	31 May	1932
Ganymed, 2B 2277-3	31 May	1932
Garden in the Rain, BVE 51621-1	12 April	1929
GARDEN IN THE RAIN, BVE 51621-2	12 April	1929

Garden Where the Praties Grow, Bb 21036-1   4 December   1930
GARDEN WHERE THE PRATIES GROW, Bb 21036-2   4 December   1930
GARDEN WHERE THE PRATIES GROW, extant broadcast transcription   17 March   1938

GATEWAY OF DREAMS, BVE 48181-1   19 November 1928
Gateway of Dreams, BVE 48181-2   19 November 1928

GENTLE MAIDEN, OEA 8851-1   9 August   1940
Gentle Maiden, OEA 8851-2   9 August   1940
GENTLE MAIDEN, extant broadcast transcription   2 January   1942

GIOCONDA, LA: BADOER QUESTA NOTTE...O GRIDO DI QUEST'ANIMA, 5206f 18 July   1911

GIOIELLI DELLA MADONNA, I: T'ERI UN GIORNA AMMALATO, HO 201 af   15 July   1912

Girl I Left Behind Me, B 20028-1   8 June   1917
Girl I Left Behind Me, B 20028-2   8 June   1917

Giunto sul passo, see MEFISTOFELE

GOD BE WITH OUR BOYS TONIGHT, B 21663-1   5 April   1918
GOD BE WITH OUR BOYS TONIGHT, B 21663-2   30 April   1918
GOD BE WITH OUR BOYS TONIGHT, B 21663-3   1 May   1918

God Bless America, OEA 9666-1   16 December 1941
God Bless America, OEA 9666-2   16 December 1941
GOD BLESS AMERICA, OEA 9666-3   23 December 1941

GOD GAVE ME FLOWERS, PBVE 61097-1, (extant test pressing)   6 July   1931
GOD GAVE ME FLOWERS, PBVE 61097-2, (extant test pressing)   6 July   1931

GOD KEEP YOU IS MY PRAYER, OEA 9082-1   28 January   1941

GOD SAVE IRELAND, Sterling 612 (cylinder)   5 July   1906
GOD SAVE IRELAND, Lx 1566   4 December   1906

God's Hand, B 16763-1   10 November 1915
GOD'S HAND, B 16763-2, (extant test pressing)   10 November 1915

GOLDEN LOVE, B 14670-1   7 April   1914

GOODBYE, C 13219-1   1 May   1913

GOODBYE, SWEETHEART, GOODBYE, Lx 3169   7 September 1909
GOODBYE, SWEETHEART, GOODBYE, Lx 3169   2 May   1913

GREEN BUSHES, OEA 9458-1   26 August   1941

GREEN ISLE OF ERIN, Edison 13153 (cylinder)   12 September 1904
Green Isle of Erin, 5926b   24 September 1904
GREEN ISLE OF ERIN, 5927b   24 September 1904
GREEN ISLE OF ERIN, Edison Bell 6443-I (cylinder)   3 November 1904
GREEN ISLE OF ERIN, Edison Bell 6443-II (cylinder)   3 November 1904
GREEN ISLE OF ERIN, Edison Bell 6443-III (cylinder)   10 November 1904
GREEN ISLE OF ERIN, Edison Bell 6443-IV (cylinder)   10 November 1904
GREEN ISLE OF ERIN, Lx 1576   5 December   1906
GREEN ISLE OF ERIN, Lxx 3160   7 September 1909
Green Isle of Erin, C 11818-1   2 April   1912
Green Isle of Erin, C 11818-2   5 April   1912
GREEN ISLE OF ERIN, 2EA 2748-1   31 March   1936

Green Pastures, OEA 419-1   29 August   1934
GREEN PASTURES, OEA 419-2   29 August   1934

HAIL, GLORIOUS SAINT PATRICK, extant broadcast transcription   17 March   1938

Happy Morning Waits, B 10136-1   30 March   1911
HAPPY MORNING WAITS, B 10136-2   31 March   1911

HARK! HARK! THE LARK!, part of CVE 49214-1, (extant test pressing)28 November 1928
Hark! Hark! the Lark!, part of CVE 49214-2   28 November 1928
Hark! Hark! the Lark!, part of CVE 49214-3   6 December 1928
HARK! HARK! THE LARK!, part of CVE 49214-4   7 December 1928
Hark! Hark! the Lark!, part of CVE 49214-5   7 December 1928

Harp That Once Through Tara's Halls, 6472a   23 September 1904
HARP THAT ONCE THROUGH TARA'S HALLS, B 11833-1   5 April   1912
HARP THAT ONCE THROUGH TARA'S HALLS, Bb 21037-1   4 December   1930

HAS SORROW THY YOUNG DAYS SHADED, 5940b	26 September 1904
HAS SORROW THY YOUNG DAYS SHADED, Lx 2840	3 October 1908
HAS SORROW THY YOUNG DAYS SHADED, C 8753-1	25 March 1910
HEAVY HOURS ARE ALMOST PAST, extant broadcast transcription	18 October 1933
HERE IN THE QUIET HILLS, OEA 9657-1	3 December 1941
Here in the Quiet Hills, OEA 9657-2	3 December 1941
Herr, was trägt der Boden hier, BRC-HQ 34-1	2 November 1931
Herr, was trägt der Boden hier, BRC-HQ 34-2	2 November 1931
HERR, WAS TRÄGT DER BODEN HIER, OEA 2134-1	28 June 1935
HOLY CHILD, BVE 37147-1	17 December 1926
HOLY CHILD, BVE 37147-2,(extant test pressing)	17 December 1926
HOLY CHILD, extant broadcast transcription	1 January 1927
Holy City, B 12709-1	11 December 1912
Holy God We Praise Thy Name, B 29870-1	9 April 1924
HOLY GOD WE PRAISE THY NAME, B 29870-2	9 April 1924
Holy Night, part of CVE 49237-1	6 December 1928
Holy Night, part of CVE 49237-2	6 December 1928
HOLY NIGHT, part of CVE 49237-3	6 December 1928
HOME TO ATHLONE, Edison Bell 10085-A (cylinder)	2 October 1905
HOME TO ATHLONE, Edison Bell 10085-B (cylinder)	2 October 1905
HOME TO ATHLONE, Edison Bell 10085-C (cylinder)	2 October 1905
HOME TO ATHLONE, Edison Bell 10085-D (cylinder)	2 October 1905
HONOR AND LOVE, B 23756-1	4 March 1920
Honor and Love, B 23756-2	4 March 1920
Horch! Horch! Die Lerche!, see Hark! Hark! The Lark!	
Hour of Love, B 15840-1	29 March 1915
HOUSE LOVE MADE FOR YOU AND ME, OEA 425-1	29 August 1934
HOW FAIR THIS SPOT, Bb 5101-1	19 September 1924
How Fair This Spot, Bb 5101-1	19 September 1924
Hurdy Gurdy Man, see The Organ Grinder	
Hymn to Christ the King, 2B 3419-1	27 May 1932
HYMN TO CHRIST THE KING, 2B 3419-2	27 May 1932
I FEEL YOU NEAR ME, Song O' My Heart (35mm)	1929
I Feel You Near Me, Song O' My Heart (70mm)	1929
I Feel You Near Me, BVE 58587-1	19 February 1930
I Feel You Near Me, BVE 58587-2	19 February 1930
I FEEL YOU NEAR ME, BVE 58587-3	21 February 1930
I Hear a Thrush at Eve, B 13218-1	1 May 1913
I HEAR A THRUSH AT EVE, B 13218-2	1 May 1913
I HEAR YOU CALLING ME, Lxx 2852	3 October 1908
I HEAR YOU CALLING ME, Lxx 2854	3 October 1908
I HEAR YOU CALLING ME, B 8695-1	10 March 1910
I HEAR YOU CALLING ME, B 8695-2	16 March 1911
I HEAR YOU CALLING ME, B 8695-3	16 June 1921
I HEAR YOU CALLING ME, BVE 40172-1	12 October 1927
I HEAR YOU CALLING ME, BVE 40172-2, (extant test pressing)	12 October 1927
I HEAR YOU CALLING ME, Song O' My Heart (35mm)	1929
I Hear You Calling Me, Song O' My Heart (70mm)	1929
I KNOW OF TWO BRIGHT EYES, Lx 2845	3 October 1908
I KNOW OF TWO BRIGHT EYES, B 11823-1	3 April 1912
I KNOW OF TWO BRIGHT EYES, OB 3856-1, (extant test pressing)	16 September 1932
I Know of Two Bright Eyes, OB 5310-1	13 September 1933
I KNOW OF TWO BRIGHT EYES, OB 5310-2	13 September 1933
I Know of Two Bright Eyes, OB 5310-3	13 September 1933
I Know of Two Bright Eyes, OB 5310-4	13 September 1933
I Look Into Your Garden, BVE 32539-1	24 April 1925
I LOOK INTO YOUR GARDEN, BVE 32539-2	24 April 1925

```
I Love to Hear You Singing, BVE 51613-1              10 April      1929
I LOVE TO HEAR YOU SINGING, BVE 51613-2              10 April      1929

I Met an Angel, OEA 2131-1                           28 June       1935
I MET AN ANGEL, OEA 2131-2                           28 June       1935

I Need Thee Every Hour, B 14695-1                     9 April      1914
I Need Thee Every Hour, B 14695-2                     9 April      1914

I SAW FROM THE BEACH, Bb 5119-1                      24 September  1924
I Saw From the Beach, Bb 5119-2                      24 September  1924
I SAW FROM THE BEACH, Bb 5119-3, (extant test pressing) 24 September 1924
I Saw From the Beach, Bb 5119-4                      24 September  1924

I SENT MY LOVE TWO ROSES, Lx 2545                    29 February   1908

I Wait Beneath Thy Window, Love, see Serenata

IDEALE, Lx 3157                                       7 September  1909
Ideale, B 21813-1                                     1 May        1918
Ideale, B 21813-2                                     1 May        1918

IF I KNOCK THE 'L' OUT OF KELLY, no matrix, (private)  9 May      1917

IF I SHOULD FALL IN LOVE AGAIN, extant broadcast transcription    1940

Il fior che avevi a me, see CARMEN
Il mio tesoro, see DON GIOVANNI

I'll Sing Thee Songs of Araby, Lx 2796              31 August     1908
I'LL SING THEE SONGS OF ARABY, Lx 2796-2            31 August     1908
I'LL SING THEE SONGS OF ARABY, B 12760-1             2 January    1913

I'LL WALK BESIDE YOU, OEA 8323-1                    30 November   1939
I'll Walk Beside You, OEA 8323-2                    30 November   1939
I'LL WALK BESIDE YOU, extant broadcast transcription              1940
I'LL WALK BESIDE YOU, extant broadcast transcription 2 January    1942

I'm Falling in Love With Someone, C 10062-1         16 March      1911
I'M FALLING IN LOVE WITH SOMEONE, B 10062-1         17 March      1911

Immenso vienteso...A vien al boscaglia, see LAKME
In a Persian Garden, see Ah, Moon of My Delight

In an Old Fashioned Town, B 18386-1                 20 September  1916
In an Old Fashioned Town, B 18386-2                 20 September  1916

Indiana Moon, B 29864-1                              8 April      1924
INDIANA MOON, B 29864-2                              8 April      1924

In Flanders' Fields, B 22254-1                      24 September  1918

In her simplicity, see MIGNON

In Old Madrid, C 18389-1                            20 September  1916

IN SWEET CONTENT, OEA 2746-1                        31 March      1936
In Sweet Content, OEA 2746-2                        31 March      1936

In Waldeseinsamkeit, Bb 5032-1                       4 September  1924
IN WALDESEINSAMKEIT, Bb 5032-2                       4 September  1924

IRELAND, MOTHER IRELAND, Song O' My Heart (35mm)                  1929
Ireland, Mother Ireland, Song O' My Heart (70mm)                  1929
Ireland, Mother Ireland, BVE 56192-1               17 October    1929
IRELAND, MOTHER IRELAND, BVE 56192-2, (extant test pressing) 17 October 1929
Ireland, Mother Ireland, BVE 56192-3               21 February   1930
IRELAND, MOTHER IRELAND, BVE 56192-4               21 February   1930

IRELAND, MY SIRELAND, B 19447-1                      5 April      1917
Ireland, My Sireland, B 19447-2                      5 April      1917

IRISH EMIGRANT, Edison 13145 (cylinder)            12 September  1904
IRISH EMIGRANT, 6470a                              23 September  1904
Irish Emigrant, 5943b                              26 September  1904
IRISH EMIGRANT, C 10060-1                           16 March      1911
IRISH EMIGRANT, BVE 41544-1                         13 January    1928
IRISH EMIGRANT, BVE 41544-2                         13 January    1928

IS SHE NOT PASSING FAIR, OB 3853-1                  16 September  1932
```

IT'S A LONG WAY TO TIPPERARY, B 15415-1   23 November   1914
It's a Long Way to Tipperary, B 15415-2   23 November   1914
IT'S A LONG WAY TO TIPPERARY, no matrix, (private)   31 March   1915

Jeannie With the Light Brown Hair, OEA 412-1   24 August   1934
JEANNIE WITH THE LIGHT BROWN HAIR, OEA 412-2   24 August   1934

JEANNINE, I DREAM OF LILAC TIME, BVE 48179-1   19 November   1928
Jeannine, I Dream of Lilac Time, BVE 48179-2   19 November   1928
Jeannine, I Dream of Lilac Time, BVE 48179-3   19 November   1928

Jehova, Du mein Vater, see CHRIST ON THE MOUNT OF OLIVES
Jehovah, hear me, see CHRIST ON THE MOUNT OF OLIVES

JERUSALEM, OEA 9497-1   6 November   1941

JESU, JOY OF MAN'S DESIRING, from BWV 147, OEA 9100-1   6 March   1941

JESUS CHRIST, THE SON OF GOD, from BWV 4, OEA 9099-1   6 March   1941
Jesus Christ, the Son of God, from BWV 4, OEA 9099-2   6 March   1941

Jesus, My Lord, My God, My All, B 27031-1   17 October   1922
Jesus, My Lord, My God, My All, B 27031-2   17 October   1922
Jesus, My Lord, My God, My All, B 27031-3   20 October   1922
JESUS, MY LORD, MY GOD, MY ALL, B 27031-4   20 October   1922

JOCELYN: BENEATH THE QUIVERING LEAVES (BERCEUSE), C 14626-1   25 March   1914

JOSEPH EN ÉGYPTE: CHAMPS PATERNELS!, C 20898-1   23 October   1917
JOSEPH EN ÉGYPTE: Champs Paternels!, C 20898-2   23 October   1917

JUNE BROUGHT THE ROSES, BVE 32536-1   23 April   1925
JUNE BROUGHT THE ROSES, BVE 32536-2, (extant test pressing)   23 April   1925

Jungling an der Quelle, Der, B 28611-1   26 September 1923

JUST A CORNER OF HEAVEN TO ME, BVE 56189-1, (extant test pressing)16 October   1929
JUST A CORNER OF HEAVEN TO ME, BVE 56189-2, (extant test pressing)16 October   1929

Just a Cottage Small, BVE 33819-1   27 October   1925
Just a Cottage Small, BVE 33819-2   27 October   1925
JUST A COTTAGE SMALL, BVE 33819-3   27 October   1925

JUST FOR TODAY, BVE 36363-1   28 September 1926
Just For Today, BVE 36363-2   28 September 1926
Just For Today, Song O' My Heart (35mm)   1929
Just For Today, Song O' My Heart (70mm)   1929
JUST FOR TODAY, extant broadcast transcription   11 October   1936
JUST FOR TODAY, extant broadcast transcription   1 February 1937

KASHMIRI SONG, OEA 8820-1   11 July   1940

Kathleen Mavourneen, 5946b   26 September 1904
KATHLEEN MAVOURNEEN, 5947b   26 September 1904
KATHLEEN MAVOURNEEN, Edison Bell 6446-I (cylinder)   3 November   1904
KATHLEEN MAVOURNEEN, Edison Bell 6446-II (cylinder)   3 November   1904
KATHLEEN MAVOURNEEN, Edison Bell 6446-III (cylinder)   10 November   1904
KATHLEEN MAVOURNEEN, Edison Bell 6446-IV (cylinder)   10 November   1904
Kathleen Mavourneen, Lx 1577   5 December   1906
KATHLEEN MAVOURNEEN, Lx 1577-2   5 December   1906
KATHLEEN MAVOURNEEN, C 10061-1   16 March   1911
Kathleen Mavourneen, CVE 39889-1   11 October   1927
Kathleen Mavourneen, CVE 39889-2   11 October   1927
KATHLEEN MAVOURNEEN, CVE 39889-3   11 October   1927

Keep the Home Fires Burning, B 20017-1   7 June   1917
KEEP THE HOME FIRES BURNING, B 20017-2   7 June   1917

KERRY DANCE, C 17648-1   9 May   1916
Kerry Dance, 2EA 2749-1   31 March   1936
KERRY DANCE, 2EA 2749-2   31 March   1936

KILLARNEY, Edison 13152 (cylinder)   12 September 1904
KILLARNEY, 6466a   23 September 1904
KILLARNEY, 5930b   24 September 1904
KILLARNEY, 5933b   24 September 1904
KILLARNEY, Edison Bell 6445-I (cylinder)   3 November   1904

```
KILLARNEY, Edison Bell 6445-II (cylinder)                    3 November   1904
KILLARNEY, Edison Bell 6445-III (cylinder)                  10 November   1904
KILLARNEY, Edison Bell 6445-IV (cylinder)                   10 November   1904
KILLARNEY, Lx 1582                                           5 December   1906
KILLARNEY, C 8594-1                                          3 January    1910
KILLARNEY, film (Wings of the Morning)                                    1936

Kingdom Within Your Eyes, B 27044-1                         20 October    1922
KINGDOM WITHIN YOUR EYES, B 27044-2                         20 October    1922

KITTY, MY LOVE, WILL YOU MARRY ME, Song O' My Heart (35mm)                1929
Kitty, My Love, Will You Marry Me, Song O' My Heart (70mm)                1929

KOMM BALD, Bb 5094-1, (extant test pressing)               19 September   1924
KOMM BALD, Bb 5094-2                                        19 September   1924


Lady Divine, BVE 51614-1                                    10 April      1929
Lady Divine, BVE 51614-2                                    10 April      1929

LAKME: IMMENSO VIENTESO...A VIEN AL BOSCAGLIA, B 8750-1     25 March      1910

Land of Might Have Been, B 27084-1                          20 November   1922
Land of Might Have Been, B 27084-2                          20 November   1922
Land of Might Have Been, B 27084-3                          20 November   1922

Larboard Watch, B 18392-1                                   21 September  1916
Larboard Watch, B 18392-2                                   21 September  1916

LASS WITH THE DELICATE AIR, OEA 8822-1                      11 July       1940

LAST HOUR, B 24036-1                                         5 May        1920
Last Hour, B 24036-2                                         5 May        1920

Last Rose of Summer, B 8684-1                                4 March      1910
Last Rose of Summer, Bb 5037-1                               4 September  1924
Last Rose of Summer, Bb 5037-2                               4 September  1924
Last Rose of Summer, BRC-HQ 32-1                             2 November   1931

LAST WATCH, Lxx 3164                                         7 September  1909

Learn to Smile, B 25351-1                                   16 June       1921
Learn to Smile, B 25351-2                                   16 June       1921
LEARN TO SMILE, B 25351-3, (extant test pressing)          17 June       1921
LEARN TO SMILE, B 25351-4                                   17 June       1921

LEGEND: CHRIST IN HIS GARDEN, OEA 8888-1                    25 October    1940

Leggenda Volacca, La, see Angel's Serenade
Leiermann, Der, see The Organ Grinder

LIEBE HAT GELOGEN, B 28610-1                                26 September  1923
Liebe hat gelogen, Bb 11343-1                                2 September  1927
LIEBE HAT GELOGEN, Bb 11343-2                                2 September  1927

Life Lesson, OEA 421-1                                      29 August     1934
LIFE LESSON, OEA 421-2                                      29 August     1934

Light in Your Eyes, see The Rainbow of Love

Light of the Sunset Glow, OEA 9069-1                        17 December   1940
LIGHT OF THE SUNSET GLOW, OEA 9069-2                        17 December   1940

LIKE STARS ABOVE, Lx 2487                                   31 January    1908
LIKE STARS ABOVE, C 11814-1                                  2 April      1912
Like Stars Above, C 11814-2                                  5 April      1912

LILIES OF LORRAINE, BVE 36374-1                             30 September  1926
Lilies of Lorraine, BVE 36374-2                             30 September  1926

LILY OF KILLARNEY: EILY MAVOURNEEN, Edison Bell 6447-I (cylinder)  3 November  1904
LILY OF KILLARNEY: EILY MAVOURNEEN, Edison Bell 6447-II (cylinder) 3 November  1904
LILY OF KILLARNEY: EILY MAVOURNEEN, Edison Bell 6447-III(cylinder)10 November  1904
LILY OF KILLARNEY: EILY MAVOURNEEN, Edison Bell 6447-IV (cylinder)10 November  1904

LILY OF KILLARNEY: THE MOON HATH RAISED HER LAMP ABOVE, B 14693-1  9 April     1914
LILY OF KILLARNEY: The moon hath raised her lamp above, B 14693-2  9 April     1914

LINDEN LEA, OEA 9326-1                                      25 June       1941

LITTLE BIT OF HEAVEN, B 16764-1                             10 November   1915
```

LITTLE BOATS, OEA 9328-1	25 June	1941
Little Boats, OEA 9328-2	25 June	1941
Little Boy Blue, B 17650-1	9 May	1916
LITTLE BOY BLUE, B 17650-2	9 May	1916
LITTLE BOY BLUE, Song O' My Heart (35mm)		1929
Little Boy Blue, Song O' My Heart (70mm)		1929
Little Boy Blue, BVE 58595-1	21 February	1930
LITTLE BOY BLUE, BVE 58595-2	21 February	1930
LITTLE CHILD OF MARY, OEA 2122-1	27 June	1935
Little Child of Mary, OEA 2122-2	27 June	1935
Little Grey Home in the West, B 14666-1	6 April	1914
LITTLE GREY HOME IN THE WEST, B 14666-2	6 April	1914
LITTLE HOUSE I PLANNED, OEA 2132-1	28 June	1935
Little Love, A Little Kiss, B 13220-1	1 May	1913
LITTLE LOVE, A LITTLE KISS, B 13220-2	1 May	1913
Little Love, A Little Kiss, B 13220-3	6 April	1914
Little Mother of Mine, B 21810-1	30 April	1918
LITTLE MOTHER OF MINE, B 21810-2	30 April	1918
Little Pal, BVE 51620-1	12 April	1929
LITTLE PAL, BVE 51620-2	12 April	1929
Little Pal, BVE 51620-3	12 April	1929
Little Prayer For Me, OEA 420-1	29 August	1934
LITTLE PRAYER FOR ME, OEA 420-2	29 August	1934
Little Silver Ring, see The Silver Ring		
LITTLE TOWN IN THE OLD COUNTY DOWN, B 25353-1, (test pressing)	17 June	1921
LITTLE TOWN IN THE OLD COUNTY DOWN, B 25353-2	17 June	1921
LITTLE WOODEN HEAD, OEA 8526-1	12 April	1940
Little Wooden Head, OEA 8526-2	12 April	1940
LITTLE YVETTE, B 29867-1	8 April	1924
Little Yvette, B 29867-2	8 April	1924
LOLITA, Lxx 2962	5 December	1908
Lolita, Lx 3150	7 September	1909
LOLITA, Lx 3150-2	7 September	1909
Londonderry Air, see O Mary Dear, Would God I Were the Tender Apple Blossom		
LORD IS MY LIGHT, Lx 2558	2 March	1908
LORD IS MY LIGHT, B 20899-1	23 October	1917
LOST CHORD, C 27043-1	20 October	1922
Lost Chord, C 27043-2	20 October	1922
Love Bells, B 18388-1	20 September	1916
Love Bells, B 18388-2	20 September	1916
Love, Here is My Heart, B 18384-1	20 September	1916
LOVE, HERE IS MY HEART, B 18384-2	20 September	1916
LOVE ME AND I'LL LIVE FOREVER, BVE 34159-1	17 December	1925
Love Me and I'll Live Forever, BVE 34159-2	17 December	1925
LOVE ME AND I'LL LIVE FOREVER, BVE 34159-3	17 December	1925
Love Sends a Little Gift of Roses, B 28601-1	24 September	1923
LOVE SENDS A LITTLE GIFT OF ROSES, B 28601-2	24 September	1923
LOVE SONG, B 29866-1	8 April	1924
Love Song, B 29866-2	8 April	1924
LOVE THEE DEAREST, Edison 13154	12 September	1904
LOVE THEE DEAREST, 6462a	23 September	1904
LOVE THEE DEAREST, OEA 9869-1	26 May	1942
Love Thee Dearest, OEA 9869-2	26 May	1942
LOVELIEST OF TREES, OEA 9203-1	6 March	1941
Lover, Come Back to Me, BVE 51622-1	12 April	1929
LOVER, COME BACK TO ME, BVE 51622-2	12 April	1929

LOVE'S GARDEN OF ROSES, B 21812-1	1 May	1918
Love's Garden of Roses, B 21812-2	1 May	1918
LOVE'S GOLDEN TREASURY, Lx 2432	28 November	1907
LOVE'S GOLDEN TREASURY, Lx 2432-2	28 November	1907
Love's Old Sweet Song, CVE 40165-1	11 October	1927
LOVE'S OLD SWEET SONG, CVE 40165-2	11 October	1927
LOVE'S PHILOSOPHY, Lx 2965	5 December	1908
Love's Roses, OB 5307-1	7 September	1933
LOVE'S ROSES, OB 5307-2	7 September	1933
LOVE'S ROSES, extant broadcast transcription	20 August	1935
LOVE'S SECRET, BVE 35893-1	1 October	1926
LOVE'S SECRET, Bb 21032-1	3 December	1930
LOVE'S SECRET, OEA 2180-1	23 July	1935
Love's Secret, OEA 2180-2	23 July	1935
LOW BACKED CAR, B 13031-1	28 March	1913
Low Backed Car, B 13031-2	28 March	1913
LUCIA DI LAMMERMOOR: FRA POCO A ME RICOVERO, C 8535-1	3 January	1910
LUCIA DI LAMMERMOOR: TU CHE A DIO SPIEGASTI, C 8740-1	23 March	1910

Lullaby, see JOCELYN
Lunge da lei per me...De'miei bollenti spiriti, see LA TRAVIATA

LUOGHI SERENI E CARI, Bb 5033-1, (extant test pressing)	4 September	1924
LUOGHI SERENI E CARI, Bb 5033-2	4 September	1924
LUOGHI SERENI E CARI, Bb 5033-3, (extant test pressing)	4 September	1924
Luoghi Sereni e Cari, BVE 34160-1	17 December	1925
LUOGHI SERENI E CARI, BVE 34160-2	17 December	1925
LUOGHI SERENI E CARI, Song O' My Heart (35mm)		1929
Luoghi Sereni e Cari, Song O' My Heart (70mm)		1929
MACUSHLA, B 10134-1	30 March	1911
MAGIC OF YOUR LOVE, OEA 8574-1	12 April	1940
MAGPIE'S NEST, Song O' My Heart (35mm)		1929
Magpie's Nest, Song O' My Heart (70mm)		1929
MAIDEN OF MORVEN, OEA 9068-1	17 December	1940
Mainacht, Bb 5031-1	4 September	1924
MAINACHT, Bb 5031-2	4 September	1924
MAIRE, MY GIRL, C 11813-1	2 April	1912

Maison Grise, La, see FORTUNIO: J'amais la vieille maison grise

MANON: Chiudo gli occhi, B 12764-1	3 January	1913
MANON: CHIUDO GLI OCCHI, B 12764-2	3 January	1913

M'appari, see MARTA

Marcheta, B 29865-1	8 April	1924
MARCHETA, B 29865-2	8 April	1924
MARCHETA, BVE 29865-3	12 April	1927
Marinari, B 10137-1	31 March	1911
Marinari, B 10137-2	4 April	1911
MARINARI, B 10137-3	4 April	1911
MARITANA: THERE IS A FLOWER THAT BLOOMETH, Lx 2844	3 October	1908
MARITANA: There is a flower that bloometh, B 12710-1	11 December	1912
MARITANA: THERE IS A FLOWER THAT BLOOMETH, B 12710-2	11 December	1912
MARTA: M'appari, B 17009-1	14 January	1916

Mary Dear, see O Mary Dear

MARY OF ALLENDALE, Lx 2850	3 October	1908
MARY OF ARGYLE, B 14674-1	7 April	1914
Mary of Argyle, B 14674-2	7 April	1914
MATTINATA, Lx 2793, (extant test pressing)	31 August	1908

MATTINATA, Lx 2793-2	31 August	1908
Mattinata, B 12766-1	3 January	1913
Mattinata, B 12766-2	3 January	1913
MAUREEN, extant broadcast transcription	17 April	1938
MAUREEN, OEA 9461-1	26 August	1941
Mavis, B 15420-1	23 November	1914
MAVIS, B 15420-2	23 November	1914
MEETING OF THE WATERS, Edison 13142 (cylinder)	12 September	1904
MEETING OF THE WATERS, 5925b	24 September	1904
MEETING OF THE WATERS, OEA 8850-1	9 August	1940
Meine Seele ist erschüttert, see CHRIST ON THE MOUNT OF OLIVES		
MEISTERSINGER, DIE: Morning was gleaming, C 16089-1	10 June	1915
MEISTERSINGER, DIE: Morning was gleaming, C 16089-2	10 June	1915
MEISTERSINGER, DIE: MORNING WAS GLEAMING, C 17656-1	10 May	1916
MEFISTOFELE: DAI CAMPI, DAI PRATI, B 12705-1	11 December	1912
MEFISTOFELE: GIUNTO SUL PASSO, B 12706-1	11 December	1912
Mi par d'udir ancora, see LA PÊCHEURS DE PERLES		
MIGHTY LAK' A ROSE, OEA 8604-1	2 May	1940
Mighty Lak' a Rose, OEA 8604-2	2 May	1940
MIGNON: IN HER SIMPLICITY, Lx 2797	31 August	1908
Minnelied, see All'mein Gedanken		
MINSTREL BOY, 6471a	23 September	1904
MINSTREL BOY, 5945b	26 September	1904
MINSTREL BOY, Edison Bell 6448-I (cylinder)	3 November	1904
MINSTREL BOY, Edison Bell 6448-II (cylinder)	3 november	1904
MINSTREL BOY, Edison Bell 6448-III (cylinder)	10 November	1904
MINSTREL BOY, Edison Bell 6448-IV (cylinder)	10 November	1904
MINSTREL BOY, B 8590-1	1 February	1910
MIRA LA BIANCA LUNA, 5203f	18 July	1911
MOLLY BAWN, Edison 13144 (cylinder)	12 September	1904
MOLLY BAWN, 5928b	24 September	1904
MOLLY BAWN, C 8752-1	25 March	1910
MOLLY BAWN, C 8752-2	17 March	1911
MOLLY BRANNIGAN, B 12765-1	3 January	1913
Moon hath raised her lamp above, see THE LILY OF KILLARNEY		
Moonlight and Roses, BVE 32535-1	23 April	1925
MOONLIGHT AND ROSES, BVE 32535-2	23 April	1925
Moonlight and Roses, BVE 32535-3	23 April	1925
Morgen, Bb 5115-1	24 September	1924
Morgen, Bb 5115-2	24 September	1924
MORGEN, Bb 5115-3	24 September	1924
MORNING, B 15847-1	30 March	1915
Morning was gleaming, see DIE MEISTERSINGER		
Mother in Ireland, B 27030-1	17 October	1922
MOTHER IN IRELAND, B 27030-2	17 October	1922
Mother in Ireland, B 27030-3	17 October	1922
MOTHER MACHREE, B 10069-1	17 March	1911
Mother Machree, BVE 40173-1	12 October	1927
MOTHER MACHREE, BVE 40173-2	12 October	1927
MOTHER MY DEAR, BVE 33821-1	27 October	1927
Mother My Dear, BVE 33821-2	27 October	1927
Mother My Dear, BVE 33821-3	27 October	1927
MOTHER O' MINE, B 13034-1	28 March	1913
MOUNTAIN LOVERS, Lxx 3135	5 September	1909
MUSIC OF THE NIGHT, OEA 404-1, (extant test pressing)	24 August	1934

MUSIC OF THE NIGHT, OEA 404-2   24 August   1934

Musicke of Sundrie Kindes, see Since First I Saw Your Face, Passing By
My commander as envoy bids me come...No country can my own outvie, see NATOMA

MY DARK ROSALEEN, Lx 2132   1 June   1907
My Dark Rosaleen, Lxx 3151   7 September   1909
MY DARK ROSALEEN, Lxx 3151-2   7 September   1909

MY DREAMS, B 12758-1   2 January   1913

My heart is sore within me, see CHRIST ON THE MOUNT OF OLIVES

MY IRISH SONG OF SONGS, B 21809-1   30 April   1918
My Irish Song of Songs, B 21809-2   30 April   1918

MY LAGAN LOVE, B 8751-1   25 March   1910

MY MOONLIGHT MADONNA, OB 5309-1   7 September   1933

MY QUEEN, Lxx 3163   7 September   1909

MY TREASURE, OEA 8605-1   2 May   1940

MY WILD IRISH ROSE, B 14667-1   6 April   1914

Myrra, see I Know of Two Bright Eyes

Nacht und Träume, see Holy Night

NATION ONCE AGAIN, Sterling 614 (cylinder)   5 July   1906
NATION ONCE AGAIN, Lx 1565   4 December   1906

NATOMA: My commander as envoy...No country can, C 11822-1   3 April   1912

NEARER, MY GOD, TO THEE, B 13225-1   1 May   1913

NECKLACE OF LOVE, OEA 422-1   29 August   1934

NEUES ANDACHTIGES KINDELWIEGEN, OEA 408-1   24 August   1934

NEXT MARKET DAY, part of B 23904-1   2 April   1920

Night Hymn at Sea, BVE 34166-1   18 December   1925
Night Hymn at Sea, BVE 34166-2   18 December   1925
Night Hymn at Sea, BVE 34166-3   18 December   1925
NIGHT HYMN AT SEA, BVE 34166-4, (extant test pressing)   24 December   1925
NIGHT HYMN AT SEA, BVE 34166-5 (extant test pressing)   24 December   1925
Night Hymn at Sea, BVE 34166-6   24 December   1925
NIGHT HYMN AT SEA, extant broadcast transcription   1 January   1926
Night Hymn at Sea, 2EA 9651-1   25 November   1941
NIGHT HYMN AT SEA, 2EA 9651-2, (extant test pressing)   25 November   1941

NIL, LE, C 14625-1   25 March   1914

NINA (TRE GIORNI SON CHE NINA), OEA 8807-1   19 June   1940

NIRVANA, C 12708-1   11 December   1912

NO, NOT MORE WELCOME, OEA 9330-1, (extant test pressing)   25 June   1941

NON É VER, B 17651-1   9 May   1916

NONE BUT THE LONELY HEART, BVE 40170-1, (extant test pressing) 12 October   1927
NONE BUT THE LONELY HEART, BVE 40170-2   12 October   1927

Norah O'Neale, BVE 56198-1   18 October   1929
NORAH O'NEALE, BVE 56198-2   18 October   1929

NORAH, THE PRIDE OF KILDARE, 6467a   23 September   1904

NOW SLEEPS THE CRIMSON PETAL, Bb 11346-1   2 September   1927
NOW SLEEPS THE CRIMSON PETAL, Bb 11346-2   2 September   1927

O CEASE THY SINGING, MAIDEN FAIR, B 23906-1   2 April   1920
O Cease Thy Singing, Maiden Fair, B 23906-2   2 April   1920
O Cease Thy Singing, Maiden Fair, B 23906-3   2 April   1920

O Come All Ye Faithful, see Adeste Fideles

O DEL MIO AMATO BEN, Bb 5035-1   4 September   1924

O Dry Those Tears, C 13224-1   1 May   1913

O Dry Those Tears, B 24034-1	5 May	1920
O Dry Those Tears, B 24034-2	5 May	1920

O il meglio mi scordavo...Numero quindici, see IL BARBIERE DI SIVIGLIA
O Lola, see CAVALLERIA RUSTICANA

O LOVELY NIGHT, Lxx 3158	7 September	1909
O MARY DEAR, BVE 56188-1, (extant test pressing)	16 October	1929
O Mary Dear, BVE 56188-2	18 October	1929
O MARY DEAR, Song O' My Heart (35mm), (Spanish version only)		1929
O Mary Dear, Song O' My Heart (70mm)		1929
O MARY DEAR, OEA 2128-1, (extant test pressing)	28 June	1935
O MARY DEAR, OEA 2128-2	28 June	1935
O MARY DEAR, extant broadcast transcription	19 November	1936
O MEN FROM THE FIELDS (CRADLE SONG), OEA 2183-1	23 July	1935
O PROMISE ME, OEA 9487-1	6 October	1941

O Sing to Me the Auld Scotch Sangs, see Auld Scotch Sangs
O Sleep! Why dost thou leave me, see SEMELE
O soave fanciulla, see LA BOHEME
O Souverain, O Juge, O Pere, see LE CID

OFF TO PHILADELPHIA, OEA 9655-1	3 December	1941
OFT IN THE STILLY NIGHT, Lx 2135	1 June	1907
OFT IN THE STILLY NIGHT, Lx 3166	7 September	1909
OFT IN THE STILLY NIGHT, OEA 8849-1	9 August	1940
Oft in the Stilly Night, OEA 8849-2	9 August	1940
OH, COULD I BUT EXPRESS IN SONG MY SORROW, OEA 9065-1	17 December	1940
OH GATHERING CLOUDS, OEA 2121-1	27 June	1935
OH, HOW I MISS YOU TONIGHT, BVE 33465-1	14 October	1925
Oh, How I Miss You Tonight, BVE 33465-2	14 October	1925
OH! THAT IT WERE SO!, Bb 5100-1, (extant test pressing)	19 September	1924
OH! WHAT BITTER GRIEF IS MINE, extant broadcast transcription	27 December	1936
OH! WHAT BITTER GRIEF IS MINE, OEA 9064-1	17 December	1940
Oh! What Bitter Grief is Mine, OEA 9064-2	17 December	1940
OLD HOUSE, OEA 8320-1	30 November	1939
Old House, OEA 8320-2	30 November	1939
Old Refrain, B 17008-1	14 January	1916
OLD REFRAIN, B 17008-2	14 January	1916
OLD SACRED LULLABY, OEA 407-1	24 August	1934
ON WINGS OF SONG, extant broadcast transcription	1 January	1927

On with the motley, see I PAGLIACCI

ONCE AGAIN, Edison Bell 6449-I (cylinder)	3 November	1904
ONCE AGAIN, Edison Bell 6449-II (cylinder)	10 November	1904
ONCE AGAIN, Edison Bell 6449-III (cylinder)	10 November	1904
ONCE AGAIN, Edison Bell 6449-IV (cylinder)	10 November	1904
Once in a Blue Moon, OB 3851-1	16 September	1932
ONCE IN A BLUE MOON, OB 3851-2	16 September	1932
ONE LOVE FOREVER, OEA 9887-1	10 August	1942
One Love Forever, OEA 9887-2	10 August	1942
ONE SUMMER MORN, extant broadcast transcription	2 January	1938
Only You, B 22693-1	16 April	1919
ONLY YOU, B 22693-2	16 April	1919
Onward Christian Soldiers, B 29871-1	9 April	1924
ONWARD CHRISTIAN SOLDIERS, B 29871-2, (extant test pressing)	9 April	1924
Ora pro nobis, B 17645-1	9 May	1916
Organ Grinder, part of CVE 49213-1	28 November	1928
Organ Grinder, part of CVE 49213-2	28 November	1928
ORGAN GRINDER, part of CVE 49213-3	28 November	1928

OULD PLAID SHAWL, Lx 3167   7 September 1909

OULD TURF FIRE, extant broadcast transcription   11 October   1936
OULD TURF FIRE, extant broadcast transcription   2 January   1938

Our Finest Hour, OEA 9460-1   26 August   1941
Our Finest Hour, OEA 9460-2   17 September 1941
OUR FINEST HOUR, OEA 9460-3   17 September 1941
Our Finest Hour, OEA 9460-4   17 September 1941

Out of Sight But Ever in My Mind, see Ever in My Mind

Padraic the Fiddler, Bb 5118-1   24 September 1924
PADRAIC THE FIDDLER, Bb 5118-2   24 September 1924
PADRAIC THE FIDDLER, Bb 5118-3, (extant test pressing)   24 September 1924

PAGLIACCI: TO ACT! WITH MY HEART...ON WITH THE MOTLEY, Lx 2489   31 January   1908

PAIR OF BLUE EYES, Song O' My Heart (35mm)   1929
Pair of Blue Eyes, Song O' My Heart (70mm)   1929
PAIR OF BLUE EYES, BVE 58588-1   19 February 1930
PAIR OF BLUE EYES, BVE 58588-2, (extant test pressing)   19 February 1930

Palms, see Les Rameaux

Panis Angelicus, CVE 38733-1   6 May   1927
PANIS ANGELICUS, CVE 38733-2   6 May   1927
PANIS ANGELICUS, CR 1497-1   5 September 1927
Panis Angelicus, CR 1497-2   5 September 1927
Panis Angelicus, CR 1497-3   5 September 1927
PANIS ANGELICUS, extant broadcast transcription   26 June   1932
PANIS ANGELICUS, extant broadcast transcription   4 April   1933

Parigi, o cara, see LA TRAVIATA
Parle moi de ma mère, see CARMEN: Votre mère avec moi...Ma mère je la vois

PARTED, Lx 2963, (Scott)   5 December 1908

PARTED, B 17010-1, (Tosti)   14 January   1916

PASSING BY, OEA 8824-1   11 July   1940

PASTOR FIDO: CARO AMOR, 2EA 2764-1   7 April   1936

PÊCHEURS DE PERLES, LA: Del tempio al limitar, C 8738-1   23 March   1910
PÊCHEURS DE PERLES, LA: DEL TEMPIO AL LIMITAR, C 8738-2   31 March   1911
PÊCHEURS DE PERLES, LA: Del tempio al limitar, B 8738-1   31 March   1911
PÊCHEURS DE PERLES, LA: DEL TEMPIO AL LIMITAR, B 8738-2   4 April   1911

PÊCHEURS DE PERLES, LA: MI PAR D'UDIR ANCORA, B 12707-1   11 December 1912

Per viver vicino a Maria, see LA FILLE DU REGIMENT
Perfect Spring, see The Awakening of a Perfect Spring

PIANTO DEL CORE, Lxx 2799   31 August   1908

PLAISIR D'AMOUR, Song O' My Heart (35mm)   1929
Plaisir d'Amour, Song O' My Heart (70mm)   1929
PLAISIR D'AMOUR, OEA 8806-1   19 June   1940
Plaisir d'Amour, OEA 8806-2   19 June   1940

Pleading, B 13003-1   19 March   1913

POOR BUTTERFLY, no matrix, (private)   9 May   1917

POOR MAN'S GARDEN, OEA 410-1   24 August   1934

PORTRAIT, B 13235-1   2 May   1913

Praise Ye the Lord, OEA 9316-1   29 May   1941
PRAISE YE THE LORD, OEA 9316-2   29 May   1941

Prayer Perfect, Bb 20691-1   5 December   1930
PRAYER PERFECT, Bb 20691-2   5 December   1930

PRAYER TO OUR LADY, BVE 35892-1, (extant test pressing)   1 October   1926
Prayer to Our Lady, OB 3854-1   16 September 1932
PRAYER TO OUR LADY, OB 3854-2   16 September 1932

Procession, Cc 11335-1   1 September 1927
PROCESSION, Cc 11335-2   1 September 1927

PUR DICESTI, O BOCCA, BOCCA BELLA, B 28609-1, (test pressing)   26 September 1923
PUR DICESTI, O BOCCA, BOCCA BELLA, B 28609-2   26 September 1923

Questa o quella, see RIGOLETTO

QUIETEST THINGS, OEA 426-1   29 August   1934

Rainbow of Love, B 20021-1   8 June   1917
RAINBOW OF LOVE, B 20021-2   8 June   1917

RAMEAUX, LES, CVE 36384-1   4 October   1926
Rameaux, Les, CVE 36384-2   4 October   1926

Recondita armonia, see TOSCA

REMEMBER THE ROSE, B 27032-1   17 October   1922
Remember the Rose, B 27032-2   17 October   1922
Remember the Rose, B 27032-3   17 October   1922

Remembering You, see As I Sit Here

RIDENTE LA CALMA, Bb 5096-1, (extant test pressing)   19 September 1924
RIDENTE LA CALMA, Bb 5096-2   19 September 1924

RIGOLETTO: BELLA FIGLIA DELL'AMORE (QUARTET), 4189f   12 May   1910
RIGOLETTO: Bella figlia dell'amore (Quartet), C 14657-1   2 April   1914
RIGOLETTO: Bella figlia dell'amore (Quartet), C 14657-2   2 April   1914
RIGOLETTO: Bella figlia dell'amore (Quartet), C 14657-3   2 April   1914
RIGOLETTO: Bella figlia dell'amore (Quartet), C 14657-4   8 April   1914
RIGOLETTO: BELLA FIGLIA DELL'AMORE (QUARTET), C 14657-5   8 April   1914

RIGOLETTO: LA DONNA E MOBILE, Lx 2491   31 January   1908
RIGOLETTO: La donna e mobile, Lx 2491-2   31 January   1908
RIGOLETTO: LA DONNA E MOBILE, Lx 2491-3, (extant test pressing) 31 August   1908
RIGOLETTO: LA DONNA E MOBILE, Lx 2491-4   31 August   1908
RIGOLETTO: La donna e mobile, B 13222-1   1 May   1913

RIGOLETTO: QUESTA O QUELLA, Lx 2559, (extant test pressing)   2 March   1908
RIGOLETTO: Questa o quella, Lx 2559-2   2 March   1908
RIGOLETTO: QUESTA O QUELLA, Lx 2559-3   5 September 1909
RIGOLETTO: QUESTA O QUELLA, B 13223-1   1 May   1913

RISE, DAWN OF LOVE, OEA 2133-1   28 June   1935

Road That Brought Me to You, B 23043-1   1 July   1919
ROAD THAT BROUGHT ME TO YOU, B 23043-2   1 July   1919

ROMEO ET JULIETTE: Ah! lève toi, soleil, C 11832-1   5 April   1912

Rosary, B 11825-1   3 April   1912
ROSARY, B 11825-2   5 April   1912
ROSARY, B 11825-3   30 March   1915
Rosary, BVE 40171-1   12 October   1927
ROSARY, BVE 40171-2   12 October   1927

Rose For Every Heart, BVE 36375-1   30 September 1926
ROSE FOR EVERY HEART, BVE 36375-2   30 September 1926
ROSE FOR EVERY HEART, BVE 36375-3, (extant test pressing)   30 September 1926

Rose Marie, B 31526-1   17 December 1924
Rose Marie, B 31526-2   17 December 1924
ROSE MARIE, B 31526-3   17 December 1924

Rose of My Heart, B 23042-1   1 July   1919
ROSE OF MY HEART, B 23042-2   1 July   1919

ROSE OF TRALEE, Song O' My Heart (35mm)   1929
Rose of Tralee, Song O' My Heart (70mm)   1929
Rose of Tralee, BVE 58586-1   19 February 1930
ROSE OF TRALEE, BVE 58586-2   19 February 1930

Rose Still Blooms in Picardy, OEA 9489-1   6 October   1941
ROSE STILL BLOOMS IN PICARDY, OEA 9489-2   6 November 1941
Rose Still Blooms in Picardy, OEA 9489-3   6 November 1941

ROSES, Lx 2798-1   31 August   1908

ROSES OF PICARDY, B 22691-1   16 April   1919
Roses of Picardy, B 22691-2   16 April   1919

Roses of Picardy, BVE 41545-1   13 January   1928
ROSES OF PICARDY, BVE 41545-2   13 January   1928

Salve dimora casta e pura, see FAUST
Sängers Trost, see The Singer's Consolation

SAVOURNEEN DEELISH, Lx 2133   1 June   1907
SAVOURNEEN DEELISH, Lx 2133-2   3 October   1908

SAY A LITTLE PRAYER, OEA 9888-1   10 August   1942
Say a Little Prayer, OEA 9888-2 (?)   10 August   1942

SAY "AU REVOIR" BUT NOT "GOODBYE", B 13033-1   28 March   1913

Schlafendes Jesuskind, BVE 32538-1   24 April   1925
SCHLAFENDES JESUSKIND, BVE 32538-2   24 April   1925
SCHLAFENDES JESUSKIND, Bb 21031-1   3 December   1930
SCHLAFENDES JESUSKIND, 2EA 2767-1   7 April   1936

Se il mio nome, see IL BARBIERE DI SIVIGLIA

SEE AMID THE WINTER SNOW, OEA 8891-1   25 October   1940

See here thy flower (Flower Song in English), see CARMEN
Seems Lák' to Me, see Since You Went Away

SEMELE: O SLEEP! WHY DOST THOU LEAVE ME, B 23902-1   1 April   1920
SEMELE: O Sleep! Why dost thou leave me, B 23902-2   1 April   1920

SEMELE: WHER'ER YOU WALK, 2EA 2765-1   7 April   1936
SEMELE: WHER'ER YOU WALK, extant broadcast transcription   1940

SEND ME AWAY WITH A SMILE, B 20546-1   7 September   1917
SEND ME AWAY WITH A SMILE, B 20546-2, (extant test pressing)   7 September   1917
SEND ME AWAY WITH A SMILE, B 20546-3   23 October   1917
Send Me Away With a Smile, B 20546-4   23 October   1917

Serenade, B 17654-1, (Raff)   10 May   1916
SERENADE, B 17654-2, (Raff)   10 May   1916

SERENADE (STÄNDCHEN), C 14651-1, (SCHUBERT)   31 April   1914
SERENADE (STÄNDCHEN), CVE 49210-1, (SCHUBERT)   27 November   1928
SERENADE (STÄNDCHEN), CVE 49210-2, (SCHUBERT)   27 November   1928

SERENATA, B 16090-1   10 June   1915
Serenata, B 16090-2   10 June   1915

SHANNON RIVER, OEA 2130-1   28 June   1935
SHANNON RIVER, OEA 2130-2, (extant test pressing)   28 June   1935
SHANNON RIVER, extant broadcast transcription   13 May   1937

SHE IS FAR FROM THE LAND, C 10138-1   31 March   1911
SHE IS FAR FROM THE LAND, 2EA 2750-1   31 March   1936

SHE MOVED THROUGH THE FAIR, OEA 9329-1   25 June   1941

SHE RESTED BY THE BROKEN BROOK, BVE 35891-1,(extant test pressing) 1 October 1926
SHE RESTED BY THE BROKEN BROOK, OEA 2181-1   23 July   1935
She Rested By the Broken Brook, OEA 2181-2   23 July   1935
SHE RESTED BY THE BROKEN BROOK, OEA 9086-1   28 January   1941

Siciliana, see CAVALLERIA RUSTICANA

SILENT HOUR OF PRAYER, extant broadcast transcription   27 December   1936

SILENT NIGHT, OEA 8887-1   25 October   1940

SILENT NOON, OEA 9202-1   6 March   1941

SILVER RING, Bb 11345-1   2 September   1927

SILVER THREADS AMONG THE GOLD, B 11834-1   5 April   1912
Silver Threads Among the Gold, B 11834-2   5 April   1912
SILVER THREADS AMONG THE GOLD, B 11834-3   3 January   1913
SILVER THREADS AMONG THE GOLD, BVE 11834-4   23 December   1925
Silver Threads Among the Gold, BVE 11834-5   23 December   1925

Since First I Saw Your Face, Bb 11340-1   2 September   1927
SINCE FIRST I SAW YOUR FACE, Bb 11340-2   2 September   1927
SINCE FIRST I SAW YOUR FACE, OEA 9066-1   17 December   1940

Since First I Met Thee, see Come Back My Love

Since You Went Away, B 24037-1	5 May	1920
SINCE YOU WENT AWAY, B 24037-2	5 May	1920
Singer's Consolation, B 23799-2	2 April	1920
SINGER'S CONSOLATION, B 23799-2	2 April	1920
Sing, Sing, Birds on the Wing, B 16762-1	10 November	1915
SING, SING, BIRDS ON THE WING, B 16762-2	10 November	1915
Sing, Sing, Birds on the Wing, B 16762-3	10 November	1915
Smiles, B 22255-1	24 September	1918
Smiles, B 22255-2	24 September	1918
SMILIN' THRO',.OEA 9478-1	6 October	1941
Smilin' Thro', OEA 9478-2	6 October	1941
SNOWY BREASTED PEARL, Edison 13124 (cylinder)	12 September	1904
SNOWY BREASTED PEARL, 5924b	24 September	1904
SNOWY BREASTED PEARL, Lx 1570	4 December	1906
SNOWY BREASTED PEARL, C 8741-1	23 March	1910
SNOWY BREASTED PEARL, extant broadcast transcription	8 December	1938
SO DEEP IS THE NIGHT, OEA 8399-1	2 May	1940
So Deep is the Night, OEA 8399-2	2 May	1940
SO DO I LOVE YOU, extant broadcast transcription	13 May	1937

Softly Through the Night is Calling, see Serenade (Schubert)
Sogno, Il, see MANON

Soldat, Der, Bb 5099-1	19 September	1924
Sometime I'll Hear Your Sweet Voice, B 28607-1	25 September	1923
SOMETIME I'LL HEAR YOUR SWEET VOICE, B 28607-2	25 September	1923
SOMETIME YOU'LL REMEMBER ME, B 21814-1	1 May	1918
Somewhere, B 23523-1	10 December	1919
SOMEWHERE, B 23523-2	11 December	1919
SOMEWHERE A VOICE IS CALLING, B 15419-1	23 November	1914
Somewhere a Voice is Calling, BVE 15419-2	12 April	1927
SOMEWHERE A VOICE IS CALLING, BVE 15419-3	12 April	1927
SOMEWHERE IN THE WORLD, B 28603-1	24 September	1923
Somewhere in the World, B 28603-2	24 September	1923
Song of Thanksgiving, B 23793-1	30 March	1920
Song of Thanksgiving, B 23793-2	30 March	1920
Song of Thanksgiving, B 23793-3	1 April	1920
Song of Thanksgiving, B 23793-4	1 April	1920
SONG OF THE NIGHT, BVE 48180-1	19 November	1928
Song of the Night, BVE 48180-2	19 November	1928
SONG O' MY HEART, BVE 58690-1	10 March	1930
Song Remembered, BVE 41561-1	17 January	1928
SONG REMEMBERED, OEA 405-1	24 August	1934
Song Remembered, OEA 405-2	24 August	1934
SONG TO THE SEALS, OEA 2126-1	27 June	1935
Sonny Boy, BVE 48178-1	19 November	1928
Sonny Boy, BVE 48178-2	19 November	1928
SONNY BOY, BVE 48178-3	19 November	1928
SOSPIRI MIEI, ANDATE OVE VI MANDO, B 13032-1	28 March	1913
SOUTH WINDS, OB 5308-1, (extant test pressing)	7 September	1933
SOUTH WINDS, OB 5308-2	7 September	1933
Southern Song, Lxx 3134	5 September	1909
SOUTHERN SONG, Lxx 3134-2	5 September	1909

Spir'to gentil, see LA FAVORITA
Ständchen, see Serenade (Schubert)

STAR OF THE COUNTY DOWN, extant broadcast transcription	11 October	1936

STAR OF THE COUNTY DOWN, extant broadcast transcription	27 December	1936
STAR OF THE COUNTY DOWN, extant broadcast transcription	25 April	1938
STAR OF THE COUNTY DOWN, OEA 8322-1	30 November	1939
Star of the County Down, OEA 8322-2	30 November	1939
STAR OF THE COUNTY DOWN, extant broadcast transcription		1940
Star Spangled Banner, B 19534-1	29 March	1917
Star Spangled Banner, B 19534-2	29 March	1917
STAR SPANGLED BANNER, B 19534-3	29 March	1917
Still as the Night, B 16093-1, (Bohm)	10 June	1915
STILL AS THE NIGHT, B 16093-2, (BOHM)	10 June	1915
STILL AS THE NIGHT, OEA 9652-1, (GOETZE)	25 November	1941
Still Night, Holy Night, see Silent Night		
STREET SOUNDS TO THE SOLDIERS' TREAD, OEA 9201-1	6 March	1941
SUNSHINE OF YOUR SMILE, B 18383-1	20 September	1916
Sunshine of Your Smile, B 18383-2	20 September	1916
SWANS, B 28613-1	26 September	1923
Sweet Genevieve, B 12759-1	2 January	1913
SWEET GENEVIEVE, B 12759-2	2 January	1913
Sweet Peggy O'Neill, B 23791-1	30 March	1920
SWEET PEGGY O'NEILL, B 23791-2	30 March	1920
Sweetest Call, BVE 32537-1	23 April	1925
SWEETEST CALL, BVE 32537-2	23 April	1925
SWEETEST FLOWER THAT BLOWS, OEA 8825-1, (extant test pressing)	11 July	1940
Sweetest Flower That Blows, OEA 8825-2	11 July	1940
SWEETLY SHE SLEEPS, MY ALICE FAIR, OEA 411-1	24 August	1934
TAKE, OH TAKE THOSE LIPS AWAY, Lx 3137-1	5 September	1909
TAKE, OH TAKE THOSE LIPS AWAY, B 11815-1	2 April	1912
Take a Look at Molly, B 28604-1	25 September	1923
TAKE A LOOK AT MOLLY, B 28604-2	25 September	1923
TALES OF HOFFMAN, see CONTES D'HOFFMAN		
Te sol quest'anima, see ATTILA		
Tenting on the Old Campground, B 15416-1	23 November	1914
Tenting on the Old Campground, B 15416-2	23 November	1914
Tenting on the Old Campground, B 15416-3	31 March	1915
TERENCE'S FAREWELL TO KATHLEEN, Lx 2134	1 June	1907
TERENCE'S FAREWELL TO KATHLEEN, OEA 423-1	29 August	1934
T'eri un giorna, see I GIOIELLI DELLA MADONNA		
Thank God For a Garden, B 23524-1	11 December	1919
THANK GOD FOR A GARDEN, B 23524-2	11 December	1919
Thank God For a Garden, B 23524-3	11 December	1919
Thanks Be to God, B 28606-1	25 September	1923
THANKS BE TO GOD, B 28606-2	25 September	1923
That Tumble Down Shack in Athlone, B 23456-1	5 November	1919
That Tumble Down Shack in Athlone, B 23456-2	5 November	1919
That Tumble Down Shack in Athlone, B 23456-3	5 November	1919
That Tumble Down Shack in Athlone, B 23456-4	10 December	1919
THAT TUMBLE DOWN SHACK IN ATHLONE, B 23456-5	10 December	1919
Then You'll Remember Me, see THE BOHEMIAN GIRL		
THERE, Bb 21026-1, (extant test pressing)	3 December	1930
THERE, Bb 21026-2	3 December	1930
There is a flower that bloometh, see MARITANA		
THERE IS A GREEN HILL, OEA 9062-1	17 December	1940
There is not in the Wide World, see The Meeting of the Waters		
THERE'S A LONG LONG TRAIL A'WINDING, B 20018-1	7 June	1917

There's a Long Long Trail A'Winding, B 20018-2	7 June	1917
THORA, Lx 2500	3 February	1908
Three Aspects, Bb 21029-1	3 December	1930
THREE ASPECTS, Bb 21029-2	3 December	1930
Three O'Clock in the Morning, B 27029-1	17 October	1922
Three O'Clock in the Morning, B 27029-2	17 October	1922
THREE O'CLOCK IN THE MORNING, B 27029-3	17 October	1922
Three Shadows, B 20027-1	8 June	1917
Three Shadows, B 20027-2	8 June	1917
THROUGH ALL THE DAYS TO BE, BVE 33820-1, (extant test pressing)	27 October	1925
Through All the Days to Be, BVE 33820-2	27 October	1925
THROUGH ALL THE DAYS TO BE, BVE 33820-3	27 October	1925
TICK, TICK, TOCK, BVE 38732-1	6 May	1927
Tick, Tick, Tock, BVE 38732-2	6 May	1927
TILL I WAKE, OEA 8821-1	11 July	1940
Till I Wake, OEA 8821-2	11 July	1940
Tis an Irish Girl I Love, B 23755-1	4 March	1920
TIS AN IRISH GIRL I LOVE, B 23755-2	4 March	1920
TO CHLOE, OEA 9277-1	10 September	1942
TOMMY LAD, B 18385-1	20 September	1916
TOSCA: E LUCEVAN LE STELLE, Lx 2501	3 February	1908
TOSCA: E LUCEVAN LE STELLE, Lx 2501-2	5 September	1909
TOSCA: Recondita armonia, B 8818-1	8 April	1910
To the Children, B 27047-1	20 October	1922
To the Children, B 27085-1	20 November	1922
TO THE CHILDREN, B 27085-2, (extant test pressing)	20 November	1922
To the Children, Bb 5117-1	24 September	1924
TO THE CHILDREN, Bb 5117-2	24 September	1924
To the Children, BVE 27085-3	17 December	1925
TO THE CHILDREN, BVE 27085-4	17 December	1925
To the Lyre, part of CVE 49237-1	6 December	1928
To the Lyre, part of CVE 49237-2	6 December	1928
TO THE LYRE, part of CVE 49237-3	6 December	1928
TRÄUME, 2EA 2766-1	7 April	1936
Träume, 2EA 2766-2	7 April	1936
TRAVIATA, LA: LUNGE SA LEI...DE'MIEI BOLLENTI SPIRITI, C 8693-1	10 March	1910
TRAVIATA, LA: Parigi, o cara, C 14686-1	8 April	1914
TRAVIATA, LA: PARIGI, O CARA, C 14686-2	8 April	1914
TRAVIATA, LA: Duet (title uncertain), 4187f	12 May	1910
Tre giorni son che Nina, see Nina		
TREES, OEA 8809-1	19 June	1940
Trees, OEA 8809-2	19 June	1940
TRISTAN UND ISOLDE: O KÖNIG, BVE TEST 426-1,(extant test pressing)	15 October	1929
TRISTAN UND ISOLDE: O KÖNIG, CVE 58692-1	10 March	1930
TRIUMPH OF TIME AND TRUTH: DRYADS AND SYLVANS, extant broadcast	2 January	1938
TROTTING TO THE FAIR, Lx 2843	3 October	1908
TROVATORE, IL: Ai nostri monti, Lx 1578, (with Lily McCormack)	5 December	1906
Trumpet Call, B 20016-1	7 June	1917
TRUMPET CALL, B 20016-2	7 June	1917
TRUMPETER, C 15845-1	30 March	1915
Tu che a Dio spiegasti l'ali, see LUCIA DI LAMMERMOOR		
TURN YE TO ME, C 15848-1	30 March	1915
Tutto è finito...O terra addio, see AIDA		
Two Brown Eyes, BRC-HQ 31	2 November	1931

ULTIMA CANZONE, Lx 3162   7 September 1909

Una furtiva lagrima, see L'ELISIR D'AMORE

UND WILLST DU DEINEM LIEBSTEN STERBEN SEHEN, BRC-HQ 33, (test)   2 November 1931

Underneath the Window, BVE 34167-1   18 December 1925
UNDERNEATH THE WINDOW, BVE 34167-2   18 December 1925
Underneath the Window, BVE 34167-3   18 December 1925
Underneath the Window, BVE 34167-4   18 December 1925

Under the Spell of the Rose, BVE 38386-1   4 May   1927
UNDER THE SPELL OF THE ROSE, BVE 38386-2, (extant test pressing) 4 May   1927
UNDER THE SPELL OF THE ROSE, BVE 49240-1   7 December 1928
Under the Spell of the Rose, BVE 49240-2   7 December 1928
Under the Spell of the Rose, BVE 49240-3   7 December 1928

Unter'm Fenster, see Underneath the Window

Until, B 15844-1   30 March   1915
UNTIL, B 15844-2   30 March   1915

Vacant Chair, B 15417-1   23 November 1914
Vacant Chair, B 15417-2   31 March   1915
VACANT CHAIR, B 15417-3   31 March   1914

Venetian Song, B 16765-1   10 November 1915
VENETIAN SONG, B 16765-2   10 November 1915

VESPERS, OB 5306-1   7 September 1933
Vespers, OB 5306-2   7 September 1933

Victor, C 23522-1   10 December 1919
Victor, C 23522-2   10 December 1919

Vieni al content, see LAKME: Immenso vienteso...A vien al boscaglia

VILLAGE THAT NOBODY KNOWS, OEA 9315-1   29 May   1941

Voi Dormite, Signora, Lx 3153   7 September 1909
VOI DORMITE, SIGNORA, Lx 3153-2   7 September 1909

Votre mère avec moi...Ma mère je la vois, see CARMEN

WAITING FOR YOU, OEA 9278-1   10 September 1942

WEARING OF THE GREEN, Edison Bell 6451-I (cylinder)   10 November 1904
WEARING OF THE GREEN, Edison Bell 6451-II (cylinder)   10 November 1904
WEARING OF THE GREEN, Edison Bell 6451-III (cylinder)   10 November 1904
WEARING OF THE GREEN, Edison Bell 6451-IV (cylinder)   10 November 1904
WEARING OF THE GREEN, B 11826-1   3 April   1912

West's Awake, 5941b   26 September 1904
West's Awake, 5942b   26 September

What a Wonderful World It Would Be, BVE 32540-1   24 April   1925
What a Wonderful World It Would Be, BVE 32540-2   24 April   1925

When, B 23903-1   1 April   1920
When, B 23903-2   1 April   1920
WHEN, B 29872-1   9 April   1924
When, B 29872-2   9 April   1924

When coldness or deceit, see THE BOHEMIAN GIRL: When other lips

WHEN I AWAKE, OEA 9084-1   28 January   1941
When I Awake, OEA 9084-2   28 January   1941

WHEN I HAVE SUNG MY SONGS, OEA 2125-1   27 June   1935

When Ireland Comes into Her Own, B 23044-1   1 July   1919

When Irish Eyes Are Smiling, B 18387-1   20 September 1916
WHEN IRISH EYES ARE SMILING, B 18387-2   20 September 1916

When My Ships Come Sailing Home, C 15839-1   29 March   1915
WHEN MY SHIPS COME SAILING HOME, C 15839-2   29 March   1915

WHEN NIGHT DESCENDS, B 23905-1   2 April   1920
When Night Descends, B 23905-2   2 April   1920

When Night Descends, B 23905-3	2 April	1920
When Night Descends, BVE 56197-1	18 October	1929
When Night Descends, BVE 56197-2	18 October	1929

When other lips, see THE BOHEMIAN GIRL

When Pershing's Men Go Marching into Picardy, B 23900-1	2 April	1920
When Pershing's Men Go Marching into Picardy, B 23900-2	2 April	1920
WHEN SHADOWS GATHER, Lxx 2853	3 October	1908
WHEN Shadows Gather, Lxx 3136	5 September	1909
WHEN SHADOWS GATHER, Lxx 3136-2	5 September	1909
WHEN SHADOWS GATHER, B 8696-1	10 March	1910

When Shall I Again See Ireland, see Ireland, My Sireland

WHEN SHALL THE DAY BREAK IN ERIN, Edison 13143 (cylinder)	12 September	1904
WHEN SHALL THE DAY BREAK IN IRELAND, 6464a	23 September	1904
WHEN THE CHILDREN SAY THEIR PRAYERS, OEA 2123-1	27 June	1935
When the Dew is Falling, B 15850-1	31 March	1915
WHEN THE DEW IS FALLING, B 15850-2	31 March	1915
WHEN TWILIGHT COMES I'M THINKING OF YOU, BVE 36362-1, (test)	28 September	1926
WHEN TWILIGHT COMES I'M THINKING OF YOU, BVE 36362-2, (test)	28 September	1926
WHEN TWILIGHT COMES I'M THINKING OF YOU, BVE 36362-3	28 September	1926
When You and I Were Seventeen, BVE 32534-1	23 April	1925
When You and I Were Seventeen, BVE 32534-2	23 April	1925
When You and I Were Seventeen, BVE 32534-3	23 April	1925
WHEN YOU AND I WERE SEVENTEEN, BVE 32534-4	23 April	1925
When You and I Were Young, Maggie, B 23525-1	11 December	1919
WHEN YOU AND I WERE YOUNG, MAGGIE, B 23525-2	11 December	1919
When You and I Were Young, Maggie, BVE 23525-3	17 December	1925
WHEN YOU AND I WERE YOUNG, MAGGIE, BVE 23525-4	17 December	1925
WHEN YOU AND I WERE YOUNG, MAGGIE, extant broadcast transcription	1 January	1926
When You Come Back, B 22256-1	24 September	1918
WHEN YOU COME BACK, B 22256-2	25 September	1918
When You Come Back, B 22256-3	25 September	1918
When You Gave Your Heart to Me, B 25352-1	16 June	1921
When You Gave Your Heart to Me, B 25352-2	16 June	1921
When You Look in the Heart of a Rose, B 22690-1	16 April	1919
WHEN YOU LOOK IN THE HEART OF A ROSE, B 22690-2	16 April	1919
WHEN YOU WISH UPON A STAR, OEA 8525-1	12 April	1940
When You Wish Upon a Star, OEA 8525-2	12 April	1940
When You're in Love, BVE 38731-1	6 May	1927
WHEN YOU'RE IN LOVE, BVE 38731-2	6 May	1927
Where Blooms the Rose, B 24035-1	5 May	1920
Where Blooms the Rose, B 24035-2	5 May	1920
Where the Rainbow Ends, B 28602-1	24 September	1923
WHERE THE RAINBOW ENDS, B 28602-2	24 September	1923
Where the River Shannon Flows, B 12761-1	2 January	1913
WHERE THE RIVER SHANNON FLOWS, B 12761-2	2 January	1913

Where the River Shannon Meets the Sea, see Shannon River
Wher'er you walk, see SEMELE

WHITE IN THE MOON THE LONG ROAD LIES, OEA 9204-1	6 March	1941
WHITE PEACE, OEA 9327-1	25 June	1941
White Peace, OEA 9327-2	25 June	1941
WHO IS SYLVIA, Bb 11342-1, (extant test pressing)	2 September	1927
WHO IS SYLVIA, Bb 11342-2	2 September	1927
WHO IS SYLVIA, part of CVE 49214-1, (extant test pressing)	28 November	1928
Who is Sylvia, part of CVE 49214-2	28 November	1928
Who is Sylvia, part of CVE 49214-3	6 December	1928
WHO IS SYLVIA, part of CVE 49214-4	7 December	1928
Who is Sylvia, part of CVE 49214-5	7 December	1928

WHO KNOWS, B 14665-1	6 April	1914
Who Knows, B 14665-2	6 April	1914
WIDMUNG, B 28612-1	26 September	1923

Wild Rose Lane, see Under the Spell of the Rose

Will You Go With Me, OEA 9488-1	6 October	1941
Will You Go With Me, OEA 9488-2	6 October	1941
WILL YOU GO WITH ME, OEA 9488-3	8 November	1941
WITHIN THE GARDEN OF MY HEART, B 12762-1	3 January	1913
WO FIND ICH TROST, Cc 5029-1	4 September	1924
WO FIND ICH TROST, Cc 5029-2, (extant test pressing)	4 September	1924
Wo find ich Trost, BVE 58691-1	10 March	1930
WO FIND ICH TROST, BVE 58691-2, (extant test pressing)	10 March	1930
Wonderful One, B 28600-1	24 September	1923
Wonderful One, B 28600-2	24 September	1923
WONDERFUL ONE, B 28600-3	24 September	1924
Wonderful World of Romance, B 23794-1	30 March	1920
Wonderful World of Romance, B 23794-2	30 March	1920
WONDERFUL WORLD OF ROMANCE, B 23794-3	1 April	1920
Wonderful World of Romance, B 23794-4	1 April	1920
Would God I Were the Tender Apple Blossom, B 28608-1	26 September	1923
WOULD GOD I WERE THE TENDER APPLE BLOSSOM, B 28608-2	26 September	1923
YE BANKS AND BRAES, OEA 9067-1	17 December	1940
YOU FORGOT TO REMEMBER, BVE 33464-1	14 October	1925
You Forgot to Remember, BVE 33464-2	14 October	1925
You Forgot to Remember, BVE 33464-3	14 October	1925
Your Eyes, B 17649-1	9 May	1916
YOUR EYES, B 17649-2	9 May	1916
Your Eyes Have Told Me So, B 23455-1	5 November	1919
Your Eyes Have Told Me So, B 23455-2	5 November	1919
Your Eyes Have Told Me So, B 23455-3	11 December	1919
YOUR EYES HAVE TOLD ME SO, B 23455-4	11 December	1919
Your Eyes Have Told Me So, B 23455-5	11 December	1919

Microgroove Reissues

RCA VICTOR

ARM 1 4997. RCA Victor Red Seal. "John McCormack, The Irish Minstrel: A Collection
    of His Legendary Songs and Ballads. A Centennial Tribute."

B 21812-1	Love's Garden of Roses	1 May	1918
B 15419-1	Somewhere a Voice is Calling	23 November	1914
B 8590-1	The Minstrel Boy	1 February	1910
C 8753-1	Has Sorrow Thy Young Days Shaded?	25 March	1910
BVE 41546-2	By the Short Cut to the Rosses	13 January	1928
BVE 56192-4	Ireland, Mother Ireland	21 February	1930
B 19447-1	Ireland, My Sireland	5 April	1917
BVE 58586-2	The Rose of Tralee	19 February	1930
Bb 21027-3	The Fairy Tree	3 December	1930
Bb 21028-1	Far Apart	3 December	1930
Bb 11346-1	Now Sleeps the Crimson Petal	2 September	1927
BVE 40166-2	Bird Songs at Eventide	11 October	1927
BVE 40178-2	The Auld Scotch Sangs	13 October	1927
B 28613-1	Swans	26 September	1923
B 13035-1	Down in the Forest	28 March	1913
Bb 21026-2	There	3 December	1930
BVE 40172-1	I Hear You Calling Me	12 October	1927
Bb 21032-1	Love's Secret	3 December	1930
Bb 21040-2	The Bitterness of Love	4 December	1930
Bb 21029-2	Three Aspects	3 December	1930
B 15847-1	Morning	30 March	1915

CAL 407. RCA Camden. "John McCormack Sings Irish Songs."

B 25353-2	Little Town in the Auld County Down	17 June	1921
B 10134-1	Macushla	30 March	1911
B 12761-2	Where the River Shannon Flows	2 January	1913
B 15419-1	Somewhere a Voice is Calling	23 November	1914
B 14677-2	THE BOHEMIAN GIRL: When other lips	11 May	1916
B 12767-1	The Foggy Dew	3 January	1913
B 18387-2	When Irish Eyes Are Smiling	20 September	1916
B 12710-2	MARITANA: There is a flower that bloometh	11 December	1912
C 8752-2	Molly Bawn	17 March	1911
B 12765-1	Molly Brannigan	3 January	1913
BVE 40173-2	Mother Machree	12 October	1927
CVE 39889-3	Kathleen Mavourneen	11 October	1927
BVE 58586-2	The Rose of Tralee	19 February	1930
BVE 40172-1	I Hear You Calling Me	12 October	1927

CAL 512. RCA Camden. "John McCormack in Opera and Song."

C 20898-1	JOSEPH EN ÉGYPTE: Champs paternels!	23 October	1917
B 12764-2	MANON: Chiudo gli occhi	3 January	1913
C 8694-1	FAUST: Salve dimora	10 March	1910

C 8589-2	LA BOHEME: Che gelida manina	1 February	1910
C 8538-1	CARMEN: Il fior che avevi a me	7 January	1910
B 13037-1	Sospiri Miei, Andate Ove vi Mando	28 March	1913
B 12705-1	MEFISTOFELE: Dai campi, dai prati	11 December	1912
B 12706-1	MEFISTOFELE: Giunto sul passo estremo	11 December	1912
B 12707-1	LA PÊCHEURS DE PERLES: Mi par d'udir ancora	11 December	1912
C 17651-1	Non è Ver	9 May	1916
B 8749-1	LAKME: Immenso vienteso...A vien al boscaglia	25 March	1910
C 11822-1	NATOMA: My commander as envoy...No country can	3 April	1912

CAL 635. RCA Camden. "John McCormack Sings Sacred Music."

B 29870-2	Holy God We Praise Thy Name	9 April	1924
BVE 40171-2	The Rosary	12 October	1927
C 14624-2	Ave Maria (Bach-Gounod), with Kreisler	31 March	1914
CVE 58684-1	CHRIST ON THE MOUNT OF OLIVES: Jehovah, Hear Me	27 February	1930
CVE 58685-1	CHRIST ON THE MOUNT OF OLIVES: My heart is sore	27 February	1930
CVE 38733-2	Panis Angelicus	6 May	1927
CVE 38388-1	Christ Went Up into the Hills	4 May	1927
C 14633-1	Ave Maria (Schubert), with Kreisler	25 March	1914
B 20899-1	The Lord is My Light	23 October	1917
B 13225-1	Nearer, My God, to Thee	1 May	1913
BVE 37147-1	The Holy Child	17 December	1926
BVE 36363-1	Just For Today	28 September	1926
B 28606-2	Thanks Be to God	25 September	1926

CAS 407(e). RCA Camden. "John McCormack Sings Irish Songs."

Same contents as CAL 407: simulated stereo.

CDN 1002. RCA Camden. "John McCormack Sings Irish Songs." (UK).

Same contents as CAL 407.

CDN 1023. RCA Camden. "John McCormack in Opera and Song." (UK).

Same contents as CAL 512.

CDN 1029. RCA Camden. "John McCormack Sings Sacred Music." (UK).

Same contents as CAL 635.

CDN 1057. RCA Camden. "John McCormack in Opera and Song." (UK).

Same contents as CAL 512, but omits C 8589-2 and C 11822-1.

CRM 1 2472. RCA Legendary Performer. "John McCormack - A Legendary Performer."
Recordings digitally reprocessed by Soundstream, Inc., U.S.A.

B 23902-1	SEMELE: Oh Sleep! Why dost thou leave me?	1 April	1920
C 17647-1	DON GIOVANNI: Il mio tesoro	9 May	1916
B 12707-1	LA PÊCHEURS DE PERLES: Mi par d'udir ancora	11 December	1912
C 8739-1	LA FILLE DU REGIMENT: Per viver vicino a Maria	23 March	1910
B 13032-1	Sospiri Miei, Andate Ove vi Mando	28 March	1913
B 13235-1	Le Portrait	2 May	1913
B 23799-2	The Singer's Consolation	2 April	1920
B 23905-1	When Night Descends	2 April	1920
B 16765-2	Venetian Song	10 November	1915
B 14676-2	A Dream	7 April	1914
C 15846-1	Come Into the Garden, Maude	30 March	1915
C 10063-1	Ah, Moon of My Delight	16 March	1911
B 14668-2	Bonnie Wee Thing	6 April	1914
B 23904-1	The Next Market Day / A Ballynure Ballad	2 April	1920
B 23792-2	The Bard of Armagh	30 March	1920

CRM 8 5177. RCA Red Seal. "100 Years, 100 Singers: Metropolitan Opera Centennial, 1883 - 1983."

C 8693-1	LA TRAVIATA: Lunge da lei per me...De miei bollenti	10 March	1910

ERAT 17. RCA Red Seal. "John McCormack in Opera." (7 inch, 45 rpm).

B 23902-1	SEMELE: Oh Sleep! Why dost thou leave me?	1 April	1920
C 8535-1	LUCIA DI LAMMERMOOR: Fra poco a me ricovero	3 January	1910
C 14658-4	LA BOHEME: O soave fanciulla, with Bori	8 April	1914
C 14686-1	LA TRAVIATA: Parigi, o cara, with Bori	8 April	1914

ERAT 18. RCA Red Seal. "McCormack Sings Irish Songs." (7 inch, 45 rpm).

B 18387-2	When Irish Eyes Are Smiling	20 September	1916
2EA 2749-2	Kerry Dance	31 March	1936
C 10061-1	Kathleen Mavourneen	16 March	1911
BVE 40173-2	Mother Machree	12 October	1927

ERAT 45. RCA Red Seal. "Four Tenors, Four Arias." (7 inch, 45 rpm).

C 8693-1	LA TRAVIATA: Lunge da lei per me...De miei bollenti	10 March	1910

F 7-OH-7606/7. RCA (7 inch, 45 rpm).

CVE 58684-1	CHRIST ON THE MOUNT OF OLIVES: Jehovah, hear me	27 February	1930
CVE 58685-1	CHRIST ON THE MOUNT OF OLIVES: My heart is sore	27 February	1930

L 4509. RCA Program Transcription (1931, 33 1/3 rpm). "Schubert Melodies."

CVE 49209-2	Ave Maria	27 November	1928
CVE 49210-2	Serenade	27 November	1928
CVE 49213-3	The Organ Grinder / Farewell	28 November	1928

LCT 1004. RCA Red Seal. "Golden Duets."

B 14658-4	LA BOHEME: O soave fanciulla, with Bori	8 April	1914

LCT 1005. RCA Red Seal. "Sacred Songs."

CVE 38733-2	Panis Angelicus	6 May	1927
C 14623-1	Angel's Serenade, with Kreisler	25 March	1914

LCT 1006. RCA Red Seal. "Golden Age at the Met."

C 17647-1	DON GIOVANNI: Il mio tesoro	9 May	1916

LCT 1008. RCA Red Seal. "Golden Voices Sing Light Music."

BVE 56198-1	Norah O'Neale	18 October	1929
BVE 35893-1	Love's Secret	1 October	1926

LCT 1036. RCA Red Seal. "McCormack in Opera and Song."

C 8535-1	LUCIA DI LAMMERMOOR: Fra poco a me ricovero	3 January	1910
CVE 58692-1	TRISTAN UND ISOLDE: O König, das kann ich dir	10 March	1930
2EA 2766-1	Träume	7 April	1936
Bb 21027-3	The Fairy Tree	3 December	1930
C 14626-1	JOCELYN: Beneath the quivering leaves...Angels	25 March	1914
C 8536-2	L'ELISIR D'AMORE:Una furtiva lagrima	1 February	1910
BVE 40172-1	I Hear You Calling Me	12 October	1927
CVE 36606-1	Adeste Fideles	1 October	1926

LCT 1037. RCA Red Seal. "Famous Duets."

C 14686-1	LA TRAVIATA: Parigi, o cara, with Bori	8 April	1914

LCT 1121. RCA Red Seal. "Caruso and McCormack Sing Christmas Music."

CVE 38733-2	Panis Angelicus	6 May	1927
C 14626-1	JOCELYN: Beneath the quivering leaves...Angels	25 March	1914
C 14633-1	Ave Maria (Schubert), with Kreisler	25 March	1914
BVE 37147-1	The Holy Child	17 December	1926
CVE 36606-1	Adeste Fideles	1 October	1926

LCT 1158. RCA Red Seal. "Critic's Choice - Chosen by Paul Hume."

B 23906-1	O Cease Thy Singing, Maiden Fair, with Kreisler	2 April	1920

LCT 6701. RCA Red Seal. "Fifty Years of Great Operatic Singing."

   C 13028-3   CARMEN: Votre mère avec moi...Ma mère je la vois, 1 May   1913
               with Marsh
   C 20898-1   JOSEPH EN ÉGYPTE: Champs paternels!   23 October 1917

LM 1202. RCA Red Seal. "Ten Tenors, Ten Arias."

   C 17647-1   DON GIOVANNI: Il mio tesoro   9 May   1916

LM 2372. RCA Red Seal. "Fifty Years of Great Operatic Singing - Tenors."

   C 20898-1   JOSEPH EN ÉGYPTE: Champs paternels!   23 October 1917

LM 2627. RCA Red Seal. "Golden Voices Sing Light Music."

   B 10134-1   Macushla   30 March   1911

LM 2628. RCA Red Seal. "Great Love Duets."

   B 14658-4   LA BOHEME: O soave fanciulla, with Bori   8 April   1914

LM 2631. RCA Red Seal. "Great Tenor Arias."

   C 17647-1   DON GIOVANNI: Il mio tesoro   9 May   1916

LM 2755. RCA Red Seal. "Songs of Sentiment."

B 8819-1	Dear Little Shamrock	8 April	1910
B 13031-1	The Low Back'd Car	28 March	1913
B 13034-1	Mother o' Mine	28 March	1913
C 27043-1	The Lost Chord	20 October	1922
B 23525-2	When You and I Were Young, Maggie	11 December	1919
B 23758-2	Beneath the Moon of Lombardy	4 March	1920
B 12704-1	At Dawning	11 December	1912
B 13233-1	Goodbye, Sweetheart, Goodbye	2 May	1913
B 11815-1	Take, Oh Take Those Lips Away	2 April	1912
B 12762-1	Within the Garden of My Heart	3 January	1913
B 14671-1	Because	7 April	1914
B 15417-3	The Vacant Chair	31 March	1915
B 14674-1	Mary of Argyle	7 April	1914
B 23901-1	The Barefoot Trail	1 April	1920
B 20019-2	Any Place is Heaven if You Are Near Me	8 April	1914

LM 6099. RCA Red Seal. "Fritz Kreisler in Immortal Performances."

C 14626-1	JOCELYN: Beneath the quivering leaves...Angels	25 March	1914
B 23906-1	O Cease Thy Singing, Maiden Fair	2 April	1920
B 23905-1	When Night Descends	2 April	1920

LM 6705. RCA Red Seal. "Ten Great Singers."

C 17647-1	DON GIOVANNI: Il mio tesoro	9 May	1916
B 12707-1	LA PÊCHEURS DE PERLES: Mi par d'udir ancora	11 December	1912
B 12764-2	MANON: Chiudo gli occhi	3 January	1913
C 20898-1	JOSEPH EN ÉGYPTE: Champs paternels!	23 October	1917
B 10134-1	Macushla	30 March	1911
B 18387-2	When Irish Eyes Are Smiling	20 September	1916
BVE 40173-2	Mother Machree	12 October	1927
BVE 58586-2	The Rose of Tralee	19 February	1930

LM 20114. RCA (Italy). "L'Epocha D'Oro Melodramma, Volume 1."

   C 8739-1   LA FILLE DU REGIMENT: Per viver vicino a Maria   23 March   1910

LM 20115. RCA (Italy). "L'Epocha D'Oro Melodramma, Volume 2."

   C 8737-1   LA BOHEME: Ah Mimi, tu piu non torni, with   23 March   1910
                 Sammarco

RB 6506. RCA Red Seal. "Golden Voices Sing Light Music."

   Same contents as LM 2627.

RB 6515. RCA Red Seal. "Great Tenor Arias."

    Same contents as LM 2631.

RB 6516. RCA Red Seal. (Anthology).

    B 14658-4   LA BOHEME: O soave fanciulla, with Bori   8 April   1914

RB 6525. RCA Red Seal. "Fritz Kreisler in Immortal Performances."

    Same contents as LM 6099.

RB 6632. RCA Red Seal. "Songs of Sentiment."

    Same contents as LM 2755

RB 16198. RCA Red Seal. "Fifty Years of Great Operatic Singing - Tenors."

    Same contents as LM 2372.

RCA, 45 rpm, 449-0172. (7 inch).

B 18387-2	When Irish Eyes Are Smiling	20 September	1916
BVE 40173-2	Mother Machree	12 October	1927

RCX 208. RCA. "John McCormack Sings Irish Songs I." (7 inch).

B 10134-1	Macushla	30 March	1911
B 18387-1	When Irish Eyes Are Smiling	20 September	1916
B 25353-2	Little Town in the Auld County Down	17 June	1921
BVE 56192-4	Ireland, Mother Ireland	21 February	1930

RCX 209. RCA. "John McCormack Sings Irish Songs II." (7 inch).

BVE 58586-2	The Rose of Tralee	19 February	1930
B 15419-1	Somewhere a Voice is Calling	23 November	1914
BVE 40173-2	Mother Machree	12 October	1927
CVE 39889-3	Kathleen Mavourneen	11 October	1927

RCX 210. RCA. "John McCormack Sings Irish Songs III." (7 inch).

B 8751-1	My Lagan Love	25 March	1910
BVE 40171-2	The Rosary	12 October	1927
B 12765-1	Molly Brannigan	3 January	1913
BVE 40172-1	I Hear You Calling Me	12 October	1927

RCX 1042. RCA. "Adeste Fideles." (7 inch).

CVE 36606-1	Adeste Fideles	1 October	1926
BVE 37147-1	The Holy Child	17 December	1926
C 14633-1	Ave Maria (Schubert), with Kreisler	25 March	1914
CVE 38733-2	Panis Angelicus	6 May	1927

RL 12472. RCA Legendary Performer. "John McCormack - A Legendary Performer."

    Same Contents as CRM 1 2472.

RL 84997W. RCA Red Seal. "John McCormack, The Irish Minstrel: A Collection
               of His Legendary Songs and Ballads."

    Same contents as ARM 1 4997.

(The above thirteen entries are RCA issues in the UK.)

RVC 1578. RCA Gold Seal. "The Marvelous Duets." (Japan). All with Kreisler.

C 14624-2	Ave Maria (Bach-Gounod)	31 March	1914
C 14626-1	JOCELYN: Beneath the quivering leaves...Angels	25 March	1914
B 17655-1	CONTES D'HOFFMAN: Beauteous night (Barcarolle)	10 May	1916
C 14633-1	Ave Maria (Schubert)	25 March	1914
B 14651-1	Serenade (Schubert)	31 March	1914
B 16090-1	Serenata (Moszowski)	10 June	1915
C 14623-1	Angel's Serenade	25 March	1914

B 16091-2	Carmé	10 June	1915
B 14652-1	Ave Maria (Mascagni)	31 March	1914
B 24036-1	The Last Hour	5 May	1920
C 14625-1	Le Nil	25 March	1914
B 16093-2	Still as the Night	10 June	1915
B 23906-1	O Cease Thy Singing, Maiden Fair	2 April	1920
B 23905-1	When Night Descends	2 April	1920

SP 33-22. RCA Camden. "This is Stereo."

| BVE 58586-2 The Rose of Tralee | 19 February | 1930 |

VIC 1393. RCA Victrola. "A John McCormack Collection of Arias, Duets, and Songs."

C 8693-1	LA TRAVIATA: Lunge da lei per me...De'miei bollenti	10 March	1910
C 8739-1	LA FILLE DU REGIMENT: Per viver vicino a Maria	23 March	1910
B 13223-1	RIGOLETTO: Questa o quella	1 May	1913
C 8737-2	LA BOHEME: Ah Mimi, tu piu non torni, with Sammarco	23 March	1910
C 14694-1	AIDA: Tutto è finito...O terra addio, with Marsh	9 April	1914
C 8535-1	LUCIA DI LAMMERMOOR: Fra poco a me ricovero	3 January	1910
C 8740-1	LUCIA DI LAMMERMOOR: Tu che a Dio spiegasti	23 March	1910
B 8738-2	LA PÊCHEURS DE PERLES: Del tempio al limitar with Sammarco	4 April	1911
C 17656-1	DIE MEISTERSINGER: Morning was gleaming	10 May	1916
C 8536-2	L'ELISIR D'AMORE: Una furtiva lagrima	1 February	1910
B 23902-1	SEMELE: Oh Sleep! Why dost thou leave me?	1 April	1920
B 28609-2	Pur Dicesti, O bocca bella	26 September	1923
B 26809-1	Swans	26 September	1923
B 28610-1	Die Liebe hat gelogen	26 September	1923
BVE 34160-2	Luoghi sereni e cari	17 December	1925
BVE 37148-1	All'mein Gedanken	17 December	1926
BVE 35893-1	Love's Secret	1 October	1926
BVE 27085-4	To the Children	17 December	1925
BVE 41546-2	By the Short Cut to the Rosses	13 January	1928

VIC 1472. RCA Victrola. "John McCormack - Arias."

C 17647-1	DON GIOVANNI: Il mio tesoro	9 May	1916
C 20898-1	JOSEPH EN ÉGYPTE: Champs paternels!	23 October	1917
C 8538-1	CARMEN: Il fior che avevi a me	7 January	1910
B 12707-1	LA PÊCHEURS DE PERLES: Mi par d'udir ancora	11 December	1912
C 8694-1	FAUST: Salve dimora	10 March	1910
B 8749-1	LAKME: Immemso vienteso...A vien al boscaglia	25 March	1910
B 12764-2	MANON: Chiudo gli occhi	3 January	1913
C 8589-2	LA BOHEME: Che gelida manina	1 February	1910
B 12705-1	MEFISTOFELE: Dai campi, dai prati	11 December	1912
B 12706-1	MEFISTOFELE: Giunto sul passo estremo	11 December	1912
C 11822-1	NATOMA: My commander as envoy...No country can	3 April	1912
B 12710-2	MARITANA: There is a flower that bloometh	11 December	1912
B 14677-2	THE BOHEMIAN GIRL: When other lips	11 May	1916
CVE 58692-1	TRISTAN UND ISOLDE: O König, das kann ich dir	10 March	1930

VIC 1622. RCA Victrola. "Songs of Sentiment."

Same contents as LM 2755.

VIC 1682. RCA Victrola. "A Golden Age Christmas."

| CVE 36606-1 Adeste Fideles | 1 October | 1926 |
| BVE 37147-1 The Holy Child | 17 December | 1926 |

WCT 8. RCA Red Seal. "Sacred Songs." (45 rpm, 7 inch, boxed set).

| CVE 38733-2 Panis Angelicus | 6 May | 1927 |
| C 14623-1   Angel's Serenade, with Kreisler | 25 March | 1914 |

WCT 10. RCA Red Seal. "Golden Age at the Met." (45 rpm, 7 inch, boxed set).

Same contents as LCT 1006.

WCT 12. RCA Red Seal. "Golden Voices Sing Light Music." (45 rpm, 7 inch, boxed set).
   Same contents as LCT 1008.

WCT 53. RCA Red Seal. "McCormack in Opera and Song." (45 rpm, 7 inch, boxed set).
   Same contents as LCT 1036.

WCT 57. RCA Red Seal. "Famous Duets." (45 rpm, 7 inch, boxed set).
   Same contents as LCT 1037.

WCT 1121. RCA Red Seal. "Caruso and McCormack Sing Christmas Music." (45 rpm, 7 inch, boxed set).
   Same contents as LCT 1121.

WDM 1626. RCA Red Seal. "Ten Tenors, Ten Arias." (45 rpm, 7 inch, boxed set).
   Same contents as LM 1202.

THE GRAMOPHONE CO. LTD. / E.M.I.

BLP 1084. "Favorite Songs by John McCormack." (10 inch).

BVE 40172-1	I Hear You Calling Me	12 October	1927
OEA 412-1	Jeannie With the Light Brown Hair	24 August	1934
BVE 58588-1	A Pair of Blue Eyes	19 February	1930
BVE 58586-2	The Rose of Tralee	19 February	1930
OEA 8323-1	I'll Walk Beside You	30 November	1939
OEA 2129-1	Believe Me If All Those Endearing Young Charms	28 June	1935
CVE 40165-2	Love's Old Sweet Song	11 October	1927
OB 3850-1	Bless This House	16 September	1932

BLP 1107. "John McCormack Sings to the Children." (10 inch).

Bb 11344-2	A Fairy Story By the Fire	2 September	1927
OEA 421-2	A Life Lesson	29 August	1934
OEA 422-1	Necklace of Love	29 August	1934
OEA 2123-1	When the Children Say Their Prayers	27 June	1935
OEA 8526-1	Little Wooden Head	12 April	1940
Bb 5117-2	To the Children, with Kreisler	24 September	1924
OEA 2124-1	Baby Aroon	27 June	1935
OEA 2183-1	O Men From the Fields (Cradle Song)	23 July	1935
OEA 8605-1	My Treasure	2 May	1940
Oea 8604-1	Mighty Lak' a Rose	2 May	1940

CSLP 501. "Fifty Years of Great Operatic Singing, Volume II, 1910 - 1920."
   Same contents as RCA LCT 6701.

CSLP 508. "Sacred Music Sung by Enrico Caruso and John McCormack."
   Same contents as RCA LCT 1121.

CSLP 518. "Operatic Duets."

C 14686-2	LA TRAVIATA: Parigi, o cara, with Bori	8 April	1914

7 EB 6029. "Songs of Ireland." (45 rpm, 7 inch).

OEA 8322-1	Star of the County Down	30 November	1939
Bb 21037-1	The Harp That Once Through Tara's Halls	4 December	1930
Bb 21036-2	Garden Where the Praties Grow	4 December	1930
OEA 423-1	Terence's Farewell to Kathleen	29 August	1934

7 EB 6034. "Songs of Pure Delight." (45 rpm, 7 inch).

OEA 412-2	Jeannie with the Light Brown Hair	24 August	1934
2EA 2750-1	She Is Far From the Land	31 March	1936

2EA 2751-1 Drink to Me Only With Thine Eyes   31 March   1936
OEA 411-1   Sweetly She Sleeps, My Alice Fair   24 August   1934

7 ER 5054. "Count John McCormack." (45 rpm, 7 inch).

OEA 8824-1 Passing By   11 July   1940
OEA 8822-1 Lass With the Delicate Air   11 July   1940
OEA 9315-1 The Village That Nobody Knows   29 May   1941
OEA 9458-1 The Green Bushes   26 August   1941
OEA 9461-1 Maureen   26 August   1941

7 ER 5066. "Songs From the Emerald Isle." (45 rpm, 7 inch).

B 18387-2   When Irish Eyes Are Smiling   20 September 1916
2EA 2749-2   Kerry Dance   31 March   1936
CVE 39889-3 Kathleen Mavourneen   11 October   1927
BVE 40173-2 Mother Machree   12 October   1927

7 ER 5181. "John McCormack's Favorite Songs." (45 rpm, 7 inch).

OEA 412-1   Jeannie With the Light Brown Hair   24 August   1934
2EA 2750-1 She Is Far From the Land   31 March   1936
2EA 2751-1 Drink to Me Only With Thine Eyes   31 March   1936
OEA 411-1   Sweetly She Sleeps, My Alice Fair   24 August   1934

7 ER 5188. "Songs of Ireland." 45 rpm, 7 inch).

Bb 21036-2 Garden Where the Praties Grow   4 December   1930
Bb 21037-1 The Harp That Once Through Tara's Halls   4 December   1930
OEA 423-1   Terence's Farewell to Kathleen   29 August   1934
OEA 8322-1 The Star of the County Down   30 November 1939

EX 29 0007 3. HMV Treasury. "John McCormack – Popular Songs and Irish Ballads."

Disc 1:
Bb 21036-2 Garden Where the Praties Grow   4 December   1930
Bb 21037-1 The Harp That Once Through Tara's Halls   4 December   1930
OEA 423-1   Terence's Farewell to Kathleen   29 August   1934
OEA 2129-1 Believe Me If All Those Endearing Young Charms 28 June   1935
2EA 2748-1 Green Isle of Erin   31 March   1936
2EA 2749-2 Kerry Dance   31 March   1936
OEA 2128-2 O Mary Dear   28 June   1935
OEA 8322-1 The Star of the County Down   30 November 1939

OEA 8849-1 Oft in the Stilly Night   9 August   1940
2EA 2750-1 She is Far From the Land   31 March   1936
OEA 8850-1 Meeting of the Waters   9 August   1940
OEA 8852-1 The Bard of Armagh   9 August   1940
OEA 9085-1 Down By the Sally Gardens   28 January   1941
OEA 9329-1 She Moved Thro' the Fair   25 June   1941
OEA 9458-1 The Green Bushes   26 August   1941
OEA 9655-1 Off to Philadelphia   3 December   1941
OEA 9459-1 Bantry Bay   26 August   1941

Disc 2:
OB 3850-1   Bless This House   16 September 1932
OEA 8323-1 I'll Walk Beside You   30 November 1939
2EA 2751-1 Drink to Me Only With Thine Eyes   31 March   1936
OB 5310-2   I Know of Two Bright Eyes   13 September 1933
OEA 412-2   Jeannie With the Light Brown hair   24 August   1934
OEA 9203-1 Loveliest of Trees   6 March   1941
OEA 9326-1 Linden Lea   25 June   1941
OEA 8824-1 Passing By   11 July   1940
OEA 2126-1 Song to the Seals   27 June   1935

OEA 8887-1 Silent Night   25 October   1940
OEA 8399-1 So Deep is the Night   2 May   1940
OEA 9065-1 O Could I But Express in Song   17 December 1940
OEA 8525-1 When You Wish Upon a Star   12 April   1940
OEA 8526-1 Little Wooden Head   12 April   1940
Bb 11345-1 The Silver Ring   2 September 1927
OEA 9202-1 Silent Noon   6 March   1941
OEA 2182-1 The Cloths of Heaven   23 July   1935
OEA 8320-1 The Old House   30 November 1939

EX 29 0056 3. "The Art of John McCormack."

Disc 1:

OEA 8806-1	Plaisir d'Amour	19 June	1940
OEA 8807-1	Nina	19 June	1940
2EA 2765-1	SEMELE: Wher'er you walk	7 April	1936
2EA 2764-1	IL PASTOR FIDO: Caro amor	7 April	1936
OEA 9316-2	Praise Ye the Lord	29 May	1941
Bb 5034-1	ATALANTA: Come My Beloved	4 September	1924
OEA 9100-1	Jesu, Joy of Man's Desiring	6 March	1941
OEA 9064-1	Oh, What Bitter Grief is Mine	17 December	1940
Bb 5096-2	Ridente la Calma	19 September	1924
OEA 9277-1	To Chloe	10 September	1942
Bb 11342-2	Who is Sylvia?	2 September	1927
2EA 2766-1	Träume	7 April	1936
Bb 5031-2	Die Mainacht	4 September	1924
Bb 5095-1	Feldeinsamkeit	19 September	1924
Bb 11339-2	Allerseelen	1 September	1927
Bb 5115-3	Morgen	24 September	1924
Bb 11338-2	Du meines Herzens Krönelein	1 September	1927

Disc 2:

OEA 2135-1	Auch kleine Dinge	28 June	1935
OEA 2134-1	Herr, Was trägt der Boden hier	28 June	1935
Bb 21031-1	Schlafendes Jesuskind	3 December	1930
Bb 21030-2	Anakreons Grab	3 December	1930
Cc 5029-1	Wo Find ich Trost	4 September	1924
OEA 8888-1	Legend: Christ in His Garden	25 October	1925
Bb 5116-2	Before My Window	24 September	1924
Bb 5101-1	How Fair This Spot	19 September	1924
Bb 5117-2	To the Children	24 September	1924
Bb 20690-2	Ave Maria (Cornelius)	5 December	1930
Cc 11335-2	La Procession	1 September	1927
OB 3852-1	L'Automne	16 September	1932
Bb 5035-1	O del Mio Amato Ben	4 September	1924
Bb 5033-2	Luoghi Sereni e Cari	4 September	1924
OEA 8822-1	Lass With the Delicate Air	11 July	1940
OB 3853-1	Is She Not Passing Fair?	16 September	1932
Bb 11346-1	Now Sleeps the Crimson Petal	2 September	1927
OEA 411-1	Sweetly She Sleeps, My Alice Fair	24 August	1934

HLM 7004. HMV Treasury. "Great Tenors."

Bb 5034-1	ATALANTA: Come My Beloved	4 September	1924

HLM 7037. HMV Treasury. "John McCormack, Tenor."

Bb 5117-2	To the Children	24 September	1924
Bb 5101-1	How Fair This Spot	19 September	1924
Cc 5030-2	Du bist die Ruh'	4 September	1924
Bb 5095-1	Feldeinsamkeit	19 September	
Bb 5094-2	Komm bald	19 September	1924
Cc 5029-1	Wo find ich Trost	4 September	1924
Bb 21030-2	Anakreons Grab	3 December	1930
2EA 2766-1	Träume	7 April	1936
Bb 20690-2	Ave Maria (Cornelius)	5 December	1930
OB 3853-1	Is She Not Passing Fair?	16 September	1932
OEA 426-1	The Quietest Things	29 August	1934
OEA 2180-1	Love's Secret	23 July	1935
OEA 2183-1	O Men From the Fields (Cradle Song)	23 July	1935
OEA 2181-1	She Rested By the Broken Brook	23 July	1935
OEA 9326-1	Linden Lea	25 June	1941
OEA 9327-1	The White Peace	25 June	1941
OEA 9316-2	Praise Ye the Lord	29 May	1941

HLM 7093. HMV Treasury. "Music Makers: An Anthology of Music by Friends of the Musicians' Benevolent Fund."

OEA 2182-1	The Cloths of Heaven	23 July	1935

HQM 1176. "John McCormack, Tenor."
Same contents as HLM 7037.

HQM 1228. "Famous British Tenors."

Bb 21026-2	There	3 December	1930
Bb 21029-2	Three Aspects	3 December	1930

7 P 211. (45 rpm, 7 inch).

OEA 8323-1	I'll Walk Beside you	30 November	1939
OEA 8322-1	The Star of the County Down	30 November	1939

7 P 238. (45 rpm, 7 inch).

OEA 8320-1	The Old House	30 November	1939
OEA 8321-1	A Child's Prayer	30 November	1939

7 P 276. (45 rpm, 7 inch).

OEA 2128-2	O Mary Dear	28 June	1935
OEA 2129-1	Believe Me If All Those Endearing Young Charms	28 June	1935

RLS 716. HMV Treasury. "L'Exquise Maggie Teyte."

2EA 9652-1	Still as the Night, with Teyte	25 November	1941

RLS 719. HMV Treasury. "Nellie Melba - The London Recordings, 1904 - 1926."

4188f	FAUST: All'erta! All'erta!, with Melba and Sammarco	12 May	1910
4189f	RIGOLETTO: Bella figlia, with Melba, Thornton, and Sammarco	12 May	1910
4190f	FAUST: All'erta! All'erta!, with Melba and Sammarco	12 May	1910

RLS 743. HMV Treasury. "The Record of Singing."

Lx 2797	MIGNON: In her simplicity	31 August	1908
Bb 5116-2	Before My Window, with Kreisler	24 September	1924

RLS 759. HMV Treasury. "The Hugo Wolf Society Recordings."

2B 2276-3	Ganymed	31 May	1932
2B 2277-2	Beherzigung	31 May	1932

RLS 766. HMV Treasury. "Schubert Lieder on Record, 1898 - 1952."

Cc 5030-2	Du bist die Ruh'	4 September	1924
Bb 11343-2	Die Liebe hat gelogen	2 September	1927

RLS 154 7003. HMV Treasury. "Schumann and Brahms Lieder on Record, 1901 - 1952."

Bb 5032-2	In Waldeseinsamkeit	19 September	1924
Bb 5094-1	Komm bald	19 September	1924
BVE 34167-2	Unter'm Fenster, with Bori	18 December	1925

E.M.I. AFFILIATED LABELS

Angel COLH 123. Great Recordings of the Century. "John McCormack - Classical Arias and German Lieder."

Bb 5034-1	ATALANTA: Come my Beloved	4 September	1924
Bb 5096-2	Ridente la Calma	19 September	1924
Bb 5033-2	Luoghi Sereni e Cari	4 September	1924
Bb £035-1	O Del Mio Amato Ben	4 September	1924
2EA 2765-1	SEMELE: Wher'er you walk	7 April	1936
2EA 2764-1	IL PASTOR FIDO: Caro amor	7 April	1936
OEA 8807-1	Nina	19 June	1940
OEA 9277-1	To Chloe	10 September	1942
Bb 5031-2	Die Mainacht	4 September	1924
Bb 5032-2	In Waldeseinsamkeit	4 September	1924

Bb 11343-2	Die Liebe hat gelogen	2 September	1927
Bb 11339-2	Allerseelen	1 September	1927
2B 2276-3	Beherzigung	31 May	1932
2B 2277-2	Ganymed	31 May	1932
OEA 2135-1	Auch kleine Dinge	28 June	1935
OEA 2134-1	Herr, was trägt der Boden hier	28 June	1935
2EA 2767-1	Schlafendes Jesuskind	7 April	1936

Angel COLH 124. Great Recordings of the Century. "John McCormack - Irish Songs and Ballads."

Bb 11346-1	Now Sleeps the Crimson Petal	2 September	1927
Bb 21036-2	Garden Where the Praties Grow	4 December	1930
OEA 423-1	Terence's Farewell to Kathleen	29 August	1934
OEA 412-2	Jeannie With the Light Brown Hair	24 August	1934
OEA 411-1	Sweetly She Sleeps, My Alice Fair	24 August	1934
OEA 2129-1	Believe Me If All Those Endearing Young Charms	28 June	1935
OEA 8322-1	The Star of the County Down	30 November	1939
OEA 8320-1	The Old House	30 November	1939
OEA 8852-1	The Bard of Armagh	9 August	1940
OEA 8850-1	Meeting of the Waters	9 August	1940
OEA 9067-1	Ye Banks and Braes	17 December	1940
OEA 8824-1	Passing By	11 July	1940
OEA 9202-1	Silent Noon	6 March	1941
OEA 9329-1	She Moved Thro' the Fair	25 June	1941
OEA 9458-1	The Green Bushes	26 August	1941
OEA 8851-1	The Gentle Maiden	9 August	1940
OEA 9869-1	Love Thee, Dearest, Love Thee	26 May	1942
OEA 9655-1	Off to Philadelphia	3 December	1941
OEA 8849-1	Oft in the Stilly Night	9 August	1940

Angel NP-4. Great Recordings of the Century. (Sampler).

2EA 2765-1	SEMELE: Wher'er you walk	7 April	1936

Note: The above three discs in the "Great Recordings of the Century" series were issued under the same numbers on various other E.M.I. labels.

Angel Seraphim 60113. Great Recordings of the Century. (Sampler).

Same contents as Angel NP-4

Angel Seraphim 60206. Great Recordings of the Century. "Great Tenors."

Same contents as HMV Treasury HLM 7004.

Arabesque 8105-2. "John McCormack - Arias and Art Songs." Issued by Caedmon Records.

Disc 1:

Lxx 3173	AIDA: Celeste Aida	7 September	1909
Lx 2491-4	RIGOLETTO: La donna e mobile	31 August	1908
Lx 2559-3	RIGOLETTO: Questa o quella	5 September	1909
Lxx 3152-2	LA FAVORITA: Spir'to gentil	7 September	1909
Lx 2501-2	TOSCA: E lucevan le stelle	5 September	1909
Lxx 2791-1	LA BOHEME: Che gelida manina	29 August	1908
Lxx 3138	CARMEN: Il fior che avevi a me	5 September	1909
2EA 2764-1	IL PASTOR FIDO: Caro amor	7 April	1936
2EA 2765-1	SEMELE: Wher'er you walk	7 April	1936
Lx 2795	CARMEN See here thy flower	31 August	1908
Lx 2797	MIGNON: In her simplicity	31 August	1908
Lx 2488	CAVALLERIA RUSTICANA: O Lola	31 January	1908
4189f	RIGOLETTO: Bella figlia, with Melba, Thornton, and Sammarco		
		12 May	1910
5205f	IL BARBIERE DI SIVIGLIA: O il meglio...Numero quindici,		
	with Sammarco	18 July	1911
5206f	LA GIOCONDA: Badoer questa notte...O grido di quest'anima		
	with Sammarco	18 July	1911
HO 201f	I GIOIELLI DELLA MADONNA: T'eri un giorna, with Kirkby-Lunn		
		15 July	1912

Disc 2:

OEA 2135-1	Auch kleine Dinge	28 June	1935
Bb 21031-1	Schlafendes Jesuskind	3 December	1930
Cc 5029-1	Wo find'ich Trost	4 September	1924
Cc 5030-2	Du bist die Ruh'	4 September	1924
Bb 11343-2	Die Liebe hat gelogen	2 September	1927
Bb 11342-2	Who is Sylvia?	2 September	1927
OEA 9277-1	To Chloe	10 September	1942
Bb 5031-2	Die Mainacht	4 September	1924
Bb 5032-2	In Waldeseinsamkeit	4 September	1924
Bb 5115-3	Morgen	24 September	1924
Bb 11339-2	Allerseelen	1 September	1927
Bb 11338-2	Du meines Herzens Krönelein	1 September	1927
OEA 8822-1	Lass With the Delicate Air	11 July	1940
OEA 8824-1	Passing By	11 July	1940

Arabesque 8124. "John McCormack - A Treasury of Irish Melodies." Issued by Caedmon Records.

Bb 21036-2	The Garden Where the Praties Grow	4 December	1930
Bb 21037-1	The Harp That Once Through Tara's Halls	4 December	1930
OEA 2129-1	Believe Me If All Those Endearing Young Charms	28 June	1935
Lx 1579	Come Back to Erin	5 December	1906
Lx 1582	Killarney	5 December	1909
Lx 2134	Terence's Farewell to Kathleen	1 June	1907
2EA 2749-2	Kerry Dance	31 March	1936
OEA 8322-1	The Star of the County Down	30 November	1939
2EA 2749-1	Green Isle of Erin	31 March	1936
OEA 2126-1	Song to the Seals	27 June	1935
Bb 11347-1	The Cloths of Heaven	2 September	1927
OEA 9063-1	The Blind Ploughman	17 December	1940
OEA 9084-1	When I Awake	28 January	1941
OEA 9314-1	The Dawn Will Break	29 May	1941
OEA 9328-1	The Little Boats	25 June	1941
OEA 9487-1	O Promise Me	6 October	1941
OEA 9278-1	Waiting for You	10 September	1942
2EA 9652-1	Still Is the Night, with Teyte	25 November	1941

E.M.I. Australia OXLP 7644. "The Great John McCormack."

2EA 2749-2	Kerry Dance	31 March	1936
OEA 8820-1	Kashmiri Song	11 July	1940
OEA 9085-1	Down by the Sally Gardens	28 January	1941
OEA 9100-1	Jesu, Joy of Man's Desiring	6 March	1941
OEA 8809-1	Trees	19 June	1940
OEA 2126-1	Song to the Seals	27 June	1935
OEA 8604-1	Mighty Lak' a Rose	2 May	1940
OEA 9459-1	Bantry Bay	26 August	1941
OEA 9478-1	Smilin' Thro'	6 October	1941
OEA 8806-1	Plaisir d'Amour	19 June	1940
OEA 8399-1	So Deep is the Night	2 May	1940
OEA 9082-1	"God Keep You" Is My Prayer	28 June	1941

Fiesta FLPS 1840. "John McCormack. Turn Ye to Me." (From E.M.I. Ireland).

C 15848-1	Turn Ye to Me	30 March	1915
B 8683-1	Annie Laurie	4 March	1910
B 14693-1	LILY OF KILLARNEY: The moon hath raised her lamp above, with Werrenrath	9 April	1914
C 17647-1	DON GIOVANNI: Il mio tesoro	9 May	1916
C 14686-1	LA TRAVIATA: Parigi, o cara, with Bori	8 April	1914
C 14657-5	RIGOLETTO: Bella figlia, with Bori, Jacoby, and Werrenrath	8 April	1914
Lx 3135	The Fairy Glen	7 September	1909
Lx 2843	Trottin' to the Fair	3 October	1908
B 11834-1	Silver Threads Among the Gold	5 April	1912
B 12759-2	Sweet Genevieve	2 January	1913
B 14675-2	Ben Bolt	7 April	1914

Bb 11344-2   A Fairy Story By the Fire   2 September 1927
BVE 58595-2 Little Boy Blue   21 February 1930

Fiesta FLPS 1856. "The Great John McCormack." (From E.M.I. Ireland).

Same contents as E.M.I. Australia OXLP 7644.

Isle 3001. "Golden Songs." (From E.M.I. Ireland).

Same contents as E.M.I. Australia OXLP 7644.

Music For Pleasure MFP 1090. "The Great John McCormack Sings Your Favorite Songs."

Same contents as E.M.I. Australia OXLP 7644.

Music For Pleasure MFP 50331. "The Great John McCormack."

Same contents as E.M.I. Australia OXLP 7644.

Talisman STAL 1057. "John McCormack. Turn Ye to Me."

Same contents as Fiesta FLPS 1840.

Tralee MKER 2002. "John McCormack - Irish Songs and Ballads."

Same contents as Angel COLH 124.

World Records P 69. "John McCormack." (Limited Edition Four Disc Set).

Disc 1:

Bb 21306-2	The Garden Where the Praties Grow	4 December	1930
Bb 21307-1	The Harp That Once Through Tara's Halls	4 December	1930
OEA 412-2	Jeannie With the Light Brown Hair	24 August	1934
OEA 423-1	Terence's Farewell to Kathleen	29 August	1934
OEA 2129-1	Believe Me If All Those Endearing Young Charms	28 June	1935
2EA 2748-1	Green Isle of Erin	31 March	1936
2EA 2749-2	Kerry Dance	31 March	1936
OEA 2128-2	O Mary Dear	28 June	1935
OEA 8322-1	The Star of the County Down	30 November	1939
OEA 8849-1	Oft in the Stilly Night	9 August	1940
2EA 2750-1	She Is Far From the Land	31 March	1936
OEA 8850-1	Meeting of the Waters	9 August	1940
OEA 8852-1	The Bard of Armagh	9 August	1940
OEA 9085-1	Down By the Sally Gardens	28 January	1941
OEA 9329-1	She Moved Thro' the Fair	25 June	1941
OEA 9458-1	The Green Bushes	26 August	1941
OEA 9655-1	Off to Philadelphia	3 December	1941
OEA 9459-1	Bantry Bay	26 August	1941

Disc 2:

Lxx 2852	I Hear You Calling Me	3 October	1908
Lxx 2962	Lolita	5 December	1908
Bb 11346-1	Now Sleeps the Crimson Petal	2 September	1927
Bb 11345-1	The Silver Ring	2 September	1927
OB 5308-2	South Winds	7 September	1933
OB 5310-2	I Know of Two Bright Eyes	13 September	1933
OEA 407-1	An Old Sacred Lullaby	24 August	1934
OEA 411-1	Sweetly She Sleeps, My Alice Fair	24 August	1934
OEA 2125-1	When I Have Sung My Songs	27 June	1935
OEA 2126-1	Song to the Seals	27 June	1935
2EA 2751-1	Drink to Me Only With Thine Eyes	31 March	1936
OEA 2127-1	Earl Bristol's Farewell	27 June	1935
OEA 2182-1	The Cloths of Heaven	23 July	1935
OEA 8320-1	The Old House	30 November	1939
OEA 8399-1	So Deep Is the Night	2 May	1940
OEA 8820-1	Kashmiri Song	11 July	1940
OEA 8821-1	Till I Wake	11 July	1940
OEA 8822-1	Lass With the Delicate Air	11 July	1940
OEA 8824-1	Passing By	11 July	1940

Disc 3:

OEA 8887-1	Silent Night	25 October	1940

OEA 9100-1	Jesu, Joy of Man's Desiring	6 March	1941
OEA 9064-1	Oh, What Bitter Grief is Mine	17 December	1940
OEA 9063-1	The Blind Ploughman	17 December	1940
OEA 9065-1	Oh, Could I But Express in Song	17 December	1940
OEA 9102-1	Silent Noon	6 March	1941
OEA 9326-1	Linden Lea	25 June	1941
OEA 9203-1	Loveliest of Trees	6 March	1941
OEA 9327-1	The White Peace	25 June	1941
OEA 9497-1	Jerusalem	6 November	1941
2EA 2765-1	SEMELE: Wher'er you walk	7 April	1936
2EA 2764-1	IL PASTOR FIDO: Caro amor	7 April	1936
OEA 8806-1	Plaisir d'Amour	19 June	1940
Bb 11343-2	Who is Sylvia?	2 September	1927
4189f	RIGOLETTO: Bella figlia, with Melba, Thornton, and Sammarco	12 May	1910
CR 1497-1	Panis Angelicus	5 September	1927
Cc 11335-2	La Procession	1 September	1927
Bb 5117-2	To the Children	24 September	1924

Disc 4:

OB 3850-1	Bless This House	16 September	1932
OB 3851-2	Once in a Blue Moon	16 September	1932
OB 5307-2	Love's Roses	7 September	1933
OEA 409-1	Friend o' Mine	24 August	1934
OEA 410-1	Poor Man's Garden	24 August	1934
OEA 419-2	Green Pastures	29 August	1934
OEA 420-2	A Little Prayer for Me	29 August	1934
OEA 426-1	The Quietest Things	29 August	1934
OEA 422-1	A Necklace of Love	29 August	1934
OEA 8323-1	I'll Walk Beside You	30 November	1939
OEA 8525-1	When You Wish Upon a Star	12 April	1940
OEA 8526-1	Little Wooden Head	12 April	1940
OEA 8574-1	Magic of Your Love	12 April	1940
OEA 8604-1	Mighty Lak' a Rose	2 May	1940
OEA 8809-1	Trees	19 June	1940
OEA 9069-2	Light of the Sunset Glow	17 December	1940
OEA 9082-1	"God Keep You" is My Prayer	28 January	1941
OEA 9888-1	Say a Little Prayer	10 August	1942

World Records SH 110. "John McCormack. Wher'er You Walk."

Same contents as Angel COLH 123.

World Records SH 306. "The Young John McCormack Sings Songs of Old Ireland."

Lx 1565	A Nation Once Again	4 December	1906
Lx 1566	God Save Ireland	4 December	1906
Lx 1567	The Boys of Wexford	4 December	1906
Lx 1568	The Croppy Boy	4 December	1906
Lx 1569	Dear Little Shamrock	4 December	1906
Lx 1570	The Snowy Breasted Pearl	4 December	1906
Lx 1576	Green Isle of Erin	5 December	1906
Lx 1577	Kathleen Mavourneen	5 December	1906
Lx 1579	Come Back to Erin	5 December	1906
Lx 1582	Killarney	5 December	1906
Lx 2132	My Dark Rosaleen	1 June	1907
Lx 2134	Terence's Farewell to Kathleen	1 June	1907
Lx 2842	The Foggy Dew	3 October	1908
Lx 2843	Trotting to the Fair	3 October	1908
Lx 2133-2	Savourneen Deelish	3 October	1908
Lx 3156	Eileen Aroon	7 September	1909

World Records SH 399. "John McCormack in Opera, 1907 - 1912."

Lx 2488	CAVALLERIA RUSTICANA: O Lola	31 January	1908
Lx 2489	PAGLIACCI: To act!...On with the motley	31 January	1908
Lx 2501-2	TOSCA: E lucevan le stelle	5 September	1909
Lxx 2791-1	LA BOHEME: Che gelida manina	29 August	1908
Lx 2797	MIGNON: In her simplicity		

Lxx 3138	CARMEN: Il fior che avevi a me	5 September 1909
Lxx 3152-2	LA FAVORITA: Spir'to gentil	7 September 1909
Lxx 3173	AIDA: Celeste Aida	7 September 1909

Lx 2559-3	RIGOLETTO: Questa o quella	5 September 1909
Lx 2491-4	RIGOLETTO: La donna è mobile	31 August 1908
4189f	RIGOLETTO: Bella figlia, with Melba, Thornton, and Sammarco	
		12 May 1910
4188f	FAUST: All'erta! All'erta!, with Melba and Sammarco	
		12 May 1910
5205f	IL BARBIERE DI SIVIGLIA: O il meglio ...	
	Numero quindici, with Sammarco	
		18 July 1911
5206f	LA GIOCONDA: Badoer questa notte... O grido di	
	quest'anima, with Sammarco	18 July 1911
HO 201af	I GIOIELLI DELLA MADONNA: T'eri un giorna,	
	with Kirkby-Lunn	15 July 1912
5203f	Mira la bianca luna, with Destinn	18 July 1911

PEARL HISTORICAL RECORDINGS / PAVILION RECORDS

GEMM 132. "Fritz Kreisler - Encores."

C 14624-2	Ave Maria (Bach-Gounod)	31 March	1914
B 14651-1	Serenade (Schubert)	31 March	1914
B 17655-1	CONTES D'HOFFMAN: Beauteous night (Barcarolle)	10 May	1916

GEMM 155 - 160. "Count John McCormack - The Years of Triumph." (Six Disc Set).

GEMM 155:

Lxx 3152-2	LA FAVORITA: Spir'to gentil	7 September	1909
C 8536-2	L'ELISIR D'AMORE: Una furtiva lagrima	1 February	1910
C 8535-1	LUCIA DI LAMMERMOOR: Fra poco a me ricovero	3 January	1910
C 8740-1	LUCIA DI LAMMERMOOR: Tu che a Dio Spiegasti l'ali	23 March	1910
C 8739-1	LA FILLE DU REGIMENT: Per viver vicino a Maria	23 March	1910
B 10137-3	Li Marinari, with Sammarco	4 April	1911
5203f	Mira la Bianca Luna, with Destinn	18 July	1911
5205f	IL BARBIERE DI SIVIGLIA: O il meglio...Numero		
	quindici, with Sammarco	18 July	1911

Lxx 3173-1	AIDA: Celeste Aida	7 September	1909
C 14694-1	AIDA: Tutto e finito...O terra addio, with Marsh	9 April	1914
C 8693-1	LA TRAVIATA: Lunge da lei...De'miei bollenti	10 March	1910
C 14686-1	LA TRAVIATA: Parigi, o cara, with Bori	8 April	1914
B 13223-1	RIGOLETTO: Questa o quella	1 May	1913
Lx 2491-1	RIGOLETTO: La donna è mobile	31 January	1907
4189f	RIGOLETTO: Bella figlia, with Melba, Thornton, and		
	Sammarco	12 May	1910
C 14657-5	RIGOLETTO: Bella figlia, with Bori, Jacobi, and		
	Werrenrath	8 April	1914

GEMM 156:

C 8589-2	LA BOHEME: Che gelida manina	1 February	1910
B 14658-4	LA BOHEME: O soave fanciulla, with Bori	8 April	191
C 8737-1	LA BOHEME: Ah Mimi tu piu non torni, with Sammarco		
		23 March	1910
B 12705-1	MEFISTOFELE: Dai campi, dai prati	11 December	1912
5206f	LA GIOCONDA: Badoer questa notte...O grido di quest'		
	anima, with Sammarco	18 July	1911
B 14693-1	LILY OF KILLARNEY: The moon hath raised her lamp above,		
	with Werrenrath	9 April	1914
B 14677-2	THE BOHEMIAN GIRL: When other lips	11 May	1916
B 12710-2	MARITANA: There is a flower that bloometh	11 December	1912
C 8694-1	FAUST: Salve dimora	10 March	1910
4190f	FAUST: All'erta! All'erta!, with Melba and Sammarco		
		12 May	1910
B 8738-2*	LA PÊCHEURS DE PERLES: Del tempio al limitar	4 April	1911
B 12707-1	LA PÊCHEURS DE PERLES: Mi par d'udir ancora	11 December	1912

B 12764-2	MANON: Chiudo gli occhi	3 January	1913
B 8750-1	LAKME: Immenso vienteso...A vien al boscaglia	25 March	1910
C 13028-3	CARMEN: Votre mère avec moi...Ma mère je la vois	1 May	1913
C 8538-1	CARMEN: Il fior che avevi a me	7 January	1910
C 20898-1	JOSEPH EN ÉGYPTE: Champs paternels!	23 October	1917
B 8738-2*	LA PÊCHEURS DE PERLES: Del tempio al limitar		
	with Sammarco	4 April	1911

*This disc contains two transfers of B 8738-2. The second transfer is erroneously labelled C 8738-2.

GEMM 157 (All with Kreisler):

C 14623-1	Angel's Serenade	25 March	1914
C 14625-1	Le Nil	25 March	1914
C 14626-1	JOCELYN: Beneath the quivering leaves	25 March	1914
C 14633-1	Ave Maria (Schubert)	31 March	1914
C 14624-2	Ave Maria (Bach-Gounod)	31 March	1914
B 14651-1	Serenade (Schubert)	31 March	1914
B 14652-1	Ave Maria (Mascagni)	31 March	1914
B 16090-1	Serenata	10 June	1915
B 16091-2	Carmé	10 June	1915
B 16093-2	Still as the Night	10 June	1915
B 17654-1	Serenade (Raff)	10 May	1916
B 17655-1	CONTES D'HOFFMAN: Beauteous Night	10 May	1916
B 24036-1	The Last Hour	5 May	1920
B 23905-1	When Night Descends	2 April	1920
B 23906-1	O Cease Thy Singing, Maiden Fair	2 April	1920
Bb 5116-2	Before My Window	24 September	1924
Bb 5117-2	To the Children	24 September	1924
Bb 5115-3	Morgen	24 September	1924
Bb 5118-2	Padraic the Fiddler	24 September	1924
Bb 5119-1	I Saw From the Beach	24 September	1924

GEMM 158:

C 17647-1	DON GIOVANNI: Il mio tesoro	9 May	1916
Bb 5096-2	Ridente la Calma	19 September	1924
Bb 5031-2	Die Mainacht	4 September	1924
Bb 5032-2	In Waldeseinsamkeit	4 September	1924
Bb 5094-2	Komm bald	19 September	1924
Bb 5095-1	Feldeinsamkeit	19 September	1924
Cc 5029-1	Wo find ich Trost	4 September	1924
BVE 32538-2	Schlafendes Jesuskind	24 April	1925
Bb 5101-1	How Fair This Spot	19 September	1924
BVE 27085-4	To the Children	17 December	1925
BVE 40170-2	None But a Lonely Heart	12 October	1927
Bb 11338-2	Du meines Herzens Krönelein	1 September	1927
Bb 11339-2	Allerseelen	1 September	1927
B 28610-1	Die Liebe hat gelogen	26 September	1923
Cc 5030-2	Du bist die Ruh'	4 September	1924
Bb 11342-2	Who is Sylvia?	2 September	1927
Bb 11343-2	Die Liebe hat gelogen	2 September	1927
CVE 49209-1	Ave Maria (Schubert)	27 November	1928
CVE 49210-2	Serenade (Schubert)	27 November	1928
CVE 49237-3	Holy Night / To the Lyre	6 December	1928
CVE 49214-4	Hark! Hark! The Lark! / Who is Sylvia?	7 December	1928
CVE 49213-3	The Organ Grinder / Farewell	28 November	1928

GEMM 159:

B 18391-3	Crucifix, with Werrenrath	8 June	1917
B 20899-1	The Lord is My Light	23 October	1917
C 27043-1	The Lost Chord	20 October	1922
BVE 37147-1	The Holy Child	17 December	1926
BVE 36363-1	Just For Today	28 September	1926
BVE 36384-1	Les Rameaux	4 October	1926
CVE 38388-1	Christ Went Up into the Hills	4 May	1927
Cc 11335-2	La Procession	1 September	1927
CR 1497-1	Panis Angelicus	5 September	1927
C 15849-1	Adeste Fideles	31 March	1915

B 23902-1	SEMELE: Oh Sleep! Why dost thou leave me?	1 April	1920
Bb 5034-1	ATALANTA: Come my Beloved	4 September	1924
HO 201 af	I GIOIELLI DELLA MADONNA: T'eri un giorno,		
	with Kirkby-Lunn	15 July	1912
Bb 5033-2	Luoghi Sereni e cari	4 September	1924
BVE 34160-2	Luoghi Sereni e cari	17 December	1925
BVE 37149-1	All'mein Gedanken	17 December	1926
BVE 35893-1	Love's Secret	1 October	1926
Bb 11337-1	A Dream of Spring	1 September	1927
Bb 11336-1	Desolation	1 September	1927
Bb 11340-2	Since First I Saw Your Face	2 September	1927
Bb 5035-1	O Del Mio Amato Ben	4 September	1924

GEMM 160:

B 28609-2	Pur Dicesti	26 September	1923
B 28613-1	Swans	26 September	1923
B 11815-1	Take, O Take Those Lips Away	2 April	1912
C 8587-3	Drink to Me Only With Thine Eyes	4 March	1910
B 8696-1	When Shadows Gather	10 March	1910
B 8695-2	I Hear You Calling Me	16 March	1911
B 15415-1	It's a Long Way to Tipperary	23 November	1914
B 20017-2	Keep the Home Fires Burning	7 June	1917
C 11822-1	NATOMA: My commander as envoy...No country can	3 April	1912
C 17656-1	DIE MEISTERSINGER: Morning was gleaming	10 May	1916

Lxx 2962	Lolita	5 December	1908
Lx 2500	Thora	3 February	1908
5931b	Believe Me If All Those Endearing Young Charms	24 September	1904
B 29871-2	Onward Christian Soldiers	9 April	1924
B 28612-1	Widmung	26 September	1923
B 23799-2	The Singer's Consolation	2 April	1920
C 11813-1	Maire, My Girl	2 April	1912
C 11817-1	Asthore	2 April	1912
C 17648-1	Kerry Dance	9 May	1916
Bb 11344-2	A Fairy Story By the Fire	2 September	1927
Bb 11345-1	The Silver Ring	2 September	1927
Bb 11346-1	Now Sleeps the Crimson Petal	2 September	1927
(Film)	Kitty My Love, Will You Marry Me?		1929

GEMM 164. "Great Voices Sing Great Operas."

| C 17647-1 | DON GIOVANNI: Il mio tesoro | 9 May | 1916 |

GEMM 1763. "Panis Angelicus."

Contents of Side 1 are the same as Side 1 of GEMM 159.
Contents of Side 2 are the same as Side 2 of GEMM 160.

GEMM 183 - 188. "Count John McCormack - The Gentle Minstrel." (Six Disc Set).

GEMM 183:

(Broadcast)	Just For Today	11 October	1936
(Broadcast)	The Ould Turf Fire	11 October	1936
(Broadcast)	The Star of the County Down	11 October	1936
(Broadcast)	O Mary Dear	19 November	1936
(Broadcast)	Ever in My Mind	19 November	1936
(Broadcast)	Oh, What Bitter Grief is Mine	27 December	1936
(Broadcast)	The Star of the County Down	27 December	1936
(Broadcast)	The Silent Hour of prayer	27 December	1936

5934b	Come Back to Erin	23 September	1904
Lx 1569	The Dear Little Shamrock	4 December	1906
Lx 2132	My Dark Rosaleen	1 June	1907
Lx 2133	Savourneen Deelish	1 June	1907
Lx 2134	Terence's Farewell to Kathleen	1 June	1907
Lx 2135	Oft in the Stilly Night	1 June	1907
Lx 2843	Trotting to the Fair	3 October	1908
Lxx 3160	Green Isle of Erin	7 September	1909
C 8588-1	Come Back to Erin	1 February	1910
C 8741-1	The Snowy Breasted Pearl	23 March	1910

GEMM 184:

B 8751-1	My Lagan Love	25 March	1910
B 8819-1	Dear Little Shamrock	8 April	1910
B 8587-3	Believe Me If All Those Endearing Young Charms	16 March	1911
C10060-1	The Irish Emigrant	16 March	1911
C 10061-1	Kathleen Mavourneen	16 March	1911
C 8752-2	Molly Bawn	17 March	1911
B 10069-1	Mother Machree	17 March	1911
B 10134-1	Macushla	30 March	1911
C 10138-1	She Is Far From the Land	31 March	1911
B 11824-2	Eileen Aroon	3 April	1912
B 11833-1	The Harp That Once Through Tara's Halls	5 April	1912
B 12761-2	Where the River Shannon Flows	2 January	1913
B 12765-1	Molly Brannigan	3 January	1913
B 12767-1	The Foggy Dew	3 January	1913
B 13031-1	The Low Back'd Car	28 March	1913
B 13231-1	Eileen Allannah	2 May	1913
B 14667-1	My Wild Irish Rose	6 April	1914
B 14673-1	Avourneen	7 April	1914
C 15846-1	Come Into the Garden, Maude	30 March	1915

GEMM 185:

B 18387-2	When Irish Eyes Are Smiling	20 September	1916
B 19448-2	Eileen	5 April	1917
B 21809-1	My Irish Song of Songs	30 April	1918
B 23456-5	That Tumble Down Shack in Athlone	10 December	1919
B 23791-2	Sweet Peggy O'Neill	30 March	1920
B 23792-2	The Bard of Armagh	30 March	1920
B 23904-1	Next Market Day / Ballynure Ballad	2 April	1920
B 25353-2	Little Town in the Old County Down	17 June	1921
B 27031-4	Jesus, My Lord, My God, my All	20 October	1922
B 28608-2	Would God I Were the Tender Apple Blossom	26 September	1923
B 29870-2	Holy God, We Praise Thy Name	9 April	1924
BVE 32539-2	I Look Into Your Garden	24 April	1925
BVE 36362-3	When Twilight Comes	28 September	1926
CVE 39889-3	Kathleen Mavourneen	11 October	1927
CVE 40165-2	Love's Old Sweet Song	11 October	1927
BVE 40166-2	Bird Songs At Eventide	11 October	1927
BVE 40167-2	Beloved I Am lonely	11 October	1927
BVE 41544-2	The Irish Emigrant	13 January	1928
BVE 41546-1	By the Short Cut to the Rosses	13 January	1928
BVE 56198-2	Norah O'Neale	18 October	1929

GEMM 186:

B 10062-1	I'm Falling in Love With Someone	17 March	1911
C 10135-1	An Evening Song	30 March	1911
B 13033-1	Say "Au Revoir" But not "Goodbye"	28 March	1913
B 13220-2	A Little Love, A Little kiss	1 May	1913
B 18384-2	Love, Here Is my Heart	20 September	1916
B 14676-2	A Dream	7 April	1914
C 15839-2	When My Ships Come Sailing Home	29 March	1915
B 16762-2	Sing! Sing! Birds on the Wing	10 November	1915
B 17646-1	Dreams	9 May	1916
B 21808-2	Calling Me Home to You	30 April	1918
B 22253-1	Dream On, Little Soldier Boy	24 September	1918
B 22690-2	When You Look in the Heart of a Rose	16 April	1919
B 25351-4	Learn to Smile	17 June	1921
B 27029-3	Three O'Clock in the Morning	17 October	1922
B 29864-2	Indiana Moon	8 April	1924
B 29865-2	Marcheta	8 April	1924
B 31523	All Alone	17 December	1924
B 31526-3	Rose Marie	17 December	1924
BVE 32534-4	When You and I Were Seventeen	23 April	1925

GEMM 187:

BVE 32535-2	Moonlight and Roses	23 April	1925
BVE 32536-1	June Brought the Roses	23 April	1925

BVE 32537-2	The Sweetest Call	23 April	1925
BVE 33464-1	You Forgot to Remember	14 October	1925
BVE 33465-1	Oh, How I Miss you Tonight	14 October	1925
BVE 33819-3	Just a Cottage Small by a Waterfall	27 October	1925
BVE 33820-3	Through All the Days to Be	27 October	1925
BVE 33821-1	Mother My Dear	27 October	1925
BVE 23525-4	When You and I Were Young, Maggie	17 December	1925
BVE 11834-4	Silver Threads Among the Gold	23 December	1925
BVE 34176-2	A Brown Bird Singing	23 December	1925
BVE 36361-1	The Far Away Bells	28 September	1926
BVE 36374-1	Lilies of Lorraine	30 September	1926
BVE 36375-2	A Rose For Every Heart	30 September	1926
BVE 36376-2	Calling Me Back to You	30 September	1926
BVE 37148-2	Because I Love You	17 December	1926
BVE 15419-3	Somewhere a Voice is Calling	12 April	1927
BVE 38387-3	Falling Leaves	4 May	1927
BVE 38731-2	When You're in Love	6 May	1927
BVE 40171-2	The Rosary	12 October	1927
BVE 41543-2	Dear Old Pal of Mine	13 January	1928
BVE 41545-2	Roses of Picardy	13 January	1928

GEMM 188:

BVE 48178-3	Sonny Boy	19 November	1928
BVE 48179-1	Jeannine, I Dream of Lilac Time	19 November	1928
BVE 48180-1	Song of the Night	19 November	1928
BVE 48181-1	Gateway of Dreams	19 November	1928
BVE 49240-1	Under the Spell of the Rose	7 December	1928
BVE 51613-2	I Love to Hear You Singing	10 April	1929
BVE 51621-2	Garden in the Rain	12 April	1929
BVE 51622-2	Lover, Come Back to Me	12 April	1929
	(Soundtrack to the movie, Song O' My Heart:)		
(Film)	THE BOHEMIAN GIRL: When coldness or deceit		1929
(Film)	A Fairy Story by the Fire	August	1929
(Film)	Just For Today	August	1929
(Film)	I Feel You Near Me		1929
(Film)	Kitty, my Love, Will You Marry Me		1929
(Film)	The Magpie's Nest		1929
(Film)	The Rose of Tralee		1929
(Film)	Luoghi Sereni e Cari		1929
(Film)	Little Boy Blue		1929
(Film)	Plaisir d'Amour		1929
(Film)	All'mein Gedanken		1929
(Film)	Ireland, Mother Ireland		1929
(Film)	I Hear You Calling Me		1929
(Film)	A Pair of Blue Eyes		1929

GEMM 219. "Echo of Naples."

C 14623-1	Angel's Serenade	25 March	1914
B 14679-1	Funiculi, Funicula	8 April	1914

GEMM 233. "Kreisler plays Encores."

B 24037-2	Since You Went Away	5 May	1920
B 16092-1	Flirtation	10 June	1915

GEMM 240 - 245. "John McCormack - The Voice That Calls Across the Years."
                (Six Disc Set).

GEMM 240:

CVE 58684-1	CHRIST ON THE MOUNT OF OLIVES: Jehovah Hear Me	27 February	1930
CVE 58685-1	CHRIST ON THE MOUNT OF OLIVES: My Heart is Sore	27 February	1930
CVE 58684-2	CHRIST ON THE MOUNT OF OLIVES: Jehovah, Du mein Vater		
		27 February	1930
CVE 58692-1	TRISTAN UND ISOLDE: O König, das kann ich dir	10 March	1930
C 8738-2	LA PECHEURS DE PERLES: Del tempio al limitar		
	with Sammarco	31 March	1911
B 16092-1	Flirtation, with Kreisler	10 June	1915
B 24037-2	Since You Went Away	5 May	1920

Bb 21029-2	Three Aspects	3 December	1930
Bb 21026-2	There	3 December	1930
Bb 21030-2	Anakreons Grab	3 December	1930
Bb 21031-1	Schlafendes Jesuskind	3 December	1930
Bb 20690-2	Ave Maria (Cornelius)	5 December	1930
Bb 20691-2	The Prayer Perfect	5 December	1930
Bb 21032-1	Love's Secret	3 December	1930
Bb 21040-2	The Bitterness of Love	4 December	1930
Bb 21037-1	The Harp That Once Through Tara's Halls	4 December	1930
Bb 21036-2	The Garden Where the Praties Grow	4 December	1930
Bb 21028-1	Far Apart	3 December	1930
Bb 21037-3	The Fairy Tree	3 December	1930

GEMM 241:

B 10136-2	The Happy Morning Waits	31 March	1911
B 16765-2	Venetian Song	10 November	1915
B 12758-1	My Dreams	2 January	1913
B 17010-1	Parted (Tosti)	14 January	1916
C 13219-1	Goodbye	1 May	1913
B 13032-1	Sospiri miei Andate Ove Vi Mando	28 March	1913
C 17651-1	Non é Ver	9 May	1916
BVE 40178-2	The Auld Scotch Sangs	13 October	1927
BVE 40177-2	Annie Laurie	13 October	1927
B 14674-1	Mary of Argyle	7 April	1914
C 15848-1	Turn Ye to Me	30 March	1915
B 14668-2	Bonnie Wee Thing	6 April	1914
B 8683-1	Annie Laurie	4 March	1910
B 14675-2	Ben Bolt	7 April	1914

GEMM 242:

B 12763-1	Dear Love Remember Me	3 January	1913
B 14670-1	Golden Love	7 April	1914
B 15838-3	Evening Song	30 March	1915
B 16760-1	Forgotten	10 November	1915
B 23524-2	Thank God For a Garden	11 December	1919
B 15850-2	When the Dew is Falling	31 March	1915
B 22693-2	Only You	16 April	1919
B 17649-2	Your Eyes	9 May	1916
B 21812-1	Love's Garden Roses	1 May	1918
B 21810-2	Little Mother of mine	30 April	1918
B 11816-1	A Child's Song	2 April	1912
C 11814-1	Like Stars Above	2 April	1912
B 11819-1	A Farewell	2 April	1912
B 15420-2	Mavis	23 November	1914
B 23758-2	Beneath the Moon of Lombardy	4 March	1920
B 13218-2	I Hear a Thrush at Eve	1 May	1913
B 20019-2	Any Place is Heaven If You Are Near Me	7 June	1917
B 23901-1	The Barefoot Trail	1 April	1920
B 23523-2	Somewhere	11 December	1919
B 15847-1	Morning	30 March	1915

GEMM 243:

B 16764-1	A Little Bit of Heaven Fell From Out the Sky	10 November	1915
BVE 40173-2	Mother Machree	12 October	1927
B 19447-1	Ireland, My Sireland	5 April	1917
B 14667-1	My Wild Irish Rose	6 April	1914
B 23043-2	The Road That Brought Me to You	1 July	1919
BVE 38732-1	Tick, Tick, Tock	6 May	1927
B 12762-1	Within the Garden of My Heart	3 January	1913
B 28605-2	Dream Once Again	25 September	1923
B 28606-2	Thanks Be to God	25 September	1923
B 21811-2	Dear Old Pal of Mine	1 May	1918
B 17008-2	The Old Refrain	14 January	1916
B 17672-2	Cradle Song 1915	11 May	1916
B 29866-1	A Love Song	8 April	1924
B 29867-1	Little Yvette	9 April	1924
B 29872-1	When	9 April	1924

B 29873-3	Bridal Dawn	9 April	1924
B 23794-3	Wonderful World of Romance	1 April	1920
BVE 18385-1	Tommy Lad	20 September	1916
BVE 58595-2	Little Boy Blue	21 February	1930
BVE 58690-1	Song Of My Heart	10 March	1930
BVE 56189-2	Just a Corner of Heaven to Me	16 October	1929

GEMM 244:

B 19534-3	The Star Spangled Banner	29 March	1917
B 11825-2	The Rosary	5 April	1912
B 11834-1	Silver Threads Among the Gold	5 April	1912
B 15419-1	Somewhere a Voice is Calling	23 November	1914
C 15845-1	The Trumpeter	30 March	1915
B 13035-1	Down in the Forest	28 March	1913
B 12760-1	I'll Sing Thee Songs of Araby	2 January	1913
B 11823-1	I Know of Two Bright Eyes	3 April	1912
C 10063-1	Ah, Moon of My Delight	16 March	1911
B 18383-1	The Sunshine of Your Smile	20 September	1916
B 15417-3	The Vacant Chair	31 March	1915
B 14671-1	Because	7 April	1914
B 12704-1	At Dawning	11 December	1912
B 14669-1	Beautiful Isle of Somewhere	6 April	1914
C 12708-1	Nirvana	11 December	1912
B 13034-1	Mother of Mine	28 March	1913
B 13233-1	Goodbye, Sweetheart Goodbye	2 May	1913
B 14666-2	Little Grey Home in the West	6 April	1914
B 22691-1	Roses of Picardy	16 April	1919
B 12759-2	Sweet Genevieve	2 January	1913

GEMM 245:

B 8590-1	The Minstrel Boy	1 February	1910
5932b	Believe Me If All Those Endearing Young Charms	24 September	1904
5930b	Killarney	24 September	1904
C 8753-1	Has Sorrow Thy Young Days Shaded?	25 March	1910
C 8752-1	Molly Bawn	25 March	1910
BVE 41546-2	By the Short Cut to the Rosses	13 January	1928
BVE 58586-2	The Rose of Tralee	19 February	1930
BVE 56192-4	Ireland, Mother Ireland	21 February	1930
B 13235-1	Le Portrait	2 May	1913
4188f	FAUST: All'erta! All'erta!, with Melba and Sammarco	12 May	1910
BVE 61097-2	God Gave Me Flowers	6 July	1931
BVE 34166-5	Night Hymn at Sea, with Bori	24 December	1925
CVE 36606-1	Adeste Fideles	1 October	1926
B 14678-2	Come Where My Love Lies Dreaming	8 April	1914
B 28600-3	Wonderful One	24 September	1923
B 28601-2	Love Sends a Little Gift of roses	24 September	1923
B 20016-2	The Trumpet Call	7 June	1917
B 15844-2	Until	30 March	1915
B 23756-1	Honour and love	4 March	1920
B 22692-2	The First Rose of summer	16 April	1919

GEMM 252 - 256. "The Tenors." (Five Record Set).

B 23902-1	SEMELE: Oh Sleep!Why dost thou leave me?	1 April	1920
Bb 5034-1	ATALANTA: Come my Beloved	4 September	1924
B 18385-1	Tommy Lad	20 September	1916

GEMM 274 - 275. "A Centenary Celebration: Count John McCormack – The Light of Other Days."

GEMM 274:

2B 3419-2	Hymn to Christ the King	27 May	1932
2B 2276-3	Beherzigung	31 May	1932
2B 2277-2	Ganymed	31 May	1932
OB 3850-1	Bless This House	16 September	1932
OB 3851-2	Once in a Blue moon	16 September	1932
OB 3852-1	L'Automne	16 September	1932

OB 3853-1	Is She Not Passing Fair	16 September 1932
OB 3854-2	A Prayer to Our Lady	16 September 1932
OB 3855-1	Charm Me Asleep	16 September 1932
OB 3856-1	I Know of Two Bright Eyes	16 September 1916
OB 5305-4	As I Sit Here	7 September 1933
OB 5306-1	Vespers	7 September 1933
OB 5307-2	Love's Roses	7 September 1933
OB 5308-2	South Winds	7 September 1933
OB 5309-1	My Moonlight Madonna	7 September 1933
OB 5310-2	I Know of Two Bright Eyes	13 September 1933
OB 5308-1	South Winds	7 September 1933
(Broadcast)*Love's Roses		20 August 1935
(Broadcast)*Believe Me If All Those Endearing Young Charms		20 August 1935

*The final two items on this side are erroneously
labelled on the album jacket. They both derive from
the same broadcast from 1935 as shown here.

GEMM 275:

Bb 5094-1	Komm bald	19 September 1924
BVE TEST-426-1	TRISTAN UND ISOLDE: O König, das kann ich dir	15 October 1929
CVE 49209-2	Ave Maria (Schubert)	27 November 1928
CVE 49210-1	Serenade (Schubert)	27 November 1928
Bb 11341-2	FORTUNIO: J'amais la vieille maison grise	2 September 1927
CVE 38733-2	Panis Angelicus	6 May 1927
B 11825-3	The Rosary	30 March 1915
B 13225-1	Nearer My God to Thee	1 May 1913
5927b	Green Isle of Erin	24 September 1904
5938b	Eileen Allannah	26 September 1904
5945b	The Minstrel Boy	26 September 1904
B 28609-1	Pur Dicesti	26 September 1923
BVE 34159-3	Love Me and I'll Live Forever	17 December 1925
BVE 32541-2	Devotion	24 April 1925
B 27032-1	Remember the Rose	17 October 1922
B 23042-2	Rose of My Heart	1 July 1919
B 8695-3	I Hear You Calling Me	16 June 1921
B 17650-2	Little Boy Blue	9 May 1916
B 28602-2	Where the Rainbow Ends	24 September 1923
B 22256-2	When You Come Back	25 September 1918
B 20546-1	Send Me Away With a Smile	7 September 1917
B 21663-1	God Be With Our Boys Tonight	5 April 1918
BVE 38386-2	Under the Spell of the Rose	4 May 1927
B 27044-2	Kingdom Within Your Eyes	20 October 1922
B 28609-1	Pur Dicesti	26 September 1923

PPR 1. "Count John McCormack." (Broadcasts of 1938). (45 rpm, 7 inch).

(Broadcast) Garden Where the Praties Grow	17 March 1938
(Broadcast) Hail, Glorious Saint Patrick	17 March 1938
(Broadcast) The Bard of Armagh	25 April 1938
(Broadcast) The Star of the County Down	25 April 1938

This disc was included in set GEMM 183 - 188.

MISCELLANEOUS LABELS

Allegro 1718. "Musical Antique - McCormack: Songs of Ireland and England."

Lxx 3151-2	My Dark Rosaleen	7 September 1909
Lx 3156	Eileen Aroon	7 September 1909
Lx 1569	Dear Little Shamrock	4 December 1906
Lx 2841	Avenging and Bright	3 October 1908
Lx 1568	The Croppy Boy	4 December 1906
Lx 2133-2	Savourneen Deelish	3 October 1908
Lx 3166	The Ould Plaid Shawl	7 September 1909
Lx 2840	Has Sorrow Thy Young Days Shaded	3 October 1908
Lxx 2852	I Hear You Calling Me	3 October 1908

Lxx 2853	When Shadows Gather	3 October	1908
Lx 2796-2	I'll Sing Thee Songs of Araby	31 August	1908
Lx 2545	I Sent My Love Two Roses	29 February	1908
Lx 3137	Take, O Take Those Lips Away	5 September	1909
Lx 2850	Mary of Allendale	3 October	1908
Lxx 3158	O Lovely Night	7 September	1909
Lx 3168	Bay of Biscay	7 September	1909
Lx 2502	A Child's Song	3 February	1908

Allegro 1721. "Caruso and McCormack Antique."

Lx 2559-3	RIGOLETTO: Questa o quella	5 September	1909
Lx 2795	CARMEN: See here thy flower	31 August	1908
Lx 2797	MIGNON: In her simplicity	31 August	1908
Lx 2844	MARITANA:There is a flower that bloometh	3 October	1908
Lx 2619	THE BOHEMIAN GIRL: When other lips	30 March	1908
Lx 2793-2	Mattinata	31 August	1908
Lxx 2962	Lolita	5 December	1908
Lx 3153-2	Voi Dormite, Signora	7 September	1909
Lx 2963	Parted	5 December	1908

Allegro LEG 9022. "John McCormack - I Hear You Calling Me."

Lxx 2852	I Hear You Calling Me	3 October	1908
Lxx 2853	When Shadows Gather	3 October	1908
Lx 2796-2	I'll Sing Thee Songs of Araby	31 August	1908
Lx 2545	I Sent My Love Two Roses	29 February	1908
Lx 3137	Take, O Take Those Lips Away	5 September	1909
Lx 2850	Mary of Allendale	3 October	1908
Lxx 3158	O Lovely Night	7 September	1909
Lx 3168	Bay Biscay	7 September	1909
Lxx 3151-2	My Dark Rosaleen	7 September	1909
Lx 3156	Eileen Aroon	7 September	1909
Lx 1569	Dear Little Shamrock	4 December	1906
Lx 2841	Avenging and Bright	3 October	1908
Lx 1568	The Croppy Boy	4 December	1906
Lx 2133-2	Savourneen Deelish	3 October	1908
Lx 3167	The Ould Plaid Shawl	7 September	1909
Lx 2840	Has Sorrow Thy Young Days Shaded	3 October	1908

Allegro Royale 1555. "John McCormack."

Lx 2491-4	RIGOLETTO: La donna e mobile	31 August	1908
Lx 2501-2	TOSCA: E lucevan le stelle	5 September	1909
Lxx 3173	AIDA: Celeste Aida	7 September	1909
Lxx 2791-1	LA BOHEME: Che gelida manina	29 August	1908
Lxx 3152-2	LA FAVORITA: Spir'to gentil	7 September	1909
Lxx 3138	CARMEN: Il fior che avevi a me	5 September	1909
Lx 2489	PAGLIACCI: To act!...On with the motley	31 January	1908
Lx 2488	CAVALLERIA RUSTICANA: O Lola	31 January	1908
Lx 3162	L'Ultima Canzone	7 September	1909
Lx 3157	Ideale	7 September	1909
Lxx 2799	I Pianto del Core	31 August	1908

Allegro Royale 1595. "Ten Top Tenors."

| Lx 2501-2 | TOSCA: E lucevan le stelle | 5 September 1909 |

Allegro Royale 1902.

| Lx 2559-3 | RIGOLETTO: Questa o quella | 5 September 1909 |

Anna 1026. "John McCormack Recital."

(Broadcast)	SEMELE: Wher'er you walk		1940
(Broadcast)	The Star of the County Down		1940
(Broadcast)	I'll Walk Beside You		1940
(Broadcast)	If I Should Fall in Love Again, with Laye		1940
B 29870-2	Holy God We Praise Thy Name	9 April	1924
B 23799-2	The Singer's Consolation	2 April	1920

B 28610-1	Die Liebe hat gelogen	26 September	1923
B 22253-1	Dream on Little Soldier Boy	24 September	1918
OEA 9328-1	The Little Boats	25 June	1941
OEA 8851-1	The Gentle Maiden	9 August	1940
OEA 9314-1	The Dawn Will Break	29 May	1941
OEA 8849-1	Oft in the Stilly Night	9 August	1940
OEA 9487-1	O Promise Me	6 October	1941
OEA 9084-1	When I Awake	28 January	1941
OEA 9278-1	Waiting For You	10 September	1942
OEA 9063-1	The Blind Ploughman	17 December	1940
BVE 49240-1	Under the Spell of the Rose	7 December	1928
BVE 58690-1	Song of My Heart	10 March	1930
BVE 38731-2	When You're in Love	6 May	1927
BVE 38387-3	The Fallen Leaf	4 May	1927

Anna 1058. "One Hundred Recordings of 'Che gelida manina'."

| Lxx 2791-1 | LA BOHEME: Che gelida manina | 29 August | 1908 |

Asco A 110. "John McCormack in Opera and Song." (Notes by Lily McCormack).

Disc 1:

Lxx 3173	AIDA: Celeste Aida	7 September	1909
Lxx 3152-2	LA FAVORITA: Spir'to gentil	7 September	1909
Lxx 2791-2	LA BOHEME: Che gelida manina	29 August	1908
Lx 2501-2	TOSCA: E lucevan le stelle	5 September	1909
Lx 2491-1	RIGOLETTO: La donna e mobile	31 January	1908
C 8693-1	LA TRAVIATA: Lunge da lei...De'miei bollenti	10 March	1910
Lxx 3138	CARMEN: Il fior che avevi a me	5 September	1909
4190f	FAUST: All'erta! All'erta!, with Melba and Sammarco	12 May	1910

(Broadcast)	O Mary Dear	19 November	1936
(Broadcast)	The Star of the County Down	27 December	1936
OEA 9655-1	Off to Philadelphia	3 December	1941
(Broadcast)	The Ould Turf Fire	11 October	1936
OEA 8851-1	The Gentle Maiden	9 August	1940
OEA 9668-1	By the Lakes of Killarney	26 May	1942
(Broadcast)	The Garden Where the Praties Grow	17 March	1938
OEA 9083-1	At the Mid Hour of the Night	28 January	1941
OEA 9869-1	Love Thee Dearest	26 May	1942

Disc 2:

5205f	IL BARBIERE DI SIVIGLIA: O il meglio...Numero quindici, with Sammarco	18 July	1911
5206f	LA GIOCONDA:Badoer questa notte...O grido di quest' anima, with Sammarco	18 July	1911
5203f	Mira la Bianca Luna, with Destinn	18 July	1911
HO 201 af	I GIOIELLI DELLA MADONNA: T'eri un giorna, with Kirkby-Lunn	15 July	1912
C 8738-2	LA PÊCHEURS DE PERLES: Del tempio al limitar with Sammarco	31 March	1911
4189f	RIGOLETTO: Bella figlia, with Melba, Thornton, and Sammarco	12 May	1910

(Broadcast)	O, What Bitter Grief is mine	27 December	1936
(Broadcast)	SEMELE: Wher'er you walk		1940
OEA 8849-1	Oft in the Stilly Night	9 August	1940
(Broadcast)	The Silent Hour of Prayer	27 December	1936
(Broadcast)	So Do I Love You	13 May	1937
(Broadcast)	Shannon River	13 May	1937

Asco A 114. "Italian Vocal Music - An Anthology."

| 5205f | IL BARBIERE DI SIVIGLIA: O il meglio...Numero quindici, with Sammarco | 18 July | 1911 |

Associated Record Company, Disc No. 53. (45 rpm, 7 inch).

| C 8535-1 | LUCIA DI LAMMERMOOR: Fra poco a me ricovero | 3 January | 1910 |
| C 8740-1 | LUCIA DI LAMMERMOOR: Tu che a Dio spiegasti | 23 March | 1910 |

Lxx 3138	CARMEN: Il fior che avevi a me	5 September	1909
C 8536-2	L'ELISIR D'AMORE: Una furtiva lagrima	1 February	1910

Associated Record Company FDY 2064. "Voices From the Golden Age."

C 8694-1	FAUST: Salve dimora	10 March	1910
B 8750-1	LAKMĘ: Immenso vienteso...A vien al boscaglia	25 March	1910
B 8738-2	LA PÊCHEURS DE PERLES: Del tempio al limitar with Sammarco	4 April	1911
C 8739-1	LA FILLE DU REGIMENT: Per viver vicino a Maria	23 March	1910

Associated Record Company FDY 2068. "The Golden Voice of John McCormack."

Lxx 3138	CARMEN: Il fior che avevi a me	5 September	1909
Lxx 3173	AIDA: Celeste Aida	7 September	1909
LX 2491-1	RIGOLETTO: La donna e mobile	31 January	1908
B 8750-1	LAKME: Immenso vienteso...A vien al boscaglia	25 March	1910
Lx 2797	MIGNON: In her simplicity	31 August	1908
C 8694-1	FAUST: Salve dimora	10 March	1910
C 8536-2	L'ELISIR D'AMORE: Una furtiva lagrima	1 February	1910
B 8738-2	LA PÊCHEURS DE PERLES: Del tempio al limitar with Sammarco	4 April	1911
C 8535-1	LUCIA DI LAMMERMOOR: Fra poco a me ricovero	3 January	1910
C 8740-1	LUCIA DI LAMMERMOOR: Tu che a Dio spiegasti	23 March	1910
Lx 2844	MARITANA: There is a flower that bloometh	3 October	1908
C 8739-1	LA FILLE DU REGIMENT: Per viver vicino a Maria	23 March	1910
5205f	IL BARBIERE DI SIVIGLIA: O il meglio...Numero quindici, with Sammarco	18 July	1911

Audio Rarities LPA 2340. "The Glorious Years of Opera, 1900 – 1910."

Lxx 3173	AIDA: Celeste Aida	7 September	1909
Lx 2501-2	TOSCA: E lucevan le stelle	5 September	1909

AU Records AU 4792. "John McCormack Memorial – On the Air, On the Screen, and on Records."

(Broadcast)	Just For Today	11 October	1936
(Broadcast)	The Ould Turf Fire	11 October	1936
(Broadcast)	The Star of the County Down	11 October	1936
(Broadcast)	Oh, What Bitter Grief is Mine	27 December	1936
(Broadcast)	The Star of the County Down	27 December	1936
(Broadcast)	The Silent Hour of Prayer	27 December	1936
BVE 40166-2	Bird Songs at Eventide	11 October	1927
Bb 11344-2	A Fairy Story By the Fire	2 September	1927
BVE 41546-2	By the Short Cut to the Rosses	13 January	1928
Bb 21040-2	The Bitterness of Love	4 December	1930
Bb 21032-1	Love's Secret	3 December	1930
Bb 21027-3	The Fairy Tree	3 December	1930
	Musical selections from Wings of the Morning:		
(Film)	Believe Me If All Those Endearing Young Charms	Summer	1936
(Film)	Killarney	Summer	1936
(Film)	The Dawning of the Day	Summer	1936
OEA 424-2	The Dawning of the Day	29 August	1934
Bb 21028-1	Far Apart	3 December	1930
2EA 9651-2	Night Hymn at Sea, with Teyte	25 November	1941
OEA 9099-1	Jesus Christ the Son of God, BWV 4	6 March	1941
OEA 9100-1	Jesu, Joy of Man's Desiring, BWV 147	6 March	1941
OEA 9326-1	Linden Lea	25 March	1941
OEA 9478-1	Smilin' Thro'	6 October	1941
OEA 2126-1	Song to the Seals	27 June	1935

Avoca AV 112. "A John McCormack Concert."

(Broadcast)	O Mary Dear	19 November	1936
OEA 9668-1	By the Lakes of Killarney	26 May	1942
(Broadcast)	The Silent Hour of Prayer	27 December	1936
OEA 9083-1	At the Mid Hour of the Night	28 January	1941
(Broadcast)	The Ould Turf Fire	11 October	1936
OEA 8851-1	The Gentle Maiden	9 August	1940

(Broadcast)	The Star of the County Down	27 December	1936
OEA 9655-1	Off to Philadelphia	3 December	1941
(Broadcast)	O What Bitter Grief is Mine	27 December	1936
OEA 9869-1	Love Thee Dearest	26 May	1942
(Broadcast)	The Garden Where the Praties Grow	17 March	1938
OEA 8849-1	Oft in the Stilly Night	9 August	1940

Inauthentic applause added to conclusion of each selection. See note for broadcast of 27 December 1936. Also available in simulated stereo on ST 112.

Avoca AV 133. "Irish Tenors Through the Years."

| OEA 2128-2 | O Mary Dear | 28 June | 1935 |
| OEA 8322-1 | The Star of the County Down | 30 November | 1939 |

Belcantodisc AB 11. "John McCormack." (7 inch).

CVE 58684-1	CHRIST ON THE MOUNT OF OLIVES: Jehovah, Hear Me	27 February	1930
CVE 58685-1	CHRIST ON THE MOUNT OF OLIVES: My Heart is Sore	27 February	1930
B 8750-1	LAKME: Immenso vienteso...A vien al boscaglia	25 March	1910
B 12705-1	MEFISTOFELE: Dai campi, dai prati	11 December	1912
B 23902-1	SEMELE: Oh Sleep! Why dost thou leave me	1 April	1920

Belcantodisc BC 231. "John McCormack."

Lx 2559-3	RIGOLETTO: Questa o quella	5 September	1909
Lx 2491-1	RIGOLETTO: La donna e mobile	31 January	1908
Lxx 3173	AIDA: Celeste Aida	7 September	1909
Lxx 3152-2	LA FAVORITA: Spir'to gentil	7 September	1909
Lx 2797	MIGNON: In her simplicity	31 August	1908
5206f	LA GIOCONDA: Badoer questa notte...O grido di quest' anima, with Sammarco	18 July	1911
Lx 2619	THE BOHEMIAN GIRL: When other lips	30 March	1908
C 8739-1	LA FILLE DU REGIMENT: Per viver vicino a Maria	23 March	1910
Lx 3138	CARMEN: Il fior che avevi a me	5 September	1909
C 13219-1	Goodbye	1 May	1913
B 28609-2	Pur Dicesti	26 September	1923
B 28613-1	Swans	26 September	1923
B 10137-3	Li Marinari, with Sammarco	4 April	1911

Belcantodisc BC 233. "Dame Nellie Melba."

| 4189f | RIGOLETTO: Bella figlia, with Melba, Thornton, and Sammarco | 12 May | 1910 |
| 4190f | FAUST: All'erta! All'erta!, with Melba and Sammarco | 12 May | 1910 |

Belcantodisc EB 12. "John McCormack." (7 inch).

Lx 2487	Like Stars Above	31 January	1908
Lx 2558	The Lord is My Light	2 March	1908
Lx 2500	Thora	3 February	1908
Lx 2135	Oft in the Stilly Night	1 June	1907

Belcantodisc EB 22. "John McCormack." (7 inch).

Lx 3162	L'Ultima Canzone	7 September	1909
Lx 3157	Ideale	7 September	1909
Lx 2490	Awakening of a Perfect Spring	31 January	1908
BVE 56189-2	Just a Corner of Heaven to Me	16 October	1929

Belcantodisc EB 36. "John McCormack in Opera." (7 inch).

Lx 2797	MIGNON: In her simplicity	31 August	1908
Lx 2491-1	RIGOLETTO: La donna e mobilé	31 January	1908
Lxx 3173	AIDA: Celeste Aida	7 September	1909
Lxx 3152-2	LA FAVORITA: Spir'to gentil	7 September	1909

Belcantodisc FB 1. "John McCormack." (7 inch).

Same contents as Belcantodisc AB 11.

Boulevard 4074. "John McCormack Sings Irish Songs and Other Favorites."

B 14674-1	Mary of Argyle	7 April	1914
B 11823-1	I Know of Two Bright Eyes	3 April	1912
B 13220-2	A Little Love, A Little Kiss	1 May	1913
B 11824-2	Eileen Aroon	3 April	1912
C 11817-1	Asthore	2 April	1912
C 8753-1	Has Sorrow Thy Young Days Shaded	25 March	1910
B 8683-1	Annie Laurie	4 March	1910
B 13031-1	The Low Backed Car	28 March	1913
B 13935-1	Down in the Forest	28 March	1913
B 12758-1	My Dreams	2 January	1913
B 14671-1	Because	7 April	1914
C 13219-1	Goodbye	1 May	1913
B 12760-1	I'll Sing Thee Songs of Araby	2 January	1913

Bulldog BDL 2019. "Twenty Golden Pieces of John McCormack."

C 15846-1	Come Into the Garden, Maude	30 March	1915
B 15838-3	Evening Song	30 March	1915
B 15844-2	Until	30 March	1915
B 15850-2	When the Dew is Falling	31 March	1915
B 14676-2	A Dream	7 April	1914
B 14679-1	Funiculi, Funicula	8 April	1914
B 18383-1	The Sunshine of Your Smile	20 September	1916
C 15839-2	When My Ships Come Sailing Home	29 March	1915
C 15848-1	Turn Ye to Me	30 March	1915
B 14675-2	Ben Bolt	7 April	1914
B 15847-1	Morning	30 March	1915
B 12759-2	Sweet Genevieve	2 January	1913
B 13035-1	Down in the Forest	28 March	1913
B 15420-2	Mavis	23 November	1914
B 19448-2	Eileen	5 April	1917
C 15845-1	The Trumpeter	30 March	1915
B 23525-2	When You and I Were Young, Maggie	11 December	1919
B 14666-2	Little Grey Home in the West	6 April	1914
B 11834-3	Silver Threads Among the Gold	3 January	1913
B 12704-1	At Dawning	11 December	1912

Cantilena 6207. "Nellie Melba Program."

| 4188f | FAUST: All'erta! All'erta!, with Melba and Sammarco | | |
| | | 12 May | 1910 |

Collectors' Records CRE 2 (Dublin). "John McCormack." (7 inch).

Same contents as Belcantodisc EB 12.

Collectors' Records CRE 5 (Dublin). "John McCormack." (7 inch).

Same contents as Belcantodisc EB 22.

Collectors C.C. Series CCS 1004. "John McCormack – Leo Slezak." (45 rpm, 7 inch).

| Lxx 3152-2 | LA FAVORITA: Spir'to gentil | 7 September | 1909 |
| Lxx 3173 | AIDA: Celeste Aida | 7 September | 1909 |

Columbia OL 5003. "Fritz Kreisler Violin Recital." (Japan).

C 14626-1	JOCELYN: Beneath the quivering leaves	25 March	1914
B 16093-2	Still as the Night	10 June	1915
B 23905-1	When Night Descends	2 April	1920
B 16091-2	Carmé	10 June	1915

Connoisseur CEN 1003. "John McCormack – Music of Ireland." (45 rpm, 7 inch).

Lx 2133-2	Savourneen Deelish	3 October	1908
Lx 1577-2	Kathleen Mavourneen	5 December	1906
5934b	Come Back to Erin	24 September	1904
5930b	Killarney	24 September	1904

Court Opera Classics CO 348. "Mario Sammarco." (Austria).

5206f	LA GIOCONDA: Badoer questa notte...O grido di quest'		
	anima, with Sammarco	18 July	1911

Court Opera Classics CO 374. "Louise Kirkby-Lunn." (Austria).

HO 201 af	I GIOIELLI DELLA MADONNA: T'eri un giorna, with		
	Kirkby-Lunn	15 July	1912

Court Opera Classics CO 382. "John McCormack." (Austria).

C 8536-2	L'ELISIR D'AMORE: Una furtiva lagrima	7 January	1910
C 8535-1	LUCIA DI LAMMERMOOR: Fra poco a me ricovero	3 January	1910
C 8740-1	LUCIA DI LAMMERMOOR: Tu che a Dio spiegasti l'ali	23 March	1910
C 8739-1	LA FILLE DU REGIMENT: Per viver vicino a Maria	23 March	1910
C 8693-1	LA TRAVIATA: Lunge da lei...De'miei bollenti	10 March	1910
C 14686-1	LA TRAVIATA: Parigi, o cara, with Bori	8 April	1914
B 13223-1	RIGOLETTO: Questa o quella	1 May	1913
B 12705-1	MEFISTOFELE: Dai campi, dai prati	11 December	1912
C 20898-1	JOSEPH EN ÉGYPTE: Champs paternels!	23 October	1917
B 8738-2	LA PÊCHEURS DE PERLES: Del tempio al limitar		
	with Sammarco	4 April	1911
B 12707-1	LA PÊCHEURS DE PERLES: Mi par d'udir ancora	11 December	1912
C 8538-1	CARMEN: Il fior che avevi a me	7 January	1910
B 8750-1	LAKME: Immenso vienteso...A vien al boscaglia	25 March	1910
B 12764-2	MANON: Chiudo gli occhi	3 January	1913
B 14658-4	LA BOHEME: O soave fanciulla, with Bori	8 April	1914
C 8737-1	LA BOHEME: O Mimi, tu piu non torni	23 March	1910

Delta TQD 3009. "John McCormack in Opera."

C 8694-1	FAUST: Salve dimora	10 March	1910
C 8693-1	LA TRAVIATA: Lunge da lei...De'miei bollenti	10 March	1910
C 8538-1	CARMEN: Il fior che avevi a me	7 January	1910
5205f	IL BARBIERE DI SIVIGLIA: O il meglio...Numero		
	quindici, with Sammarco	18 July	1911
C 8535-1	LUCIA DI LAMMERMOOR: Fra poco a me ricovero	3 January	1910
Lx 2491-4	RIGOLETTO: La donna e mobilé	31 August	1908
C 8536-2	L'ELISIR D'MORE: Una furtiva lagrima	1 February	1910
C 8740-1	LUCIA DI LAMMERMOOR: Tu che a Dio spiegasti l'ali	23 March	1910
5206f	LA GIOCONDA: Badoer questa notte...O grido di quest'		
	anima, with Sammarco	18 July	1911
Lxx 3173	AIDA: Celeste Aida	7 September	1909
C 8739-1	LA FILLE DU REGIMENT: Per viver vicino a Maria	23 March	1910
B 8750-1	LAKME: Immenso vienteso...A vien al boscaglia	25 March	1910

Delta TQD 3023. "John McCormack Sings Ballads."

Lx 2132	My Dark Rosaleen	1 June	1907
Lxx 2852-1	I Hear You Calling Me	3 October	1908
Lxx 3158	O Lovely Night	7 September	1909
C 8587-3	Drink to Me Only With Thine Eyes	4 March	1910
B 8751-1	My Lagan Love	25 March	1910
C 10063-1	Ah Moon of My Delight	16 March	1911
B 10137-3	Li Marinari, with Sammarco	4 April	1911
C 11814-1	Like Stars Above	2 April	1912
B 11816-1	A Child's Song	2 April	1912
B 11819-1	A Farewell	2 April	1912
B 11815-1	Take, O Take Those Lips Away	2 April	1912
B 11826-1	Wearing of the Green	3 April	1912
B 11833-1	The Harp That Once Through Tara's Halls	5 April	1912

Delta ATL 4078. "Nellie Melba."

Same contents as Belcantodisc BC 233. This disc was marketed on the Delta, Fidelio, and Leonora labels, all with the record number ATL 4078.

Demesne DRLP 007. "John McCormack Sings Irish Favorites."

Same contents as RCA Camden CAL 407.

Demesne DRLP 008. "John McCormack Sings Songs of Praise."

B 29870-2	Holy God We Praise Thy Name	9 April	1924
CVE 36606-1	Adeste Fideles	1 October	1926
BVE 37147-1	The Holy Child	17 December	1926
BVE 40171-2	The Rosary	12 October	1927
C 14624-2	Ave Maria (Bach-Gounod), with Kreisler	31 March	1914
B 13225-1	Nearer My God to Thee	1 May	1913
PBVE61097-2	God Gave Me Flowers	6 July	1931
CVE 38733-2	Panis Angelicus	6 May	1927
BVE 36363-1	Just For Today	28 September	1926
CVE 38388-1	Christ Went Up into the Hills	4 May	1927
B 20899-1	The Lord is My Light	23 October	1917
B 28606-2	Thanks Be to God	25 September	1923
C 14633-1	Ave Maria (Schubert), with Kreisler	25 March	1914

Design DLP 121. "The Greatest Voices of a Golden Era, Volume I."

Lx 2501-2	TOSCA: E lucevan le stelle	5 September	1909

Dolphin DOLB 7020. "The Golden Voice of John McCormack."

Same contents as Avoca AV 112, not including the inauthentic applause on that disc. Spoken introductions deleted from broadcast selections.

Dolphin DOLM 5023. "Memories of John McCormack."

B 11819-1	A Farewell	2 April	1912
B 18384-2	Love Here is My Heart	20 September	1916
B 21808-2	Calling Me Home to You	30 April	1918
BVE 32536-1	June Brought the Roses	23 April	1925
BVE 32539-2	I Look into Your Garden	24 April	1925
BVE 32537-2	The Sweetest Call	23 April	1925
BVE 33821-1	Mother, My Dear	27 October	1925
BVE 36361-1	The Far Away Bells	28 September	1926
BVE 36362-3	When Twilight Comes I'm Thinking of You	28 September	1926
BVE 36374-1	Lilies of Lorraine	30 September	1926
BVE 36375-2	A Rose for Every Heart	30 September	1926
BVE 40166-2	Bird Songs at Eventide	11 October	1927
Bb 11345-1	The Silver Ring	2 September	1927
BVE 40167-1	Beloved I Am Lonely	11 October	1927
BVE 49240-3	Under the Spell of the Rose	7 December	1928

Egmont EGM 7015. "Enrico Caruso - Operatic Arias / John McCormack - Irish Songs."

Lx 2133-2	Savourneen Deelish	3 October	1908
Lx 1567	The Boys of Wexford	4 December	1906
Lx 1568	The Croppy Boy	4 December	1906
Lx 1570	The Snowy Breasted Pearl	4 December	1906
Lx 2841	Avenging and Bright	3 October	1908
Lx 1566	God Save Ireland	4 December	1906

Ember 3400. "John McCormack Sings Irish Songs."

B 12761-2	Where the River Shannon Flows	2 January	1913
B 14667-1	My Wild Irish Rose	6 April	1914
B 13034-1	Mother O' Mine	28 March	1913
B 14693-1	LILY OF KILLARNEY: The moon hath raised her lamp above, with Reinald Werrenrath	9 April	1914
B 8683-1	Annie Laurie	4 March	1910
B 10134-1	Macushla	30 March	1911
C 8594-1	Killarney	3 January	1910
B 10069-1	Mother Machree	17 March	1911
B 13031-1	The Low Backed Car	28 March	1913
B 12765-1	Molly Brannigan	3 January	1913
B 13231-1	Eileen Allannah	2 May	1913
B 11826-1	The Wearing of the Green	3 April	1912

Ember GVC 11. "John McCormack Sings Irish Songs."

Same contents as Ember 3400.

Ember GVC 15. "John McCormack – Volume 2."

C 15846-1	Come Into the Garden, Maude	30 March	1915
B 15838-3	Evening Song	30 March	1915
B 15844-2	Until	30 March	1915
B 15850-2	When the Dew is Falling	31 March	1915
B 14676-2	A Dream	7 April	1914
B 14679-1	Funiculi, Funicula	8 April	1914
B 18383-1	The Sunshine of Your Smile	20 September	1916
C 15839-2	When My Ships Come Sailing Home	29 March	1915
C 15848-1	Turn Ye to Me	30 March	1915
B 14675-2	Ben Bolt	7 April	1914
B 15847-1	Morning	30 March	1915
B 12759-2	Sweet Genevieve	2 January	1915
B 13035-1	Down in the Forest	28 March	1913
B 15420-2	Mavis	23 November	1914
B 19448-2	Eileen	5 April	1917
C 15845-1	The Trumpeter	30 March	1915

Ember GVC 30. "John McCormack – Volume 3."

B 28608-2	Would God I Were the Tender Apple Blossom	26 September	1923
B 11825-3	The Rosary	30 March	1915
B 17008-2	The Old Refrain	14 January	1916
B 20018-1	There's a Long Long Trail A'Winding	7 June	1917
B 22693-2	Only You	16 April	1919
B 14668-2	Bonnie Wee Thing	6 April	1914
B 16760-1	Forgotten	10 November	1915
B 23523-2	Somewhere	11 December	1919
B 22691-1	Roses of Picardy	16 April	1919
B 23906-1	O Cease Thy Singing, Maiden Fair	2 April	1920
B 14674-1	Mary of Argyle	7 April	1914
B 17010-1	Parted	14 January	1916
B 17645-1	Dreams	9 May	1916
B 16762-2	Sing, Sing, birds on the Wing	10 November	1915
B 14665-1	Who Knows?	6 April	1914
B 21812-1	Love's Garden of Roses	1 May	1918

Ember GVC 51. "John McCormack – Volume 4."

B 23525-2	When You and I Were Young, Maggie	11 December	1919
B 12704-1	At Dawning	11 December	1912
B 14666-2	Little Grey Home in the West	6 April	1914
B 11834-3	Silver Threads Among the Gold	3 January	1913
B 13032-1	Sospiri miei, Andate Ove vi Mando	28 March	1913
B 15419-1	Somewhere a Voice is Calling	23 November	1914
B 16090-1	Serenata, with Kreisler	10 June	1915
B 14669-1	Beautiful Isle of Somewhere	6 April	1914
C 14626-1	JOCELYN: Beneath the quivering leaves, with Kreisler	25 March	1914
B 13033-1	Say "Au Revoir" But not "Goodbye"	28 March	1913
B 18385-1	Tommy Lad	20 September	1916
B 23791-2	Sweet Peggy O'Neill	30 March	1920
B 17672-2	Cradle Song 1915	11 May	1916
B 21810-2	Little Mother of Mine	30 April	1918
B 23524-2	Thank God For a Garden	11 December	1919

Eterna 469. "John McCormack – Operatic Recital." (10 inch).

Lxx 3152-2	LA FAVORITA: Spir'to gentil	7 September	1909
Lx2501-2	TOSCA: E lucevan le stelle	5 September	1909
Lx 2795	CARMEN: See here thy flower	31 August	1908
Lx 2488	CAVALLERIA RUSTICANA: O Lola	31 January	1907
Lxx 3173	AIDA: Celeste Aida	7 September	1909
Lx 2491-4	RIGOLETTO: La donna e mobilé	31 August	1908

Eterna 496. "John McCormack – Recital No. 2." (10 inch).

Lx 3162	L'Ultima Canzone	7 September	1909

Lx 3157	Ideale	7 September	1909
Lx 2799	I Pianto del Core	31 August	1908
Lxx 3138	CARMEN: Il fior che avevi a me	5 September	1909
Lxx 3135	Mountain Lovers	5 September	1909

Eterna 731. "John McCormack Recital."

Lxx 3173	AIDA: Celeste Aida	7 September	1909
Lx 2488	CAVALLERIA RUSTICANA: O Lola	31 January	1908
Lx 3162	L'Ultima Canzone	7 September	1909
B 12764-2	MANON: Chiudo gli occhi	3 January	1913
Lx 3157	Ideale	7 September	1909
C 17656-1	DIE MEISTERSINGER: Morning was gleaming	10 May	1916
Lxx 3152-2	LA FAVORITA: Spir'to gentil	7 September	1909
Lxx 3138	CARMEN: Il fior che avevi a me	5 September	1909
B 16091-2	Carmé, with Kreisler	10 June	1915
Lxx 3135	Mountain Lovers	5 September	1909
Lxx 2791-2	LA BOHEME: Che gelida manina	29 August	1908
Lx 2491-4	RIGOLETTO: La donna e mobile	31 August	1908
Lxx 2799	I Pianto del Core	31 August	1908
Lx 2501-2	TOSCA: E lucevan le stelle	5 September	1909

Eterna 739. "Gaetano Donizetti - Operatic Highlights."

C 8536-2	L'ELISIR D'AMORE: Una furtiva lagrima	1 february	1910

Everest 3258. "The Young Fritz Kreisler."

C 14626-1	JOCELYN: Beneath the quivering leaves	25 March	1914
B 16093-2	Still as the Night	10 June	1915
B 23905-1	When Night Descends	2 April	1920
B 16091-2	Carmé	10 June	1915

Famous Records of the Past FRP 1.

Lx 2491-4	RIGOLETTO: La donna e mobile	31 August	1908

Fidelio ATL 4050. "A Golden Treasury of the Past, Volume I."

C 8737-1	LA BOHEME: Ah Mimi, tu piu non torni, with Sammarco	23 March	1910

Fidelio ATL 4052. "A Golden Treasury of the Past, Volume III."

C 8694-1	FAUST: Salve dimora	10 March	1910
4190f	FAUST: All'erta! All'erta!, with Melba and Sammarco	12 May	1910

Fidelio ATL 4078. "Nellie Melba Program."

Same contents as Belcantodisc BC 233. Also marketed with this number on the Delta and Leonore labels.

Fidelio ATL 4085. "John McCormack Sings Irish Songs."

C 10060-1	The Irish Emigrant	16 March	1911
C 8753-1	Has Sorrow Thy Young Days Shaded	25 March	1910
C 10061-1	Kathleen Mavourneen	16 March	1911
C 8594-1	Killarney	3 January	1910
C 8588-1	Come Back to Erin	1 February	1910
Lx 3167	The Ould Plaid Shawl	7 September	1909
Lx 2133-2	Savourneen Deelish	3 October	1908
Lx 1567	The Boys of Wexford	4 December	1906
Lx 1568	The Croppy Boy	4 December	1906
C 8741-1	The Snowy Breasted Pearl	23 March	1910
Lx 2841	Avenging and Bright	3 October	1908
Lx 1566	God Save Ireland	4 December	1906

Fidelio ATL 4088. "Great Voices."

C 8741-1	The Snowy Breasted Pearl	23 March	1910

C 10061-1	Kathleen Mavourneen	16 March	1911
Lx 2491-4	RIGOLETTO: La donna e mobile	31 August	1908
Lxx 3173	AIDA: Celeste Aida	7 September	1909
C 8538-1	CARMEN: Il fior che avevi a me	7 January	1910
Lx 1566	God Save Ireland	4 December	1906

Galaxy 4834. "Caruso and McCormack Antique."

Same contents as Allegro 1721.

Golden Age of Opera EJS 295. "Potpourri 18."

| (Broadcast) Love's Roses | 20 August | 1935 |
| (Broadcast) Believe Me If All Those Endearing Young Charms | 20 August | 1935 |

Golden Age of opera EJS 478. "Maggie Teyte."

| 2EA 9652-2 | Still as the Night, with Teyte | 25 November | 1941 |

Golden Jubilee Record GJR 7. (7 inch).

Sterling Cylinders:
(612)	God Save Ireland	5 July	1906
(613)	The Boys of Wexford	5 July	1906
(682)	Come Back to Erin	5 July	1906

Edison Bell Cylinders:
(6449)	Once Again	November	1904
(6446)	Kathleen Mavourneen	November	1904
(6442)	The Dear Little Shamrock	November	1904

Note: Announcements omitted from these transfers. It is not known which takes of the Edison Bell recordings were used for side 2. This was a privately issued disc of which 100 copies were distributed.

Halo 50324. "John McCormack Antique. Irish Love Songs and English Ballads."

Same contents as Allegro 1718. Outer jacket also marked "Ultraphonic."

Heritage HER 509. "The Art of John McCormack." (45 rpm, 7 inch).

C 8535-1	LUCIA DI LAMMERMOOR: Fra poco a me ricovero	3 January	1910
C 8740-1	LUCIA DI LAMMERMOOR: Tu che a Dio spiegasti l'ali	23 March	1910
C 8538-1	CARMEN: Il fior che avevi a me	7 January	1910
C 8536-2	L'ELISIR D'AMORE: Una furtiva lagrima	1 February	1910

Hudson 225. "An Antique: McCormack – Caruso."

Same contents as side 1 of Allegro 1718.

ID Records IDLP 2005. "John McCormack Rarities."

BVE 56198-1	Norah O'Neale	18 October	1929
B 11816-1	A Child's Song	2 April	1912
B 23904-1	Next Market Day / A Ballynure Ballad	2 April	1912
BVE 33819-3	Just a Cottage Small By a Waterfall	27 October	1925
B 18383-1	The Sunshine of Your Smile	20 September	1916
B 23456-5	That Tumble Down Shack in Athlone	10 December	1919
B 27029-3	Three O'Clock in the Morning	17 October	1922
BVE 32534-4	When You and I Were Seventeen	23 April	1925
B 14669-1	Beautiful Isle of Somewhere	6 April	1914
BVE 33464-1	You Forgot to Remember	14 October	1925
B 21809-1	My Irish Song of Songs	30 April	1918
B 10062-1	I'm Falling in Love With Someone	17 March	1911
Bb 5119-1	I Saw from the Beach, with Kreisler	24 September	1924
B 22690-2	When You Look in the Heart of a Rose	16 April	1919

International Award Series AK 168. "The Greatest Voices of a Golden Era, Volume I."

| Lx 2501-2 | TOSCA: E lucevan le stelle | 5 September | 1909 |

Jay 3002. "John McCormack Sings Irish Songs."

| Lxx 3151-2 | My Dark Rosaleen | 7 September | 1909 |

Lx 2840	Has Sorrow Thy Young Days Shaded	3 October	1908
Lx 2133-2	Savourneen Deelish	3 October	1908
Lx 3167	The Ould Plaid Shawl	7 September	1909
Lx 2841	Avenging and Bright	3 October	1908
Lx 1569	Dear Little Shamrock	4 December	1906
Lx 3156	Eileen Aroon	7 September	1909
Lx 1568	The Croppy Boy	4 December	1906

Jay 3007. "John McCormack Sings Love Songs." (10 inch).

Lx 3168	Bay of Biscay	7 September	1909
Lx 3137	Take, O Take Those Lips Away	5 September	1909
Lx 2545	I Sent My love Two Roses	29 February	1908
Lx 2963	Parted	5 December	1908
Lxx 2962	Lolita	5 December	1908
Lx 3153-2	Voi Dormite, Signora	7 September	1909
Lxx 3158	O Lovely Night	7 September	1909

JM Records JM 201. "John McCormack in Song."

B 19447-1	Ireland, My Sireland	5 April	1917
B 19448-2	Eileen	5 April	1917
B 11824-2	Eileen Aroon	3 April	1912
B 13231-1	Eileen Allannah	2 May	1913
B 14673-1	Avourneen	7 April	1914
B 11819-1	A Farewell	2 April	1912
B 23902-1	SEMELE: O Sleep, why dost thou leave me	1 April	1920
B 11816-1	A Child's Song	2 April	1912
B 8751-1	My Lagan Love	25 March	1910
B 15847-1	Morning	30 March	1915
B 16762-2	Sing! Sing! Birds on the Wing	10 November	1915
B 15838-3	Evening Song	30 March	1915
B 11834-1	Silver Threads Among the Gold	5 April	1912
B 22693-2	Only You	16 April	1919
B 14670-1	Golden Love	7 April	1914
B 15844-2	Until	30 March	1915
B 10136-2	The Happy Morning Waits	31 March	1911

Note: The song "Until" is not listed on the label of this record.

JM Records JM 202. "John McCormack Sings."

C 15845-1	The Trumpeter	30 March	1915
C 11817-1	Asthore	2 April	1912
C 15848-1	Turn Ye to Me	30 March	1915
C 11813-1	Maire My Girl	2 April	1912
C 12708-1	Nirvana	11 December	1912
C 15846-1	Come into the Garden, Maude	30 March	1915
C 15839-2	When My Ships Come Sailing Home	29 March	1915
B 16091-2	Carmé, with Kreisler	10 June	1915
BVE 38732-1	Tick, Tick, Tock	6 May	1927
B 13235-1	Le Portrait	2 May	1913
B 16760-1	Forgotten	10 November	1915
B 13220-2	A Little Love, A Little Kiss	1 May	1913
B 21663-1	God Be With Our Boys Tonight	5 April	1918
B 23455-4	Your Eyes Have Told Me So	11 December	1919
B 12707-1	LA PÊCHEURS DE PERLES: Mi par d'udir ancora	11 December	1912

John McCormack Society of Greater Kansas City (no number). Soundtrack of Musical
Selections Sung by John McCormack in the Film Song O' My Heart.

(Film)	THE BOHEMIAN GIRL: When coldness or deceit		1929
(Film)	A Fairy Story by the Fire	August	1929
(Film)	Just For Today	August	1929
(Film)	I Feel You Near Me		1929
(Film)	Kitty, My Love, will You Marry Me		1929
(Film)	The Magpie's Nest		1929
(Film)	The Rose of Tralee		1929
(Film)	Luoghi Sereni e Cari		1929

(Film)	Little Boy Blue	1929
(Film)	Plaisir d'Amour	1929
(Film)	All'Mein Gedanken	1929
(Film)	Ireland, Mother Ireland	1929
(Film)	I Hear You Calling Me	1929
(Film)	A Pair of Blue Eyes	1929

John McCormack Society of Ireland JMcC 1. "John McCormack Sings." (7 inch).

B 12759-2	Sweet Genevieve	2 January	1913
Lx 2843	Trotting to the Fair	3 October	1908
B 11834-1	Silver Threads Among the Gold	5 April	1912
Lx 3155	The Fairy Glen	7 September	1909

John McCormack Society of Ireland JMcC 2. "John McCormack Sings." (7 inch).

C 14657-5	RIGOLETTO: Bella figlia, with Bori, Jacoby, and Werrenrath	8 April	1914
B 14693-1	LILY OF KILLARNEY: The moon hath raised her lamp above, with Werrenrath	9 April	1914
C 15848-1	Turn Ye to Me	30 March	1915
B 8683-1	Annie Laurie	4 March	1910

Leonora ATL 4078. "Nellie Melba Program."

Same contents as Belcantodisc BC 233.

Murray Hill S 4359. "The Great John McCormack Sings Irish Songs and Traditional Melodies."

This was a five disc set containing relabeled pressings of the first five Scala-Everest discs (SC 820, SC 843, SC 853, SC 873, and SC 882). It was available for the most part by mail only. Though the box states that the discs were rechanneled for stereo, this was not the case, and the Scala issue numbers may be discerned in the inner land areas of the discs.

Murray Hill 920344. "150 Songs, Jigs, Reels, and Ballads of Ireland."

One side of a disc in this five record set contains the same selections as Scala SC 873, omitting B 14693-1.

MRF Records MRF 5. "John McCormack Memorial: On the Air, On the Screen, and on Records."

Same contents as AU 4792.

New World Records NW 247. (American Art Songs).

B 28613-1	Swans	26 September	1923
Bb 21040-2	Bitterness of Love	4 December	1930

O.A.S.I. 539. "John McCormack – Down Memory Lane."

B 27029-3	Three O'Clock in the Morning	17 October	1922
B 28600-3	Wonderful One	24 September	1923
B 31523-2	All Alone	17 December	1924
B 29865-2	Marcheta	8 April	1924
BVE 32534-4	When You and I Were Seventeen	23 April	1925
BVE 32535-2	Moonlight and Roses	23 April	1925
BVE 33464-1	You Forgot to Remember	14 October	1925
BVE 33465-1	Oh, How I Miss You Tonight	14 October	1925
BVE 37148-2	Because I Love You	17 December	1926
BVE 48178-3	Sonny Boy	19 November	1928
BVE 48179-1	Jeannine I Dream of Lilac Time	19 November	1928
BVE 51621-2	A Garden in the Rain	12 April	1929
BVE 51620-2	Little Pal	12 April	1929
OEA 8525-1	When You Wish Upon a Star	12 April	1940

O.A.S.I. 603. "Emmy Destinn – Operatic and Song Recital."

5203f	Mira la Bianca Luna, with Destinn	18 July	1911

O.A.S.I. 619. "Bicentennial Celebration Offering, 1776 - 1976."

OEA 9667-3	Battle Hymn of the Republic	23 December	1941
OEA 9666-3	God Bless America	23 December	1941

O.A.S.I. "The Magic of McCormack."

Disc 1:

B 10069-1	Mother Machree	17 March	1911
B 10136-2	The Happy Morning Waits	31 March	1911
B 11834-3	Silver Threads Among the Gold	3 January	1913
C 8587-3	Drink to Me Only With Thine Eyes	4 March	1910
B 13220-2	A Little Love, A Little Kiss	1 May	1913
C 8738-2	LA PÊCHEURS DE PERLES: Del tempio al limitar with Sammarco	31 March	1911
B 14675-2	Ben Bolt	7 April	1914
B 14676-2	A Dream	7 April	1914
B 15847-1	Morning	30 March	1915
C 13028-3	CARMEN: Votre mère avec moi...Ma mère je la vois, with Marsh	1 May	1913

Disc 2:

C 13219-1	Goodbye	1 May	1913
C 15849-1	Adeste Fideles	31 March	1915
B 16091-2	Carmé, with Kreisler	10 June	1915
C 14623-1	Angel's Serenade, with Kreisler	25 March	1914
B 16764-1	A Little Bit of Heaven Fell From Out the Sky	10 November	1915
B 17010-1	Parted	14 January	1916
CVE 40165-2	Love's Old Sweet Song	11 October	1927
BVE 40166-2	Bird Songs at Eventide	11 October	1927
BVE 38732-1	Tick, Tick, Tock	6 May	1927
BVE 34159-1	Love Me and I'll Live Forever	17 December	1925
OEA 9656-1	Come Back My Love	3 December	1941

Pelican LP 110. "John McCormack - Moonlight and Roses."

BVE 32535-2	Moonlight and Roses	23 April	1925
BVE 29865-3	Marcheta	12 April	1927
BVE 41545-2	Roses of Picardy	13 January	1928
BVE 38732-1	Tick, Tick, Tock	6 May	1927
B 27029-3	Three O'Clock in the Morning	17 October	1922
BVE 48178-3	Sonny Boy	19 November	1928
BVE 34178-1	Love Me and I'll Live Forever	17 December	1925
BVE 33464-1	You Forgot to Remember	14 October	1925
BVE 58595-2	Little Boy Blue	21 February	1930
C 15845-1	The Trumpeter	30 March	1915
BVE 51620-2	Little Pal	12 April	1929
B 10062-1	I'm Falling in Love with Someone	17 March	1911
B 31526-3	Rose Marie	17 December	1924
BVE 51622-2	Lover Come Back to Me	12 April	1929

Pelican LP 101. "It's a Long Way to Tipperary."

B 15415-1	It's A Long Way to Tipperary	23 November	1914
B 20017-2	Keep the Home Fires Burning	7 June	1917
B 22691-1	Roses of Picardy	16 April	1919
B 20018-1	There's a Long Long Trail A'Winding	7 June	1917

Pelican LP 119. "Son of Tipperary - Original Songs of World War I, Volume 2."

B 20546-3	Send Me Away With a Smile	23 October	1917

Pickwick CDM 1024. "John McCormack Sings Irish Songs."

Same contents as RCA Camden CAL 407.

Pickwick CDM 1057. "John McCormack in Opera and Song."

Same contents as RCA Camden CDN 1057.

Pickwick HPE 669. "John McCormack in Irish Song."

    Same contents as Fidelio ATL 4085. Distributed on cassette as HPC 669.

Pickwick HPE 670. "John McCormack - My Dark Rosaleen and Other Popular Ballads."

    Same contents as Delta TQD 3023. Distributed on cassette as HPC 670.

Radiex RM 3. "The Best of Radio Memories, Volume 3."

(Broadcast) O Mary Dear	19 November	1936

Reader's Digest RD4 49. "Hear Them Again." (10 Disc Set).

BVE 40172-1 I Hear You Calling Me	12 October	1927

Reader's Digest RDA 57. "A Merry Christmas with World Famous Artists." (4 Disc Set).

C 14624-2	Ave Maria (Bach-Gounod), with Kreisler	31 March	1914
CVE 36606-1	Adeste Fideles	1 October	1926
CVE 38733-2	Panis Angelicus	6 May	1927

Reader's Digest RDM 2301/4. "A Merry Christmas with World Famous Artists."

    Same contents as Reader's Digest RDA 57.

Reader's Digest RDM 2678. "Golden Voices Sing Great Arias."

C 8693-1	LA TRAVIATA: Lunge da lei...De'miei bollenti	10 March	1910

Rhapsoady RHA 6001. "McCormack in Irish Song."

    Same contents as Fidelio ATL 4085.

Rhapsody RHA 6005. "John McCormack Sings Ballads."

    Same contents as Delta TQD 3023.

Rhapsody RHA 6012. "A Golden Treasury of the Past, Volume I."

    Same contents as Fidelio ATL 4050.

Rhapsody RHA 6015. "John McCormack in Opera."

    Same contents as Delta TQD 3009.

Rococo 5274. "John McCormack."

C 17647-1	DON GIOVANNI: IL mio tesoro	9 May	1916
C 8536-2	L'ELISIR D'AMORE: Una furtiva lagrima	1 February	1910
C 8535-1	LUCIA DI LAMMERMOOR: Fra poco a me ricovero	3 January	1910
C 8740-1	LUCIA DI LAMMERMOOR: Tu che a Dio spiegasti l'ali	23 March	1910
C 8739-1	FIGLIA DEL REGGIMENTO: Per viver vicino a Maria	23 March	1910
C 8693-1	LA TRAVIATA: Lunge da lei...De'miei bollenti	10 March	1910
C 14694-1	AIDA: Tutto è finito...O terra addio, with Marsh	9 April	1914
B 13223-1	RIGOLETTO: Questa o quella	1 May	1913
C 14657-5	RIGOLETTO: Bella figlia, with Bori, Jacoby, and Werrenrath	8 April	1914
B 14658-4	LA BOHEME: O soave fanciulla, with Bori	8 April	1914
C 8737-1	LA BOHEME: Ah Mimi, tu piu non torni, with Sammarco	23 March	1910
B 8738-2	LA PÊCHEURS DE PERLES: Del tempio al limitar with Sammarco	4 April	1911
C 17656-1	DIE MEISTERSINGER: Morning was gleaming	10 May	1916
B 12710-2	MARITANA: There is a flower that bloometh	11 December	1912
B 14677-2	THE BOHEMIAN GIRL: When other lips	11 May	1916
B 14693-1	THE LILY OF KILLARNEY: The moon hath raised her lamp above, with Werrenrath	9 April	1914

Rococo 5301. "John McCormack, Volume 2."

B 13032-1	Sospiri Miei, Andate Ove vi Mando	28 March	1913
B 10137-3	Li Marinari, with Sammarco	4 April	1911
C 17651-1	Non è Ver	9 May	1916

B 16765-2	Venetian song	10 November	1915
B 10062-1	I'm Falling in Love With Someone	17 March	1911
C 10135-1	An Evening Song	30 March	1911
B 13035-1	Down in the Forest	28 March	1913
B 12760-1	I'll Sing Thee Songs of Araby	2 January	1913
C 14625-1	Le Nil, with Kreisler	25 March	1914
B 13235-1	Le Portrait	2 May	1913
C 11817-1	Asthore	2 April	1912
B 14671-1	Because	7 April	1914
B 11816-1	A Child's Song	2 April	1912
B 11815-1	Take, O Take Those Lips Away	2 April	1912
C 8741-1	The Snowy Breasted Pearl	23 March	1910

Rococo 5319. "Dame Maggie Teyte."

| 2EA 9652-1 | Still as the Night, with Teyte | 25 November | 1941 |

Rococo 5321. "Lucrezia Bori."

| C 14686-1 | LA TRAVIATA: Parigi, o cara, with Bori | 8 April | 1914 |

Rococo 5343. "John McCormack, Volume 3."

Cc 5030-2	Du bist die Ruh'	4 September	1924
Bb 11342-2	Who is Sylvia?	2 September	1927
Bb 5094-2	Komm bald	19 September	1924
Bb 21030-2	Anakreons Grab	3 December	1930
Cc 5029-1	Wo find ich Trost?	4 September	1924
Bb 5115-3	Morgen, with Kreisler	24 September	1924
B 23906-1	O Cease Thy Singing, Maiden Fair, with Kreisler	2 April	1920
B 23905-1	When Night Descends, with Kreisler	2 April	1920
Bb 5116-2	Before My Window, with Kreisler	24 September	1924
C 10063-1	Ah, Moon of My Delight	16 March	1911
OEA 9201-1	The Street Sounds to the Soldiers' Tread	6 March	1941
OEA 9204-1	White in the Moon the Long Road Lies	6 March	1941
Bb 11336-1	Desolation	1 September	1927
Bb 11337-1	A Dream of Spring	1 September	1927
Bb 21032-1	Love's Secret	3 December	1930
OEA 2126-1	Song to the Seals	27 June	1935
Bb 21029-2	Three Aspects	3 December	1930
Bb 21040-2	The Bitterness of Love	4 December	1930

Rondo-Lette A 34. "Caruso – McCormack Antique."

Same contents as Allegro 1721.

Royale 18119. "John McCormack." (10 inch).

Lx 2491-1	RIGOLETTO: La donna e mobile	31 January	1908
Lxx 3173	AIDA: Celeste Aida	7 September	1909
Lxx 2791-1	LA BOHEME: Che gelida manina	29 August	1908
Lxx 3138-1	CARMEN: Il fior che avevi a me	5 September	1909
C 13219-1	Goodbye	1 May	1913
Lx 2489	PAGLIACCI: To act!...On with the motley	31 January	1908

Royale EP 324. "John McCormack." (7 inch).

C 13219-1	Goodbye	1 May	1913
Lx 3157	Ideale	7 September	1909
Lx 2491-4	RIGOLETTO: La donna e mobile	31 August	1908
Lxx 3173	AIDA: Celeste Aida	7 September	1909

Rubini GV 523. "John McCormack Recital."

CVE 49210-2	Serenade (Schubert)	27 November	1928
CVE 49209-1	Ave Maria (Schubert)	27 November	1928
CVE 49213-3	The Organ Grinder / Farewell	28 November	1928
CVE 49214-4	Hark! Hark! The Lark / Who is Sylvia?	7 December	1928
CVE 49237-3	Holy Night / To the Lyre	6 December	1928
BVE 34160-2	Luoghi Sereni e Cari	17 December	1925

Bb 11338-2	Du meines Herzens Krönelein	1 September	1927
BVE 27085-4	To the Children	17 December	1925
Bb 11336-1	Desolation	1 September	1927
Bb 11337-1	A Dream of Spring	1 September	1927
Bb 11345-1	The Silver Ring	2 September	1927
Bb 11341-1	FORTUNIO: J'amais la vieille maison grise	2 September	1927
BVE 38732-1	Tick, Tick, Tock	6 May	1927
BVE 40166-2	Bird Songs at Even tide	11 October	1927

Rubini GV 532. "John McCormack - Odeons."

Lx 2502	A Child's Song	3 February	1908
Lx 1565	A Nation Once Again	4 December	1906
Lx 1579	Come Back to Erin	5 December	1906
Lx 1582	Killarney	5 December	1906
Lx 3156	Eileen Aroon	7 September	1909
Lx 2558	The Lord is My Light	2 March	1908
Lx 2487	Like Stars Above	31 January	1908
Lx 1568	The Croppy Boy	4 December	1906
Lx 1567	The Boys of Wexford	4 December	1906
Lxx 2853	When Shadows Gather	3 October	1908
Lxx 2962	Lolita	5 December	1908
Lx 2430	I Sent My Love Two Roses	29 February	1908
Lx 3168	Bay of Biscay	7 September	1909
Lx 2796-2	I'll Sing Thee Songs of Araby	31 August	1908
Lx 1566	God Save Ireland	4 December	1906

Rubini GV 901. "John McCormack - Volume Three."

Bb 21040-2	The Bitterness of Love	4 December	1930
OB 3850-1	Bless This House	16 September	1932
OB 3851-2	Once in a Blue Moon	16 September	1932
BVE 36361-1	The Far Away Bells	28 September	1926
Bb 11345-1	The Silver Ring	2 September	1927
OB 3855-1	Charm Me Asleep	16 September	1932
BVE 23525-4	When You and I Were Young, Maggie	17 December	1925
BVE 11834-4	Silver Threads Among the Gold	23 December	1925
BVE 58586-2	The Rose of Tralee	19 February	1930
BVE 56192-4	Ireland, Mother Ireland	21 February	1930
BVE 15419-3	Somewhere a Voice is Calling	12 April	1927
Bb 21037-1	The Harp That Once Through Tara's Halls	4 December	1930
Bb 21036-2	The Garden Where the Praties Grow	4 December	1930
OB 5307-2	Love's Roses	7 September	1933
BVE 41545-2	Roses of Picardy	13 January	1928
BVE 41543-2	Dear Old Pal of Mine	13 January	1928
Bb 20691-2	The Prayer Perfect	5 December	1930

Saga 7029. "Nellie Melba."

4189f	RIGOLETTO: Bella figlia, with Melba, Thornton, and Sammarco	12 May	1910

Scala SC 820. "John McCormack, Tenor."

Lx 2501-2	TOSCA: E lucevan le stelle	5 September	1909
Lxx 3138	CARMEN: Il fior che avevi a me	5 September	1909
Lxx 3173	AIDA: Celeste Aida	7 September	1909
Lx 2491-1	RIGOLETTO: La donna e mobile	31 January	1908
Lx 2797	MIGNON: In her simplicity	31 August	1908
Lx 2488	CAVALLERIA: O Lola	31 January	1908
Lx 2489	PAGLIACCI: To act!...On with the motley	31 January	1908
Lx 2844	MARITANA: There is a flower that bloometh	3 October	1908
Lx 2502	A Child's Song	3 February	1908
Lx 3168	Bay of Biscay	7 September	1909
Lx 3167	The Ould Plaid Shawl	7 September	1909
Lx 3150-2	Lolita	7 September	1909
Lx 2793-2	Mattinata	31 August	1908
Lx 3153-2	Voi Dormite, Signora	7 September	1909
Lx 2963	Parted (Scott)	5 December	1908

Lx 3157   Ideale*   7 September 1909

*This title was not listed on some record labels.
Note: Late pressings of the Scala discs were reissued by Everest Records in
Scala-Everest jackets. Some discs had "Period" (another Everest subsidiary)
labels on the records marketed in these later jackets. See note for Murray
Hill (LP's) also.

Scala SC 843. "John McCormack Sings Irish Songs."

Lxx 2852	I Hear You Calling Me	3 October	1908
Lx 2431-2	A Farewell	28 November	1907
Lx 2432-2	Love's Golden Treasury	28 November	1907
Lx 2487	Like Stars Above	31 January	1908
Lx 2798	Roses	31 August	1908
Lx 2619	THE BOHEMIAN GIRL: When other lips	30 March	1908
Lx 2796-2	I'll Sing Thee Songs of Araby	31 August	1908
Lx 2840	Has Sorrow Thy Young Days Shaded?	3 October	1908
Lx 2430	Absent	28 November	1907
Lxx 2853	When Shadows Gather	3 October	1908
Lxx 3158	O Lovely Night	7 September	1909
Lxx 3160	Green Isle of Erin	7 September	1909
C 8741-1	The Snowy Breasted Pearl	23 March	1910
C 8588-1	Come Back to Erin	1 February	1910
C 10061-1	Kathleen Mavourneen	16 March	1911
B 13233-1	Goodbye, Sweetheart, Goodbye	2 May	1913

Scala SC 853. "John McCormack - Recital No. 3."

Lxx 2791-1	LA BOHEME: Che gelida manina	29 August	1908
Lxx 3152-2	LA FAVORITA: Spir'to gentil	7 September	1909
Lx 2559-3	RIGOLETTO: Questa o quella	5 September	1909
Lxx 2799	Pianto del Core	31 August	1908
Lx 3162	L'Ultima Canzone	7 September	1909
Lx 2841	Avenging and Bright	3 October	1908
Lx 3156	Eileen Aroon	7 September	1909
Lx 1568	The Croppy Boy	4 December	1906
Lxx 3135	Mountain Lovers	5 September	1909
Lx 1566	God Save Ireland	4 December	1906
Lx 1565	A Nation Once Again	4 December	1906
Lx 2132	My Dark Rosaleen	1 June	1907
Lx 2133-2	Savourneen Deelish	3 October	1908
Lx 3137	Take, O Take Those Lips Away	5 September	1909
Lx 2545	I Sent My Love Two Roses	29 February	1908
Lx 2850	Mary of Allendale	3 October	1908
Lx 1569	The Dear Little Shamrock	4 December	1906

Scala SC 873. "John McCormack - Volume 4: Irish Songs."

B 12761-2	Where the River Shannon Flows	2 January	1913
B 14667-1	My Wild Irish Roses	6 April	1914
B 13034-1	Mother o'Mine	28 March	1913
B 14693-1	LILY OF KILLARNEY: The moon hath raised her lamp		
	above, with Werrenrath	9 April	1914
B 8683-1	Annie Laurie	4 March	1910
B 10134-1	Macushla	30 March	1911
C 8594-1	Killarney	3 January	1910
B 10069-1	Mother Machree	17 March	1911
B 13031-1	The Low Backed Car	28 March	1913
B 12765-1	Molly Brannigan	3 January	1913
B 13231-1	Eileen Allanah	2 May	1913
B 11826-1	The Wearing of the Green	3 April	1912

Scala SC 882. "John McCormack - Songs of Romance."

B 14671-1	Because	7 April	1914
C 10135-1	An Evening Song	30 March	1911
C 8587-3	Drink to Me Only With Thine Eyes	4 March	1910
C 10063-1	Ah, Moon of My Delight	16 March	1911

B 12759-2	Sweet Genevieve	2 January	1913
C 14626-1	JOCELYN: Beneath the quivering leaves, with Kreisler	25 March	1914
B 13220-2	A Little Love, A Little Kiss	1 May	1913
B 13218-2	I Hear a Thrush at Eve	1 May	1913
B 11825-3	The Rosary	30 March	1915
B 12758-1	My Dreams	2 January	1913

Scala SC 889. "John McCormack – Love Serenades."

B 14651-1	Serenade (Schubert), with Kreisler	31 March	1914
B 17654-2	Serenade (Raff): with Kreisler	10 May	1916
B 14675-2	Ben Bolt	7 April	1914
B 14677-2	THE BOHEMIAN GIRL: When other lips	11 May	1916
B 17655-1	CONTES D'HOFFMAN: Beauteous Night, with Kreisler	10 May	1916
B 15419-1	Somewhere a Voice is Calling	23 November	1914
B 14652-1	Ave Maria (Mascagni)	31 March	1914
B 12704-1	At Dawning	11 December	1912
B 16093-2	Still as the Night, with Kreisler	10 June	1915
B 11834-3	Silver Threads Among the Gold	3 January	1913

Smithsonian RO 17. "The Music of Victor Herbert."

B 10062-1	I'm Falling in Love With Someone	17 March	1911
C 11822-1	NATOMA: My commander as envoy...No country can	3 April	1912

Summit LSE 2019. "John McCormack." (45 rpm, 7 inch).

C 8741-1	The Snowy Breasted Pearl	23 March	1910
Lx 1566	God Save Ireland	4 December	1906
Lx 1567	The Boys of Wexford	4 December	1906
C 10061-1	Kathleen Mavourneen	16 March	1911

Sutton SU 272. "The Best of John McCormack."

Lx 2841	Avenging and Bright	3 October	1908
Lx 1569	The Dear Little Shamrock	4 December	1906
Lx 3156	Eileen Aroon	7 September	1909
Lx 1568	The Croppy Boy	4 December	1906
Lxx 3151-2	My Dark Rosaleen	7 September	1909
Lx 2840	Has Sorrow Thy Young Days Shaded	3 October	1908
Lx 2133-2	Savourneen Deelish	3 October	1908
Lx 3167	The Ould Plaid Shawl	7 September	1909
Lx 3168	Bay of Biscay	7 September	1909
Lx 2963	Parted	5 December	1908

Top Artists Platters (TAP) T 321. "Twenty Great Duets of the Twentieth Century."

HO 201 af	I GIOIELLI DELLA MADONNA: T'eri un giorna, with Kirkby-Lunn	15 July	1912

Top Artists Platters T 325. "The Singers of Oscar Hammerstein the First."

Lx 2559-3	RIGOLETTO: Questa o quella	5 September	1909

Top Artists Platters T 303. "Twenty Tenors – Twenty Arias.".

Lx 2501-2	TOSCA: E lucevan le stelle	5 September	1909

Tapestry GD 7377. "Gilmour's Album: Favorite Recordings of Clyde Gilmour."

B 23902-1	SEMELE: Oh Sleep! Why dost thou leave me?	1 April	1920

Treasury GM 132. "John McCormack." (7 inch).

C 8694-1	FAUST: Salve dimora	10 March	1910
Lxx 3138	CARMEN: Il fior che avevi a me	5 September	1909
C 8738-2	I PESCATORI DI PERLE: Del tempio al limitar, with Sammarco	4 April	1911
C 8535-1	LUCIA DI LAMMERMOOR: Fra poco a me ricovero	3 January	1910

Lx 2491-4   RIGOLETTO: La donna e mobile   31 August   1908

Unique Opera Records Company UORC 107. "John McCormack, Tenor, 1930 - 1938."

Side 1:
Same contents as the disc issued by the John McCormack Society of Greater
Kansas City of the sountrack to Song O' My Heart, omitting "The Magpie's
Nest" and including a short excerpt of dialog. The sound quality is more
variable and largely poorer on UORC.

Side 2:
(Broadcast) O, What Bitter Grief is Mine   27 December   1936
(Broadcast) SEMELE: Wher'er you walk   1940
(Broadcast) O Mary Dear   19 November   1936
(Broadcast) The Star of the County Down   27 December   1936
OEA 9655-1 Off to Philadelphia   3 December   1941
(Broadcast) The Ould Turf Fire   11 October   1936
OEA 8851-1 The Gentle Maiden   9 August   1940
OEA 9668-1 By the Lakes of Killarney   26 May   1942
(Broadcast) The Garden Where the Praties Grow   17 March   1938
OEA 9083-1 At the Mid Hour of the Night   28 January   1941
OEA 9869-1 Love Thee Dearest   26 May   1942
            Note: There is a pressing flaw (recurring swish) on side 2 of many,
            if not all, copies of UORC 107.

Unique Opera Records Company UORC 151. "Potpourri No. 2."

(Broadcast) I'll Walk Beside You   2 January   1942

Voce Records 88. "Great Singers - Previously Unpublished Recordings."

B 27085-2   To the Children   20 November   1922
Bb 5116-1   Before My Window   24 September   1924
BVE TEST 426-1 TRISTAN UND ISOLDE: O König, das kann ich dir 15 October   1929
BVE 35891-1 She Rested By the Broken Brook   1 October   1926

Vocal Records Collectors Society VRCS 1968.

Bb 11338-2   Du meines Herzens Krönelein   1 September   1927

Westwood 504. "It's a Long Way to Tipperary."

Same contents as Pelican LP 101.

XTRA Records 1107. "John McCormack."

Same contents as Scala SC 882.

MICROGROOVE ADDENDA

The following information was received too late for inclusion at its proper
places in this discography: RCA CM 0700, "Golden Performances That Will Live Forever": BVE 40173-2 (12 October 1927); New World Records NW 241, "Toward an American
Opera": C 11822-1 (3 April 1912); RCA Camden CAS 535, "This is Stereo": Same as
RCA Camden SP-33-22 (which was a premium disc); TAP T 308, "Foremost Puccini Singers of the Twentieth Century": Lxx 2791-? (29 August 1908); and Music For Pleasure
MFP 1004, "The Greatest Singers, The Greatest Songs": Same contents as E.M.I. ISLE
3001, but omitting OEA 2126-1 and OEA 8806-1.

CENTENARY CASSETTE REISSUES

A set of four cassettes was offered for sale by mail under the auspices of the
English Chapter of the John McCormack Society of America to celebrate the centenary
of McCormack's birth. These tapes contained many commercial recordings, published
and unpublished, and broadcast transcriptions from fine quality originals. These
dubbings are the only form in which some of this material has been disseminated.
Where this is the case, these transfers are noted in the Recording Chronology. Further details may be obtained by writing to the Chapter at 2 Purbeck Court, 128
Oakleigh Road North, Whetstone, London N20 OTA, England.

Appendices

RCA Victor album C 3. "An Hour with Schubert." (4 12 inch 78 rpm records).

Disc 1, 6927:
CVE 49209-2	Ave Maria	27 November	1928
CVE 49210-1,2	Serenade	27 November	1928

Disc 2, 6928:
CVE 49213-3	The Organ Grinder / Farewell	28 November	1928
	(side B not McCormack)		

Note: Album C 3 also included Victor records 9307 and 9308, which contained various short compositions of Schubert played by the Victor Orchestra, conducted by Nathaniel Shilkret. Initially issued on Victrola Scroll labels, later albums had discs with Victor labels. In these later sets take 1 of the Serenade rather than the initial take 2 was used. This set did not include disc no. 6926.

RCA Victor album DM 1358. "Irish Songs By John McCormack." (3 10 inch 78 rpm discs).

Disc 1, 10-0040:
BVE 58586-2	The Rose of Tralee (rerecording)	19 February	1930
BVE 56192-4	Ireland, Mother Ireland (rerecording)	21 February	1930

Disc 2, 10-0041:
OEA 8850-1	The Meeting of the Waters	9 August	1940
BVE 41546-1	By the Short Cut to the Rosses	13 January	1928

Disc 3, 10-0042:
Bb 21037-1	The Harp That Once Through Tara's Halls	4 December	1930
OEA 2128-2	O Mary Dear	28 June	1935

Note: Sides were numbered for automatic record changer.

RCA Victor album MO 1228. "John McCormack Sings Again." (6 10 inch 78 rpm discs).

Disc 1, 10-1434:
Bb 5034-1	ATALANTA: Come my beloved	4 September	1924
Bb 5096-2	Ridente la Calma	19 September	1924

Disc 2, 10-1435:
B 28609-2	Pur Dicesti, O Bocca Bocca Bella	26 September	1923
Bb 5095-1	Feldeinsamkeit	19 September	1924

Disc 3, 10-1436:
B 8695-3	I Hear You Calling Me	16 June	1921
B 10134-1	Macushla	30 March	1911

Disc 4, 10-1437:
B 12710-2	MARITANA: There is a flower that bloometh	11 December	1912
B 13233-1	Goodbye, Sweetheart Goodbye	2 May	1913

Disc 5, 10-1438:

B 8750-1	LAKME: Immenso vienteso...A vien al boscaglia	25 March	1910
B 12705-1	MEFISTOFELE: Dai campi, dai prati	11 December	1912

Disc 6, 10-1439:

B 14658-4	LA BOHEME: O soave fanciulla	8 April	1914
B 8738-2	LA PÊCHEURS DE PERLES: Del tempio al limitar	4 April	1911

Note: These 12 sides were all pressed from original stampers, though they had lead-in and lead-out grooves added.

Music Arts Library of Victor Records, Album 3: "Concert Songs." (Df Disc no. 742).

B 12704-1	At Dawning	11 December	1912
B 13218-2	I Hear a Thrush at Eve	1 May	1913

Note: This album of nine discs contained, in addition to 742 by McCormack, 8 other discs by prominent Victor artists (discs 631, 659, 556, 507, 827, 838, 844, and 859).

Victor Heritage Series Red Seal, Gold Label Discs (Red Vinyl).

15-1009:

C 8737-1	LA BOHEME: Ah Mimi, tu piu non torni	23 March	1910
C 14686-2	LA TRAVIATA: Parigi, o cara	8 April	1914

15-1015:

C 14647-1	DON GIOVANNI: Il mio tesoro	9 May	1916
C 8739-1	LA FILLE DU REGIMENT: Per viver vicino a Maria	23 March	1910

15-1019A:

4190f	FAUST: All'erta! All'erta! (Trio)	12 May	1910
	(Side B not McCormack)		

Note: This series was sold as separate records, though special albums were provided to house the discs. These discs were pressed from original stampers.

American Gramophone Society (A.G.S.) "John McCormack Memorial." (18 Df 10 inch 78 rpm discs. Pressed by HMV for Addison Foster. Three albums in dust jacket.

AGSA 46:

B 29870-2	Holy God We Praise Thy Name	9 April	1924
Bb 5119-1	I Saw From the Beach	24 September	1924

AGSA 47:

B 23799-2	The Singer's Consolation	2 April	1920
B 28610-1	Die Liebe hat gelogen	26 September	1923

AGSA 48:

Bb 5032-2	In Waldeseinsamkeit	4 September	1924
Bb 5031-2	Die Mainacht	4 September	1924

AGSA 49:

Bb 5035-1	O Del Mio Amato Ben	4 September	1924
Bb 5033-2	Luoghi Sereni e cari	4 September	1924

AGSA 50:

Bb 5094-2	Komm bald	19 September	1924
Bb 5095-1	Feldeinsamkeit	19 September	1924

AGSA 51:

B 22253-1	Dream On, Little Soldier Boy	24 September	1918
B 28607-2	Sometime	25 September	1923

AGSA 52:

OEA 8822-1	Lass with the Delicate Air	11 July	1940
OEA 9328-1	The Little Boats	25 June	1941

AGSA 53:

OEA 9669-1	Love Thee, Dearest, Love Thee	26 May	1942
OEA 9458-1	The Green Bushes	26 August	1941

AGSA 54:

OEA 9655-1	Off to Philadelphia	3 December	1941
OEA 9461-1	Maureen	26 August	1941

AGSA 55:
| OEA 8851–1 | The Gentle Maiden | 9 August | 1940 |
| OEA 9314–1 | The Dawn Will Break | 29 May | 1941 |

AGSA 56:
| OEA 8849–1 | Oft in the Stilly Night | 9 August | 1940 |
| OEA 9487–1 | O Promise Me | 6 October | 1941 |

AGSA 57:
| OEA 8824–1 | Passing By | 11 July | 1940 |
| OB 3855–1 | Charm Me Asleep | 16 September | 1932 |

AGSA 58:
| OEA 9084–1 | When I Awake | 28 January | 1941 |
| OEA 9278–1 | Waiting For You | 10 September | 1942 |

AGSA 59:
| OEA 9315–1 | The Village That Nobody Knows | 29 May | 1941 |
| OEA 9063–1 | The Blind Ploughman | 19 December | 1940 |

AGSA 60:
| OEA 9668–1 | By the Lakes of Killarney | 26 May | 1942 |
| OEA 9083–1 | At the Mid Hour of the Night | 28 January | 1941 |

AGSA 61:
| OEA 9277–1 | To Chloe | 10 September | 1942 |
| OEA 8807–1 | Nina | 19 June | 1940 |

AGSA 62:
| BVE 49240–1 | Under the Spell of the Rose | 7 December | 1928 |
| BVE 58690–1 | Song O' My Heart | 10 March | 1930 |

AGSA 63:
| BVE 38731–2 | When You're in Love   (rerecording) | 6 May | 1927 |
| BVE 38387–3 | Fallen Leaf   (rerecording) | 4 May | 1927 |

Note: All but the last two sides were pressed from original stampers. The discs were packaged in numerical order in Volumes I through III. The set was originally sold by subscription only, though far more than the 250 sets originally advertised as a limited edition are known to exist. Many sets of records were sold without the original albums and dust jacket.

APPENDIX B

EXTANT TEST PRESSINGS

The following extant recordings were not published on commercial 78 rpm records. They all exist as test pressings on shellac or vinyl (single face). Those marked with an asterisk have been transferred to long playing disc. It is probable that other extant test pressings have escaped the notice of the compilers.

Lx 2559	RIGOLETTO: Questa o quella	2 March	1908
Lx 2793	Mattinata	31 August	1908
Lx 2491–3	RIGOLETTO: La donna e mobile	31 August	1908
4188f*	FAUST: Trio	12 May	1910
(none)	It's a Long Way to Tipperary (Cyril McCormack; John joins in refrain) (private recording)	31 March	1915
B 16763–2	God's Hand	10 November	1915
B 18391–1	Crucifix	21 September	1916
(none)	If I Knock the "L" Out of Kelly (Cyril McCormack; John may join in refrain) (private recording)	9 May	1917
(none)	Poor Butterfly (Gwendolyn McCormack; John joins in refrain) (private recording)	9 May	1917
B 20546–2	Send Me Away With a Smile	7 September	1917
B 25351–3	Learn to Smile	17 June	1921
B 25353–1	Little Town in the Auld County Down	17 June	1921
B 27045–1	A Fairy Story By the Fire	20 October	1922
B 27085–2*	To the Children	20 November	1922
B 28609–1*	Pur Dicesti	26 September	1923
B 28612–1*	Widmung	26 September	1923
B 29871–2*	Onward Christian Soldiers	9 April	1924

Cc 5029-2	Wo find ich Trost	4 September 1924
Bb 5033-1	Luoghi Sereni e Cari	4 September 1924
Bb 5033-3	Luoghi Sereni e Cari	4 September 1924
Bb 5094-1*	Komm bald	19 September 1924
Bb 5096-1	Ridente la Calma	19 September 1924
Bb 5100-1	Oh! That It Were So!	19 September 1924
Bb 5116-1*	Before My Window	24 September 1924
Bb 5116-3	Before My Window	24 September 1924
Bb 5118-3	Padraic the Fiddler	24 September 1924
Bb 5119-3	I Saw From the Beach	24 September 1924
B 31523-1	All Alone	17 December 1924
BVE 32536-2	June Brought the Roses	23 April 1925
BVE 33820-1	Through All the Days to Be	27 October 1925
BVE 34167-2*	Underneath the Window	18 December 1925
BVE 34166-4	Night Hymn at Sea	24 December 1925
BVE 34166-5*	Night Hymn at Sea	24 December 1925
BVE 36361-2	The Far Away Bells	28 September 1926
BVE 36362-1	When Twilight Comes	28 September 1926
BVE 36362-2	When Twilight Comes	28 September 1926
BVE 36375-3	A Rose For Every Heart	30 September 1926
BVE 35891-1	She Rested by the Broken Brook	1 October 1926
BVE 35892-1	A Prayer to Our Lady	1 October 1926
BVE 35893-1*	Love's Secret	1 October 1926
BVE 37147-2	The Holy Child	17 December 1926
BVE 38386-2*	Under the Spell of the Rose	4 May 1927
Bb 11336-2	Desolation	1 September 1927
Bb 11338-1	Du meines Herzens Krönelein	1 September 1927
Bb 11339-1	Allerseelen	1 September 1927
Bb 11342-1	Who is Sylvia	2 September 1927
Bb 11347-1*	The Cloths of Heaven	2 September 1927
BVE 40166-1	Bird Songs at Eventide	11 October 1927
BVE 40167-1	Beloved I Am Lonely	11 October 1927
BVE 40167-2*	Beloved I Am Lonely	11 October 1927
BVE 40170-1	None but a Lonely Heart	12 October 1927
BVE 40172-2	I Hear You Calling Me	12 October 1927
BVE 40177-1	Annie Laurie	13 October 1927
BVE 41543-3	Dear Old Pal of Mine	13 January 1928
CVE 49214-1	Hark! Hark! The Lark! / Who is Sylvia	28 November 1928
BVE TEST 426-1	TRISTAN UND ISOLDE: O König (with pf.)	15 October 1929
BVE 56188-1	O Mary Dear	16 October 1929
BVE 56189-2*	Just a Corner of Heaven to Me	16 October 1929
BVE 56190-2	FORTUNIO: J'amais la vieille maison grise	16 October 1929
BVE 56192-2	Ireland, Mother Ireland	17 October 1929
BVE 56198-1*	Norah O'Neale	18 October 1929
BVE 58588-2	A Pair of Blue Eyes	19 February 1930
BVE 58596-1	A Fairy Story By the Fire	21 February 1930
CVE 58684-1*	CHRIST ON THE MOUNT OF OLIVES: Jehovah, Hear Me	27 February 1930
CVE 58684-2*	CHRIST ON THE MOUNT OF OLIVES: Jehova! Du mein...	27 February 1930
CVE 58685-1*	CHRIST ON THE MOUNT OF OLIVES: My Heart is Sore	27 February 1930
BVE 58685-2	Wo find ich Trost	10 March 1930
CVE 58692-1*	TRISTAN UND ISOLDE: O König (with orchestra)	10 March 1930
Bb 21026-1	There	3 December 1930
Bb 21030-1	Anakreons Grab	3 December 1930
PBVE61097-1	God Gave Me Flowers	6 July 1931
PBVE61097-2*	God Gave Me Flowers	6 July 1931
BRC HQ 33-1	Und willst du deinem Liebsten sterben sehen	2 November 1931
2B 2276-2	Beherzigung	31 May 1932
OB 3856-1	I Know of Two Bright Eyes	16 September 1932
OB 5308-1*	South Winds	7 September 1933
OEA 404-1	Music of the Night	24 August 1934
OEA 408-1	Ein neues andachtiges Kindelwiegen	24 August 1934
OEA 2124-2	Baby Aroon	27 June 1935
OEA 2128-1	O Mary Dear	28 June 1935
OEA 2130-2	Shannon River	28 June 1935
OEA 8823-1	The Blind Ploughman	11 July 1940
OEA 8825-1	The Sweetest Flower That Blows	11 July 1940
OEA 9330-1	No, Not More Welcome	25 June 1941

2EA 9651-2* Night Hymn at Sea   25 November 1941
2EA 9652-1* Still as the Night   25 November 1941

Note: RCA Victor published the following matrices for the first time on long
playing discs: BVE 35893-1, BVE 56198-1, CVE 58684-1, CVE 58685-1, and
CVE 58692-1. Matrix BRC HQ 33-1 was recorded at 33 1/3 rpm with high fidelity
equipment.

APPENDIX C
AURAL DIFFERENCES FOR ALTERNATE TAKES

McCormack recorded a great many titles more than once, and a number of them several
times throughout his career. In many cases these multiple titles are easily distinguished from one another because of differences in recording process (cylinder vs.
disc, acoustic vs. electric) or accompaniment. In some cases, such as the G & T
recordings versus the Odeons, there is little doubt as to the distinction between
two recordings of the same title, but there are other pairs of recordings that are
somewhat more difficult to distinguish between upon hearing, especially if one or
the other is in the form of a microgroove transfer. For the following multiply
recorded titles aural differences are provided in order that variant takes and repeated recordings may be told apart. Minimal but decisive clues only are provided.
We have not attempted to analyze the performances. In order that owners of both
78's and LP's may utilize these descriptions, we have tried to limit them to clues
that are independent of original playing speeds, sound quality, or subjective descriptions of performances, though it is not always possible to avoid one or the
other of these.We have included only Odeon, Victor, and HMV titles, as we did not
have sufficient access to pre-1906 recordings to analyze these in detail. Neither
have we compared electrical disc recordings with any film or broadcast counterparts.
The sound quality of these latter is usually sufficient to distinguish them from
disc recordings. We have not been able to provide clues for all multiple titles
after 1906, but we have done so for as many as were available to us in satisfactory
sound.

Note: We are indebted to William R. Moran for descriptions of differences between
most of the Victor variant takes, which are taken from forthcoming volumes of the
Encyclopedic Discography of Victor Recordings (Greenwood Press), edited by himself
and Ted Fagan. We have also adapted their clear format for presenting the
descriptions. Several other correspondents gave substantive assistance in construct-
ing this appendix.

ANNIE LAURIE
BVE 40177-1 (13 October 1927)
   Second verse: "Winds" pronounced with short vowel sound.
BVE 40177-2 (13 October 1927)
   Second verse: "Winds" pronounced with long vowel sound.

AVE MARIA
CVE 49209-1 (27 November 1928)
   Final "Ave Maria": Chime is heard just before "ah" of "Maria."
CVE 49209-2 (27 November 1928)
   Final "Ave Maria": Chime is heard just after "ah" of "Maria" and is dimmer
      because masked by voice.

BEFORE MY WINDOW
Bb 5116-1 (24 September 1924)
   High B flat: Held less than one second.
Bb 5116-2 (24 September 1924)
   High B flat: Held for about three seconds.

BLIND PLOUGHMAN
OEA 8823-1 (11 July 1940)
   First verse: "the seeds they stir (run together) and..."
                 "shelter birds (unshaded) that sing..."
   Second verse: "From the shelter of your heart, Brother..." (r's not trilled)
OEA 9063-1 (17 December 1940)
   First verse: "the seeds they stir (not run together) and..."
                 "shelter birds (shaded) that sing..."
   Second verse: "From the shelter of your heart, Brother..." (r's trilled)

BOHEME: CHE GELIDA MANINA
Lxx 2791(-1) (29 August 1908)
    Final lines: "poiche v'ha preso (slight catch on pre) stanza. La dolce
        speranza..."(insecure on note after high note).
    Timing: Sluggish throughout: 4:13 at score pitch.
Lxx 2791-2 (29 August 1908)
    Final lines: poiche v'ha preso (no catch on pre) stanza. La dolce
        speranza..." (secure on note after high note).
    Timing: Faster, with more vitality: 3:30 at score pitch.
C 8589-2 (1 February 1910)
    Virtually the same as Lxx 2791-2 stylistically and musically.
    Orchestra: Different overall from Odeons.
    Recording quality: Technically better than both Odeons.

BOHEMIAN GIRL:
Lx 2619 (30 March 1908)
    Orchestral introduction: Prominent brass; no background noise.
    Last phrase: Trill on 'r' of next to last "remember."
    Orchestral closing: Two chords.
B 14677-1 (7 April 1914)
    Orchestral introduction: No brass; no background noise.
    Last phrase: No turn on final "remember."
    Orchestral closing: Two chords.
B 14677-2 (11 May 1916)
    Orchestral introduction: No brass; background noise heard twice before voice
        ends.
    Last phrase: Turn on final "remember."
    Orchestral closing: Reprise of melody.

BY THE SHORT CUT TO THE ROSSES
BVE 41546-1 (13 January 1928)
    Final phrase: "For the short cut to the rosses is (breath, but no aspirate)
        the road to fairy land." (slight wobble on "land").
BVE 41546-2 (13 January 1928)
    Final phrase: "For the short cut to the rosses is (breath, with aspirate)
        the road to fairy land." (no wobble on "land").

CARMEN: IL FIOR CHE AVEVI A ME
Lx 3138 (5 September 1909)
    Orchestral introduction: Fate theme is played by brass an octave above score.
C 8538-1 (7 January 1910)
    Orchestral introduction: Fate theme played by tuba at score pitch.

CHILD'S SONG
Lx 2502 (3 February 1908)
    Opening line: Noticeable vibrato in voice.
    Closing line: No pianissimo at end.
B 11816-1 (2 April 1912)
    Opening line: No vibrato.
    Closing line: Pianissimo trill on last note.

CLOTHS OF HEAVEN
Bb 11347-1 (2 September 1927)
    Tempo: Brisk (2:02: first note is B flat).
OEA 2128-1 (23 July 1935)
    Tempo: More relaxed (2:23: first note is B flat).

COME BACK TO ERIN
Lx 1579 (5 December 1906)
    Verses: Odeon omits second verse and repeats refrain instead.
C 8588-1 (1 February 1910)
    Verses: Victor includes second verse.

CRUCIFIX:
B 18391-1 (21 September 1916)
    Last line: Singing concludes "He sleepeth never, never."
B 18391-3 (8 June 1917)
    Last line: Singing concludes "He never sleepeth."

DEAR LITTLE SHAMROCK
Lx 1569 (4 December 1906)
   Accompaniment: Primarily brass, with enthusiastic tuba.
   Verses: Two verses sung (second omitted).
B 8819-1 (8 April 1910)
   Accompaniment: Primarily strings and woodwinds.
   Verses: Three verses sung.

EILEEN AROON
Lx 3156 (7 September 1909)
   Last line: "a rock 'mid melting snow, Eileen Aroon." (No pianissimo on "snow";
     two turns on "Eileen").
B 11824-2 (3 April 1912)
   Last line: "a rock 'mid melting snow, Eileen Aroon." (Pianissimo on "snow";
     no turn on "Eileen").

FAREWELL
Lx 2431-2 (28 November 1907)
   Third verse: "Be good, sweet maid, and let who <u>can</u> be clever;"
B 11819-1 (2 April 1912)
   Third verse: "Be good, sweet maid, and let who <u>will</u> be clever;"

FAUST: TRIO
4188f (12 May 1910)
   Last line: All voices end together.
4190f (12 May 1910)
   Last line: Melba's voice stops earlier than the other two.

FORTUNIO: J'AMAIS LA VIEILLE MAISON GRISE
Bb 11341-1 (2 September 1927)
   Surface: Issued only on HMV: usually noisy.
Bb 11341-2 (2 September 1927)
   Surface: Issued only on Victor: usually noticeably quieter.
   (The performances are virtually indistinguishable.)

GOD BE WITH OUR BOYS TONIGHT
B 21663-1 (5 April 1918)
   Second verse begins: "<u>Brave</u> ones who answered..."
   In second verse: "O waiting heart, I dare not tell, how <u>long</u> and <u>sad</u>..."
B 21663-2 (30 April 1918)
   Second verse begins: "<u>Brave</u> ones who answered..."
   In second verse: "O waiting heart, I dare not tell, how <u>sad</u> and <u>long</u>..."
B 21663-3 (1 May 1918)
   Second verse begins: "<u>Kind</u> ones who answered..."
   In second verse: "O waiting heart, I dare not tell, how <u>sad</u> and <u>long</u>..."

GOODBYE, SWEETHEART GOODBYE
Lx 3169 (7 September 1909)
   Last verse: "<u>Yet-I</u> (run together) am here..."
   Orchestral accompaniment: Woodwinds prominent.
B 13233-1 (2 May 1913)
   Last verse: "<u>Yet I</u> (not run together) am here..."
   Orchestral accompaniment: Strings prominent.

GREEN ISLE OF ERIN
Lx 1576 (5 December 1906)
   Verses: One verse, two refrains.
Lxx 3160 (7 September 1909)
   Verses: Two verses, two refrains.

HAS SORROW THY YOUNG DAYS SHADED
Lx 2840 (3 October 1908)
   Second verse sung: Begins "Has love to thy soul so tender..."
C 8753-1 (25 March 1910)
   Second verse sung: Begins "If thus the young hours have fleeted..."

I HEAR YOU CALLING ME
Lxx 2854 (3 October 1908)
   First verse: "I came. (no pause) Do you remember..."

Third verse: "I stand. (pause) Do you behold me..."
B 8695-1 (10 March 1910)
    First verse: "I came. (pause) Do you remember..."
    Third verse: "I stand. (no pause) Do you behold me..."
    Orchestra at end: No rests between final chords.
B 8695-2 (16 March 1911)
    First verse: "I came. (no pause) Do you remember..."
    Third verse: "I stand. (no pause) Do you behold me..."
    Orchestra at end: No rests between final chords.
B 8695-3 (16 June 1921)
    First verse: "I came. (pause) Do you remember..."
    Third verse: "I stand. (pause) Do you behold me..."
    Orchestra at end: Two distinct chords at end, separated by rests.

I KNOW OF TWO BRIGHT EYES
Lx 2845 (3 October 1908)
    Orchestral introduction: Slight discordance at one point.
    Orchestral playing: Prominent clarinet part audible in accompaniment,
       especially playing octaves in second verse.
    Timing: 2:42 in key of A major.
B 11823-1 (3 April 1912)
    Orchestral introduction: No discordance.
    Orchestral playing: No prominent clarinet.
    Timing: 2:29 in key of A major.

I KNOW OF TWO BRIGHT EYES
OB 3856-1 (16 September 1932)
    Last line: Momentary hoarseness at beginning of high A flat.
OB 5310-2 (13 September 1933)
    Last line: No hoarseness on high A flat.

I'LL SING THEE SONGS OF ARABY
Lx 2796-2 (31 August 1908)
    End of song: Orchestra holds same note through the end of McCormack's
       pianissimo til end of music.
B 12760-1 (2 January 1910)
    End of song: Orchestra begins a separate final chord as McCormack's
       pianissimo ends.

IRISH EMIGRANT
BVE 41544-1 (13 January 1928)
    First verse: "I'm sitting by the stile, Mary (breath), where we sat side by
       side (no breath) on a bright May morning long ago (breath) when first..."
BVE 41544-2 (13 January 1928)
    First verse: "I'm sitting by the stile, Mary (breath), where we sat side by
       side (breath) on a bright May morning long ago (breath) when first..."

KATHLEEN MAVOURNEEN
Lx 1577-2 (5 December 1906)
    Pronunciation: "Mavour<u>neen</u>" throughout the song.
    In final refrain: "<u>O</u> why art thou silent, thou voice of my heart?"
C 10061-1 (16 March 1911)
    Pronunciation: "Mavour<u>nyeen</u>" throughout the song.
    In final refrain: "<u>Then</u> why art thou silent, thou voice of my heart?"

KILLARNEY
Lx 1582 (5 December 1906)
    Orchestral accompaniment: Prominent tuba, essentially the only instrument
       audible much of the time.
C 8594-1 (3 January 1910)
    Orchestral accompaniment: Much more an orchestral sound than the band
       sound in the Odeon. Strings and woodwinds prominent.

KOMM BALD
Bb 5094-1 (19 September 1924)
Bb 5094-2 (19 September 1924)
    No significant differences in performances or timing. Both sung in key of F.
       Some take 1 test pressings are noisier than the published take 2.

LIKE STARS ABOVE
Lx 2487 (31 January 1908)
   Orchestra at end: Concludes with two chords.
C 11814-1 (2 April 1912)
   Orchestra at end: Concludes with six notes, the last one sustained.

LORD IS MY LIGHT
Lx 2558 (2 March 1908)
   Orchestral introduction: Prominent arpeggiated chords.
B 20899-1 (23 October 1917)
   Orchestral introduction: No arpeggiated chords.

LOVE ME AND I'LL LIVE FOREVER
BVE 34159-1 (17 December 1925)
   Second verse: "Love me and I'll live til heaven calls me on the final day.
               O Love, I'm yours forever, ..."
BVE 34159-3 (17 December 1925)
   Second verse: "Love me and I'll live til heaven calls me on that final day.
               Love me and I'll live forever,..."

LOVE'S SECRET
BVE 35893-1 (1 October 1926)
   Timing: 1:59 (when first note is F).
   First verse: Briskly sung; no problem on "silently.)
Bb 21032-1 (3 December 1930)
   Timing: 2:11 (when first note is F).
   First verse: More deliberately sung; slightly pinched sounding on "silently."
OEA 2180-1 (23 July 1935)
   Timing: 2:19 (when first note is E, a half step lower).
   First verse: Relaxed but quickly sung.

MARITANA: THERE IS A FLOWER THAT BLOOMETH
Lx 2844 (3 October 1908)
   Last phrase: "the memory of the past." (downward portamento connecting
     "the" and "past."
B 12710-2 (11 December 1912)
   Last phrase: Only slight portamento on "the," not connecting to "past."

MATTINATA
Lx 2793 (31 August 1908)
   Pronunciation: Sings all the words throughout the song.
Lx 2793-2 (31 August 1908)
   Pronunciation: Forgets three or four words about half way through song
     (sings "na na na na" to melody).

MOLLY BAWN
C 8752-1 (25 March 1910)
   Final words: "Catch" in voice on final "Bawn."
   Key: B flat.
C 8752-2 (17 March 1911)
   Final words: No "catch" on final "Bawn."
   Key: A

MY DARK ROSALEEN
Lx 2132 (1 June 1907)
   Third verse: Trumpets at beginning.
Lxx 3151-2 (7 September 1909)
   Third verse: No trumpets.

NIGHT HYMN AT SEA, WITH BORI
BVE 34166-4 (24 December 1924)
BVE 34166-5 (24 December 1924)
   No significant differences in performances.

NOW SLEEPS THE CRIMSON PETAL
Bb 11346-1 (2 September 1927)
Bb 11346-2 (2 September 1927)
   No significant differences in performance or timing. HMV surfaces are
    noisier than Victor.

OFT IN THE STILLY NIGHT
Lx 2135 (1 June 1907)
    Verses: Full song performed.
Lxx 3166 (7 September 1909)
    Verses: Only one verse sung.

PADRAIC THE FIDDLER
Bb 5118-2 (24 September 1924)
    Second verse: "And for them he's always <u>playin'</u>..."
Bb 5118-3 (24 September 1924)
    Second verse: "And for them he's always <u>playing</u>..."

PÊCHEURS DE PERLES: DEL TEMPIO AL LIMITAR, WITH SAMMARCO
B 8738-2 (4 April 1911)
    McCormack's solo passage (Nadir) beginning "La turba al Dio prostra..." to
    the next entrance of Sammarco (Zurga): Prominent flute playing obbligato
    together with harp.
    Balance betwwen voices: Good throughout.
    Final words: "Per sempre unir!" sung together.
C 8738-2 (31 March 1911)
    McCormack's solo passage: In the passage noted above there is a faint
    obbligato by violins, with a prominent harp.
    Balance between voices: Favors McCormack, especially in the opening passages.
    Final words: Sammarco completes the word "sempre" while McCormack is holding
    the high B flat on "sem."

PUR DICESTI
B 28609-1 (26 September 1923)
    Final refrain: Holds "pur" for nearly two seconds at beginning, noticeably
    longer than all other occurrences of this word.
B 28609-2 (26 September 1923)
    Final refrain: Holds "pur" for about same length of time throughout, less
    than one second.

RIDENTE LA CALMA
Bb 5096-1 (19 September 1924)
Bb 5096-2 (19 September 1924)
    The performances are virtually identical in performance, accompaniment, and
    timing.

RIGOLETTO: LA DONNA E MOBILE
Lx 2491 (31 January 1908)
    Orchestral introduction: Muddy, poorly recorded sound.
    Orchestra at end: Orchestra stops as voice stops.
Lx 2491-2 (31 January 1908)
    Orchestral introduction: Clearly recorded (for Odeon) sound; violins more
    defined.
    Orchestra at end: Orchestra stops abruptly a few measures after voice
    concludes. Some microgroove transfers have eliminated this orchestral
    passage.
    Note: The performances are very similar stylistically and musically. Timing
    is essentially the same. Take 3 also exists as a test pressing, but was
    unavailable to the compilers.

RIGOLETTO: QUESTA O QUELLA
Lx 2559-3 (5 September 1909)
    Performance: Significantly more portamento than Victor,
    Timing: 2:06 at score pitch.
    High B flat: Somewhat rough.
    Orchestra at end: Orchestra concludes with a single A flat chord.
B 13223-1 (1 May 1913)
    Performance: Less portamento.
    Timing: 1:56 at score pitch.
    High B flat: Clear and smooth.
    Orchestra at end: Orchestra concludes with one A flat chord (same as Odeon),
    then repeats it an octave higher.

ROSARY
B 11825-2 (5 April 1912)

Last line: "To kiss the cross with (diminuendo on high note) her..."
B 11825-3 (30 March 1915)
    Last line: "To kiss the cross with (no diminuendo) her..."

SAVOURNEEN DEELISH
Lx 2133 (1 June 1907)
    Second verse: "All my pay and booty I hoarded for you, <u>Dear</u>,"
Lx 2133-2 (3 October 1908)
    Second verse: "All my pay and booty I hoarded for you, <u>Love</u>,"

SCHLAFENDES JESUSKIND
BVE 32538-2 (24 April 1925)
    Recording quality: Voice distantly recorded.
    In middle of song: "Blume du, noch in der Knospe dämmernd..." (ä pronounced
        like long <u>a</u> vowel sound in English).
2EA 2767-2 (7 April 1936)
    Recording quality: Voice more forward relative to orchestra.
    In middle of song: "Blume du, noch in der Knospe dämmernd..." (ä pronounced
        like short <u>i</u> vowel sound in English).

SEND ME AWAY WITH A SMILE
B 20546-1 (7 September 1917)
    Orchestral opening: No snare drums.
B 20546-3 (23 October 1917)
    Orchestral opening: Prominent snare drums.

SERENADE (STÄNDCHEN)
CVE 49210-1 (27 November 1928)
    Second line: "Shades of night are swiftly falling, <u>Loved One</u>, come to me."
CVE 49210-2 (27 November 1928)
    Second line: "Shades of night are swiftly falling, <u>Dear One</u>, come to me."

SHE RESTED BY THE BROKEN BROOK
BVE 35891-1 (1 October 1926)
    Third verse: "She (no aspirate) vanished (no diminuendo) in the..."
    Final note: Not sharp ("blue").
OEA 2181-1 (23 July 1935)
    Third verse: "She (no aspirate) vanished (marked diminuendo) in the..."
    Final note: Not sharp.
OEA 9086-1 (28 January 1941)
    Third verse: "She (aspirate) vanished (slight diminuendo) in the..."
    Final note: Slightly sharp on "blue."

SILVER THREADS AMONG THE GOLD
B 11834-1 (5 April 1912)
    Third verse: "Darling, I am <u>growing old</u>..." (aspirate on "old").
B 11834-3 (3 January 1913)
    Third verse: "Darling, I am <u>growing, growing old</u>..." (no aspirate on "old").

SINCE FIRST I SAW YOUR FACE
Bb 11340-2 (2 September 1927)
    Final refrain: "I asked you leave, you bade me love, ist now a time to
        <u>wrangle</u>." (re first verse, line 3).
OEA 9066-1 (17 December 1940)
    Final refrain: "I asked you leave, you bade me love, ist now a time to
        <u>chide me</u>." (re second verse, line 3).

SNOWY BREASTED PEARL
Lx 1570 (4 December 1906)
    Verses: Omits second verse (which begins "If I sigh, a sudden fear...")
C 8741-1 (23 March 1910)
    Verses: Includes all three verses.

SOUTH WINDS
OB 5308-1 (7 September 1933)
    Last note: Neither high nor pianissimo.
OB 5308-2 (7 September 1933)
    Last note: High and pianissimo.

TAKE, O TAKE THOSE LIPS AWAY
Lx 3137-1 (5 September 1909)
   Orchestra at end: Concludes with a sustained A major chord (same chord as
      during McCormack's high A) fading away.
B 11815-1 (2 April 1912)
   Orchestra at end: Concludes with two separate and new A major chords, which
      both begin and end after McCormack has finished singing.

TOSCA: E LUCEVAN LE STELLE
Lx 2501 (3 February 1908)
   Orchestra at beginning: Strings prominent.
   Near end of aria: "<u>E</u> muoio disperato!" E muoio disperato!" (No unnatural
      resonance on first <u>E</u>).
   Final phrase: "Tant<u>o la</u> vita!" (Distinct portamento between "to" and "la").
   Timing: 2:20 at score pitch.
Lx 2501-2 (5 September 1909)
   Orchestra at beginning: Clarinet prominent.
   Near end of aria: "<u>E</u> muoio disperato!" E muoio..." (Unnatural resonance on
      first <u>E</u>, possibly stamper imperfection or momentary hoarseness).
   Final phrase: "Tanto la vita!" (No portamento between "to" and "la").
   Timing: 2:40 at score pitch.

UNDER THE SPELL OF THE ROSE
BVE 38386-2 (4 May 1927)
   Final high note: No pianissimo.
BVE 49240-1 (7 December 1928)
   Final high note: Sung with pianissimo.

WHEN SHADOWS GATHER
Lx 3136-2 (5 September 1909)
   Timing: 3:34 in key of E.
B 8696-1 (10 March 1910)
   Timing: 3:04 in key of E.

APPENDIX D

THE CANADIAN VICTOR PIRATES

In 1921 a series of six double face acoustic records was issued in Canada by
various labels by the Compo company. The titles of the twelve selections would
have been instantly recognizable to any McCormack afficionado, though the labels
mysteriously credited the performances merely to "Tenor" or "Famous Tenor." The
titles did in fact derive from Victor stampers of recordings by McCormack (pre-
sumably the common published takes).

The history of these pirated recordings is quite interesting. Herbert Berliner
(a son of Émile) was Vice President and General manager of the Berliner Gram-O-
Phone Company in Montreal. In 1918 he started a company of his own, the Compo
Company, whose activities were originally intended to be primarily the manufacture
of custom record pressings. In 1921 he resigned from the Berliner Company.
Berliner was licensed to manufacture Victor recordings in Canada, and when
Herbert left, as best as can be determined, he took the metal parts for twelve
McCormack recordings with him.

These Victor stampers were used by the Compo organization to manufacture records
that were issued on their own labels. The six discs were sold originally on the
Apex label, and shortly afterward almost certainly on the Sun and Gennett labels,
all three of which were issued by Compo. They may have been issued on the
Hectrola, Hydrola, Opera Phone, and Starr-Gennett labels, but this is unlikely.
None of the pirate issues stayed on the market very long. They were withdrawn
within a year or less and replaced with original Compo recordings of the same
titles sung by impersonators (one of whom may have been Billy Jones.) It is very
probable that the Compo replacement masters are those issued on the Pathé/Perfect
label under the credit "Mr. X." (The singer labelled "Mr. X" on Grey Gull was
usually Arthur Fields, and those records are unrelated to this problem.)

It may be surmised that those running the Compo organization knew that Victor
would almost certainly take action to have the pirate recordings suppressed, but
that even once this had transpired the records using impersonators would still be

rumored to be McCormack recordings, and people would buy them for that reason. Many same-numbered discs exist, some with McCormack, and others with an imitator. The former can sometimes be identified by vestiges of the Victor numbers under the labels, but most reliably by a comparison with genuine Victor counterparts, since the Compo replacement recordings have obvious differences in style and accompaniment.

The six discs, numbered 531 through 536 on the various Compo labels, are as follows:

Disc no. 531:
B 14666-2   Little Grey Home in the West   6 April   1914
B 14669-1   Beautiful Isle of Somewhere   6 April   1914

Disc no. 532:
B 21811-2   Dear Old Pal of Mine   1 May   1918
B 18387-2   When Irish Eyes Are Smiling   20 September 1916

Disc no. 533:
B 16764-1   A Little Bit of Heaven   10 November 1915
B 10069-1   Mother Machree   17 March   1911

Disc no. 534:
B 8695-?*   I Hear You Calling Me
B 13220-2   A Little Love, A Little Kiss   1 May   1913

Disc no. 535:
B 8683-1   Annie Laurie   4 March   1910
B 12761-2   Where the River Shannon Flows   2 January   1913

Disc no. 536:
B 11834-?* Silver Threads Among the Gold
B 23456-5   That Tumble Down Shack in Athlone   10 December 1919

*Multiple published takes of these titles exist, making it uncertain which was used by Compo.

The compilers are indebted to Steven C. Barr for the information contained in this appendix. Further information or corrections from readers would be welcomed.

APPENDIX E

FILM RECORDINGS

John McCormack appeared in two commercial motion pictures during his career. The first, Song O' My Heart (1929), was a vehicle designed especially for him to appear in a starring role. The second, Wings of the Morning (1936), was a drama in which he had a cameo appearance as himself.

Song O' My Heart was the first full length movie which starred an operatic singer. The story was built around his role as a singer whose attributes were essentially those of McCormack the man. The story by Tom Barry and Sonya Levien was that of an Irish singer who declined to continue a blossoming career in order to return to Ireland to care for the children of his childhood sweetheart, who, married to another, dies during the story. McCormack signed a contract for $500,000 with the William Fox Corporation in May of 1929 in New York City. At that time neither the script of the movie nor the title had been determined. It had originally been thought that a contract for two movies for the sum of $1,000,000 would be signed, but this plan was abandoned pending the outcome of the first effort. Incidental scenes were filmed in Ireland near Moore Abbey (McCormack's residence at the time) in August of 1929. Other scenes to be filmed in Ireland had been planned, but, except for two short sequences, the balance of the movie was filmed in Hollywood between 25 November 1929 and 16 January 1930. It has not been possible to assign precise dates to the various scenes in the movie, including those which contain musical performances by McCormack.

The filming of each scene in all cases included the recording on film at that time of any musical selections in that scene. Thus the original film is the master for the musical recordings. The entire film was shot not only on the standard 35mm film but also in separate takes in the 70mm format developed by Fox studios (known as "Fox Grandeur"). The soundtrack of the 35mm film was 2mm wide, while that of the 70mm film was 7mm wide, reputedly yielding superior sound reproduction. The

70mm format had been used in several previous Fox releases, but for <u>Song O' My Heart</u> the 70mm version is not known to have been released, and it is not known to have survived. Films to be released in the 70mm format were filmed in both 35mm and 70mm versions, and this required that each scene be filmed twice. Thus there were two separate sets of musical recordings, one for each size of film. Only the 35mm version is known to have survived for <u>Song O' My Heart</u>. The concert sequence was filmed in Los Angeles Philharmonic Auditorium. Other than the two scenes filmed in Ireland (which included "A Fairy Story by the Fire" and "Just For Today"), the remaining scenes were all filmed at the Fox Movietone Studios in Hollywood, California. The fifteen musical selections by McCormack are given in the Recording Chronology.

In its original form <u>Song O' My Heart</u> had full dialog on the soundtrack along with the musical numbers. For foreign release, however, the dialog in English was replaced by a continuous musical score which was interrupted only for McCormack's singing. Intertitles such as those used for movies in the silent era were used in the various languages of the countries in which the film was released. The no-dialog versions thus produced were known as "synchronized" versions. All of these contained two songs which the American dialog version did not: "Plaisir d'Amour" and "All'mein Gedanken." Another song recorded for the film, "O Mary Dear," is known to have been used only in that synchronized version produced with Spanish intertitles and is not known to have survived. The song "Bantry Bay" was originally intended to have been included in the film, but it is not known to have been performed for the filming.

<u>Song O' My Heart</u> premiered at the 44th Street Theatre in New York City on 11 March 1930 with much fanfare and was critically well received. However, following its engagements here and abroad, it vanished and was believed lost. A print of a synchronized version was discovered in the Fox vaults by Miles Kreuger, and soon after the movie received its first showing in nearly four decades on 16 July 1971 at New York's Museum of Modern Art. Several years later a full dialog version was discovered and presented in New York by the John McCormack Society of America on 19 October 1974, as part of their celebration of the 90th anniversary of McCormack's birth.

In 1930 the soundtrack of the movie was transferred to discs by the Victor Company for use in those theatres which could not utilize the sound-on-film of the original reels. None of these transcription discs is known to have survived. The musical selections by McCormack from the film original have been transferred three times to long playing discs. All three utilized a synchronized version of the film containing fourteen songs. The initial release on UORC had all the recordings on one side of the disc. Unfortunately this transfer suffered from variable sound quality: the volume fades in and out, final notes are clipped, and there is extraneous noise. Soon after the UORC release there was issued a far superior Lp of the music by the John McCormack Society of Greater Kansas City (no issue number). The sound quality was good throughout, and this disc included the brief selection "The Magpie's Nest," which had been omitted by UORC. It also included the closing orchestral music. The third release of the music was by Pearl Records in equally good sound.

The credits for <u>Song O' My Heart</u> are as follows:

Director	Frank Borzage
Assistant Director	Lew Borzage
Story and Dialog	Tom Barry
Continuity	Sonia Levien
Settings	Harry Oliver
Costumes	Sophie Wachner
Sound Engineer	George Costello
Photography, 35mm version	Chester Lyons and Al Brick
Photography, 70mm version	J.O. Taylor
Editor	Margaret V. Clancy

Cast:	
Sean O'Carolan	John McCormack
Mary O'Brien	Alice Joyce
Eileen O'Brien	Maureen O'Sullivan
Tad O'Brien	Tommy Clifford
Fergus O'Donnell	John Garrick
Mona	Effie Ellsler
Peter Conlon	J.M. Kerrigan

Joe Rafferty	J. Farrell MacDonald
Elizabeth Kennedy	Emily Fitzroy
Vincent Glennon	Edwin Schneider
Guido	Andres de Segurola
Dennis Fullerton	Edward Martindel

An additional song, "In the Place Where They Make the Gas," was sung by J.M. Kerrigan without accompaniment at one point in the story. The dialog version of Song O' My Heart was licensed to the John McCormack Society of Greater Kansas City for a time during the 70's. The organization has apparently now been dissolved, and inquiries to their address (1012 Baltimore, Suite 900, Kansas City, Missouri) have gone unanswered. It is to be hoped that the present day owners of the rights to the film will one day make it available to the general public, where, like so many other classic films from its era, it would undoubtedly enjoy great success before a wide audience.

The second film in which McCormack appeared, Wings of the Morning, was the first British Technicolor film and starred Henry Fonda. It's plot was intricate and improbable, and McCormack's appearance as himself in an informal concert sequence is a refreshing break in an otherwise uninteresting story. The three selections were recorded on film during the summer of 1936 on an undetermined date. Other film footage that exists of McCormack is usually silent film. The 26 June 1932 performance of "Panis Angelicus" at the Pontifical High Mass of the 31st International Eucharistic Congress (Phoenix Park, Dublin) was filmed, but the recording that survives is derived from the BBC broadcast of this service.

We are indebted to Miles Kreuger for most of the discographic and background detail regarding Song O' My Heart presented in this appendix and in the recording chronology. We would welcome further information on any other extant film recordings by McCormack.

APPENDIX F

SUMMARY OF EXTANT BROADCAST RECORDINGS

1 JANUARY 1926, NEW YORK.
    When You and I Were Young, Maggie
    Night Hymn at Sea, with Bori

1 JANUARY 1927, NEW YORK.
    Calling Me Back to You
    On Wings of Song (Never recorded commercially.)
    The Holy Child

26 JUNE 1932, DUBLIN.
    Panis Angelicus

4? APRIL 1933, NEW YORK.
    Panis Angelicus

18 OCTOBER 1933, NEW YORK.
    The Heavy Hours Are Almost Past (never recorded commercially.)

18 SEPTEMBER 1934, NEW YORK.
    FLORIDANTE: Alma mia (Never recorded commercially.)

20 AUGUST 1935, NEW YORK.
    Love's Roses
    Believe Me If All Those Endearing Young Charms

11 OCTOBER 1936, NASHVILLE.
    Just For Today
    The Ould Turf Fire (Never recorded commercially.)
    The Star of the County Down (World Premier of the Hughes' arrangement.)

19 NOVEMBER 1936, NEW YORK.
    O Mary Dear
    Ever in My Mind

27 DECEMBER 1936, NEW YORK.
    Oh! What Bitter Grief is Mine
    The Star of the County Down
    Silent Hour of Prayer (Never recorded commercially.)

2 JANUARY 1937, HOLLYWOOD.
  One Summer Morn (Never recorded commercially.)
  The Ould Turf Fire (Never recorded commercially.)
  THE TRIUMPH OF TIME AND TRUTH: Dryads and Sylvans (Never recorded com-
    mercially.)
  Come In, and Welcome (Never recorded commercially.)

1 FEBRUARY 1937, UNKNOWN LOCALE.
  Just For Today

13 MAY 1937, HOLLYWOOD.
  Shannon River
  So Do I Love You (Never recorded commercially.)

17 MARCH 1938, HOLLYWOOD.
  The Garden Where the Praties Grow
  Hail, Glorious Saint Patrick (Never recorded commercially.)

17 APRIL 1938, HOLLYWOOD.
  Maureen

25 APRIL 1938, HOLLYWOOD.
  The Bard of Armagh
  The Star of the County Down

6 or 8 DECEMBER 1938, LONDON.
  The Snowy Breasted Pearl
  The Old House (possibly)

1940, LONDON.
  SEMELE: Wher'er you walk
  The Star of the County Down
  I'll Walk Beside You
  If I Should Fall in Love Again, with Laye (Never recorded commercially.)

2 JANUARY 1942, LONDON.
  I'll Walk Beside You
  The Gentle Maiden

Note: A transcription disc (reference no. MA 1 LP 31512) in the archives of the
British Broadcasting Company contains rerecordings of various commercial recordings (unpublished on 78 rpm discs) rather than broadcast transcriptions. It was
placed there for the BBC's reference by Leonard F.X. MacDermott Roe

APPENDIX G

ODEON SHELLAC ISSUES AND REISSUES

Columns under **Original Issue Series** are 2800–RO; columns under **Affiliated Reissues** are Amer. Odeon–Other.

Matrix	2800	44000	57000	66000	84000	O	X	RO	Amer. Odeon	Ariel	Col.-Fono.	Eng. Col.	Okeh	Regal	Other
Lx 1565		44364	57556			0214 / 634			33017				70002	G 5002	
Lx 1566		44365	57554			0213			33016					G 5002	
Lx 1567		44366	57555			0213								G 5003	
Lx 1568		44367	57552			0212			33014				70006	G 5003	
Lx 1569		44368	57558			0215 / 635			33018				70001	G 5004	
Lx 1570		44369	57553			0212			33015	6231				G 5001	
Lx 1576		44374	57557			0214 / 634								G 5004	
Lx 1577-2		44375	57559			0215 / 635				6229				G 5005	
Lx 1579		44376	57560			0216			33019		F 119			G 5005	Avoca 78-2077
L 1580	2896														
L 1581	2895										F 119			G 5006	
Lx 1582		44377	57561			0216								G 5000	
Lx 2132		44889	57510			0382					F 120				
Lx 2133		44852	57550			0220			33013						
Lx 2134		44853	57551			0220								G 5001	
Lx 2135		44854	57512												
Lx 2430			57511	66066		0382			33011		F 130		70003		
Lx 2431				66067							F 131				
Lx 2431-2			57548	66067		0219									
Lx 2432			57549			0219			33012						
Lx 2432-2			57549	66068		0219									
Lx 2487			57507	66267		0410			33008		F 121				
Lx 2488			57523	66180				RO 217		5049	F 117				
Lx 2489			57524	66215				RO 217		5049					
Lx 2490			57504	66208		0390 / 998				6231					
Lx 2491			57508	66201				RO 276							
Lx 2500				66190		0919									
Lx 2501			57525	66191		942									
Lx 2502			57503	66177		0390			33006						
Lx 2545			57506	66254		0381					F 130				
Lx 2558			57505			0410			33007						
Lx 2619			57522	66256		0381 / 0741					F 118				
Lxx 2791					84205		X 3			8645					
Lxx 2791-2					84205		X 3								
Lx 2793-2			57633					RO 586 / RO 658	33028						IRCC 3101
Lx 2795			57582					RO 454							
Lx 2796-2			57583			0455			33021	6234	F 118				
Lx 2797			57581			0503									
Lx 2798			57580			0455			33020		F 121		70004		
Lxx 2799					84206		X 3			8645					IRCC 3101
Lx 2491-4			57508			0218			33009						
Lx 2133-2			57550			0538				6229				G 5000	
Lx 2840			57587			0468			33022						
Lx 2841			57590			0468									
Lx 2842			57593			0469									
Lx 2843			57594			0469									
Lx 2844			57588			0503									
Lx 2845			57591			0513					F 131				
Lx 2850			57602			0513					F 120				
Lxx 2852					84207		X 100					864			
Lxx 2853					84210		X 100						50008		
Lxx 2854					84208		X 11						50001		
Lxx 2962					84217		X 11					864			
Lx 2963			57608			0336									
Lx 2965			57704			0816									
Lx 2501-2			57525			0218					F 117				CRS 12
Lx 2559-3			57631			0218		RO 276	33026				50007		
Lxx 3134-2					84233		X 41						50007		
Lxx 3135					84226		X 75					880			
Lx 3136-2			57632					RO 317	33027						
Lx 3137			57630					RO 317	33025						
Lxx 3138					84225		X 75					863	50002		IRCC 3092
Lx 3150-2			57640					RO 658	33029				50006		
Lxx 3151-2					84240		X 44						50006		
Lxx 3152-2					84230		X 65			8647		868			IRCC 3092
Lx 3153-2			57643					RO 586	33031						
Lx 3155			57644			0716									
Lx 3156			57641			0538			33030					G 5006	
Lx 3157			57642			0336									
Lxx 3158					84229		X 41					869	50003		
Lxx 3160					84234		X 44					880	50004		
Lx 3162			57645			0741			33033						
Lxx 3163					84231		X 62								
Lxx 3164					84239		X 62			6234					
Lx 3166			57646			0716							70005		Avoca 78-2077
Lx 3167			57647			0633			33035						
Lx 3168			57648			0633			33036						
Lx 3169			57705			0816			33037						
Lxx 3173					84236		X 65			8647		863	50005		CRS 12

Bibliography

Bennett, John R., *Voices of the Past, Volume I: H.M.V. English Catalog*, Lingfield, Surrey: Oakwood Press, n.d.

Bennett, John R. and Eric Hughes, *Voices of the Past, Volume IV: The International Red Label Catalog, Part I*, Lingfield, Surrey: Oakwood Press, n.d.

Bennett, John R. and Eric Hughes, *Voices of the Past, Volume VI: The International Red Label Catalog, Part 2*, Lingfield, Surrey: Oakwood Press, n.d.

Clough, Francis F. and C.J. Cuming, *The World's Encyclopedia of Recorded Music*, Westport, Connecticut: Greenwood Press, 1966 (Reprint).

Darrell, R.D., *The Gramophone Shop Encyclopedia of Recorded Music, First Edition*, New York: Gramophone Shop, Inc., 1936

Dennis, James F.E., "Emmy Destinn Discography," *The Record Collector*, XX: 29–47, 1971.

Dennis, James F.E., "Fonotipia Information," *The Record Collector*, XVIII: 44–45, 1968.

Dolan, Peter F., "John McCormack, Mastersinger: A Short Account of his American Career," *The Sword of Light*, Spring, 1974.

Fagan, Ted, "Pre-LP Recordings of RCA at 33 1/3 rpm Through 1931 to 1934," *The Association for Recorded Sound Collections Journal*, XIII: 20–42, 1981 (Part I); XIV: 41–61, 1982 (Part 2); XV: 25–68, 1983 (Part 3).

Fawcett-Johnston, Brian, "John Count McCormack: Complete Pre-1910 Discography," *The Record Collector*, XXIX: 33–48, 1984.

Foxall, Raymond, *John McCormack*, New York: Alba House, 1963.

Frow, George L., *The Edison Disc Phonographs and the Diamond Discs - A History with Illustrations*, Sevenoaks, Kent: Frow, n.d.

Gelatt, Roland, *The Fabulous Phonograph, 1877 - 1977*, New York: Macmillan, 1977.

Greaves, Sam, "Letter Re the McCormack Odeons," *The Record Collector*, XI: 189, 1957.

Keveny, J., "Records Research: The John McCormack Edison Bell Cylinders," *Newsletter of the John McCormack Society of America*.

Key, Pierre V.R., *John McCormack - His Own Life Story*, Boston: Small, Maynard & Co., 1918.

Kutsch, K.J. and Leo Riemens, *A Concise Biographical Dictionary of Singers. From the Beginnings of Recorded Sound to the Present*, translated, expanded, and annotated by Harry Earl Jones, New York: Chilton, [1962], 1969.

Ledbetter, Gordon R., *The Great Irish Tenor*, London: Duckworth, 1977.

Leslie, George Clark, *The Gramophone Shop Encyclopedia of Recorded Music, Second edition*, New York: Simon and Schuster, 1942.

McCormack, Lily, *I Hear You Calling Me*, Westport, Connecticut: Greenwood Press, 1975 (facsimile of 1949 edition).

Moore, Jerrold Northrop, *A Matter of Records - Fred Gaisberg and the Golden Era of the Gramophone*, New York: Taplinger, 1976.

Moran, William R., "John McCormack Correction," *The Record Collector*, XIV: 95, 1961.

Morby, Paul, "The McCormack Cylinders," *The Record Collector*, XVIII: 37-42, 1968.

Moses, Julian Morton, *The Collectors' Guide to American Recordings, 1895 - 1925*, New York: Dover, 1977 (Second Edition).

Perkins, John F., Alan Kelly, and John Ward, "The Berliner (Gramophone Company) Catalog," *The Record Collector*, XXi: 270-283, 1974.

Read, Oliver and Walter L. Welch, *From Tin Foil to Stereo - Evolution of the Phonograph*, New York: Bobbs-Merrill, 1959.

Reid, Robert H., *The Gramophone Encyclopedia of Recorded Music, Third Edition*, New York: Crown, 1948.

Richards, John B., "Louise Kirkby-Lunn Discography," *The Record Collector*, XIX: 140-159, 1970.

Roden, Philip F., *A John McCormack Discography*, (Appendix to *I Hear You Calling Me* by Lily McCormack), Westport, Connecticut: Greenwood Press, 1975 (Reprint of 1949 edition).

Roden, Philip F. and Robert L. Webster, "The McCormack Odeons," *The Record Collector*, XI: 5-18, 1957.

Roe, Leonard F.X. MacDermott, *John McCormack - The Complete Discography*, London: Charles Jackson, 1956.

Roe, Leonard F.X. MacDermott, *The John McCormack Discography*, Lingfield, Surrey: Oakwood Press, 1972.

Rous, Samuel Holland, *The Victrola Book of the Opera - Fifth Edition*, Camden, New Jersey: Victor Talking Machine Company, 1919.

Sears, Richard S., *V - DISCS: A History and Discography*, Westport, Connecticut: Greenwood Press, 1980.

Strong, L.A.G., *John McCormack - The Story of a Singer*, New York: Macmillan, 1941.

Ward, John, "The Gramophone and Typewriter Company Matrix Series (1898 - 1907)," *The Record Collector*, XV: 72-80, 1962.

Ward, John, Alan Kelly, and John Perkins, "The Search for John O'Reilly - A Collectors' Mystery," *The Record Collector*, XXI: 283-286, 1974.

Artist Index

Numbers refer to pages in the Recording Chronology.
The following abbreviations are used: (c) composer,
(1) lyricist, librettist, (arr.) arranger, (trans.)
translator.

Adams, Katherine (1) 59
Adams, Sara Frances (1) 33
Adams, Stephen (c) 12, 13, 30, 72
Agnes, Sister (c) 81
Aitken, George (c) 27
Aldington, May (1) 62
Alexander, Francis (1) 84
Allen, Mary (chorus) 58
Allitsen, Frances (c) 12, 44, 47, 48
Almers, Hermann (1) 53
Alstyne, Egbert Van (1) 46, 47
Anacreon (1) 65
Anonymous (1) 14, 15, 80, 83, 85
Aquinas, Thomas (1) 60, 62, 73, 74
Arale, David L. (1) 85
Arne, Michael (c,1) 83
Ashworth-Hope, M. (1) 72
Ayer, Nathaniel D. (c) 51
   (c,1) 51
Axt, William (c,1) 64

Bach, Johann Sebastian (c) 33, 34, 86
Bain (arr.) 76
Baker, Elsie (chorus) 58
Balfe, Michael William (c) 3, 4, 5, 6,
   7, 10, 12, 20, 36, 38, 42, 57, 68,
   79
Ball, Ernest R. (c) 25, 35, 40, 42,
   47, 63
Bantock, Sir Granville (c) 58, 60, 71,
   76, 77
Barbier, Jules (1) 13, 22, 29, 41
Baring-Gould, Sabine (1) 52
Barker, G.A. (c) 3, 4, 6, 24, 63
Barnard, Charlotte Alington ("Claribel")
   (c) 4, 5, 7, 8, 9, 10, 20
Barnby, Sir Joseph (c) 50
Barnes, William (1) 86
Barr, Joan T. (1) 82
Barron, J. Francis (1) 38
Barrie, Royden (1) 53, 56, 62, 64, 75, 89
Barthelmy, R. (c) 38
Bartlett, J.C. (c) 36

Bates, Arlo (1) 49
Bath, Hubert (conductor) 3
Batten, Robert (c,1) 16
Bayard, Jean-Francois-Alfred (1) 22
Bax, Arnold (c) 86
Beaumarchais, Pierre-Augustin (1)
   27, 46
Beethoven, Ludwig van (c) 70
Benedict, Sir Julius (c) 6, 7, 37
Benham, Earl (c,1) 48, 52
Bennett, William Sterndale (c) 16, 27
Berlin, Irving (c,1) 45, 54, 55, 59,
   88
Bethune, Rev. (1) 63
Bey, Auguste Marriette (1) 19, 37
Bimboni, Alberto (c) 32
Bingham, C. Clifton (1) 3, 5, 6, 7,
   10, 18, 28, 42, 62, 78
Bizet, Georges (c) 13, 17, 20, 22, 26,
   30, 31, 33
Black, Ben (c) 55
Black, Frank (conductor) 79, 80
Black, Phyllis (1) 75
Blake, William (1) 58, 71, 77, 88
Blau, Edouard (1) 29
Blaufuss, Walter (c) 46, 47, 60
Blossom, Henry (1) 43
Blumenthal, Joseph (c) 18, 25
Bohm, Carl (c) 40
Boito, Arrigo (c) 29
   (1) 27, 29
Bok, Edward (1) 40
Bori, Lucrezia (soprano) 35, 36, 37,
   56, 57
Boucicault, Dion (1) 6, 7, 8, 28, 37
Boulton, Harold (1) 76, 84, 86, 87, 89
   (trans.) 85
Bourdon, Rosario (celeste) 43, 46, 47,
   50
   ('cello) 33, 35
   (conductor) 42, 50, 51, 52, 54, 58
   (piano) 47, 48
Bowles, Fred G. (1) 44, 45, 87, 88

ERRATA

About the Compilers

PAUL W. WORTH holds a Bachelor of Arts degree and a Master's in Education from the University of Texas at Austin. He is a teacher in the Austin Independent School District.

JIM CARTWRIGHT studied music at North Texas State University and the University of Texas at Austin, and is the owner of *Immortal Performances*, dealing in the sale of collectors' recordings. He produces and hosts a weekly radio show featuring historical, instrumental, orchestral, and vocal recordings. He has published discographies on many famous artists as supplements to record catalogs, including Arturo Toscanini, Ignace Jan Paderewski, and Amelita Galli-Curci.